Emperor Penguin

Did You Know?

- Penguins are flightless sea birds.
- The emperor penguin is the largest of the penguins, standing up to 4 feet tall.
- Penguins are good swimmers and use their wings as paddles.
- A penguin's thick layer of blubber helps insulate its body in cold Antarctic waters.

SOUTH CAROLINA

Science

Program Authors

Dr. Jay K. Hackett
Professor Emeritus of Earth Sciences
University of Northern Colorado
Greeley, CO

Dr. Richard H. Moyer
Professor of Science Education and Natural Sciences
University of Michigan-Dearborn
Dearborn, MI

Dr. JoAnne Vasquez
Elementary Science Education Consultant
NSTA Past President
Member, National Science Board and NASA Education Board

Mulugheta Teferi, M.A.
Principal, Gateway Middle School
Center of Math, Science, and Technology
St. Louis Public Schools
St. Louis, MO

Dinah Zike, M.Ed.
Dinah Might Adventures LP
San Antonio, TX

Kathryn LeRoy, M.S.
Executive Director
Division of Mathematics and Science Education
Miami-Dade County Public Schools, FL
Miami, FL

Dr. Dorothy J. T. Terman
Science Curriculum Development Consultant
Former K-12 Science and Mathematics Coordinator
Irvine Unified School District, CA
Irvine, CA

Dr. Gerald F. Wheeler
Executive Director
National Science Teachers Association

Bank Street College of Education
New York, NY

Contributing Authors

Dr. Sally Ride
Sally Ride Science
San Diego, CA

Lucille Villegas Barrera, M.Ed.
Elementary Science Supervisor
Houston Independent School District
Houston, TX

American Museum of Natural History
New York, NY

Contributing Writer

Ellen Grace
Albuquerque, NM

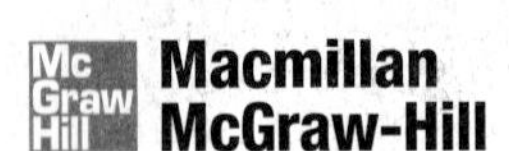

Students with print disabilities may be eligible to obtain an accessible, audio version of the pupil edition of this textbook. Please call Recording for the Blind & Dyslexic at 1-800-221-4792 for complete information.

A

The McGraw-Hill Companies

Macmillan McGraw-Hill

Published by Macmillan/McGraw-Hill, of McGraw-Hill Education, a division of The McGraw-Hill Companies, Inc., Two Penn Plaza, New York, New York 10121.

is a trademark of The McGraw-Hill Companies, Inc.

Printed in the United States of America

ISBN-13: 978-0-02-286085-1/3
ISBN-10: 0-02-286085-1/3

2 3 4 5 6 7 8 9 (058/043) 10 09 08 07

The American Museum of Natural History in New York City is one of the world's preeminent scientific, educational, and cultural institutions, with a global mission to explore and interpret human cultures and the natural world through scientific research, education, and exhibitions. Each year the Museum welcomes around four million visitors, including 500,000 schoolchildren in organized field trips. It provides professional development activities for thousands of teachers; hundreds of public programs that serve audiences ranging from preschoolers to seniors; and an array of learning and teaching resources for use in homes, schools, and community-based settings. Visit www.amnh.org for online resources.

Be a Scientist

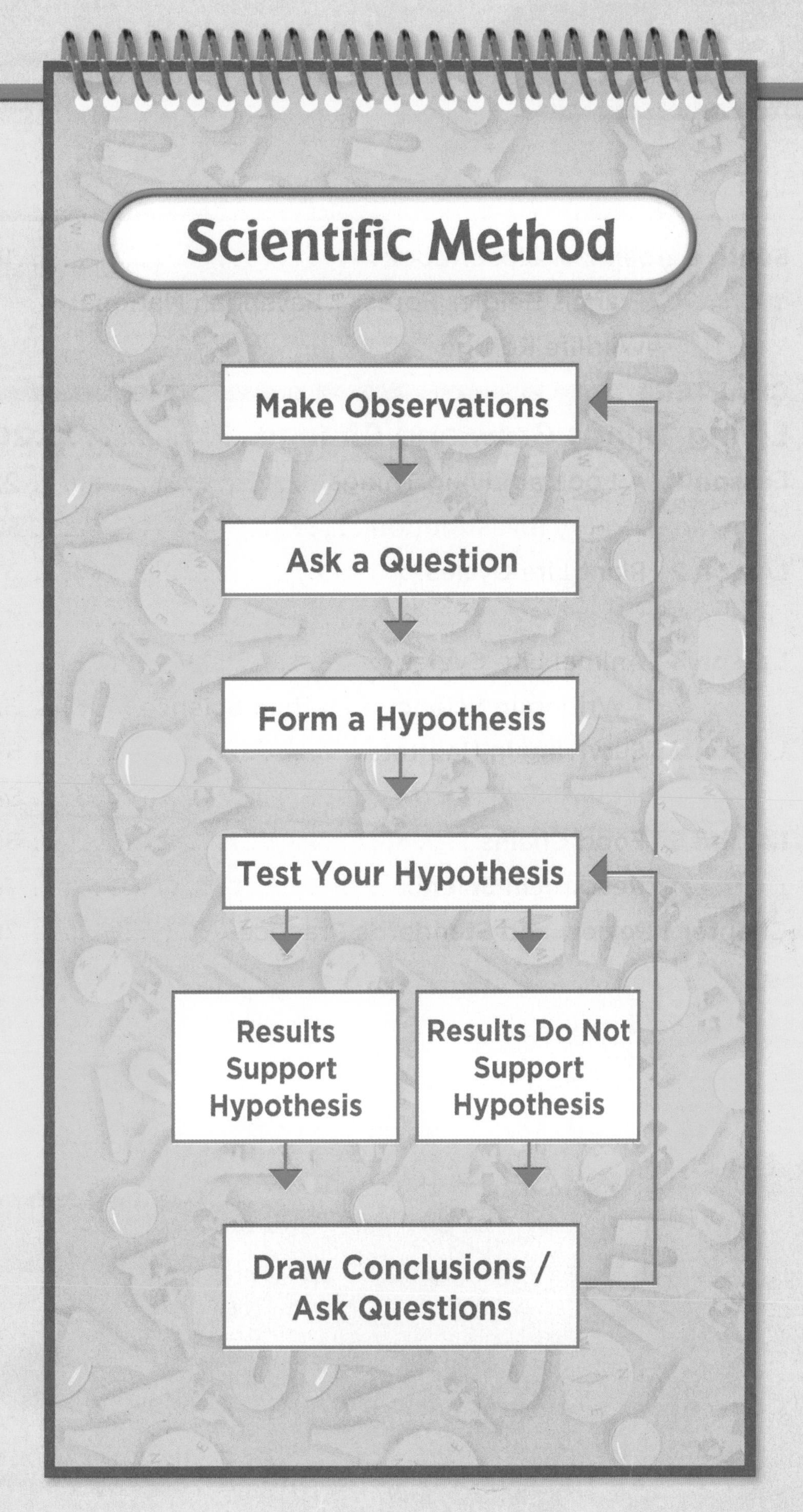
Scientific Method
Make Observations
Ask a Question
Form a Hypothesis
Test Your Hypothesis
Results Support Hypothesis
Results Do Not Support Hypothesis
Draw Conclusions / Ask Questions

Life Science

UNIT A

UNIT A

CHAPTER 2

CHAPTER 3

Earth Science

UNIT B

UNIT B

Physical Science

UNIT C

UNIT C

CHAPTER 7

Activities and Investigations

Life Science

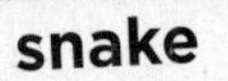
snake

Sun

hawk

Earth Science

Physical Science

CHAPTER 6

Explore Activities

Quick Labs

Inquiry Skills and Investigations

CHAPTER 7

Explore Activities

Quick Labs

Inquiry Skills and Investigations

Be a Scientist

Chameleons can change color to communicate.

Giant Madagascan chameleon

Be a Scientist

The Scientific Method

Look and Wonder

Madagascar is a tropical island off the coast of Africa. It is home to plants and animals found nowhere else on Earth! What would it be like to live on a tropical island? What kinds of things might you see there?

3-I.3. Generate questions about objects, organisms, and events in the environment and use those questions to conduct a scientific investigation. **3-I.4.** Predict the outcome of an investigation and compare the result with the prediction.

Explore

What do you know about animals that live in Madagascar?

- How do you look for animals in their natural habitat?
- What kinds of animals would you see in a forest?
- What does an animal need to live in a forest?
- How do scientists find answers to these questions?

Chris Raxworthy

Paule Razafimahatratra

Meet two scientists who are curious about the natural world and everything that lives in it. Chris Raxworthy and Paule Razafimahatratra study animals that live in Madagascar. They work at the American Museum of Natural History in New York City and at the University of Antananarivo in Madagascar.

What do scientists do?

Chris and Paule want to find out about the many amazing animals that live in Madagascar. Much of the island has never been explored by scientists. New plants and animals are discovered all the time.

The scientific method is a process that scientists use to investigate the world around them. It helps them answer questions about the natural world.

Right now, Chris and Paule are studying a lizard called a giant Madagascan chameleon. Chris has observed these chameleons in dry forests. He wants to know where else in Madagascar the chameleons live.

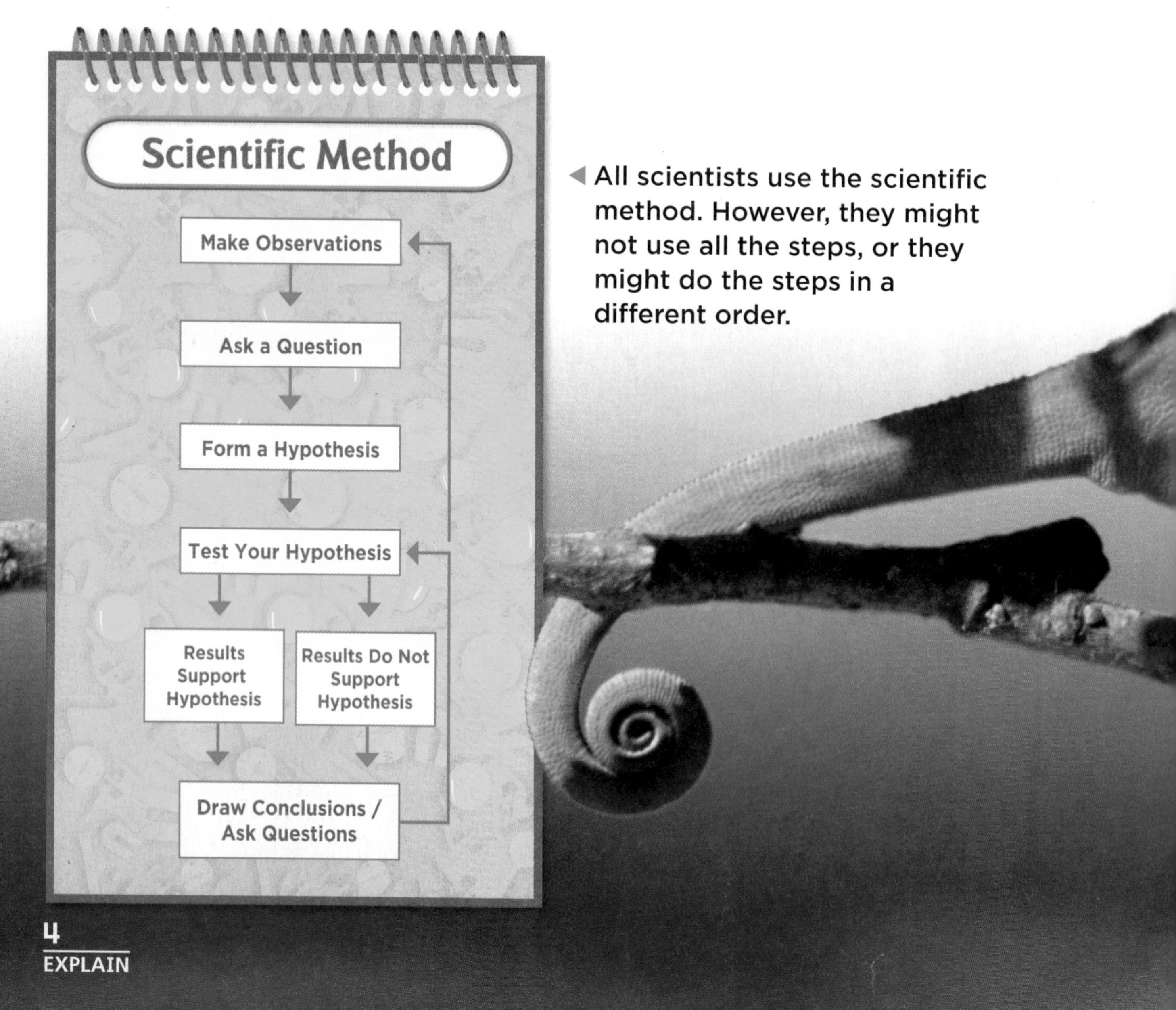

◀ All scientists use the scientific method. However, they might not use all the steps, or they might do the steps in a different order.

Chris knows that variables such as temperature and rainfall affect where animals live. A variable is something that can change.

Chris uses this information to form a hypothesis. A hypothesis is a statement that can be tested to answer a question.

Here is Chris's hypothesis. If a place has temperatures between 10 and 40 degrees Celsius and between 50 and 150 centimeters of rainfall every year, then giant Madagascan chameleons could live there.

Form a Hypothesis

1. Ask lots of "why" questions.
2. Look for connections between important variables.
3. Suggest possible explanations for those connections.

▶ **Make sure the explanations can be tested.**

giant Madagascan chameleon ▲

How do scientists test a hypothesis?

The giant Madagascan chameleon is about as long as a banana. It is hard to find in the dense forest, though, because it hides. People in Madagascar say you can never find a chameleon when you are looking for one!

Where should Chris and Paule look for chameleons? In order to find out, they study their data about temperature and rainfall. Data is information. They put this data into a computer and make a map. The computer colors yellow all the areas that are likely to have chameleons. Those areas have similar temperatures and rainfall to places where chameleons have been found before. Chris predicts that if they go to those areas, they will find giant Madagascan chameleons.

observed
predicted

▲ **The purple dots on this map show where giant Madagascan chameleons have been seen before. The yellow areas show where Chris and Paule think the chameleons live.**

◀ **Chris uses his headlamp to find chameleons at night when they sleep.**

Chris and Paule choose new places to look for chameleons. They choose places that are in the yellow areas on the map. They collect data in these places to test their hypothesis. They use procedures that other scientists can repeat. That way other scientists can check Chris's and Paule's results.

"We wear headlamps and search at night, when the chameleons are sleeping and are easier to find," Chris explains. "We look up in the branches for pale-colored comma shapes." Every time they find a chameleon, Chris and Paule make careful notes and take photographs. They record the exact date, time, and place in their field journals.

Test Your Hypothesis

1. Think about the different kinds of data that could be used to test the hypothesis.
2. Choose the best method to collect this data.
   - **perform an experiment** (in the lab)
   - **observe the natural world** (in the field)
   - **make and use a model** (on a computer)
3. Then plan a procedure and gather data.

▶ **Make sure that the procedure can be repeated.**

Chris and Paule record data when they find giant Madagascan chameleons and other lizards.

CHRIS'S FIELD JOURNAL

April 9th, 2006
Ambohibola Forest
15mm rain measured in rain gauge
Temperature range from 20-34°C
Heavy afternoon rain shower

This deciduous forest has large trees and cut tree stumps. The forest edge is burnt. Hunting and cattle grazing occur in the forest. It has many small streams that dry up in the winter.

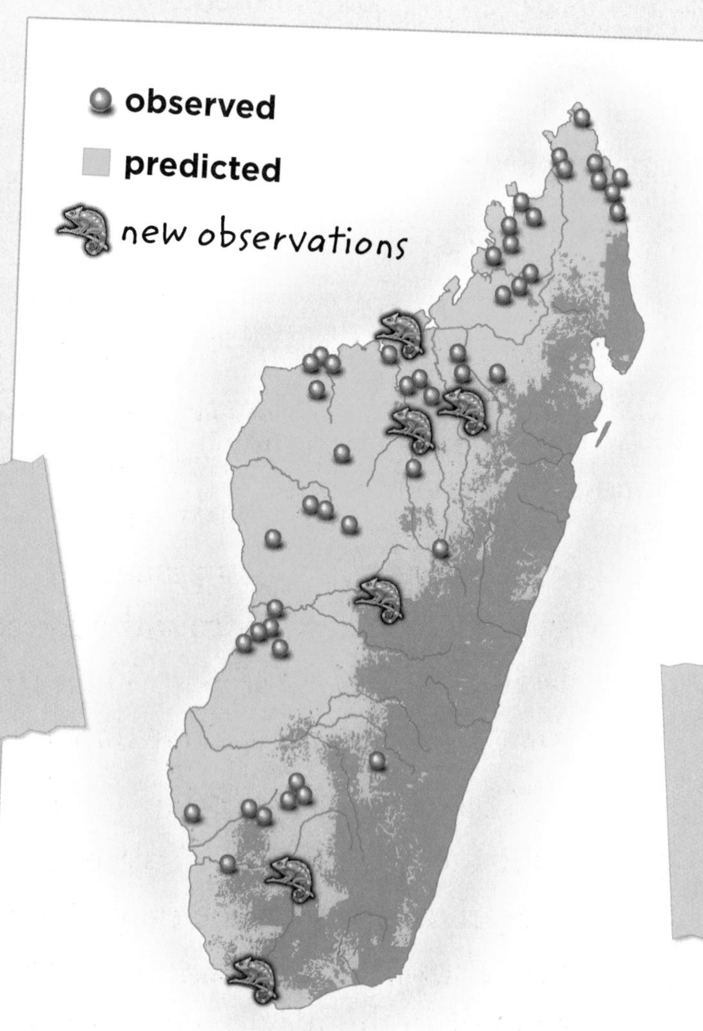

giant Madagascan chameleon
(Furcifer oustaleti)
Found at 10:45 A.M. in grassland with scattered trees. Laid 17 eggs 14x8mm.

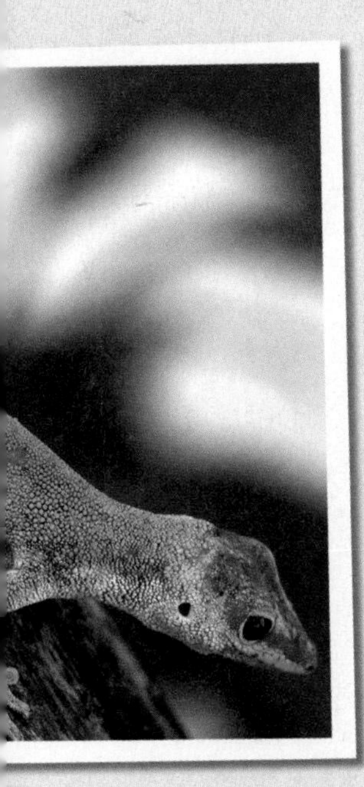

Madagascan day gecko
(Phelsuma madagascariensis)
on a tree trunk at 11:30 A.M., in a small clump of trees growing by a small stream.

Analyze the Data

1. Organize the data as a chart, table, graph, diagram, map, or group of pictures.
2. Look for patterns in the data. These patterns can show how important variables in the hypothesis affect one another.

▶ **Make sure to check the data by comparing it to data from other sources.**

How do scientists analyze data?

Part of testing a hypothesis is looking for patterns in the data that has been collected. Chris and Paule study the information from all of the locations they visited. They mark the seven places on the map where they found a giant Madagascan chameleon. Then they look for patterns in their data.

They observe that the chameleons they found were in the yellow area on the map. They talk about the temperatures and rainfall in the places where they found the chameleons.

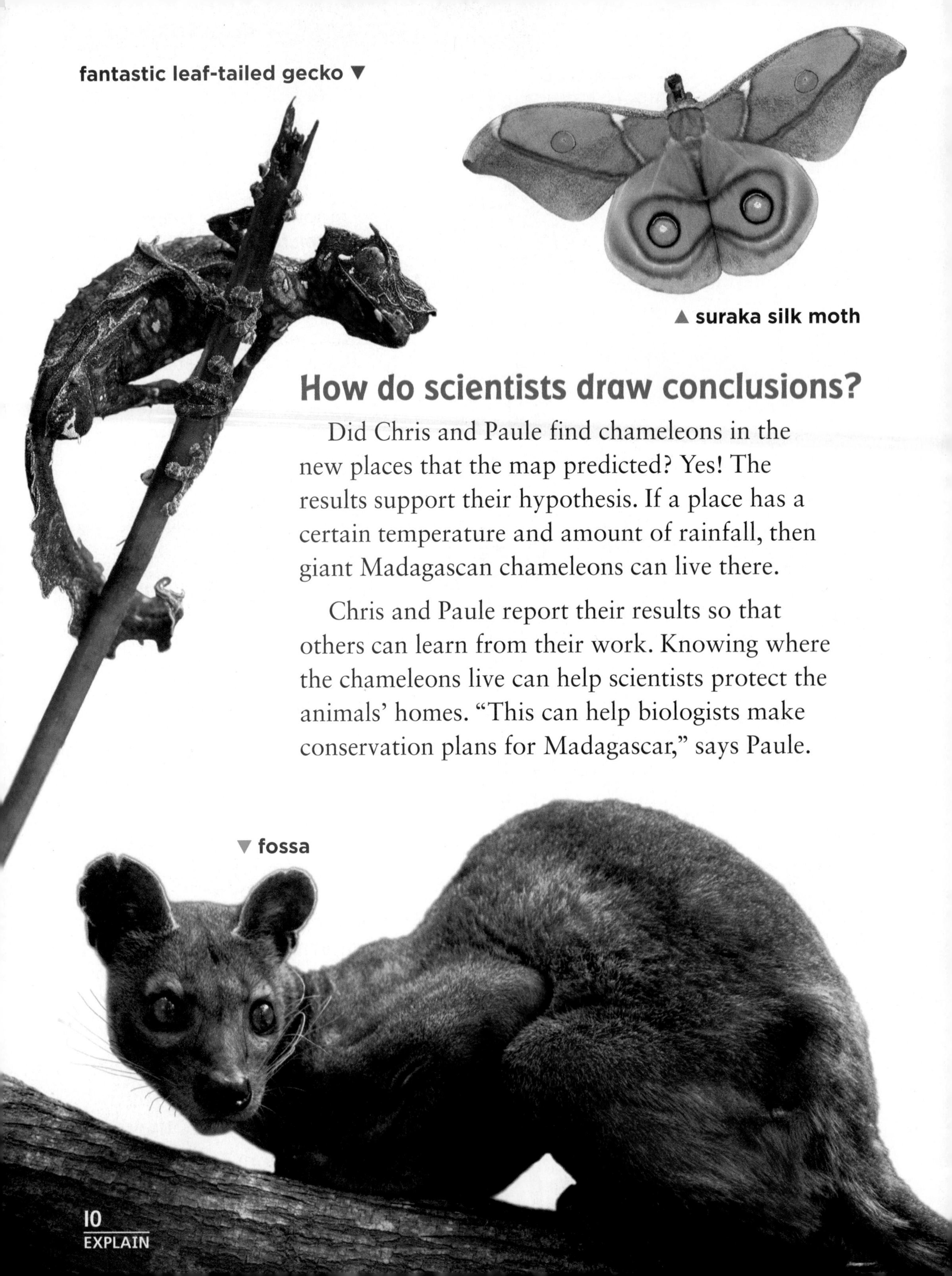

fantastic leaf-tailed gecko ▼

▲ suraka silk moth

▼ fossa

How do scientists draw conclusions?

Did Chris and Paule find chameleons in the new places that the map predicted? Yes! The results support their hypothesis. If a place has a certain temperature and amount of rainfall, then giant Madagascan chameleons can live there.

Chris and Paule report their results so that others can learn from their work. Knowing where the chameleons live can help scientists protect the animals' homes. "This can help biologists make conservation plans for Madagascar," says Paule.

Malagasy tree frog ▲

Draw Conclusions

1. Decide if the data clearly support or do not support the hypothesis.
2. If the results are not clear, rethink how the hypothesis was tested and make a new plan.
3. Write down the results to share with others.

▶ **Make sure to ask questions.**

ring-tailed lemur ▶

Chris and Paule's results lead them to new questions. What other variables affect where giant Madagascan chameleons live? The animals shown on this page all live in Madagascar. Could scientists search for these living things in the same way? Which places on the island are home to the greatest number of plants and animals? New questions can lead to a new hypothesis and to learning new things. Learning more about the animals that live in Madagascar will help protect them.

Think, Talk, and Write

1. Why is the scientific method useful to scientists?
2. What other questions about animals can you think of? Choose one and form a hypothesis that can be tested.

▼ red millipede

Focus on Skills

Scientists use many skills as they work through the scientific method. Skills help them gather information and answer questions they have about the world around us. Here are some skills they use.

Observe Use your senses to learn about an object or event.

Form a Hypothesis Make a statement that can be tested to answer a question.

Communicate Share information with others.

Classify Place things with similar properties into groups.

Use Numbers Order, count, add, subtract, multiply, and divide to explain data.

Make a Model Make something to represent an object or event.

animal	what I observed

▲ **Observe** the animals on these pages. Then make a chart to **communicate** your observations.

3-I.I. Classify objects by two of their properties (attributes).

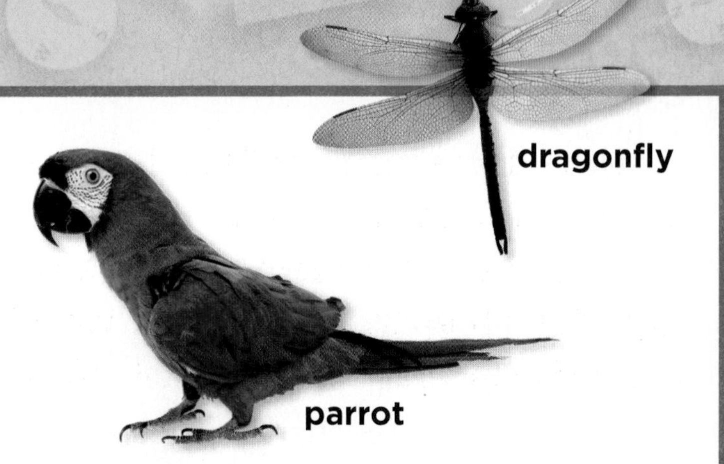

Use Variables Identify things that can control or change the outcome of an experiment.

Interpret Data Use information that has been gathered to answer questions or solve a problem.

Measure Find the size, distance, time, volume, area, mass, weight, or temperature of an object or event.

Predict State possible results of an event or experiment.

Infer Form an idea from facts or observations.

Experiment Perform a test to support or disprove a hypothesis.

snail

Animal Young

Animal	Average Number of Young
beetle	75
sea star	2,000,000
lizard	14
hedgehog	4
gazelle	1

▲ **Use this chart to infer how an animal's size affects how many young it has at a time.**

Inquiry Skill Builder

In each chapter of this book, you will find an Inquiry Skill Builder. These features will help you build the skills you need to become a great scientist.

3-I.6. Infer meaning from data communicated in graphs, tables, and diagrams.

Safety Tips

In the Classroom

- Read all of the directions. Make sure you understand them. When you see "⚠ **Be Careful,**" follow the safety rules.
- Listen to your teacher for special safety directions. If you do not understand something, ask for help.
- Wash your hands with soap and water before an activity.
- Be careful around a hot plate. Know when it is on and when it is off. Remember that the plate stays hot for a few minutes after it is turned off.
- Wear a safety apron if you work with anything messy or anything that might spill.
- Clean up a spill right away, or ask your teacher for help.
- Dispose of things the way your teacher tells you to.
- Tell your teacher if something breaks. If glass breaks, do not clean it up yourself.
- Wear safety goggles when your teacher tells you to wear them. Wear them when working with anything that can fly into your eyes or when working with liquids.
- Keep your hair and clothes away from open flames. Tie back long hair, and roll up long sleeves.
- Keep your hands dry around electrical equipment.
- Do not eat or drink anything during an experiment.
- Put equipment back the way your teacher tells you to.
- Clean up your work area after an activity, and wash your hands with soap and water.

In the Field

- Go with a trusted adult—such as your teacher, or a parent or guardian.
- Do not touch animals or plants without an adult's approval. The animal might bite. The plant might be poison ivy or another dangerous plant.

Responsibility
Treat living things, the environment, and one another with respect.

Life Science

Most salamanders are small, but some reach five feet in length.

South Carolina state amphibian: The spotted salamander

the yellow-crowned night heron

Francis Beidler Forest

Four Holes Swamp

Visiting the Francis Beidler Forest is like taking a trip back in time. In the forest you can see trees that are more than 1,000 years old.

The forest is located in Four Holes Swamp. A swamp is a forest in a very wet area. Four Holes Swamp has the largest stand of old bald cypress trees and tupelo gum trees in the world.

The Importance of Wetlands

A swamp is a type of wetland. Some of the plants and animals in Four Holes Swamp are very rare. Like all living things, they need certain conditions to live and grow. Some of the animals in Four Holes Swamp can live only in forests with old trees.

Wetlands are important for many reasons. They provide a home for a variety of living things. They also help prevent flooding. When heavy rains fall, the ground cannot absorb all the water. Wetlands act like sponges, absorbing the extra water. Wetlands also act like filters. They remove waste material from the water.

Think, Talk, and Write

Critical Thinking Why might some animals need to live in forests with old trees?

3-2.3. Recall the characteristics of an organism's habitat that allow the organism to survive there.

South Carolina

A CLOSER LOOK

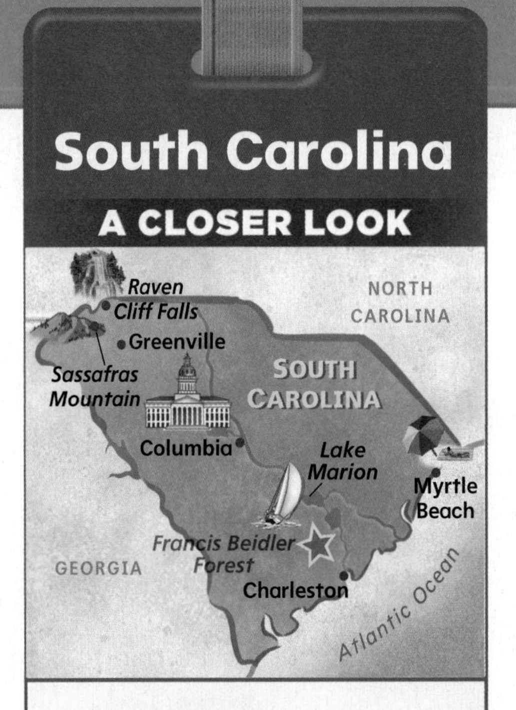

Main Idea

Wetlands provide the right conditions for certain kinds of animals and plants to live.

Activity

Classify What kinds of trees live in your area?

- Collect leaves from three different trees in your neighborhood.
- Use a field guide or key to identify the trees.
- Use research materials to find out more about your trees. Make a poster that shows what you learned.

Savannah National Wildlife Refuge

A Safe Place for Birds

For bird watchers the Savannah National Wildlife Refuge is a must-see stop. Almost 300 kinds of birds live there. Refuge means "safe place." During the winter months, many mallards, pintails, and other ducks come to the refuge.

In spring and fall, songbirds travel to and from their northern nesting grounds. They stop at the refuge to eat and rest during their journeys.

Other birds found at the refuge include geese, shorebirds, and bald eagles. However, the refuge is not just for birds. It is also home to alligators, manatees, deer, and squirrels.

An Old Rice Farm

For thousands of years, the area was used by Native Americans. Later, European settlers arrived. They used much of the land to grow rice. Rice is a crop that needs a lot of water. The settlers made ditches and dams to control water in their rice fields. Today, these old rice fields attract a great variety of birds.

Think, Talk, and Write

Critical Thinking Why do you think so many ducks stop at the refuge?

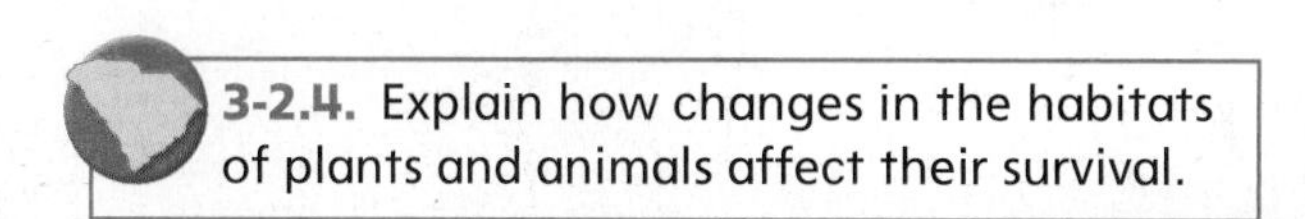

South Carolina

A CLOSER LOOK

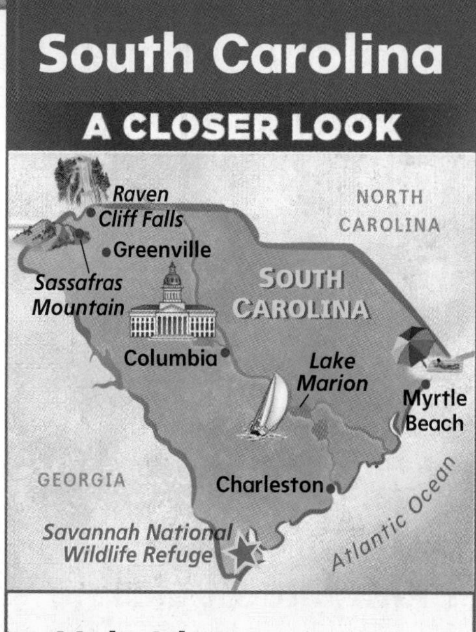

Main Idea

Human activities, such as farming, can affect which animals live in an area.

Activity

Compare What do the birds that live in the Savannah National Wildlife refuge have in common?

- Choose two types of birds that live in the refuge.
- Find out more about the birds you chose.
- Make a report to share with your classmates.

CHAPTER 1

Living Things Grow and Change

The Big Idea

How do living things get what they need to live and grow?

Gecko hatches from an egg.

Key Vocabulary

organism
a living thing (p. 24)

environment
all the living and nonliving things that surround an organism (p. 26)

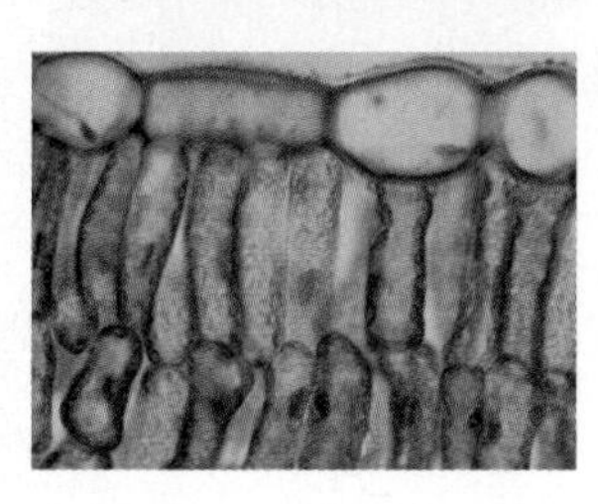

cell
the basic building block that makes up all living things (p. 28)

life cycle
all the stages in an organism's life (p. 38)

adaptation
a body part or behavior that helps one kind of living thing survive in its environment (p. 62)

food chain
a series of organisms that depend on one another for food (p. 70)

More Vocabulary

respond, p. 24
reproduce, p. 25
seed, p. 34
embryo, p. 34
flower, p. 36
pollination, p. 37
fruit, p. 37
cone, p. 39
metamorphosis, p. 47
egg, p. 47
larva, p. 47
pupa, p. 47
habitat, p. 56
climate, p. 56
soil, p. 56
structure, p. 59
shelter, p. 60
ecosystem, p. 68
producer, p. 70
consumer, p. 71
decomposer, p. 71
food web, p. 72

Lesson 1

Living Things and Their Needs

Watering hole in Namibia, Africa

Look and Wonder

Living and nonliving things can be found all over Earth. How can you tell the difference between living and nonliving things? How many of each can you see here?

3-2.1. Illustrate the life cycles of seed plants and various animals and summarize how they grow and are adapted to conditions within their habitats.

Explore

Inquiry Activity

How do living and nonliving things differ?

Purpose

Find out some characteristics of living and nonliving things.

Procedure

1. **Predict** How are all living things alike? How are nonliving things alike?
2. Make a table. Label the columns *Living Things* and *Nonliving Things*.
3. Place 4 pieces of string outside on the ground so that they form a square.
4. **Observe** Look for living things in your square area. List them in your table. Tell how you know they are living. Do the same with nonliving things that you see.

Draw Conclusions

5. **Interpret Data** What characteristics do the living things share? Which do the nonliving things share?
6. Trade tables with a partner. Do the things on your partner's table share the same characteristics as yours?
7. **Infer** How are living things different from nonliving things?

Explore More

Experiment Does the amount of sunlight affect how many living things are in an area? How could you test this?

Materials

four 1-meter pieces of string

Step 2

Living Things	Nonliving Things

Step 4

3-I.I. Classify objects by two of their properties (attributes).

Read and Learn

Main Idea 3-2.1

All living things have certain characteristics and needs in common.

Vocabulary

organism, p. 24

respond, p. 24

reproduce, p. 25

environment, p. 26

cell, p. 28

LOG ON e-Glossary at www.macmillanmh.com

Reading Skill

Main Idea and Details

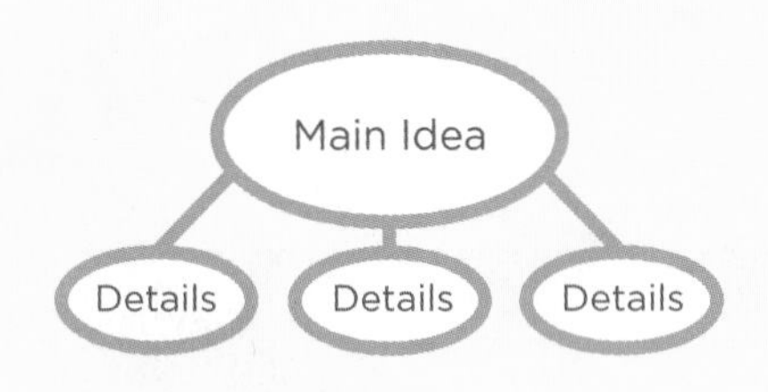

What are living things?

Look outside. Do you see any plants or animals? Plants and animals are living things. What are some characteristics that all living things share?

Living Things Grow

Living things are called **organisms** (AWR•guh•niz•uhmz). All organisms use energy to grow. To *grow* means to change with age. A young sunflower plant is small and green. Over time, it grows taller and its stem grows harder. Eventually, a flower forms. A young bird grows into an adult. It gets bigger and less fuzzy.

Living Things Respond

Living things **respond** (ri•SPOND), or react, to the world around them. When a plant is in shade, it responds by bending toward sunlight. When a bird sees a cat and senses danger, it may fly high into the trees. When a day gets hot, a lizard may go underground to keep cool.

Living Things Grow

Read a Photo

How will the small gulls change as they grow?

Clue: Young organisms grow more similar to their parents.

◀ When skinks reproduce, the female lays eggs. New skinks hatch from the eggs.

Living Things Reproduce

Living things reproduce (ree•pruh•DEWS). To **reproduce** means to make more of one's own kind. An apple tree reproduces by making apple seeds. The seeds can grow into new apple trees. A turtle reproduces by laying eggs. Young turtles hatch from the eggs.

Nonliving Things

Nonliving things are all around you. Rocks, soil, and water are nonliving things that come from nature. Cars and roads are nonliving things made by humans. Nonliving things are different from living things. They do not use energy to grow, respond, or reproduce.

Quick Check

Main Idea and Details What are some characteristics of living things?

Critical Thinking Is a toy a living thing? How can you tell?

When the weather gets cooler in autumn, this tree responds by losing its leaves. ▶

What do living things need?

Living things have needs. They need food, water, and space. Many also need gases found in air or water. A living thing will die if its needs are not met.

Living things get everything they need to survive from their environment (en•VYE•ruhn•muhnt). An **environment** is all the living and nonliving things that surround an organism.

Food

Living things need energy to live and grow. They get energy from food. Animals get food by eating other organisms. Plants make their own food using energy from sunlight.

A caterpillar gets the energy it needs to grow by eating leaves.

Water

Did you know that more than half of your body is water? All living things are full of water. They use the water in their bodies to break down food and get rid of waste. They use it to transport food throughout their bodies. Living things need a regular supply of water to stay healthy.

These plants soak up water from wet soil in their environment.

Gases

Animals need oxygen (OK•suh•juhn) to survive. *Oxygen* is a gas found in air and water. Every time you breathe, you take in oxygen from the air. Fish, clams, and most other sea animals get oxygen from the water around them.

Plants need oxygen and a gas called *carbon dioxide* (KAHR•buhn dye•OK•side). They use energy from sunlight to change carbon dioxide and water into food.

Space

Organisms need space, or room. Plants need space to grow and find water and sunlight. Animals need space to move and find food. Different organisms need different amounts of space. Whales swim for miles in oceans. Goldfish can live in tiny ponds.

▲ Some water animals, such as this manatee, must come to the surface to take in oxygen from the air.

▲ Foxes hunt in forests and fields. Small dens help them stay safe.

Quick Check

Main Idea and Details What are some things that all organisms need to survive?

Critical Thinking What might happen to an animal in a crowded environment?

Quick Lab

Observe Cells

1. **Observe** Look at a piece of onion. Then observe it using a hand lens. What do you see?
2. **Communicate** Draw how the onion looks when viewed with a hand lens.
3. **Observe** Look at a slide of an onion under a microscope. What do you see? Is there any space between the cells?

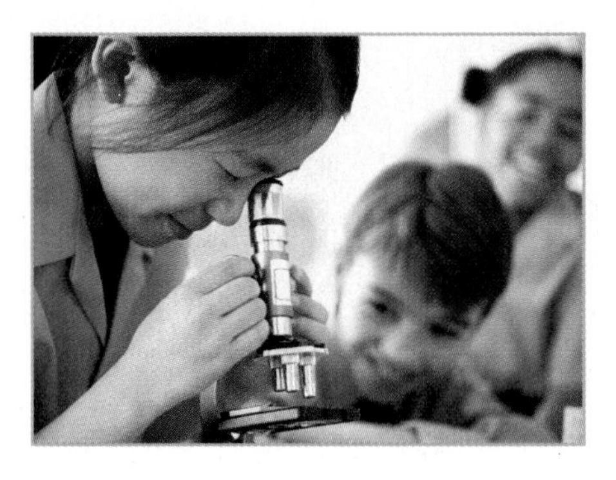

4. **Communicate** Draw how the onion looks when viewed with a microscope. Then compare your two drawings.
5. **Infer** How small are cells? What tool do you need to observe cells?

What are living things made of?

How are you like a brick building? The building is made of many small bricks. You are made of many small parts called cells. **Cells** are the building blocks of life. All organisms are made up of one or more cells.

Cells are too small to see with just your eyes. They are so small that it takes millions to make one little ant. You need a tool called a *microscope* (MYE•kruh•skohp) to observe cells. A microscope makes tiny things look larger.

Some organisms are made of a single cell. Organisms called bacteria are an example. They live in soil and water. Some live on our skin and in our bodies!

Quick Check

Main Idea and Details What are cells?

Critical Thinking What do you think cells need to survive?

◀ These cells from a lilac leaf were magnified with a microscope.

Lesson Review

Visual Summary

Living things grow, respond, and reproduce.

Living things **need** food, water, gases from air or water, and space to live.

Living things are made of **cells**.

Make a FOLDABLES™ Study Guide

Make a Three-Tab Book. Use it to summarize what you learned about living things and their needs.

Think, Talk, and Write

1. **Main Idea** How can you tell the difference between a living and nonliving thing?

2. **Vocabulary** What is an environment?

3. **Main Idea and Details** What do living things need to survive?

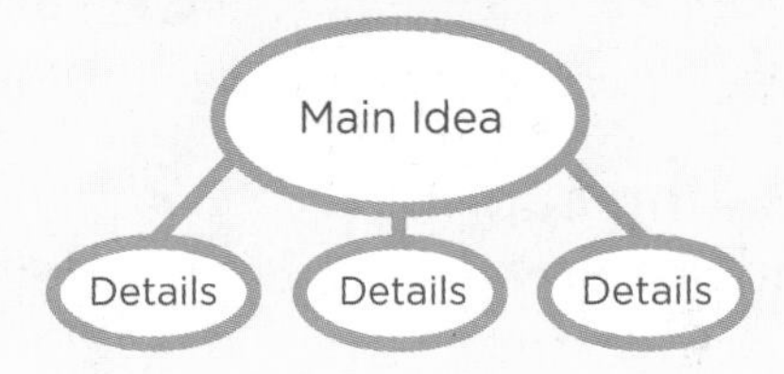

4. **Critical Thinking** Suppose you wanted to grow plants in your backyard. What would you do?

5. **Test Prep** **People need all of the following to survive EXCEPT**
   - **A** air.
   - **B** water.
   - **C** cars.
   - **D** space.

Writing Link

Write a Story
Suppose you were a bird. What would you need to live? How would your life be different? Research to learn more about birds. Write a story about life as a bird.

Health Link

Food Pyramid
People need the right balance of foods to stay healthy. The Food Guide Pyramid shows this balance. Do research to find out about the Food Guide Pyramid.

LOG ON e-Review Summaries and quizzes online at www.macmillanmh.com

Materials

4 identical plants

measuring cup and water

ruler

Structured Inquiry

What do plants need to survive?

Form a Hypothesis

Do plants need light to grow? Do they need water? Write a hypothesis. Start with "If plants do not get light and water, then . . ."

Test Your Hypothesis

Light and Water	Light and No Water
Water and No Light	No Light and No Water

1. Label four identical plants as shown.
2. **Observe** How do the plants look? How tall are they? Measure them and record your observations in a chart. Use words and pictures.

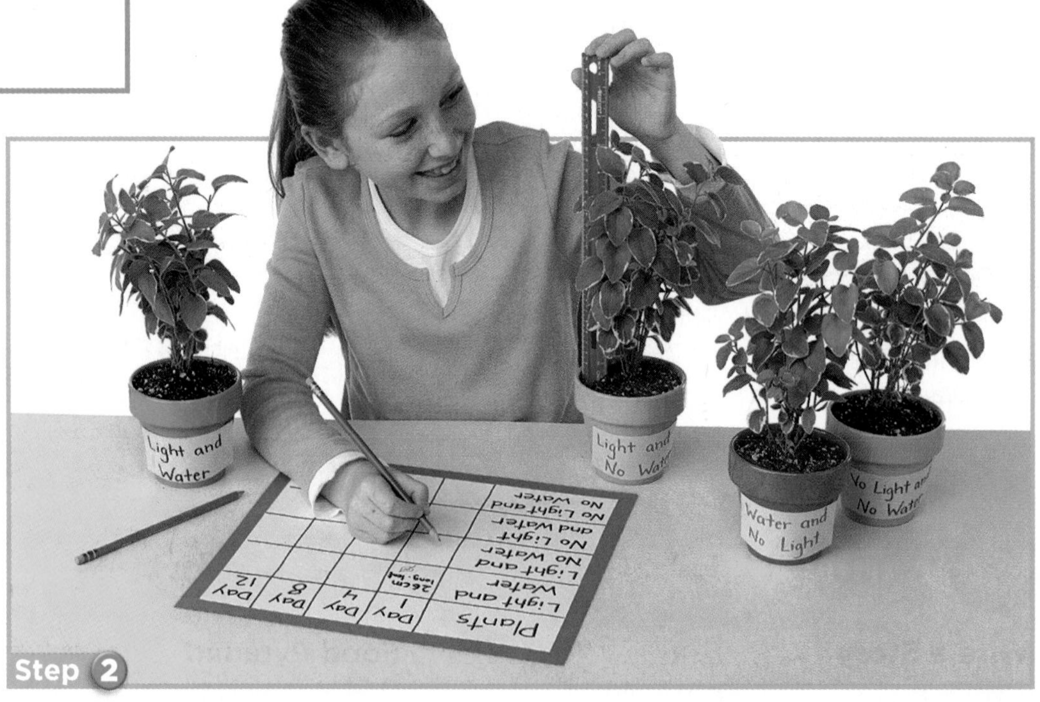

Step 2

3. Put the plants labeled *No Light* in a dark place, such as a closet. Put the plants labeled *Light* in a sunny place, such as on a windowsill.
4. **Predict** What do you think will happen to each plant? Record your predictions.

3-I.4. Predict the outcome of a simple investigation and compare the result with the prediction.

5 **Observe** Look at the plants every other day. Water each plant labeled *Water* with 200 mL of water. Measure how tall the plants grow. Record your observations in your chart using words and pictures.

Draw Conclusions

6 **Interpret Data** Which plant grew the most after two weeks? Which plant looks the healthiest? Use your chart to help you.

7 What do plants need to survive?

Guided Inquiry

What else do land plants need to survive?

Form a Hypothesis

Do plants need air? Do they need soil? Write a hypothesis about one of these.

Test Your Hypothesis

Design an experiment to test your hypothesis. Decide which of the materials below you will use. Write the steps you will follow.

- two identical plants
- petroleum jelly
- measuring cup
- water
- soil

Draw Conclusions

Did your results support your hypothesis? Why or why not? Share your results with your classmates.

Open Inquiry

What other questions do you have about plants and their needs or structures? Talk with your classmates about questions you have. Choose one question to investigate. How might you answer this question? Make sure your experiment tests only one variable at a time.

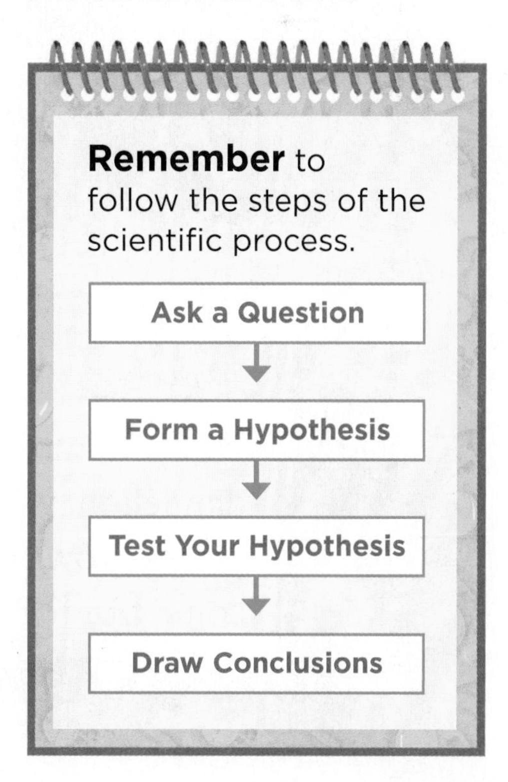

Lesson 2

Plant Life Cycles

Look and Wonder

Did you know that when you blow on a dandelion, you are helping seeds spread? New plants grow from those seeds. Where do seeds come from? How do seeds grow into plants?

3-2.1. Illustrate the life cycles of seed plants and various animals and summarize how they grow and are adapted to conditions within their habitats.

Explore Inquiry Activity

What does a seed need to grow?

Form a Hypothesis

Do seeds need water to grow? Form a hypothesis. Start with "If seeds do not get water, then . . ."

Test Your Hypothesis

1. **Observe** Look at the seeds with a hand lens. Draw what you see.
2. **Use Variables** Fold each paper towel into quarters. Then put two tablespoons of water onto one towel. Put the wet towel into a plastic bag. Label the bag *Water*. Put the dry towel into a bag. Label this bag *No Water*.
3. Place three seeds into each bag. Seal the bags and place them in a warm spot.
4. **Observe** Look at the seeds every day for a week. Record what you see with pictures and words. If the paper towel in the *Water* bag feels dry, add two tablespoons of water.

Draw Conclusions

5. **Interpret Data** Which seeds changed? How did they change?
6. **Infer** Why do you think the seeds changed?
7. Did your results support your hypothesis?

Explore More

Experiment What would happen if you wet the paper towel with something other than water? Experiment to find out.

Materials

- 6 seeds
- hand lens
- 2 paper towels
- water
- tablespoon
- 2 plastic bags

Step 1

Step 3

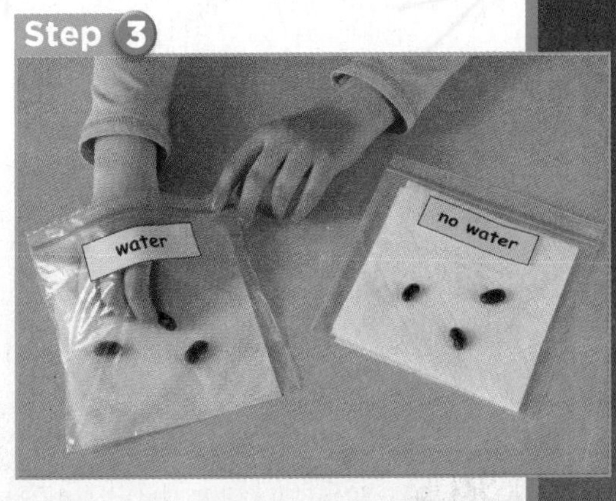

3-1.4. Predict the outcome of a simple investigation and compare the result with the prediction.

Read and Learn

Main Idea 3-2.1

A life cycle describes how an organism grows and reproduces. Most plants grow from seeds.

Vocabulary

seed, p. 34

embryo, p. 34

flower, p. 36

pollination, p. 37

fruit, p. 37

life cycle, p. 38

cone, p. 39

LOG ON e-Glossary at www.macmillanmh.com

Reading Skill

Sequence

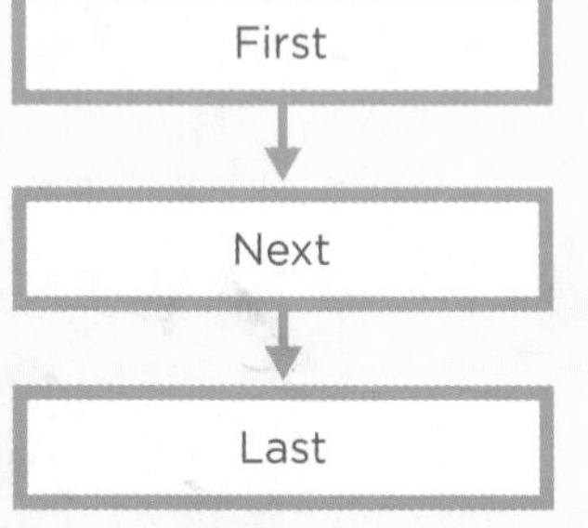

How do plants grow?

Did you know that when you eat corn, peas, or nuts, you are eating seeds? Seeds come in all shapes and sizes. Some are big like lima beans. Some are tiny like poppy seeds. Big or small, all seeds have the same function.

A **seed** is a structure that can grow into a new plant. It holds a young plant that is ready to grow. This young plant is called an **embryo** (EM•bree•oh). A seed has parts that help an embryo survive. It holds stored food that the embryo uses to grow. It has a tough covering that protects the embryo.

When a seed is planted in the soil, it can *germinate*, or begin to grow. A seed needs water, nutrients, and the right temperature to germinate. It can wait to grow for months or even years until conditions are right.

From Seed to Plant

1. A seed is planted in soil.

2. The seed germinates. Roots start growing down into the soil.

When a seed begins to germinate, it soaks up water. That makes it swell up and break through its covering. The embryo grows out of the seed. It grows into a small plant called a *seedling*. A seedling can grow into an adult plant.

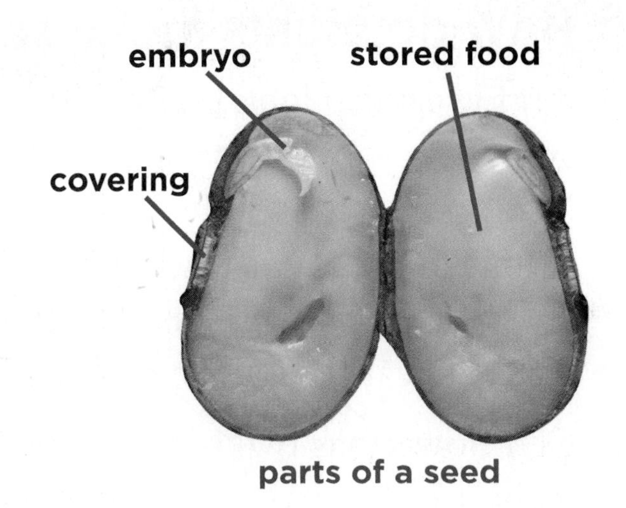

parts of a seed

Quick Check

Sequence What happens to a seed after it germinates?

Critical Thinking What might happen to a seed if it does not get enough water?

5. In time, the plant grows into an adult. Now it can reproduce and make new seeds. ▶

3. The roots grow longer, and a stem pushes up out of the ground.

4. The plant grows leaves. It starts to make its own food.

How do plants make seeds?

Flowers can look pretty and smell sweet. They also do an important job. Many plants need flowers to reproduce. A **flower** is a plant structure that makes seeds. Plants that use flowers to make seeds are called *flowering plants*.

A flower has two parts that help it make seeds, a male part and a female part. The male part makes a powder called *pollen*. The female part makes tiny eggs. When pollen and an egg come together, a seed can form.

How does pollen get to an egg? Wind may blow pollen from one flower to another. Animals such as hummingbirds, bees, and bats can carry pollen, too. Some animals are attracted to a flower's smell or bright colors. They drink a sweet liquid, called *nectar*, from the flower. Sticky pollen clings to their bodies. Then, they carry the pollen to another flower.

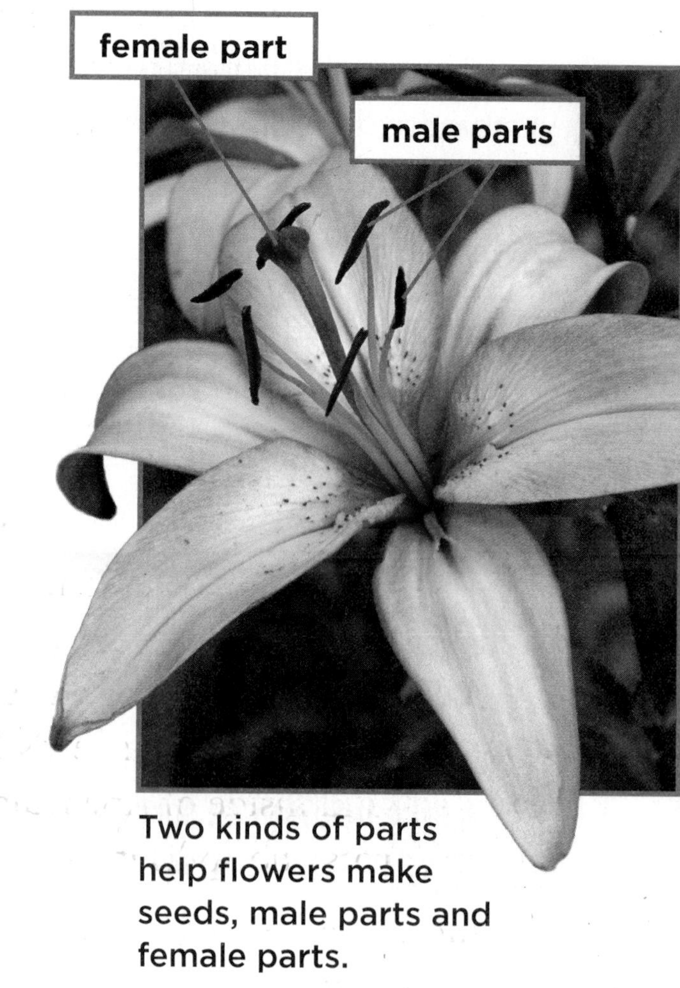

Two kinds of parts help flowers make seeds, male parts and female parts.

When a bee drinks nectar from a flower, yellow pollen sticks to its body.

The movement of pollen from the male part of a flower to the female part is called **pollination** (pol•uh•NAY•shuhn). After pollination, seeds can develop. In flowering plants, fruit forms around the seeds. **Fruit** is a structure that holds seeds.

How Seeds Travel

Before a seed can germinate, it has to find its way to the soil. How does it get there? Some seeds, such as a fuzzy dandelion's, are made to blow in the breeze. Other seeds fall to the ground inside of ripe fruit. The fruit rots and spills its seeds.

Animals can help, too. Seeds, such as acorns, may be buried by squirrels. Prickly seeds can stick to an animal's fur and be carried to a new place. When an animal eats fruit, the seeds may pass through the animal's body. They are left on the ground in the animal's waste.

Quick Lab

Fruits and Seeds

strawberry

1. **Observe** Look at the fruit from three different plants. Compare their shapes and sizes.

peach

2. Carefully cut open the fruit. How do their parts compare? Do they all have a peel or skin? Do they all have seeds?

kiwi

3. **Observe** Look at the seeds from each fruit. Compare the location of the seeds in each fruit.
4. **Infer** What do all fruit have in common? How might fruit help seeds survive and grow?

Berry seeds will pass through this ermine's body and into the soil, where they can grow.

Quick Check

Sequence How does a seed form?

Critical Thinking How do bright sweet-smelling flowers help plants?

FACT Tomatoes have seeds, so they are fruit.

What is the life cycle of some plants?

How a plant germinates, grows, and reproduces is the plant's life cycle. A **life cycle** is the stages in an organism's life. Plants grow and reproduce in different ways.

In time, adult plants die. They *decompose*, or break down, and become part of the soil. This adds nutrients to the soil that help other plants grow.

Flowering Plants

Most plants are flowering plants. Flowering plants grow from seeds into adult plants. As adults, they reproduce and make new seeds using flowers.

Life Cycle of a Cherry Tree

A young cherry tree grows.

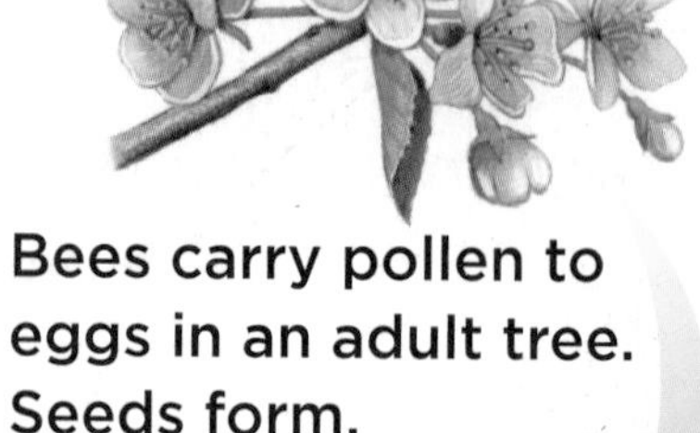

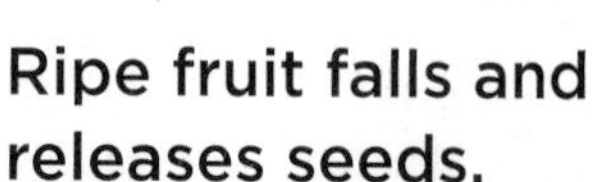

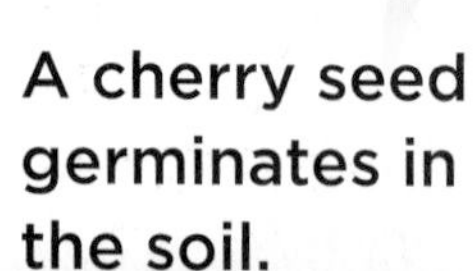

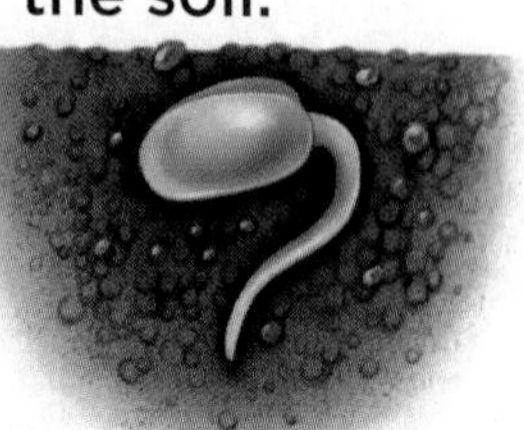

Conifers

Have you ever picked up a pine cone? **Cones** are plant structures that make seeds. Plants that reproduce with cones are called *conifers*. They include pine, spruce, and hemlock trees. Conifers have similar life cycles to flowering plants. Both grow from seeds. Both reproduce and make new seeds through pollination. However conifers make seeds inside of cones instead of flowers.

pine tree

Quick Check

Sequence How do conifers form seeds?

Critical Thinking How are flowers and cones alike? How are they different?

Life Cycle of a Pine Tree

A young pine tree grows.

An adult tree makes male and female cones. Wind blows pollen from the male cones onto the female cones.

Seeds develop inside the female cone.

When the cone is ripe, seeds fall out.

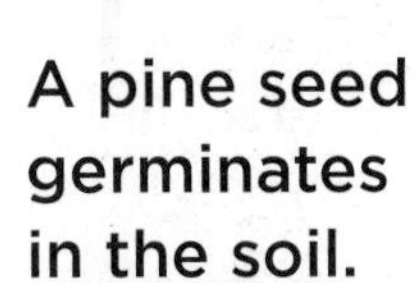
A pine seed germinates in the soil.

Read a Diagram

What are the stages of a conifer's life cycle?

Clue: Arrows help show a sequence.

Science in Motion Watch plant life cycles to learn more at **www.macmillanmh.com**

How do plants grow without seeds?

Some plants reproduce without making seeds. A type of plant called a fern never makes seeds. Instead it makes *spores*. Like a seed, a spore can fall to the ground. It can grow into a new fern plant. Unlike a seed, a spore does not have stored food.

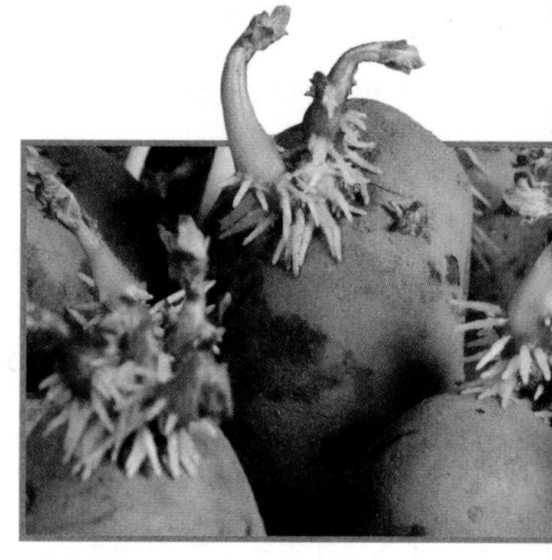

▲ New stems and leaves can grow out of the "eyes" of a potato.

New plants can also grow from parts of plants. Potato plants can grow from the white spots, or "eyes," on a potato. Other plants grow from an underground stem called a *bulb*. An onion is one type of bulb. Sometimes, a new plant can also grow from a stem or leaf that is placed in water.

Life Cycle of a Fern

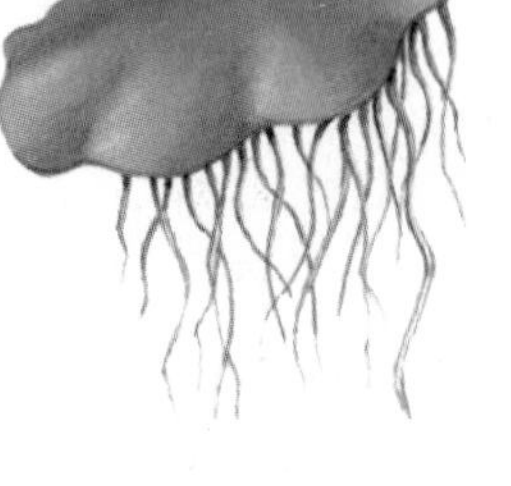

Adult ferns grow and release spores.

A spore grows into a small organism with male and female parts.

A young fern grows when cells from the male and female parts join.

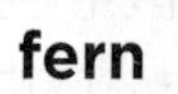

Quick Check

Sequence What is the life cycle of a fern?

Critical Thinking Would a fern survive if it landed in soil with few nutrients? Why?

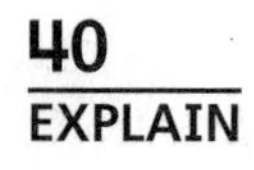

Lesson Review

Visual Summary

Plants go through a series of changes as they grow into adults.

Flowering plants and **conifers** grow from seeds and have similar life cycles.

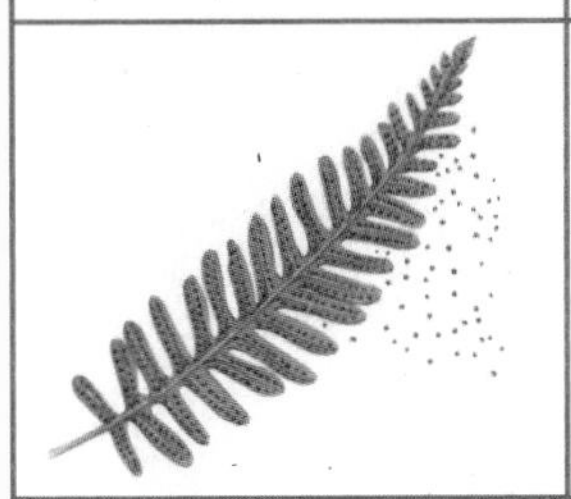

Some plants, such as **ferns**, do not grow from seeds.

Make a FOLDABLES Study Guide

Make a Layered-Look Book. Use it to summarize what you learned about plant life cycles.

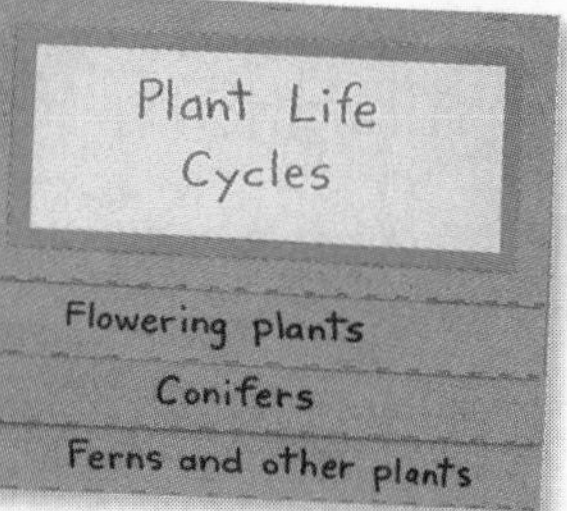

Think, Talk, and Write

1. **Main Idea** How are flowering plants, conifers, and ferns different?

2. **Vocabulary** What is fruit?

3. **Sequence** What is the life cycle of a flowering plant?

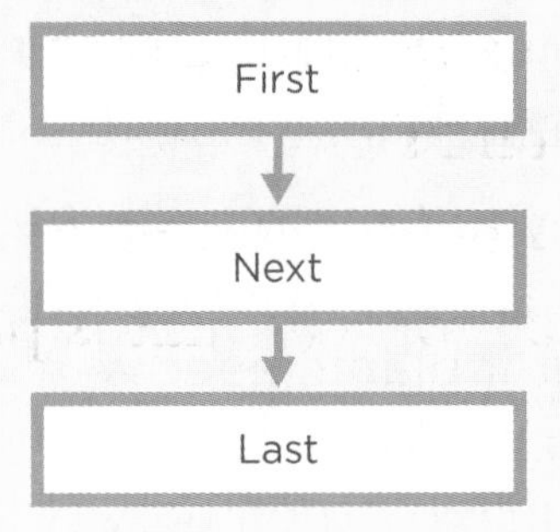

4. **Critical Thinking** How do animals help flowering plants?

5. **Test Prep** **How does a conifer reproduce?**
   A with bulbs
   B with flowers
   C with cones
   D with spores

Writing Link

Writing That Compares
Which plants grow in your community? Choose four plants around your home. Do they reproduce using flowers, cones, or spores? Write paragraphs comparing and contrasting the plants you found.

Art Link

Paint a Picture
Use the Internet or library resources to find images of flowers painted by Georgia O'Keeffe. Look closely at two of her paintings of plants. How do they make you feel? Describe them. Then make your own paintings of plants.

Focus on Skills

Inquiry Skill: Form a Hypothesis

You just learned how seeds grow into plants. Can seeds grow when the weather is cold? To answer questions like this, scientists start with what they know about plants. Then they use this information to turn their question into a testable statement. That is, they **form a hypothesis**.

▶ Learn It

When you **form a hypothesis**, you make a statement that you can test by collecting data. Suppose you want to find out if plants need sunlight. Based on what you know, you could form a hypothesis like this: If plants do not get sunlight, then they will not grow.

A good hypothesis needs to be testable. You could test the hypothesis above by placing one plant in the dark and one in sunlight. Then you could observe and record what happens. A hypothesis also needs to identify the variables. In the example above, sunlight and plant growth are variables.

▶ Try It

Form a hypothesis about what seeds need to grow. Then test that hypothesis with an experiment.

Materials **water, 2 paper towels, 6 pea seeds, 2 sealable plastic bags, 2 foam cups, ice**

1. Think about what you know about seeds. Now form a hypothesis about this question: Will pea seeds germinate more quickly in a cold spot or in a warm spot? Begin with "If I plant a pea seed in the cold, then . . ."

2. Fold two wet paper towels in half and place three seeds onto each. Place each paper towel into a plastic bag and seal the bags.
3. Place one bag into a foam cup filled with ice. Place the other into an empty cup.
4. Make a chart like the one below. Use it to record your observations. Do your results support your hypothesis?

Step 4

	Cold	Warm
Day 1		
Day 2		
Day 3		
Day 4		

▶ Apply It

Now that you have learned to think like a scientist, you can answer other questions. Do seeds germinate more quickly in the light or dark? **Form a hypothesis** about this question. Then plan an experiment to test your hypothesis.

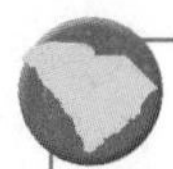

3-1.4. Predict the outcome of a simple investigation and compare the result with the prediction.

Lesson 3

Animal Life Cycles

Look and Wonder

This butterfly is going through a big change. Do you know what it used to look like? All animals change as they get older. Do all animals change in the same ways?

3-2.1. Illustrate the life cycles of seed plants and various animals and summarize how they grow and are adapted to conditions within their habitats.

Explore

Inquiry Activity

How does a caterpillar grow and change?

Make a Prediction

How does a caterpillar change as it grows? Write a prediction.

Test Your Prediction

1. **Observe** Look at the caterpillar. Draw a picture of it and label all the parts you can see. △ **Be Careful.** Handle animals with care.
2. **Measure** Find the length of your caterpillar. Record the caterpillar's length on your drawing.
3. Put your caterpillar into the kit.
4. **Observe** Once a day, observe your caterpillar and draw a picture of it. Label any changes you observe. If you can measure the caterpillar's length without disturbing it, record the length each day.

Draw Conclusions

5. **Interpret Data** What small changes did the caterpillar go through? What big changes did you observe?
6. **Infer** What are the stages in a butterfly's life cycle?

Explore More

Experiment How do tadpoles change as they grow? Make a plan to test your ideas.

Materials

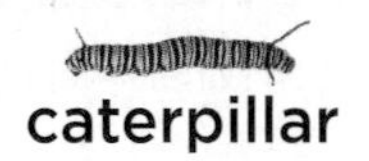
caterpillar

hand lens

ruler

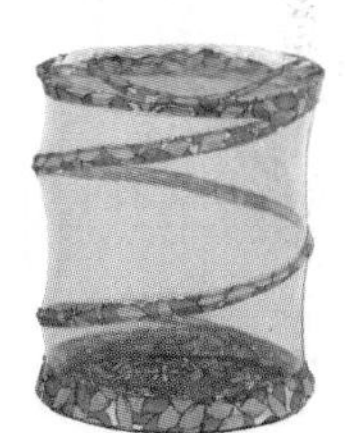
caterpillar kit

Step 1

Step 2

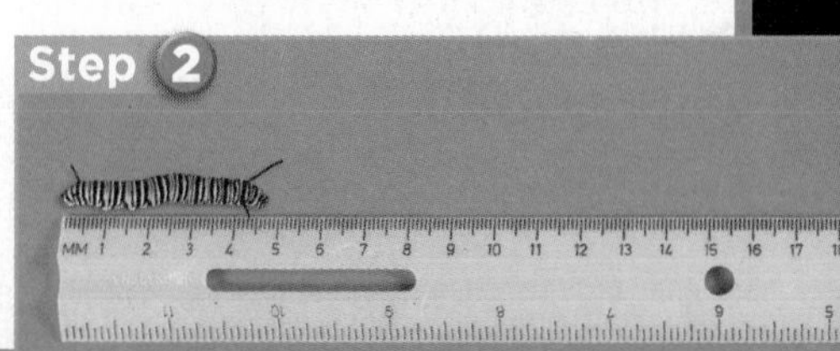

3-I.3. Generate questions about objects, organisms, and events in the environment and use those questions to conduct a scientific investigation.

Read and Learn

Main Idea 3-2.2

Animals have different life cycles. Some animals are born looking like their parents. Others change greatly as they grow.

Vocabulary

metamorphosis, p. 47

egg, p. 47

larva, p. 47

pupa, p. 47

at www.macmillanmh.com

Reading Skill

Sequence

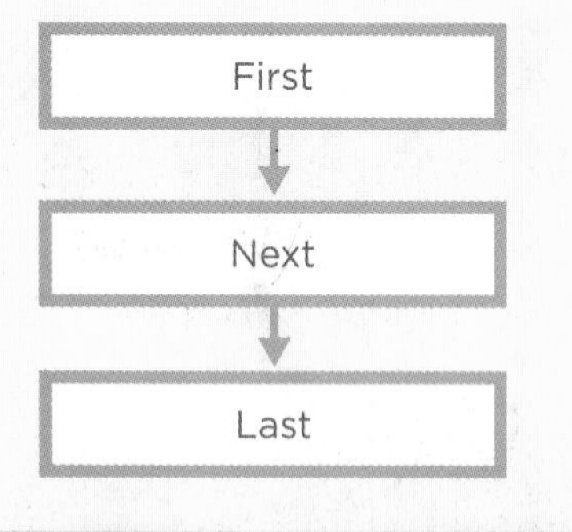

What are some animal life cycles?

Did you know that a caterpillar is actually a young butterfly? A tadpole is a young frog. These animals go through big changes as they grow. Do all animals change in the same ways?

Different types of animals change in different ways. Some animals are born looking like their parents. Others are not. These animals might change shape or color as they grow. They may even grow new structures. The way an animal changes with age is part of its life cycle.

An animal is born. It grows. It reproduces as an adult. In time it dies. Its body breaks down and becomes part of the soil. It adds nutrients to the soil that other organisms need to grow.

Life Cycle of a Frog

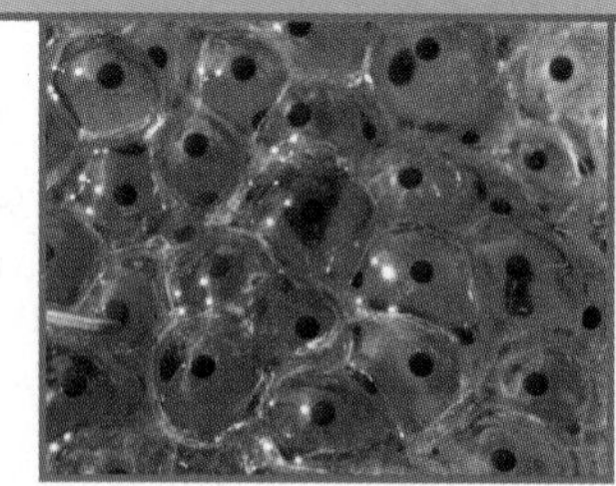

Egg Frogs lay eggs in water.

Tadpole Young frogs, or tadpoles, hatch. Like fish, they swim and breathe with gills.

Becoming an Adult A tadpole starts to grow legs and lungs.

Adult Now the frog looks like its parents. It moves onto land and can reproduce.

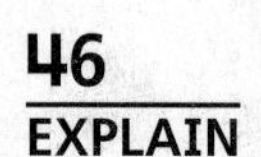

Metamorphosis

Some animals change shape through a process called **metamorphosis** (met•uh•MAWR•fuh•sis). Amphibians and most insects go through metamorphosis. Their life cycle begins with an **egg**. Eggs contain food that young animals need. Most have a shell that protects the animal.

When the young animal has grown enough, it *hatches*, or breaks out of the egg. It looks different from adults of its kind. With time, it grows into an adult that can have its own young. Most amphibians and insects do not look after their young. The young can get food on their own.

Quick Check

Sequence Name the stages in a ladybug's life cycle.

Critical Thinking Compare a frog's life cycle to a ladybug's life cycle.

Life Cycle of a Ladybug

Egg A ladybug starts life as an egg.

Larva When an insect hatches it is called a **larva**. A ladybug larva eats bugs and grows.

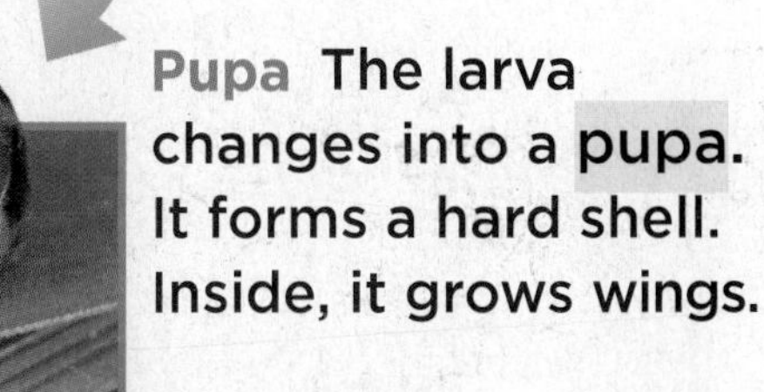

Pupa The larva changes into a **pupa**. It forms a hard shell. Inside, it grows wings.

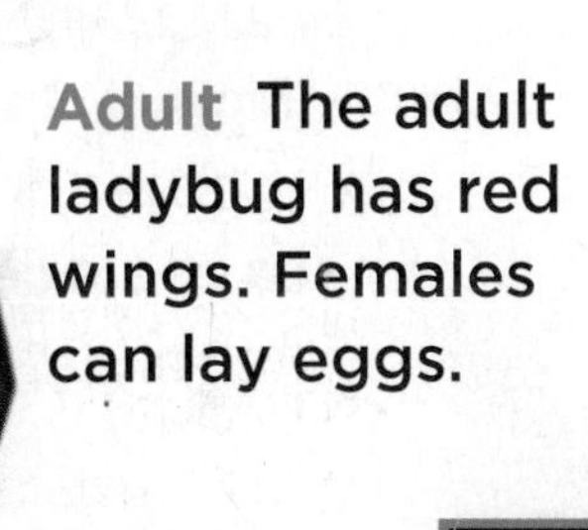

Adult The adult ladybug has red wings. Females can lay eggs.

How do reptiles, fish, and birds change as they grow?

Reptiles, fish, and birds have similar life cycles. Most of these animals lay eggs. Reptiles lay their eggs on dry land. Fish lay their eggs in water. Birds often build nests to protect their eggs. Most birds sit on their eggs until the eggs are ready to hatch.

An animal grows inside the egg. For a time it gets everything it needs to survive from the egg. When the young animal has grown enough, it hatches. Young reptiles, fish, and birds do not go through metamorphosis. They look similar to adults of their kind when they hatch.

Life Cycle of a Sea Turtle

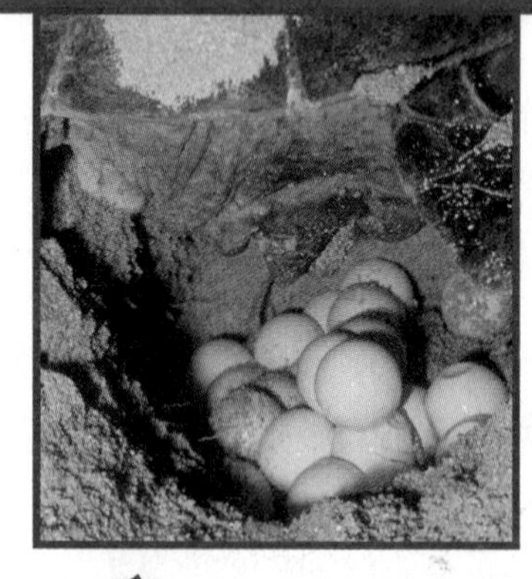

Egg Females crawl to the beach to lay eggs in the sand.

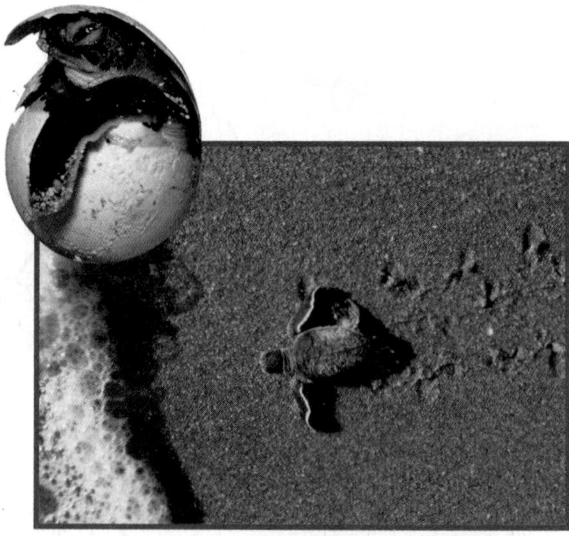

Young Sea turtles hatch on the beach and quickly crawl to the ocean.

Adult Turtles grow to 140 kg (300 lbs). Females stay in the sea until they are ready to lay eggs.

In time, young reptiles, fish, and birds grow into adults. Now they can reproduce and have young of their own. Most reptiles and fish do not look after their young. The young can find food on their own. Birds often raise their young until the young can fly and find food for themselves.

Quick Check

Sequence What happens after a fish lays eggs?

Critical Thinking How is a reptile's life cycle similar to a frog's? How does it differ?

Quick Lab

A Bird's Life Cycle

1. **Observe** Look at these three photos. Put them in order to show the life cycle of a chicken.
2. **Communicate** Describe a chicken's life cycle. How does a chicken change as it grows?
3. **Compare** How is the life cycle of a chicken similar to the turtle's? How does it differ?

Life Cycle of a Trout

Egg Fish eggs may float in water or sink to the bottom.

Young Fish hatch and begin to find food.

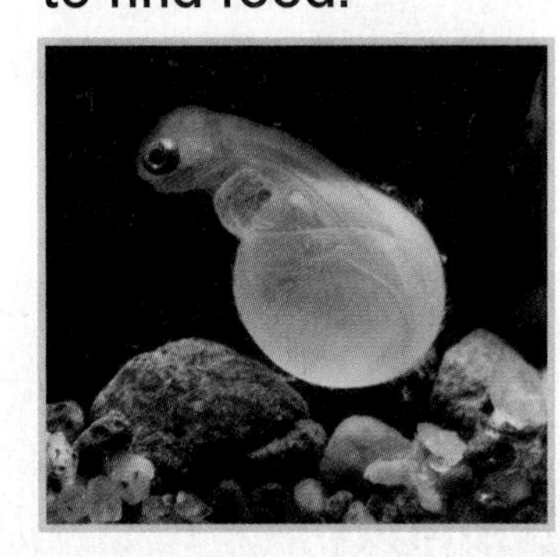

Adult Most fish continue to grow all their lives. Females may lay thousands of eggs each year!

What is the life cycle of a mammal?

Mammals do not hatch from eggs. Young mammals are born live. They look much like their parents from the start. Adult mammals feed and care for their young.

As they grow, young mammals lose fat and grow stronger. Their faces change to look more like adults. In time, they learn to survive on their own. They grow into adults that can reproduce and have their own young.

Quick Check

Sequence Which does a cheetah do first, reproduce or learn to hunt?

Critical Thinking How might growing bigger help an animal survive?

Life Cycle of a Cheetah

Cub Most female cheetahs have three to five cubs at once. They protect and feed the cubs.

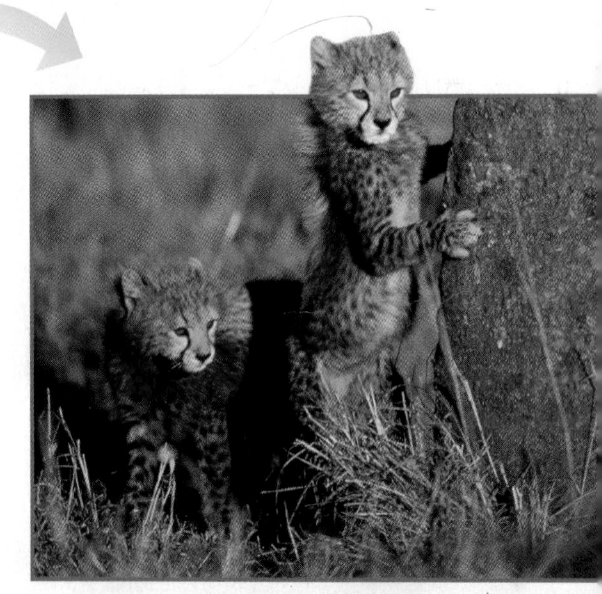

Young Cheetahs learn and practice the skills they will need to hunt.

Adult Cheetahs grow big and can reproduce. Adults are as fast as a car on a highway.

Read a Diagram

How does a cheetah change as it grows?

Clue: Arrows help show a sequence.

Lesson Review

Visual Summary

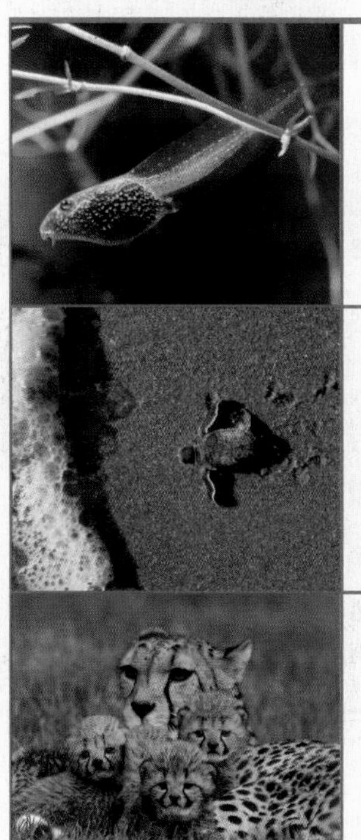

Every type of animal has its own life cycle. **Amphibians** and most **insects** go through metamorphosis.

Most **reptiles**, **birds**, and **fish** hatch from eggs. Reptiles and fish do not usually care for their young.

Mammals are born live. They depend on their parents until they can get food on their own.

Make a FOLDABLES™ Study Guide

Make a Layered-Look Book. Use it to summarize what you learned about animal life cycles.

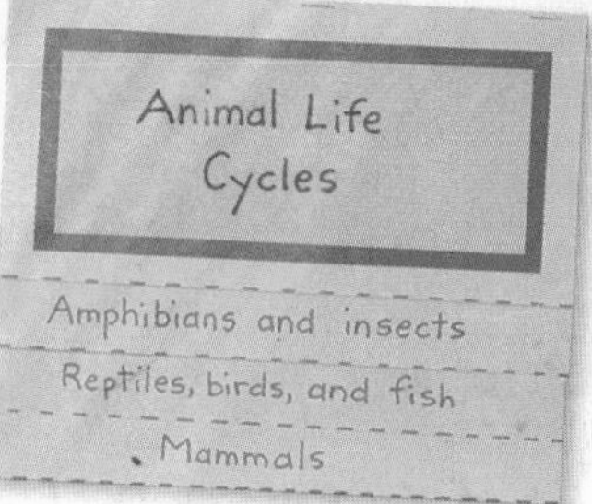

Think, Talk, and Write

1. **Main Idea** Describe the life cycles of two different animals.

2. **Vocabulary** What is metamorphosis?

3. **Sequence** Name three stages in a sea turtle's life cycle. Put them in order.

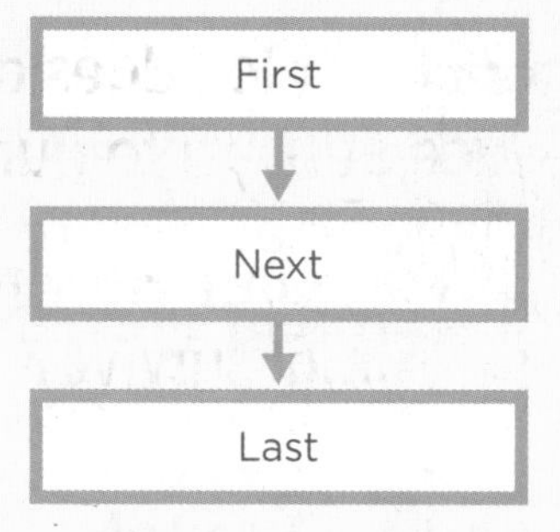

4. **Critical Thinking** Do you go through metamorphosis? How do you know?

5. **Test Prep** **An iguana's life cycle would be most like a**

A turtle's.
B cheetah's.
C fly's.
D bear's.

Writing Link

Write a Story
Choose an animal you know about. Pretend you are that animal. Describe how you change and grow as you get older.

Math Link

Solve a Problem
Female cheetahs usually give birth to a minimum of three cubs and a maximum of five cubs. What is the minimum and maximum number of cubs that five female cheetahs would have?

LOG ON e-Review Summaries and quizzes online at www.macmillanmh.com

The Little Lambs

I live on a farm, so I see animals grow up. We have chickens, cows, and sheep. I like sheep the best. When they are born, they are very small. Their wool is curly and soft. They stay close to their parents. When they get bigger, they run and play. It is fun to watch them. Their wool grows longer. Soon, we will cut their wool to make yarn. Next year they will be adult sheep.

Personal Narrative

A good personal narrative

- tells a story from the writer's own experience
- expresses the writer's feelings
- tells the events in an order that makes sense
- uses time-order words, such as *first*, *then*, or *after that*

These little lambs will grow to look like their parents.

Write About It

Personal Narrative Have you ever seen a plant or animal grow and change? Write about your experience. Describe the changes. Write what you observed and how it made you feel.

LOG ON e-Journal Write about it online at www.macmillanmh.com

Graphing Life Spans

How long do animals live? A fruit fly is likely to live for only about a month. A Galapagos tortoise can live for 150 years! Each type of animal has its own life span. A *life span* is the amount of time an organism usually lives.

You can compare the life spans of different animals. Examine the life-span data in the table below. Use the data to make a bar graph comparing the animals' life spans.

Animal	Average Life Span*
blacktail deer	10 years
American robin	13 years
rat snake	23 years
fence lizard	4 years
American toad	15 years

* under ideal conditions

American robin

Make a Bar Graph

- Title your graph. Label the left side and the bottom.
- Next, list the animals along the bottom of the graph.
- Write numbers up the left side. Start with 0 and count to the longest life span.
- Draw a bar for each animal up to the number that shows its life span.

Solve It

Make a bar graph using the data from the chart. Then use your bar graph to compare the life spans.

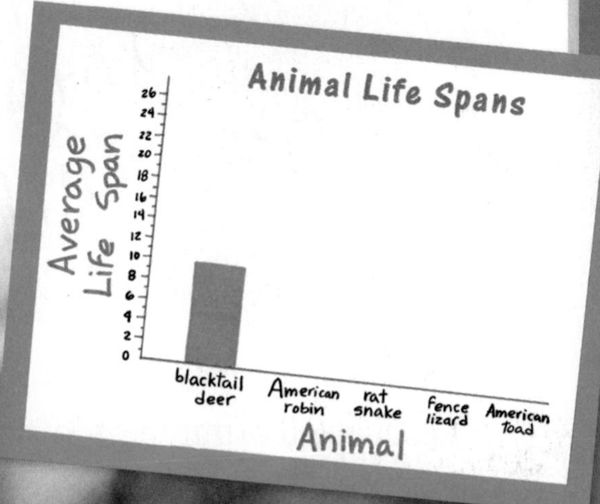

3-I.6. Infer meaning from data communicated in graphs, tables, and diagrams.

Lesson 4

Surviving in Habitats

Green sea turtles and longfin batfish

Look and Wonder

What would it feel like to be in this ocean environment? Could humans live in this salty ocean? Why is it a good place for this turtle and these fish?

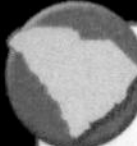

3-2.3. Recall the characteristics of an organism's habitat that allow the organism to survive there.

Explore

Inquiry Activity

Can ocean animals live and grow in fresh water?

Make a Prediction

Can brine shrimp grow in both fresh water and salt water? Write a prediction.

Test Your Prediction

1. Fill each jar with 480 mL of water. Put 2 tbsp of sea salt in one jar. Label it *Salt Water*. Label the other jar *Fresh Water*.

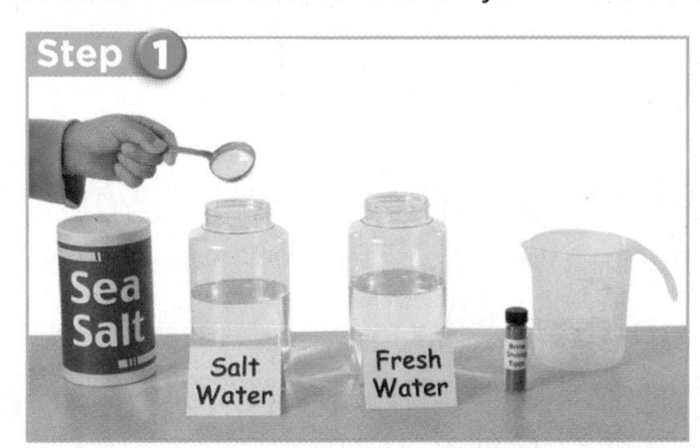

2. Add 1 tsp of brine shrimp eggs to each jar.
3. **Observe** Watch what develops in each jar over the next few days. Use a hand lens.

Draw Conclusions

4. **Interpret Data** In which jar did the brine shrimp eggs hatch? How could you tell?
5. **Infer** Can all ocean animals live and grow in fresh water? How do you know?

Explore More

Experiment Does temperature affect the hatching of brine shrimp eggs? Design an experiment to find out.

Materials

2 jars

measuring cup and water

sea salt

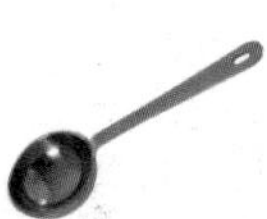

measuring spoon

brine shrimp eggs

hand lens

3-I.4. Predict the outcome of a simple investigation and compare the result with the prediction.

This northern habitat is called a tundra. Caribou dig for food in the tundra's snow.

Read and Learn

Main Idea 3-2.3

Earth has different habitats. They are classified by the types of climate, soil, plants, and animals they have.

Vocabulary

at www.macmillanmh.com

Reading Skill

Compare and Contrast

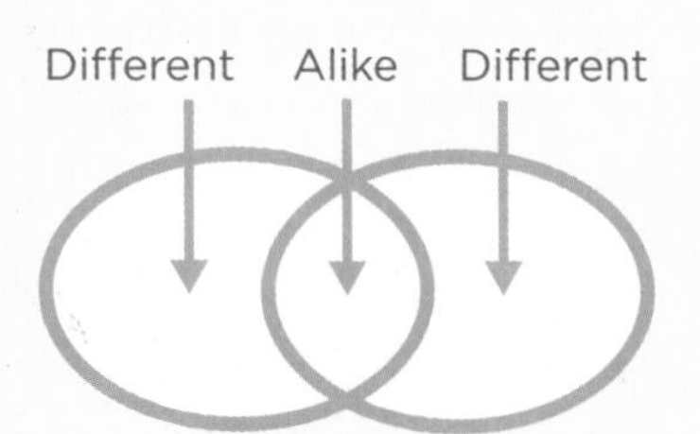

How do habitats differ?

If you could take a trip around the world, you would see that Earth has many kinds of habitats. A **habitat** is the type of environment that a living thing needs in order to survive. Habitats vary from place to place in many ways. Each of Earth's land habitats has a certain kind of climate. **Climate** is the pattern of weather in a place over a long time. Some land environments have a warm and wet climate. Others are cold and dry. Some environments are dry at some times and wet at other times.

Different habitats have different types of soil. **Soil** is made of bits of rock and humus (HYEW•muhs). *Humus* is broken-down plant and animal material. It contains nutrients and soaks up rainwater. Soil rich in humus holds plenty of water and nutrients for plants to use.

These buffalo eat grass in a grassland. This habitat is too dry for most types of trees to grow.

Earth's water habitats differ in many ways. Some have salt water. Some have fresh water. Water habitats may be warm or cool, shallow or deep.

Habitats also differ by the types of plants and animals they have. Grasslands are covered in grass, and forests are filled with trees. Oceans are filled with fish that can live only in salt water. Ponds are filled with fish that can live only in fresh water.

Ponds are freshwater habitats filled with plants, algae, and animals.

Quick Check

Compare and Contrast What are some ways in which habitats differ?

Critical Thinking Describe the habitat in which you live.

How do plants get what they need?

From the tallest white pine tree to the smallest clover, most plants have the same basic needs. They need water, sunlight, energy from food, and carbon dioxide. Carbon dioxide is a gas found in air. Plants need nutrients, too. *Nutrients* are substances that help living things grow and stay healthy. Plants must get all these things from their environment in order to survive.

Plants have structures that help them get or make what they need. A **structure** is a part of a living thing. Most plants have roots, stems, and leaves. Many plants also have flowers, fruits, and seeds. These parts help plants live, grow, and reproduce. When plants *reproduce*, they make new plants like themselves.

Quick Check

Compare and Contrast How do structures differ among plants?

Critical Thinking Why do plants not need to eat?

Leaves take in carbon dioxide from the air. They use energy from the Sun to change carbon dioxide and water into food for the plant.

Quick Lab

Observe Plant Parts

1. Get two plants to observe.
2. **Observe** Look at the parts of each plant. Does each plant have roots? How about stems and leaves?
3. **Record Data** Use pictures and words in a chart to describe each plant's parts.
4. **Compare** How are the parts of these plants alike? How are they different?

Read a Diagram

How do leaves help plants get what they need?

Clue: Bold words can help you find information.

How do animals get what they need?

Like plants, all animals have the same basic needs. Animals need water, energy from food, and oxygen. Oxygen is a gas found in air and water. Animals need shelter and safety, too. A **shelter** is a place in which animals can stay safe.

Animals have structures that help them meet their needs in their environment. Body parts, such as legs, wings, and beaks, are examples of animal structures.

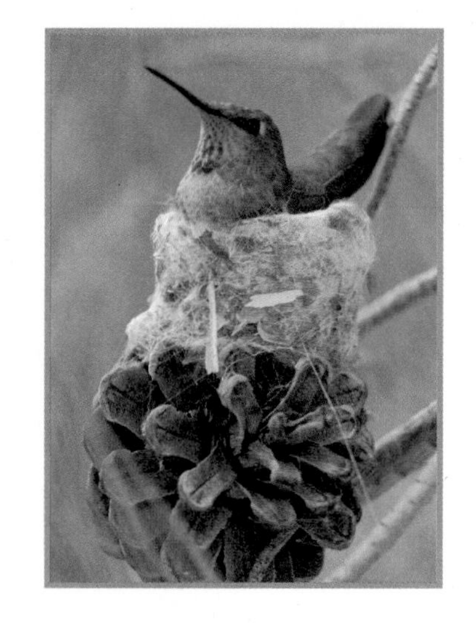

▲ Birds use nests for shelter.

Getting Food, Water, and Oxygen

Animals cannot make their own food the way plants can. Instead, they must eat plants or other animals. Legs, fins, and wings help animals move to find food. Beaks and tongues help animals catch and swallow food. They help animals drink water, too.

A lion's rough tongue helps it get water. ▶

▲ Gills help fish get oxygen.

Structures help animals breathe. Animals breathe to get oxygen. Many animals breathe with lungs. Lungs take in oxygen from the air. Fish breathe by pushing water through their gills. Gills take in oxygen from water.

Finding Shelter and Staying Safe

Some animals use trees or other plants for shelter. Other animals build their own shelters. Birds, for example, build nests as shelters for their young. Birds use their beaks and feet to gather materials and build their nests.

Some animals have structures that help them stay safe. A kangaroo's pouch helps young kangaroos stay safe. A porcupine's sharp quills help it stay safe from other animals.

▲ A young kangaroo develops in its mother's pouch. There it stays safe.

Quick Check

Compare and Contrast How are legs, fins, and wings important to different animals?

Critical Thinking How might the shape of a bird's beak affect what it eats?

What helps living things survive in their environment?

Living things live in the environment that best meets their needs. Smooth cordgrass grows in the salt marshes along the South Carolina coast. Here the salty water is just right for it to grow. The eastern redbud grows well on sunny hillsides. Here the direct sunlight provides perfect conditions for it to succeed.

Adaptations (ad•uhp•TAY•shuhns) help living things survive in their environment. An **adaptation** is a special feature or behavior that helps a living thing survive. Smooth cordgrass has many adaptations that help it live in salty water. For example, it has structures that help remove salt from its leaves.

Quick Check

Compare and Contrast How are plants adapted to different habitats?

Critical Thinking Are a bear's sharp teeth an adaptation? Explain.

A bear's claws are an adaptation that help it catch fish.

Lesson Review

Visual Summary

Living things live in different kinds of **habitats**.

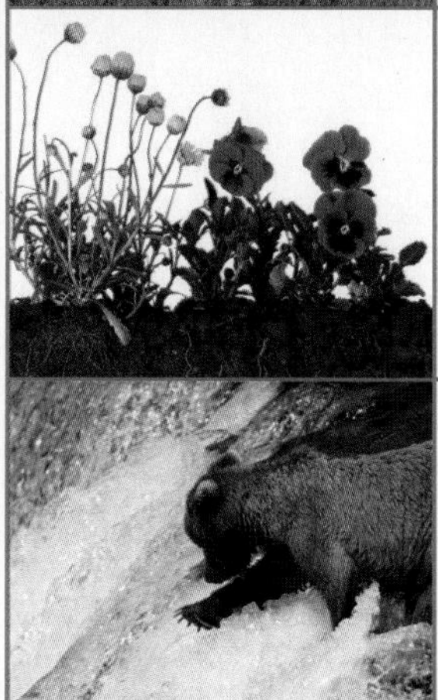

Plants and animals have **structures** that help them get what they need.

Adaptations help living things survive.

Make a FOLDABLES Study Guide

Make a Three-Tab Book. Use it to summarize what you learned.

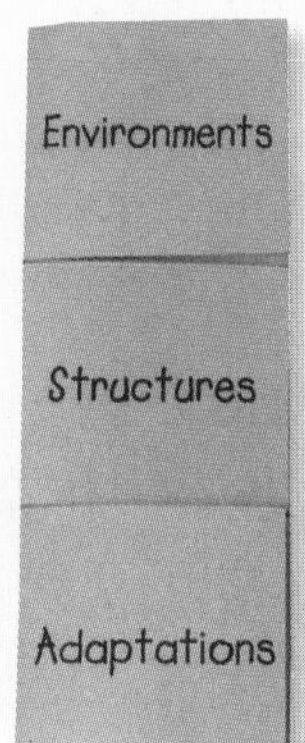

Think, Talk, and Write

1. **Main Idea** How do living things get what they need from their habitats?
2. **Vocabulary** What is climate?
3. **Compare and Contrast** How are land habitats similar to water habitats? How are they different?

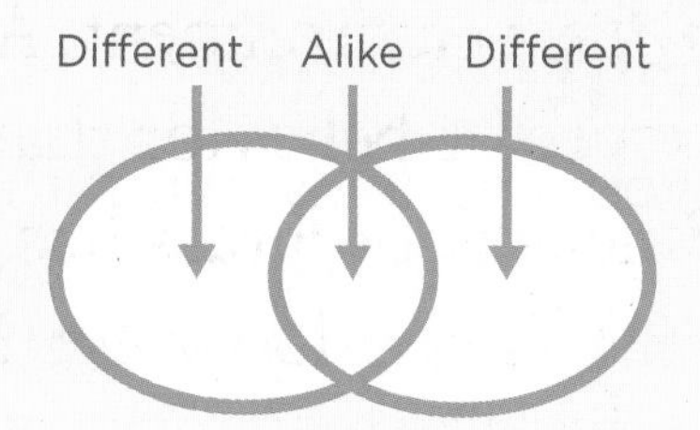

4. **Critical Thinking** You have a plant, and you need to choose a habitat to plant it in. What do you need to know about the plant before you decide where it belongs?
5. **Test Prep** **Plant nutrients include all of the following EXCEPT**
   - **A** sand.
   - **B** water.
   - **C** carbon dioxide.
   - **D** food.

Writing Link

Write a Paragraph
How do your moving parts help you survive? Make a chart. In one column list your moving parts. In the second column, tell how each helps you. Use your chart to write a paragraph.

Math Link

Make a Bar Graph
List ten plants that live near your school. Then group the plants into categories, such as grasses or trees. Make a graph to show how many of each category live near your school.

LOG ON e-Review Summaries and quizzes online at www.macmillanmh.com

Inquiry Skill: Classify

Earth is a big place. Millions of living things find homes in many different environments around our planet. With so many living things and so many environments, what can scientists do to understand life in our world? One thing they do is **classify** living things.

▶ Learn It

When you **classify**, you put things into groups that are alike. Classifying is a useful tool for organizing and analyzing things. It is easier to study a few groups of things that are alike than millions of individual things.

▶ Try It

Scientists **classify** plants. They classify animals, too. Can you?

1. To start, observe the animals shown on the next page. Look for things they have in common.
2. Then come up with a rule. What characteristic can you use to group the animals? Let's try wings. Which animals have wings? Which animals do not? Make a table to show your groups.

Wings	No Wings

I have wings!

rhea

▶ Apply It

Classify these animals using your own rule.

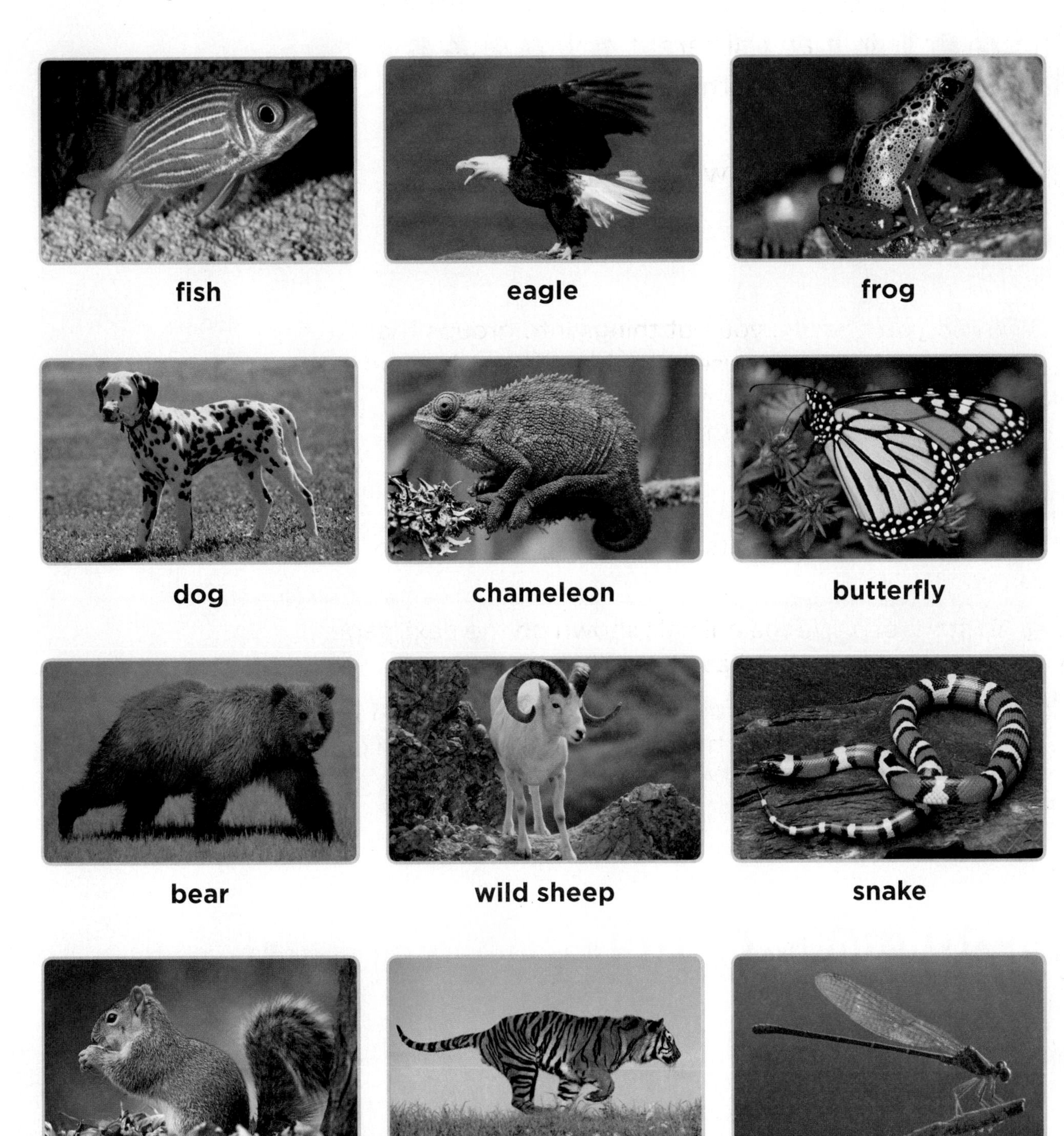

3-I.I. Classify objects by two of their properties (attributes).

Lesson 5

Food Chains

Look and Wonder

A bald eagle can fly at 200 miles per hour when diving for a fish. Bald eagles depend on fish for food. What do other animals depend on for food?

3-2.5. Summarize the organization of simple food chains (including the roles of producers, consumers, and decomposers).

Explore

Inquiry Activity

What kind of food do owls need?

Purpose

Find out what an owl eats by studying an owl pellet.

Procedure

1. Work with a partner. Put on plastic gloves. Place your owl pellet onto a paper plate.
2. **Predict** What do you expect to see inside the owl pellet? Write your prediction.
3. Using the tweezers, separate the objects in the owl pellet.
4. **Observe** What is in the owl pellet? Use the hand lens. Record your observations.

Draw Conclusions

5. **Interpret Data** What do the materials inside the owl pellet tell you about what an owl eats?
6. **Infer** What organisms might an owl eat? What might those organisms eat?

Explore More

Interpret Data Keep track of the things you eat in one day. Do most of your foods come from plants or animals?

Materials

plastic gloves

owl pellet

paper plate

tweezers

hand lens

Step 3

3-I.4. Predict the outcome of a simple investigation and compare the result with the prediction.

Read and Learn

Main Idea 3-2.5

Food chains and food webs show how organisms in an ecosystem depend on each other.

Vocabulary

ecosystem, p. 68

food chain, p. 70

producer, p. 70

consumer, p. 71

decomposer, p. 71

food web, p. 72

LOG ON e-Glossary at www.macmillanmh.com

Reading Skill ✓

Infer

Clues	What I Know	What I Infer

What is an ecosystem?

Look at the diagram below. Can you see a frog ready to snap up an insect? How about a turtle resting in the Sun? Frogs, insects, turtles, and sunlight are part of a pond ecosystem (EK•oh•sis•tuhm). An **ecosystem** is all the parts of an environment that interact. An ecosystem may be a pond, a swamp, or a field. It may be as small as a puddle or as big as an ocean.

A Pond Ecosystem

Crane flies eat plants and algae. They lay eggs in water. ▼

Big or small, ecosystems are made up of living and nonliving things. Frogs, birds, and plants are some living things in a pond. Sunlight, water, and soil are some nonliving things.

Different organisms live in different parts of an ecosystem. Fish live in the water. A cattail lives along the edge of a pond. Living things get food, water, and shelter from their ecosystems.

Quick Check

Infer Which pond animals could also survive in a land ecosystem?

Critical Thinking How might an ecosystem change if the climate suddenly became colder?

Pond plants grow well in wet soil. Animals use them as food and shelter. ▶

◀ These turtles eat snails, fish, insects, and plants. They climb out of the water to warm up.

◀ Pond snails slide along the bottom looking for plants and algae to eat.

What is a food chain?

All organisms need energy from food to live and grow. Most are a source of energy as well. They pass on energy to organisms that eat them. A **food chain** shows how energy passes from one organism to another in an ecosystem. The arrows in a food-chain diagram, like the ones below, show the flow of energy.

The first organisms in a food chain are producers (pruh•DEW•suhrz). A **producer** is an organism that makes its own food. Green plants and algae are two examples. Most producers use energy from the Sun to make their own food. This means that the energy in most food chains starts with the Sun.

The next organisms in a food chain are consumers (cuhn•SEW•muhrz). A **consumer** is an organism that eats other organisms. All animals are consumers. A food chain may have many consumers.

Next in the food chain are decomposers (dee•cuhm•POH•zuhrz). A **decomposer** is an organism that breaks down dead plant and animal material. Decomposers put nutrients back into the soil. Some worms and bacteria are decomposers.

Quick Check

Infer What might happen to grasshoppers and eagles if turtles were removed from the pond food chain?

Critical Thinking How are these food chains alike?

What is a food web?

One morning a turtle eats a pond snail. The next day, that same turtle eats a crayfish. Most animals eat several kinds of food. They are part of several food chains. Food chains can connect to form a **food web**.

The diagram below shows a pond food web. Look at the arrows from the largemouth bass to the heron and bald eagle. They show that herons and bald eagles eat bass. The bass is part of more than one food chain. The heron and the eagle are predators. *Predators* hunt other organisms for food. The organisms they hunt are *prey*.

A Pond Food Web

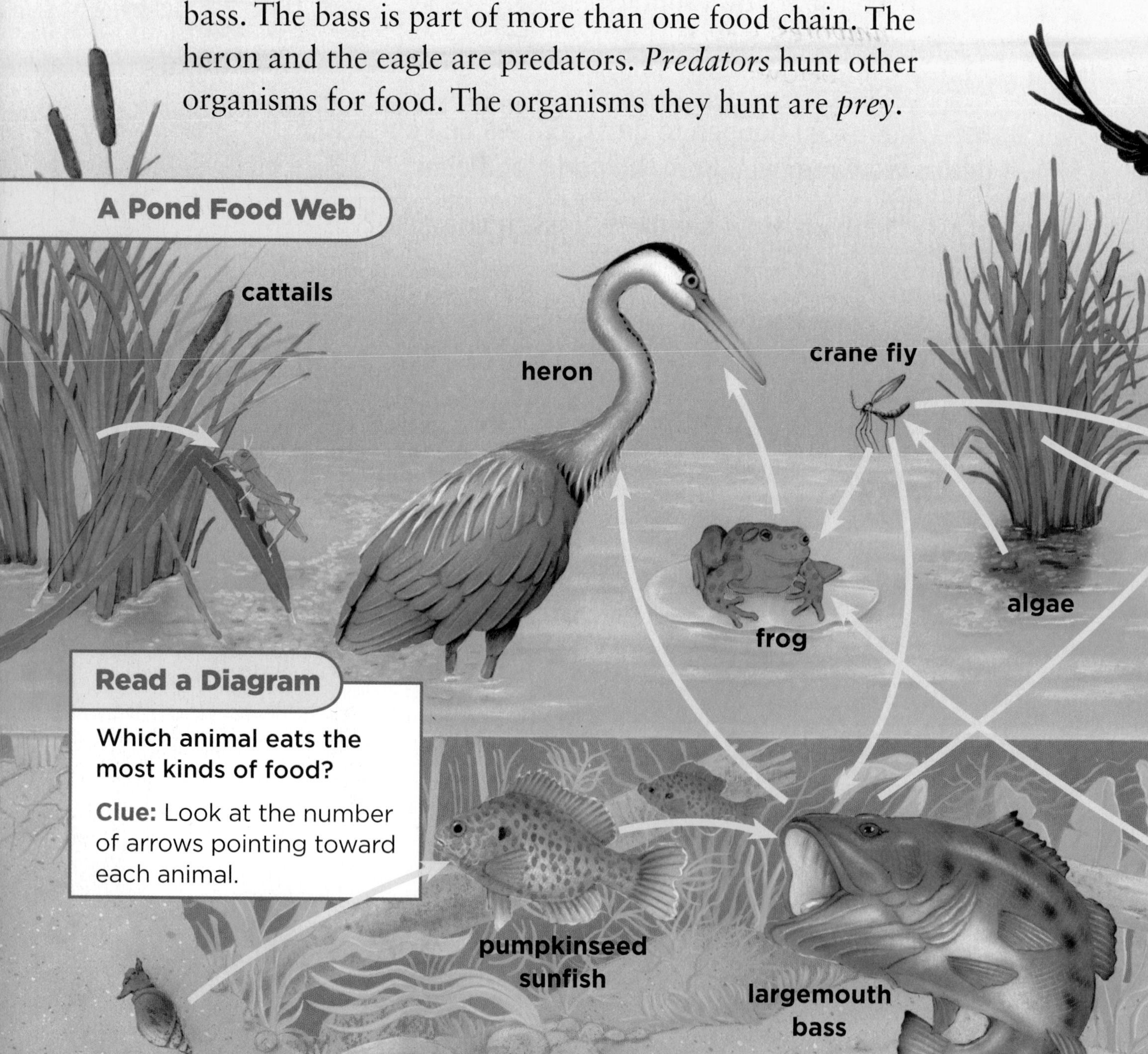

Read a Diagram

Which animal eats the most kinds of food?

Clue: Look at the number of arrows pointing toward each animal.

You can learn about living things by studying food webs. Below, you can see that the snail eats plants. Organisms that eat mostly plants are *herbivores*. Some animals, such as herons, eat mostly other animals. These organisms are *carnivores*. Animals that eat both plants and animals are *omnivores*. Can you find an omnivore below?

Food webs also show how organisms compete for food. Three animals—turtles, fish, and snakes—eat crayfish. If snakes eat all the crayfish, the others might go hungry.

Quick Check

Infer How could a heron survive if there were no more bass?

Critical Thinking Are you an herbivore, carnivore, or omnivore?

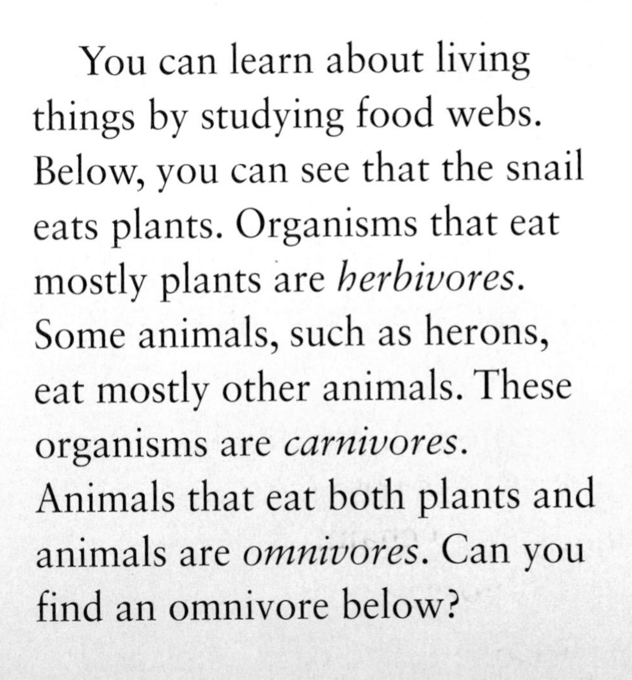

Quick Lab

Observe Decomposers

1. Put some apple pieces into a plastic bag. Seal the bag. ⚠ **Be Careful.** Do not open the sealed bag.
2. **Observe** Leave the bag in a warm, dark place for a week. Observe the pieces every day. Record the changes you see.
3. **Communicate** What happened to the pieces of apple? How did they change over time?
4. **Infer** What does this activity tell you about decomposers?

Why are decomposers important?

In a pond, dead plant and animal material drifts to the bottom. What keeps the pond from filling with dead organisms? Decomposers!

Decomposers are an important part of ecosystems. Worms, mushrooms, mold, and some insects and snails are decomposers. Many one-celled organisms are decomposers. Decomposers feed on dead material. As they eat, they release nutrients into the water or soil. These nutrients help plants and other organisms grow.

◀ These tiny decomposers were magnified 2,700 times.

These leaves will make a good meal for decomposers. ▶

Quick Check

Infer How do decomposers help a pond ecosystem?

Critical Thinking What would happen if a forest had no decomposers?

Lesson Review

Visual Summary

The living things in an **ecosystem** depend on each other to survive.

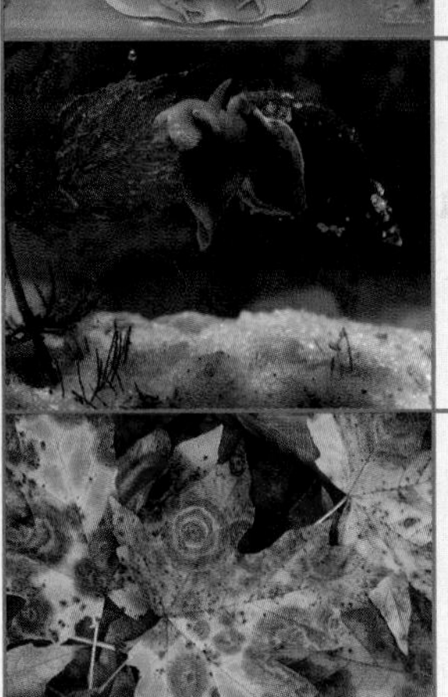

Food chains and **food webs** show how energy flows through an ecosystem.

Producers, **consumers**, and **decomposers** make up food chains and food webs.

Make a FOLDABLES™ Study Guide

Make a Trifold Book. Use it to summarize what you learned about food chains and food webs.

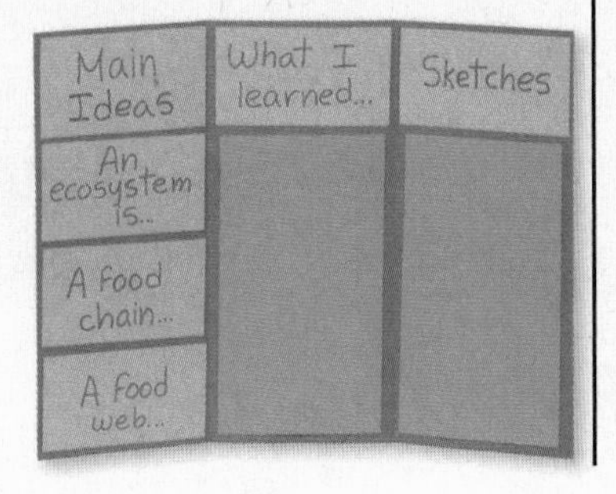

Think, Talk, and Write

1. **Main Idea** How are organisms connected in an ecosystem? How could you show this?

2. **Vocabulary** What is a consumer?

3. **Infer** How does it help an animal to be part of more than one food chain?

Clues	What I Know	What I Infer

4. **Critical Thinking** How do both plants and animals depend on decomposers?

5. **Test Prep** MOST producers get their energy from
   A sunlight.
   B consumers.
   C predators.
   D rocks.

Writing Link

Writing That Compares
Choose two animals. Find out where they live and what they eat. Find out what eats them. Then compare the animals in an essay.

Art Link

Make a Poster
Research an ecosystem near your home. Make a poster to show how organisms in that ecosystem depend on one another.

LOG ON e-Review Summaries and quizzes online at www.macmillanmh.com

EATING AWAY AT POLLUTION

You cannot see microorganisms, but they are all around you. Microorganisms are tiny living things. You need a microscope to see them. Many are made of just one cell.

Some microorganisms are harmful. They can make animals and plants sick. Others are helpful. They can eat things that are harmful to plants and animals. Some can even help clean up Earth's water, land, and air. Scientists use these tiny organisms to eat pollution.

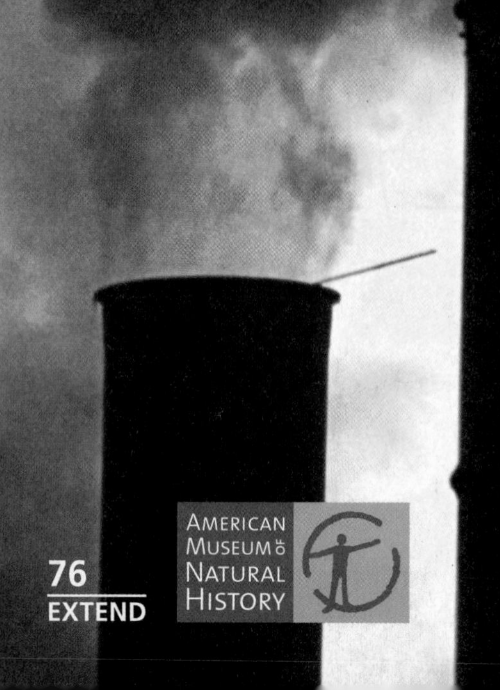

Some microorganisms eat oil. When oil spills on water or soil, the tiny creatures eat the oil. The waste they leave behind is safe for the environment. Other microorganisms can help keep air clean. Factories and power plants often produce a lot of smoke. Microorganisms can eat dangerous chemicals in the smoke that would pollute the air.

Classify

When you classify

- you compare things to see how they are alike and different
- you put things into groups based on their characteristics

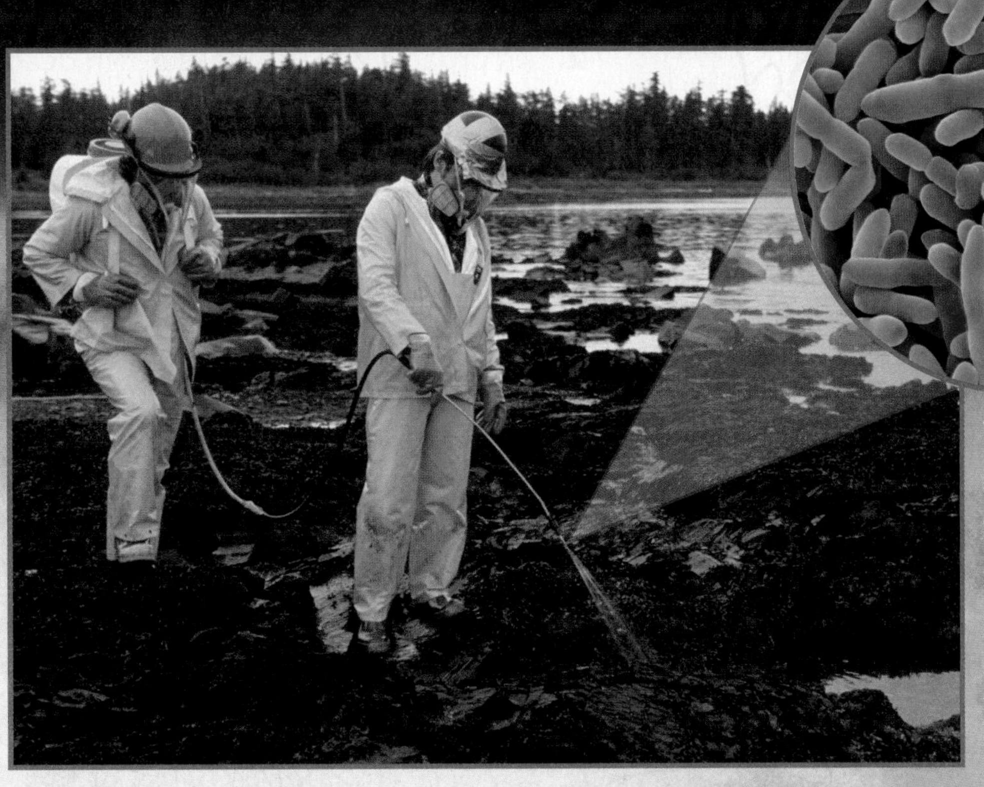

Workers spray microorganisms onto an oil spill in Alaska. The round photo shows the microorganisms as seen through a microscope.

Write About It

Classify This article explains that some microorganisms are harmful and others are helpful. This is a way to classify them. Read the article again with a partner. Look for another way to classify microorganisms. Then write about it.

LOG ON e-Journal Write about it online at www.macmillanmh.com

Visual Summary

Lesson 1 All living things have certain characteristics and needs in common.

Lesson 2 A life cycle describes how an organism grows and reproduces.

Lesson 3 Animals have different life cycles. Some animals are born looking like their parents. Others change greatly as they grow.

Lesson 4 Earth has different habitats.

Lesson 5 Food chains and food webs show how organisms in an ecosystem depend on each other.

Make a FOLDABLES Study Guide

Glue your lesson study guides to a piece of paper as shown. Use your study guide to review what you have learned in this chapter.

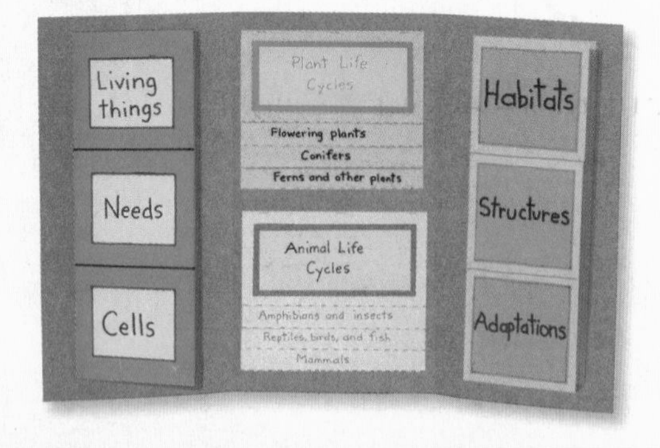

Vocabulary

Fill each blank with the best term from the list.

adaptation, p. 62	**metamorphosis**, p. 47
climate, p. 56	**organism**, p. 24
decomposer, p. 71	**producer**, p. 70
food chain, p. 70	**seed**, p. 34
life cycle, p. 38	**shelter**, p. 60

1. Animals often seek a safe place, or ________, to protect themselves.
3-2.2
2. An organism that breaks down dead plants and animals is called a(n) ________.
3-2.5
3. An organism goes through stages that make up its ________.
3-2.1
4. Some organisms, such as caterpillars, go through ________, in which their body changes shape.
3-2.1
5. An organism that makes its own food is called a(n) ________.
3-2.5
6. A structure that can grow into a new plant is called a(n) ________.
3-2.1
7. A(n) ________ shows how energy passes from one organism to another in an ecosystem.
3-2.5
8. A special structure or behavior that helps an organism survive in an environment is a(n) ________.
3-2.1
9. Each living thing is a(n) ________.
3-2.1
10. The pattern of weather in a place over a long time is its ________.
3-2.3

Skills and Concepts

Answer each of the following in complete sentences.

11. **Infer** Is it possible to have more than one producer in a food chain? Could there be more than one consumer?
3-2.5

12. **Descriptive Writing** Describe the structures that different animals use to breathe.
3-2.2

13. **Predict** A ripe apple falls to the ground. How can this help an apple tree reproduce?
3-2.1

14. **Critical Thinking** What would happen to an ecosystem if the producers were removed?
3-2.5

15. What is happening in this picture? Which part of a life cycle does this picture show?
3-2.1

The Big Idea

16. How do living things get what they need to grow and change?
3-2.1

Performance Assessment

Make a Life-Cycle Poster

chameleon

robin

- Choose two very different animals, such as a chameleon and a robin. Use this book and do library research to learn about their life cycles.
- Create a poster that shows each animal's life cycle on one half of the poster. Illustrate each stage of the life cycle with pictures. Explain each stage with words.
- Share your poster with your classmates. Learn about other animals' life cycles by looking at other posters.
- How are the life cycles of your classmates' animals similar to the ones that you picked? How are they different?

South Carolina Activity

Find out more about a wildlife community near your home. Look for a food chain. Find at least one producer, consumer, and decomposer. Draw a picture to show how energy moves through the food chain.

South Carolina Standards Practice

1 **What is one of the questions you could ask to find out whether something is living?**

A Does it grow?

B Was it made by humans?

C Does it come from nature?

D Is it made of more than one cell?

3-I.3

2 **The data table shows four different populations of snails over a three-year period.**

Snail Population Each Year			
	Year 1	**Year 2**	**Year 3**
Population 1	20	25	28
Population 2	20	23	24
Population 3	20	27	34
Population 4	20	18	16

Which snail population is surviving best in its habitat?

F population 1

G population 2

H population 3

I population 4

3-I.6

3 **Mrs. Carroll's class studied worms. They did an experiment to test how much a worm ate in a week. The students' results were different from their predictions. What should they do?**

A get new worms

B read more books about worms

C ask a gardner about worms

D do their experiment again

3-I.7

4 **To observe cells, you need a tool called a**

F graduated syringe.

G microscope.

H test tube.

I forceps.

3-I.5

5 **Which animal goes through a stage in which it can swim and breathe with gills?**

A a ladybug

B a cheetah

C a turtle

D a frog

3-2.I

6 **Which organism in the illustration below is both a consumer and a decomposer?**

F the fallen tree

G the earthworm

H the mammal

I the bird

3-2.5

7 **How do animals use camouflage to survive?**

A by standing out from their environment

B by imitating other animals

C by blending in with their environment

D by giving warning calls

3-2.2

8 **A certain food chain includes turtles, grasshoppers, grasses, and eagles. Which organisms are at the bottom of the food chain?**

F turtles

G grasshoppers

H grasses

I eagles

3-2.5

9 **Which gas do animals need to survive?**

A carbon dioxide

B helium

C hydrogen

D oxygen

3-2.3

10 **Some dinosaur fossils have structures that look like wings. What might you infer about these animals?**

F They lived in water.

G They could fly.

H They were large.

I They ate fish.

3-2.2

CHAPTER 2

Habitats and Adaptations

The Big Idea

How do adaptations help living things survive in different habitats?

A vole eats a yew berry.

Key Vocabulary

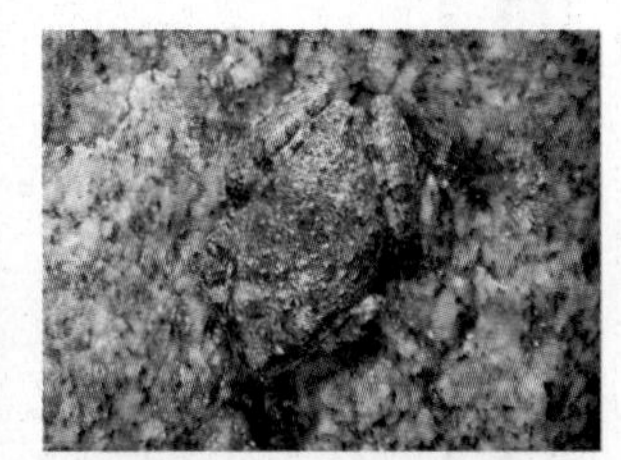

camouflage
a body covering that helps an animal blend in with its environment (p. 90)

deciduous
trees that lose their leaves in fall as the temperature gets cooler (p. 109)

coniferous
trees that make cones instead of flowers (p. 109)

mimicry
when one living thing imitates another living thing in color or shape (p. 110)

hibernate
to go into a deep sleep that lasts through winter (p. 112)

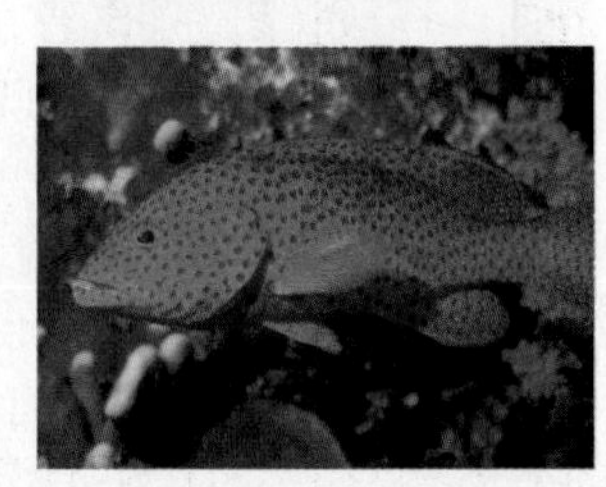

gills
body parts that fish use to get oxygen from water (p. 134)

More Vocabulary

desert, p. 86

nocturnal, p. 90

grassland, p. 96

temperate, p. 97

tropical, p. 97

forest, p. 106

arctic tundra, p. 118

permafrost, p. 119

blubber, p. 122

migrate, p. 124

ocean, p. 131

algae, p. 132

Lesson 1

Life in the Desert

Look and Wonder

Death Valley is North America's driest desert. Less than two inches of rain fall here in an entire year! What adaptations help plants and animals survive in such a dry place?

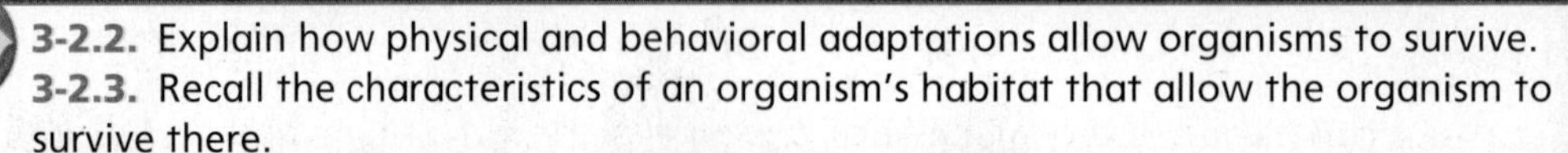

3-2.2. Explain how physical and behavioral adaptations allow organisms to survive.
3-2.3. Recall the characteristics of an organism's habitat that allow the organism to survive there.

Explore

Inquiry Activity

What adaptations help plants survive in a desert?

Make A Prediction

Why can some plants live in dry environments? How do special structures help them survive? Write a prediction.

Test Your Prediction

1. **Observe** Use a hand lens to observe each plant. What structures do they have? What are their leaves like? What are their stems like?
2. **Record Data** Make a chart to record your observations. Use words and pictures.
3. **Observe** Cut a leaf from each plant in half. Use a hand lens to look at the leaves. What are the leaves like inside?

Draw Conclusions

4. **Compare** How are the plants alike? How are they different?
5. **Infer** What special structures help a desert plant survive in its hot, dry environment?

Explore More

Experiment Put a leaf from each plant on the windowsill. How do the leaves change?

Materials

hand lens

two plants

scissors ⚠ Be Careful.

Step 1

Step 3

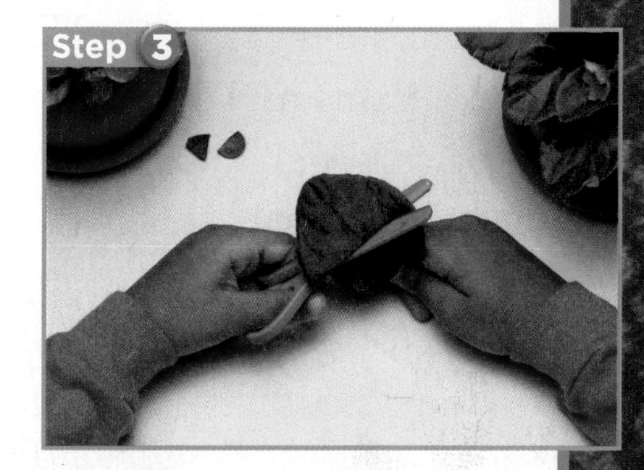

3-I.8. Use appropriate safety procedures when conducting investigations.

Read and Learn

Main Idea 3-2.2 3-2.3

Deserts have dry climates and sandy soil. Desert plants and animals have adaptations that help them survive.

Vocabulary

desert, p. 86

nocturnal, p. 90

camouflage, p. 90

e-Glossary at www.macmillanmh.com

Reading Skill

Compare and Contrast

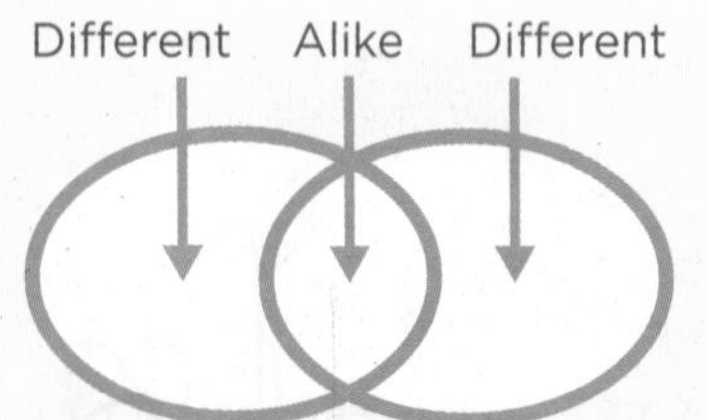

What is a desert?

A wave of heat blasts your body. You take a deep breath, and dry air stings your nose. Dust from the sandy ground covers your shoes. You are in the Sonoran Desert. This is one of the largest deserts in North America.

A **desert** is a habitat that has a dry climate. Less than 25 centimeters (10 inches) of rain falls in a desert each year. Several centimeters of rain may fall all at once within a few days. Then for months there is no rain at all.

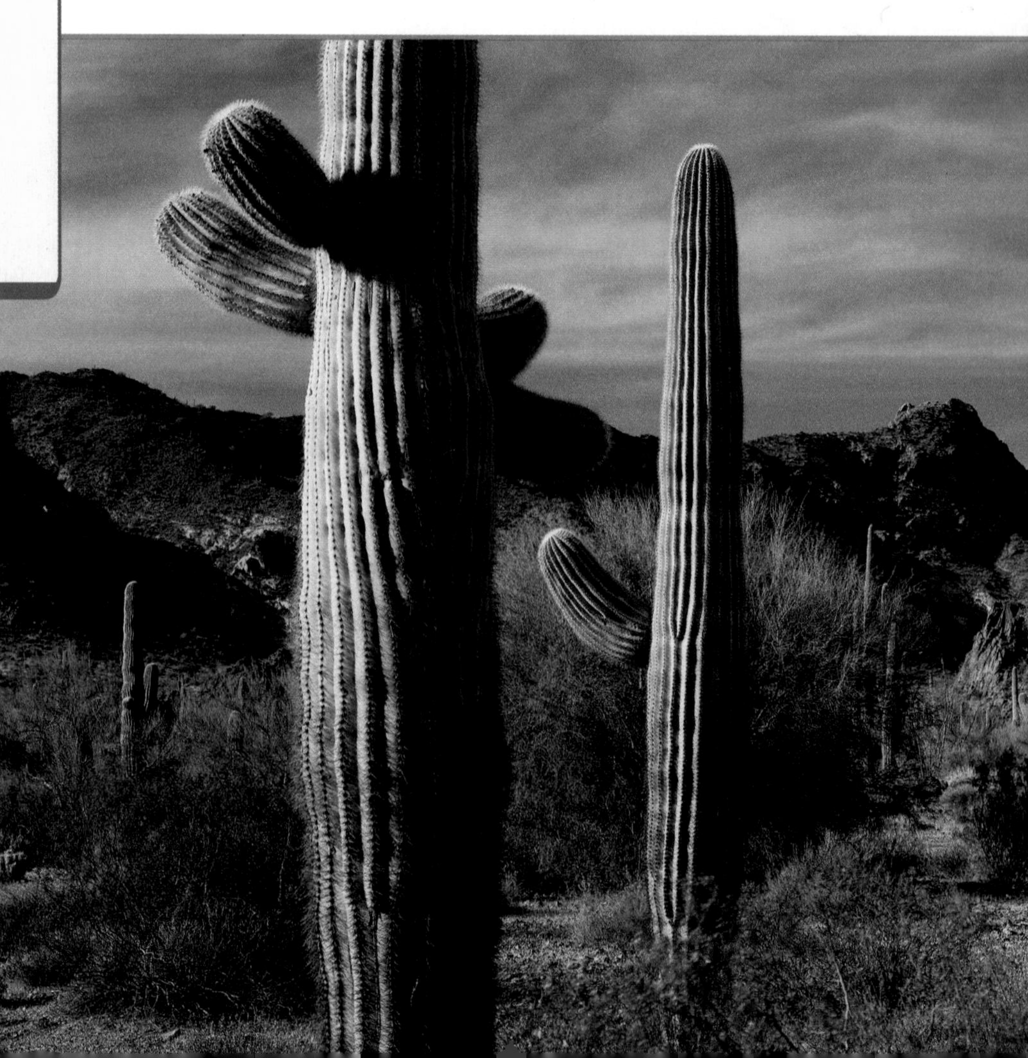

Saguaro National Park is in the Sonoran Desert. ▶

Temperatures in a desert vary widely between day and night. During the day, the Sun's heat warms the land and air. After the Sun sets, the temperature drops quickly. The desert is much cooler at night than in the day.

The soil in a desert is mostly sand. There is little humus to soak up rainwater. Rainwater trickles down through the desert sand. It goes deeper than most plants' roots can reach.

Quick Check

Compare and Contrast How do a desert's daytime and nighttime temperatures compare?

Critical Thinking What are three key features that describe deserts?

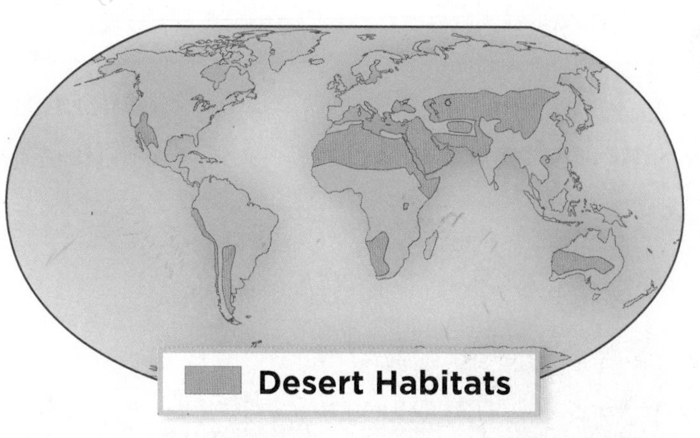

What adaptations help desert plants?

Some plants can grow in deserts. Other plants cannot. Plants that grow in deserts have adaptations that help them survive with little water. Special roots help them take in water. Special leaves and stems help them store water. Spines and thorns protect them from thirsty animals. The diagram below shows some of these adaptations.

Adaptations of Desert Plants

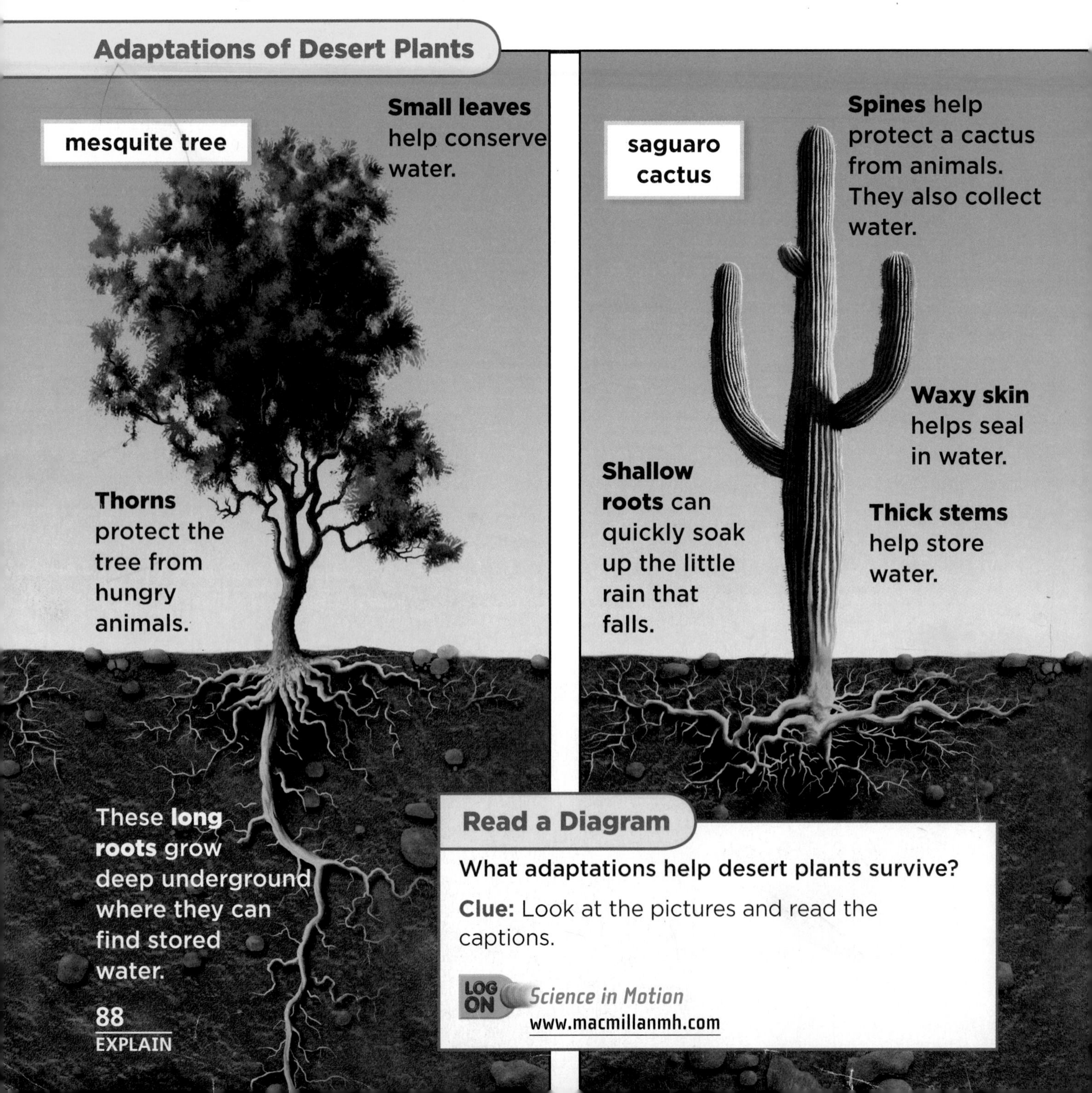

Read a Diagram

What adaptations help desert plants survive?

Clue: Look at the pictures and read the captions.

LOG ON *Science in Motion* www.macmillanmh.com

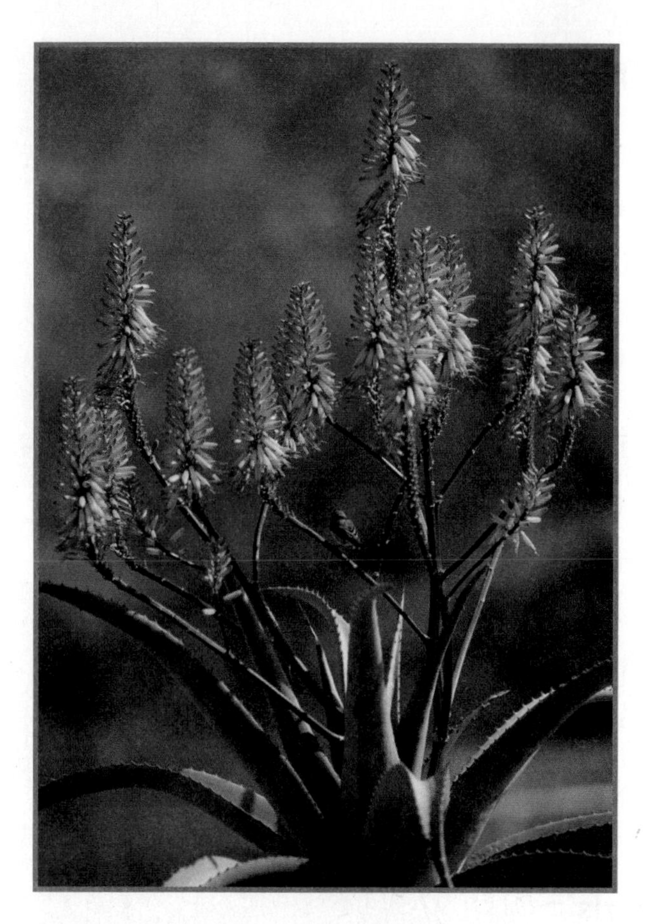

▲ Succulents, such as this aloe, are common desert plants. Their waxy skin and thick leaves are adapted to store lots of water.

Quick Lab

Desert Adaptations

1. **Make a Model** Wet two paper towels. Then wrap one in wax paper. This models a plant that has waxy skin. Use the uncovered towel to model a plant that does not have waxy skin.
2. Place your models in a sunny window.
3. **Compare** How do the paper towels feel later in the day?
4. **Draw Conclusions** How does waxy skin help desert plants survive?

Quick Check

Compare and Contrast How are the roots of a mesquite tree similar to the roots of a cactus? How are they different?

Critical Thinking A prickly pear cactus has spines, shallow roots, and waxy skin. Could it survive in a desert? Explain your answer.

prickly pear cactus ▶

What adaptations help desert animals?

Desert animals can survive in the desert because of their adaptations. Here are just a few of their many adaptations.

Sleeping the Day Away

Can you imagine sleeping all day and going to school at night? Except for going to school, this is what many desert animals do. Rattlesnakes and coyotes, among others, are nocturnal (nahk•TURN•uhl). **Nocturnal** means they sleep during the day. They come out at night when it is cooler.

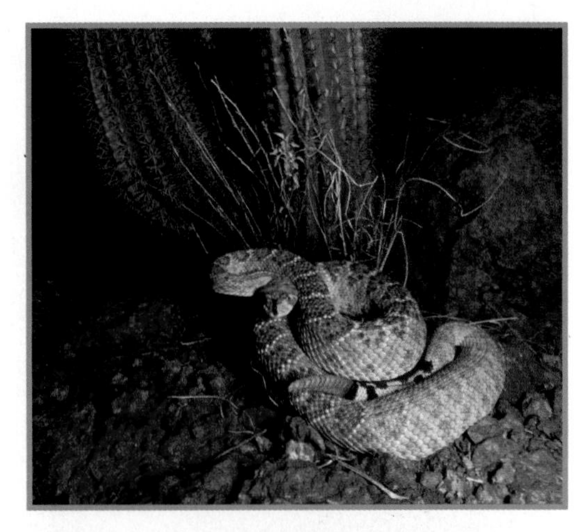

▲ Rattlesnakes are nocturnal.

Keeping Cool

Large ears and thin bodies help animals such as the desert jackrabbit stay cool. These special features are adaptations that help animals lose extra body heat.

▲ A jackrabbit's long ears help it stay cool.

Blending In

Some desert animals can hide in plain sight. Their body coverings blend in with the environment. Blending in is an adaptation called **camouflage** (KAM•uh•flahzh). Camouflage helps animals stay safe.

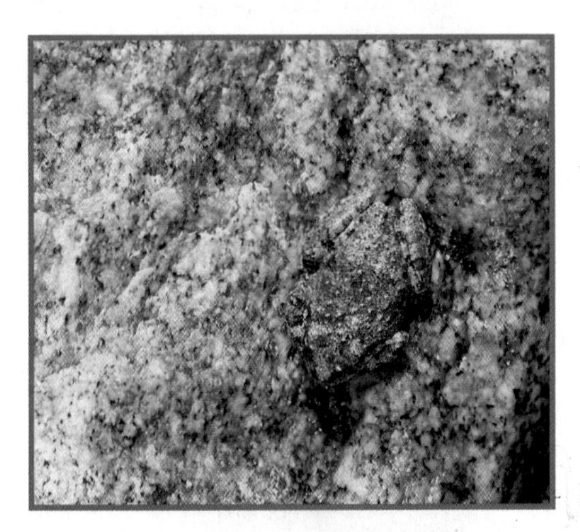

▲ Can you see the frog? Camouflage helps it blend in with the rock.

Quick Check

Compare and Contrast How are desert animals and plants similar?

Critical Thinking Could an animal with thick fur survive in a hot desert?

Lesson Review

Visual Summary

A **desert** is a habitat that has a dry climate and dry, sandy soil.

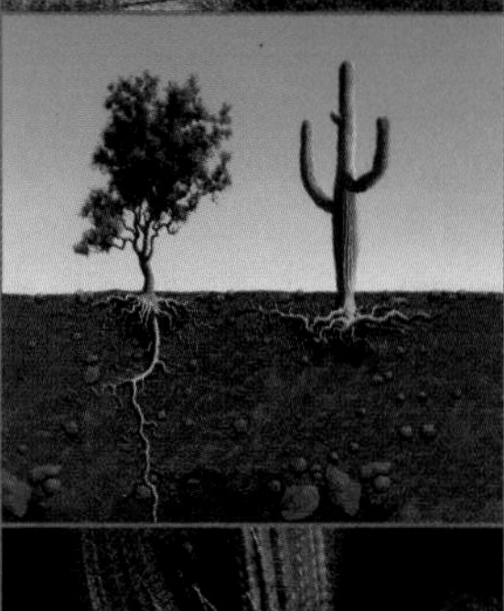

Desert plants have special roots, stems, and leaves that help them take in and store water.

Desert animals have adaptations that help them stay safe and cool.

Make a FOLDABLES™ Study Guide

Make a Pyramid Fold. Use it to summarize what you read about desert plants and animals.

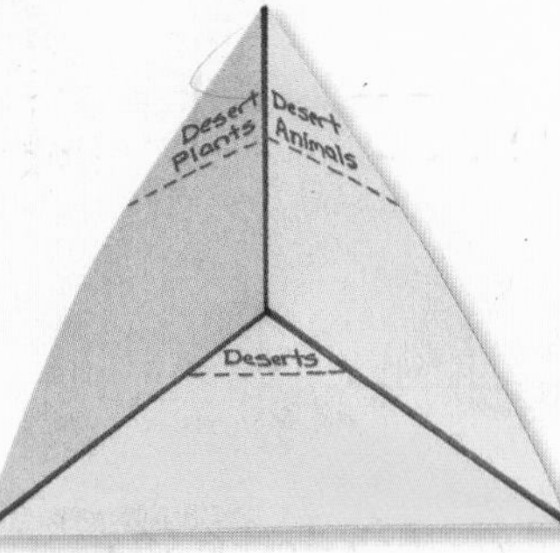

Think, Talk, and Write

1. **Main Idea** What adaptations help desert plants and animals survive?
2. **Vocabulary** What is a desert like? Describe it.
3. **Compare and Contrast** How are a cactus's adaptations similar to a mesquite tree's? How are they different?

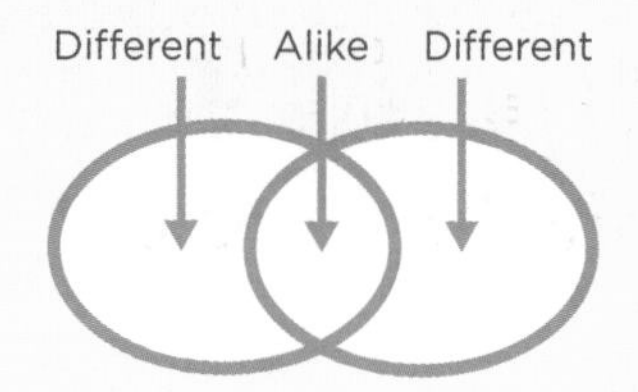

4. **Critical Thinking** Buffalo have thick, dark coats. They eat mainly grasses. Could a buffalo survive in a desert? Explain your answer.
5. **Test Prep** **Deserts are habitats with**
   - **A** cold climate and frozen soil.
   - **B** wet climate and marshy soil.
   - **C** dry climate and sandy soil.
   - **D** hot climate with lots of rainfall.

Writing Link

Writing a Story
Write a story about life in the desert. Use information from this lesson to help set the scene. Remember to include a beginning, a middle, and an end.

Math Link

Make a Chart
Use the Internet to find the average temperature for each month in Death Valley. Record the information in a chart. Write a sentence to describe Death Valley's climate.

LOG ON e-Review Summaries and quizzes online at www.macmillanmh.com

Be a Scientist

Materials

yellow paper

brown paper

stopwatch

Structured Inquiry

How does camouflage help some animals survive?

Form a Hypothesis

How does camouflage help animals stay safe? Record your hypothesis. Start with "If an animal has camouflage, then . . ."

Test Your Hypothesis

1. Cut out 20 yellow circles and 20 brown circles.
2. **Experiment** Spread out the circles on the paper to model animals with and without camouflage. Then ask a classmate to pick up as many circles as he or she can in 10 seconds.

3. **Record Data** How many of each color circle did your classmate pick up? Use a chart to record the results.
4. Repeat steps 1 and 2 with two other classmates.

Step 3

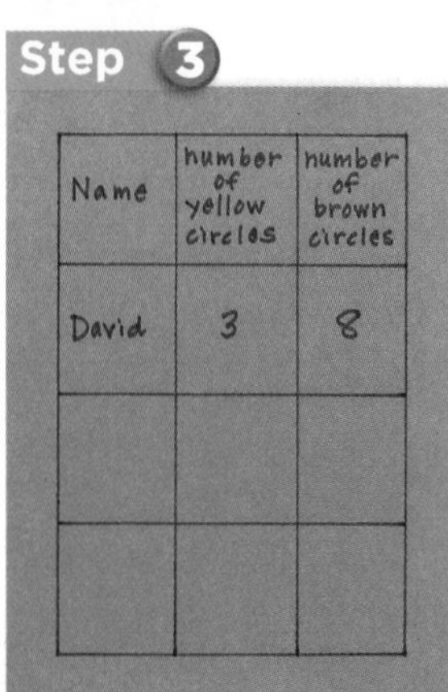

Name	number of yellow circles	number of brown circles
David	3	8

Draw Conclusions

5. **Interpret Data** Did your classmates pick up more yellow or brown circles? Which circles were harder to find?
6. How might camouflage help animals survive?

Guided Inquiry

How do pale colors help some animals survive?

Form a Hypothesis

Pale body coverings help desert animals stay cool. Why is this true? Write a hypothesis.

Test Your Hypothesis

Design a plan to test your hypothesis. Use the materials shown. Write the steps you plan to follow.

Materials

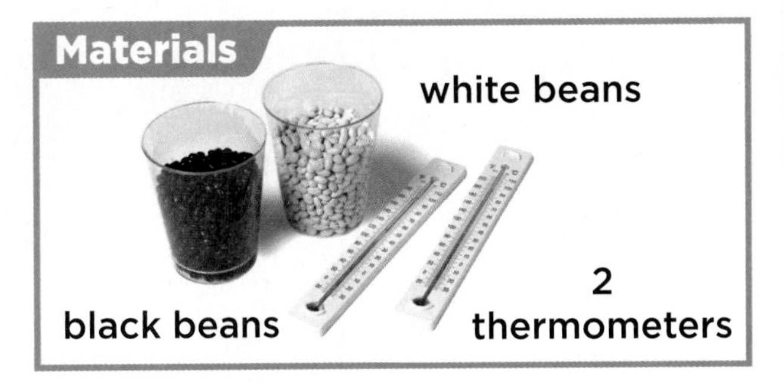

Draw Conclusions

Did your results support your hypothesis? Why or why not? Share your results with your classmates.

Open Inquiry

What other questions do you have about desert plants and animals? Talk with your classmates about questions you have. How might you find the answers to your questions?

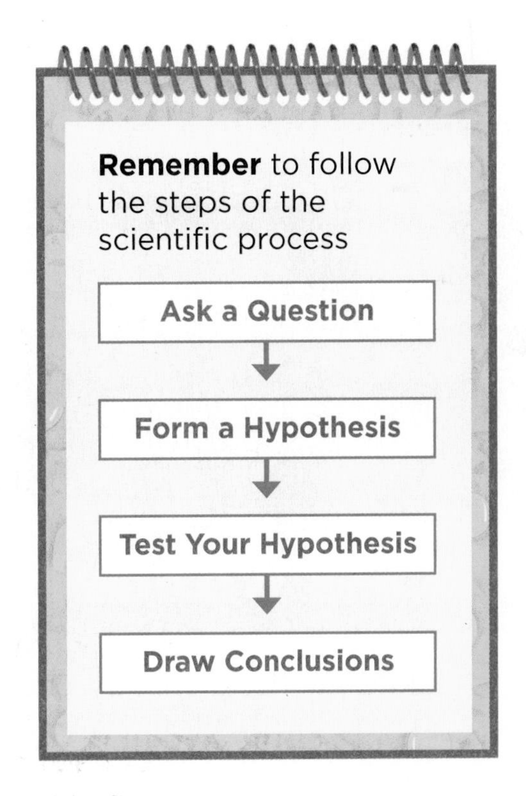

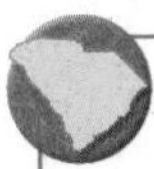

3-I.3. Generate questions about objects, organisms, and events in the environment and use those questions to conduct a simple scientific investigation.

Life in the Grasslands

Look and Wonder

Long-necked giraffes, speedy cheetahs, and watchful zebras live in Africa's Serengeti Plain. What is the Serengeti? How do these animals find food and stay safe?

3-2.2. Explain how physical and behavioral adaptations allow organisms to survive.
3-2.3. Recall the characteristics of an organism's habitat that allow the organism to survive there.

What kinds of animals live in a grassland?

Make a Prediction

Why do some animals live in grasslands? Write your prediction.

Test Your Prediction

1. Use research materials to learn about an animal that lives in a grassland habitat.
2. **Record Data** Make a picture fact card for your animal. Draw or tape a picture of the animal on the card, and label it. On the other side, write the name of the grassland habitat. List three facts you learned about it.
3. **Compare** Trade fact cards with your classmates. Do your animals live in the same grassland habitat?
4. **Classify** Group the animals according to their grassland habitats.

Draw Conclusions

5. What are some important things that would be found in grassland habitats?
6. What are some adaptations that grassland animals have in common?

Explore More

What would happen to a grassland after a month of no rain? How does rainfall affect grassland animals?

Materials

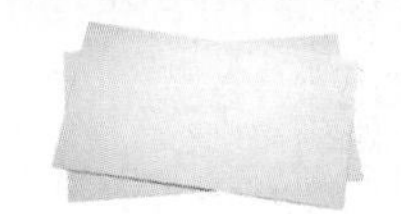

large index cards

colored pencils

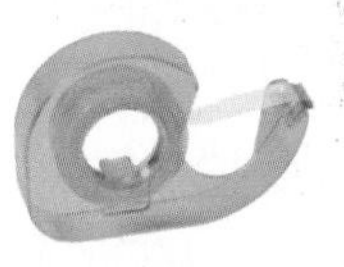

tape

Step 2

Step 3

3-1.4. Predict the outcome of a simple investigation and compare the result with the prediction.

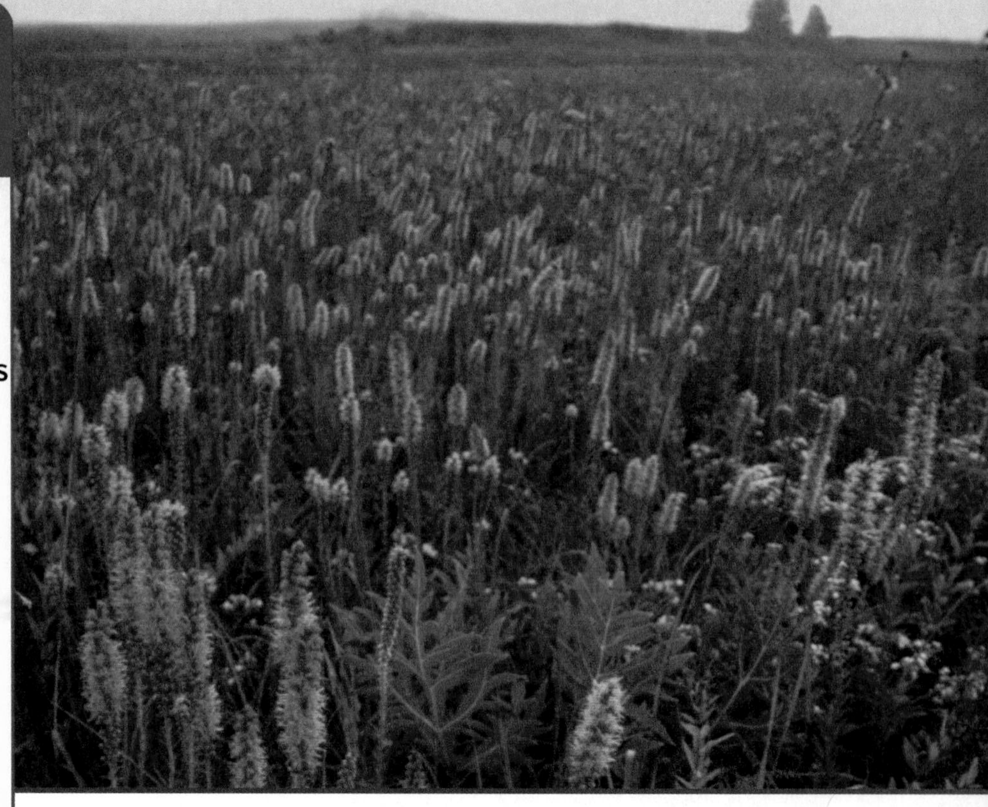

Read and Learn

Main Idea 3-2.2 3-2.3

Grasses are the main type of plant in a grassland habitat. Plants and animals that live in a grassland have structures and behaviors that help them survive.

Vocabulary

grassland, p. 96

temperate, p. 97

tropical, p. 97

at www.macmillanmh.com

Reading Skills

Compare and Contrast

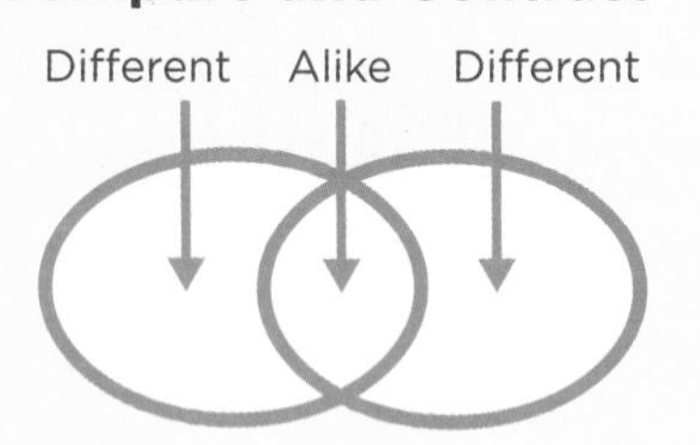

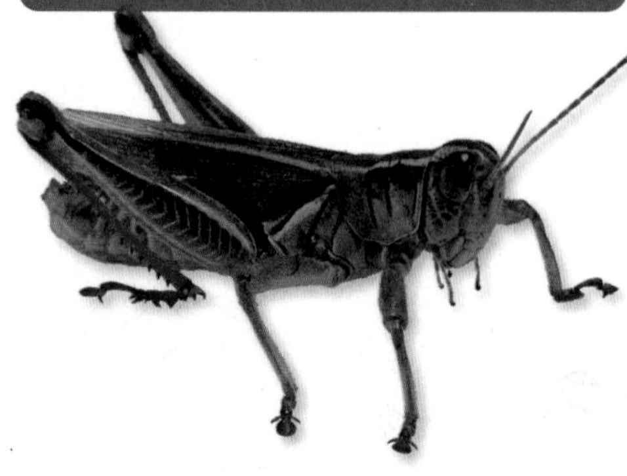

▲ Grasshoppers have back legs built for jumping.

▲ The prairies of North America are temperate grasslands.

What is a grassland?

Miles of green grass stretch out before you. Wildflowers bloom. The air is warm against your skin. Grasshoppers jump. A green snake slithers. Suddenly, the wind blows, and thousands of blades of grass make a quiet swishing sound. You are in the grasslands of North America.

A **grassland** is a habitat that is covered with grasses. Grass is everything to a grassland. Grass is food for animals. Grass is like a blanket that keeps in warmth and moisture. Grass is both a hiding place and a shelter from the wind and cold. Grass holds down soil that would otherwise blow away in the wind.

There are two types of grasslands. Temperate grasslands are one type. **Temperate** means the environment has a mild climate and four seasons. Temperate grasslands have soil that is rich in humus. The North American *prairies* are temperate grasslands.

Tropical grasslands are the second type of grasslands. **Tropical** means the environment is near the equator and is warm all year round. Tropical grasslands have a rainy season and a dry season. They usually have more trees and poorer soil than temperate grasslands. The *savanna* grasslands of Africa's Serengeti Plain are tropical grasslands.

Both temperate and tropical grasslands get about 25 to 75 centimeters (10 to 30 inches) of rain each year. With so little rain, the land can dry out. Fires can start easily. Fires form regularly in grasslands.

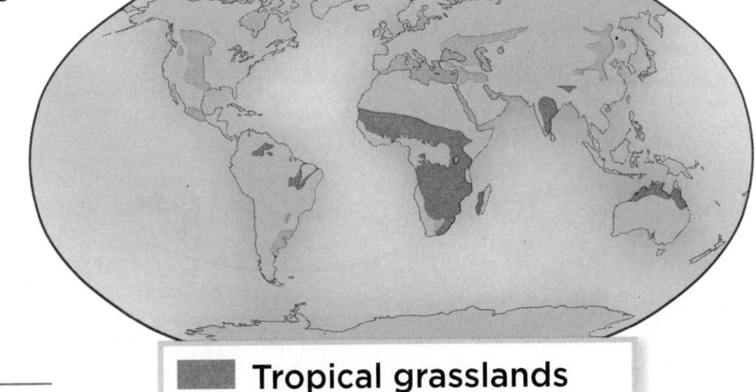

Quick Check

Compare and Contrast How are temperate and tropical grasslands different?

Critical Thinking What kind of grasslands are in North America?

The savannas of Africa are tropical grasslands.

What adaptations help grassland plants survive?

Different grasslands have different kinds of grasses. However, nearly all grassland grasses are adapted to grow well in dry conditions.

Grasses have deep roots. The roots work like a sponge, soaking up moisture and storing nutrients. When a fire burns, everything above the ground is destroyed. Down below, the roots survive. They hold on to their moisture and nutrients.

After a fire, new stalks can grow from the roots. The old, dead grass becomes part of a new layer of soil. Over time, the soil gets richer and richer.

Most grasses are adapted to grow from the bottom up. This helps them survive and grow after animals graze on the tops of the plants.

Parts of a Grass Plant

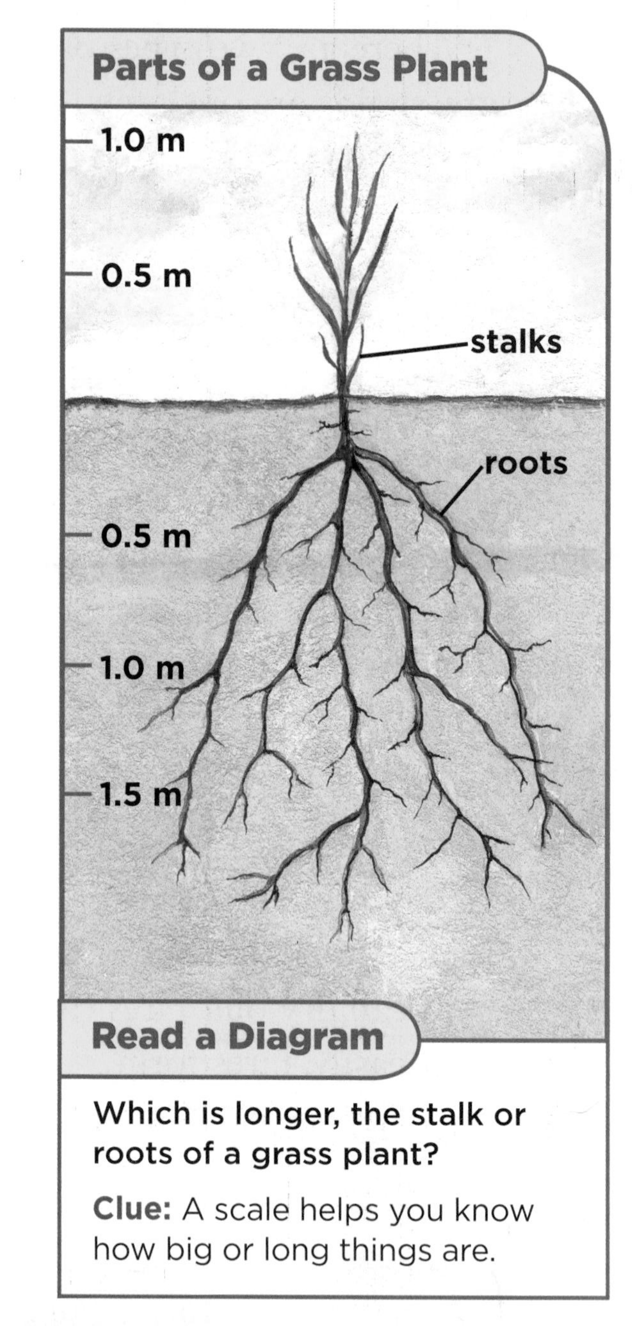

Read a Diagram

Which is longer, the stalk or roots of a grass plant?

Clue: A scale helps you know how big or long things are.

◀ Fire may burn the grass above the soil, but deep roots are not harmed. This means grass can grow back quickly after a fire.

Trees that grow in tropical grasslands also have adaptations that help them survive. The baobab tree grows in Africa's savannas. It grows leaves only during the wet season. It loses its leaves during the dry season. This adaptation helps it conserve water.

The baobab's thick trunk is adapted to store water during the long dry season. Its bark is fire resistant, making it well adapted to survive grassland fires.

Quick Check

Compare and Contrast How are tropical grassland grasses and trees alike?

Critical Thinking Could a cactus survive in a grassland? Why?

Quick Lab

How Grasses Grow

1. Put some sand or pebbles in the bottom of a plastic cup. Add potting soil almost to the top. Sprinkle grass seeds over the soil. Water the soil. Place the cup in a sunny spot.
2. **Record Data** Record when you planted the grass on a calendar.

SUN.	MON.	TUES.	WED.	THURS.	FRI.	SAT.
	1	2	3	4	5	6
7	8	9	10	11	12	13

3. **Observe** Check your grass seeds each day. Keep the soil moist. Record your observations on the calendar.
4. **Compare** Carefully uproot some grass. Measure the grass and the roots. Which is longer? Was the grass easy to pull out? Why or why not?

Baobab trees have bark that resists fire.

What adaptations help animals survive in grasslands?

Many kinds of animals live in grasslands. All of them have adaptations that help them survive.

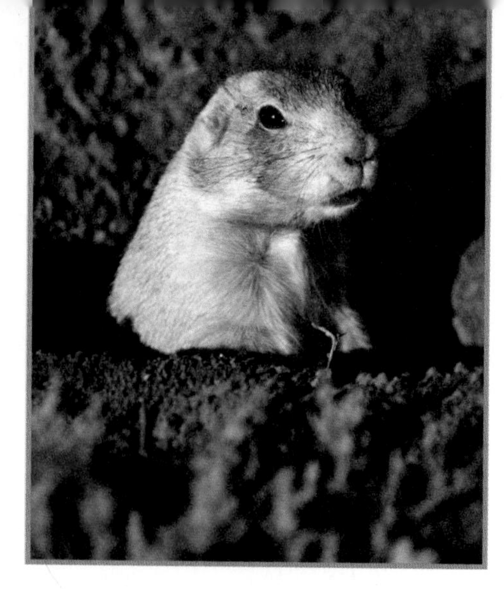

▲ Prairie dogs can escape danger quickly by hiding in their burrows.

Flat Teeth

Some grassland animals have flat teeth adapted for eating grass. Zebras bite off the tough tops of grasses. Antelopes eat the stems closest to the ground.

Burrows

Small animals can hide easily. Prairie dogs dig burrows, or holes, in the ground. They come out only during certain hours of the day.

Speed

Cheetahs can catch prey by running fast. African cheetahs can run at speeds of up to 112 kilometers (70 miles) per hour.

Quick Check

Compare and Contrast Compare how different animals survive in grasslands.

Critical Thinking Some grassland animals travel in herds. How might this help them stay safe?

Zebras bite grass easily with their flat teeth. ▼

African cheetahs have flexible spines that help them run very fast. ▼

Lesson Review

Visual Summary

A **grassland** is a habitat covered with grasses.

Grassland plants have adaptations that help them survive dry conditions and fires.

Grassland animals have special structures and behaviors that help them survive.

Make a FOLDABLES™ Study Guide

Make a Pyramid Fold. Use it to summarize what you read about grasslands.

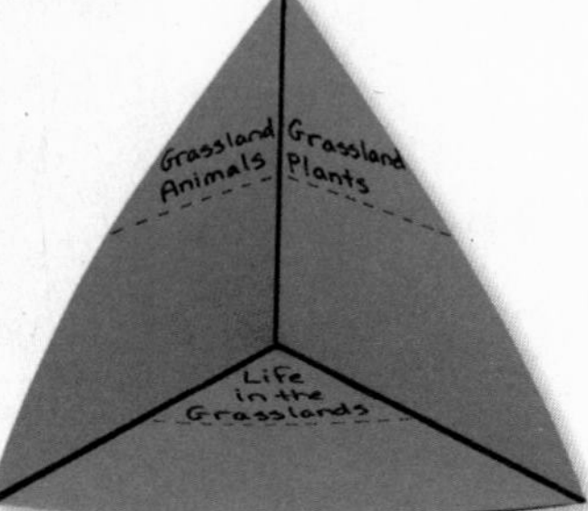

Think, Talk, and Write

1. **Main Idea** What are grasslands?

2. **Vocabulary** What word describes grasslands that are warm year-round?

3. **Compare and Contrast** How are grasslands and deserts alike? How are they different?

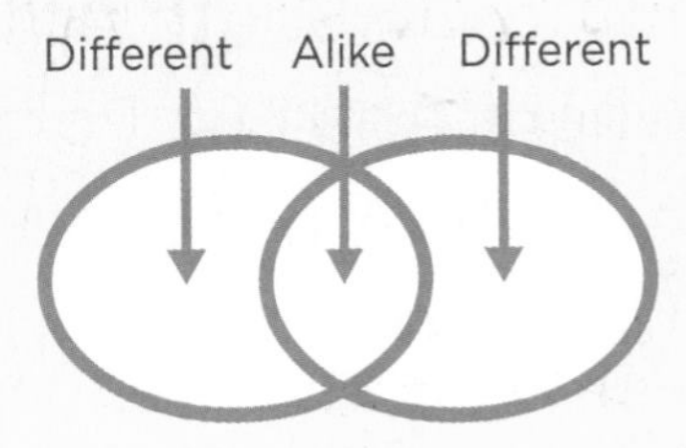

4. **Critical Thinking** The world's fastest-running land animals live in grasslands. Explain why speed is an important adaptation for grassland animals.

5. **Test Prep** **Tropical grasslands are found**
   - **A** near the North Pole.
   - **B** near the equator.
   - **C** in North America.
   - **D** in Antarctica.

Writing Link

Write a Report
Use research materials to find out more about cheetahs. Why do the people of Africa value these animals? What must be done to protect cheetahs?

Math Link

Multiply and Divide
If a cheetah runs for 4 minutes at a speed of 105 kilometers per hour, how many kilometers does the cheetah run?

Reading in Science

Meet Ana Luz Porzecanski

Grasslands, known as pampas, are common in South America. That is where Ana Luz Porzecanski, a scientist at the American Museum of Natural History, grew up.

Ana studies birds of the pampas. Some of the birds she studies are called *tinamous* (TIN•uh•mooz). Their brown and gray feathers help them blend in with the tall grass, shrubs, and bushes. This helps them hide from predators, such as foxes and hawks, that eat the birds or their eggs.

How does Ana find tinamous if they are so well hidden? She listens for their songs. Each kind of tinamou has a different song. Sometimes she has to sing or play a recording of their song to get the birds to answer back. It takes time, patience, and a little luck.

The tinamous are hard to see, but their shiny green, turquoise, or purple eggs really stand out. Ana wants to know why the eggs are so colorful. Why do you think the tinamous have such colorful eggs?

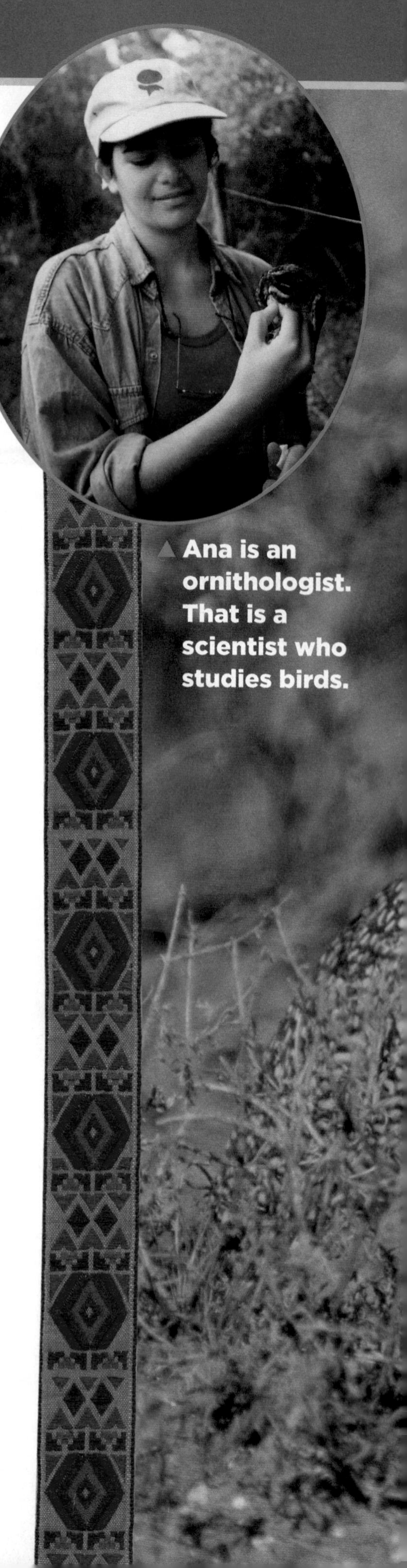

▲ Ana is an ornithologist. That is a scientist who studies birds.

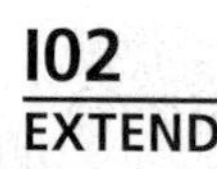

Compare and Contrast

- First, you explain how things are alike.
- Next, you explain how things are different.
- You use compare words, such as *like* and *both*, and contrast words, such as *unlike* and *but.*

Tinamou eggs are colorful.

Write About It

Compare and Contrast Work with a partner to compare the tinamou with another animal you know about. List ways the animals are alike and different in a Venn diagram. Then use your diagram to write about the animals.

LOG ON e-Journal Write about it online at www.macmillanmh.com

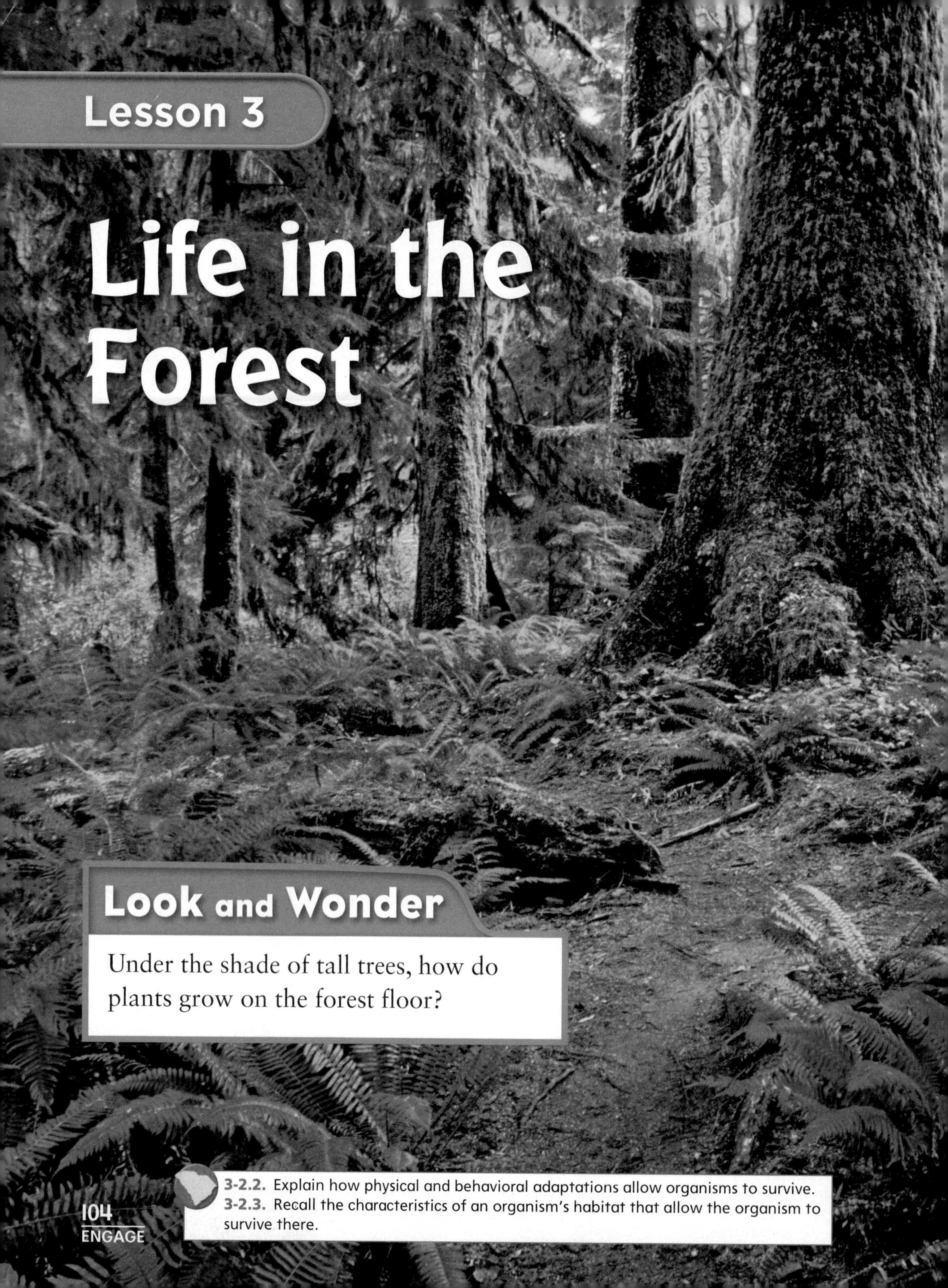

Lesson 3

Life in the Forest

Look and Wonder

Under the shade of tall trees, how do plants grow on the forest floor?

3-2.2. Explain how physical and behavioral adaptations allow organisms to survive.
3-2.3. Recall the characteristics of an organism's habitat that allow the organism to survive there.

Explore

Inquiry Activity

Will a plant grow toward light?

Make a Prediction

Plants need sunlight to survive. If something is blocking the light, how will a plant respond?

Test Your Prediction

1. Cut a hole in one end of a shoe box.
2. Cut two dividers from the cardboard as tall as the shoe box but 1 in. narrower than its width.
3. Tape the dividers upright along the inside of the box. The first divider should be attached to the same side as the hole that was cut into the box in step 1. The other divider should be on the other side.
4. Put your plant in the end of the box opposite the hole. Then put the lid on the box, and turn the hole toward bright sunlight.
5. **Observe** Every three or four days, remove the lid to water your plant and observe its growth. Do this for several weeks.

Draw Conclusions

6. How does the plant change after a few weeks? How does it get the light it needs?
7. **Infer** How might this be similar to what happens on the forest floor?

Explore More

Observe plants around your school. Which kinds live in the shade? Which kinds live in direct sunlight?

Materials

scissors

large shoe box

heavy cardboard

masking tape

small potted plant

Step 4

3-1.4. Predict the outcome of a simple investigation and compare the result with the prediction.

Read and Learn

Main Idea 3-2.2 3-2.3

Forests are habitats that have many trees. Forest plants and animals have adaptations that help them survive in their environment.

Vocabulary

forest, p. 106

deciduous, p. 109

coniferous, p. 109

mimicry, p. 110

hibernate, p. 112

at www.macmillanmh.com

Reading Skills 

Main Idea and Details

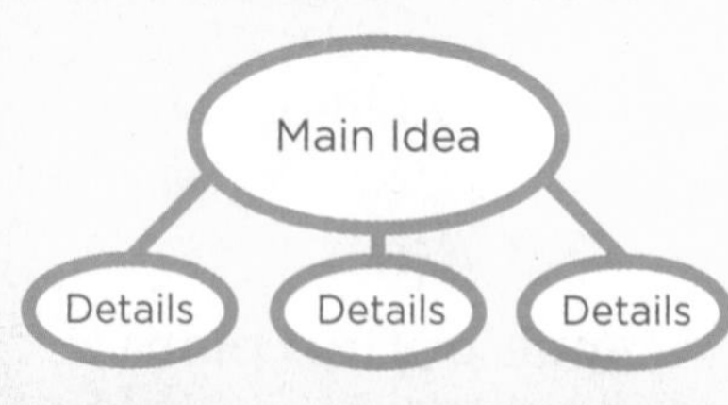

What is a forest?

It is dark and damp. Tall trees surround you. Raindrops drip from overhead. The hot, moist air feels heavy around you. Insects buzz. Birds sing. You are in the Amazon rain forest.

A **forest** is a habitat that has many trees. Different types of forests can be found in different parts of the world.

Tropical Rain Forests

A *tropical rain forest* is a forest habitat found near the equator. Tropical rain forests are green, rich forests. They have more kinds of living things than any other land habitat.

Tropical rain forests are hot and wet. About 200 to 460 centimeters (80 to 180 inches) of rain falls here in a single year. The temperature usually stays between 68°F and 93°F (20°C and 34°C) all year round.

Tropical rain forests are hot, wet forest habitats near the equator.

The soil in a tropical rain forest is not very rich in plant nutrients. This is because nutrients are quickly absorbed by rain-forest plants. The nutrients are only in a thin, top layer of soil. Hard clay lies below.

Temperate Forests

A *temperate forest* is a forest habitat found in North America, Europe, and Asia. Unlike tropical rain forests, temperate forests have four seasons: winter, spring, summer, and fall. Temperatures and rainfall change from season to season. Winters are cold and dry. Summers are warm and wet. About 76 to 127 centimeters (30 to 50 inches) of rain fall each year.

The soil in a temperate forest is rich in humus. Humus helps keep the soil moist. It also supplies nutrients for plants to grow.

Quick Check

Main Idea and Details What are two types of forests?

Critical Thinking Compare a tropical rain forest to a temperate forest.

Temperate forests are forest habitats that have four seasons.

What adaptations help forest plants survive?

Forest plants grow in layers. The plants in each layer are adapted to grow toward the light. They also have other adaptations that help them survive.

Tropical Rain-Forest Plants

Many tropical trees grow very tall. Their branches spread out in the canopy or emergent layer. Although tall, many of these trees have shallow roots. Buttresses help support their tall size. *Buttresses* are special root structures that spread out from the trunk.

Trees and smaller plants that grow in the canopy or understory often have leaves with drip tips. This adaptation helps them lose extra rainwater.

Very little sunlight reaches the understory and forest floor. Most plants that grow here have very large leaves. This adaptation helps plants soak in as much sunlight as possible.

Read a Diagram

What are the layers of a rain forest?

Clue: Bold words can help you find information.

Temperate Forest Plants

The tall trees of the temperate forest are mostly deciduous (di•SI•juh•wuhs) or coniferous (coh•NI•fuh•ruhs). **Deciduous** trees lose their leaves in fall as the temperature gets cooler. The leaves grow back in spring and summer. This adaptation helps them conserve energy during cold winters. **Coniferous** trees make cones instead of flowers. Coniferous trees are often called evergreens. They stay green all year. Their thin, needlelike leaves are tough and waxy. This adaptation helps them conserve water during cold, dry winters.

▲ A pine cone holds the seeds of a coniferous tree.

Quick Check

Main Idea and Details What are some adaptations of forest plants?

Critical Thinking Could temperate-forest trees survive in a tropical rain forest? Explain.

Leaves on deciduous trees change from green to yellow, orange, and red in the fall. They fall off, and then they grow back in spring.

How do animals survive in a tropical rain forest?

Many kinds of animals swing, swoop, dart, and jump in the rain-forest canopy. Each kind of animal has adaptations that help it survive.

▲ The poison arrow frog's bright colors warn predators to stay away.

Warning Colors

How does this bright-colored frog stay safe in the rain forest? You would think predators would notice its bright colors and attack. Predators do notice the brilliant colors. However, these colors are a warning that say, "I am poisonous!" so predators stay away.

Blending In

Can you find the mantis in the photograph on the right? The orchid mantis is well disguised. It stays safe in its environment by looking like the flower of an orchid. This adaptation is called mimicry (MI•mi•kree). **Mimicry** is when one living thing imitates another living thing in color or shape.

Mimicry helps this orchid mantis stay safe. ▼

Getting Away

What if you were stuck on a branch with a predator closing in? If you were an iguana, you would fall. Iguanas can fall 18 meters (60 feet) or more from a high branch without getting hurt. Iguanas often sit on tree limbs that hang over water. When an enemy comes, they just drop into the water!

An iguana's long tail helps it balance in the high branches of a tropical rain forest.

Quick Lab

Hiding Out

1. **Make a Model** Fold a piece of colored construction paper in half. Draw a butterfly outline. Cut out two butterflies.
2. Select a piece of fabric or wrapping paper to be your butterfly habitat.
3. Draw two large spots or "eyes" on one butterfly's wings. Color the other butterfly to look like the habitat.
4. **Observe** Place your butterflies on the habitat. Which one can you find quickly? Which one looks like it does not belong there?
5. **Infer** Why would blending in help a butterfly stay safe? Would having large spots or other markings help protect a butterfly? Why do you think so?

Quick Check

Main Idea and Details What are some adaptations of tropical rain-forest animals?

Critical Thinking How might an animal's appearance protect it from predators?

How do animals survive in a temperate forest?

Temperate-forest animals have adaptations that help them survive the changing seasons. They also have adaptations that keep them safe.

▲ Dormice hibernate during winter.

Surviving Winter

When the weather gets cool in fall, some animals eat extra food. They store energy for winter, when food is harder to find. Some animals also grow thicker coats to keep them warm during winter.

Some animals hibernate (HIGH•buhr•nayt). **Hibernate** means "to go into a deep sleep that lasts through winter." The animals live off energy stored in their bodies.

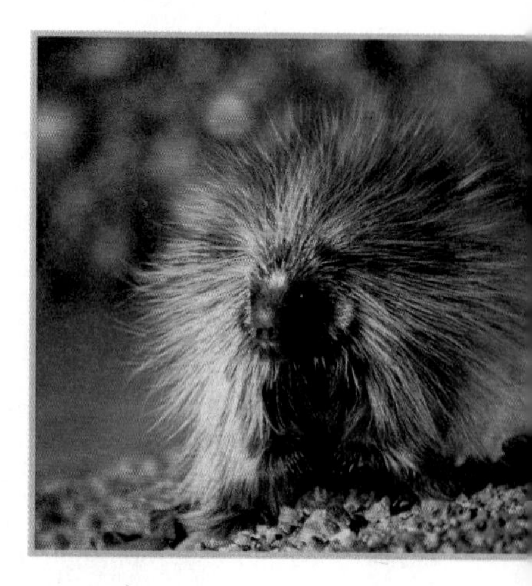

▲ A porcupine's sharp quills help it stay safe.

Staying Safe

Skunks and porcupines have unusual ways to stay safe. Skunks spray a stinky chemical if an enemy gets too close. It also stings the predator's eyes. Porcupines have needlelike quills that they raise when an enemy comes near. If the attack continues, the enemy gets stuck with sharp quills!

Quick Check

Main Idea and Details How do adaptations help animals in temperate forests?

Critical Thinking Why do some animals hibernate?

Skunks spray a smelly chemical to keep predators away. ▼

Lesson Review

Visual Summary

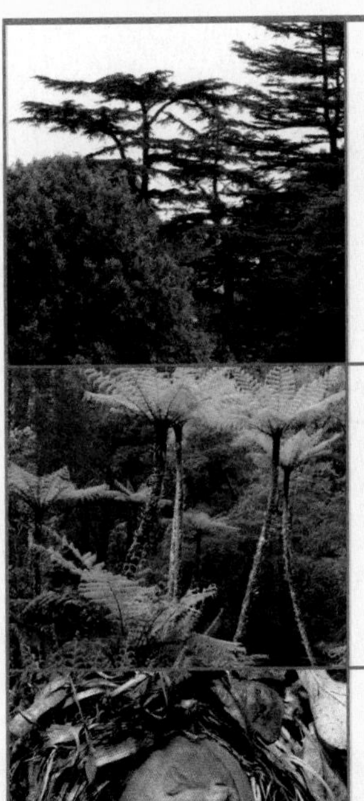

A **forest** has mostly trees. Tropical rain forests and temperate forests are types of forests.

Forest plants have special structures that help them survive.

Forest animals have adaptations that help them grow and survive.

Make a FOLDABLES™ Study Guide

Make a Pyramid Fold. Use it to summarize what you read about forests.

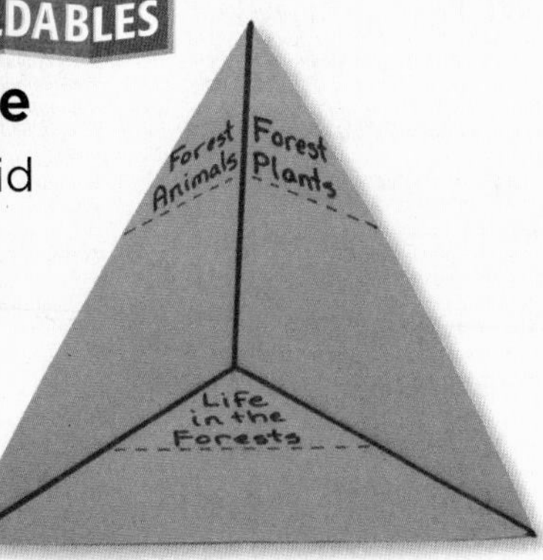

Think, Talk, and Write

1. **Main Idea** How are tropical rain forests different from temperate forests? In what ways are these two types of forests similar?

2. **Vocabulary** What is mimicry?

3. **Main Idea and Details** What adaptations help plants and animals survive cold winters in a temperate forest?

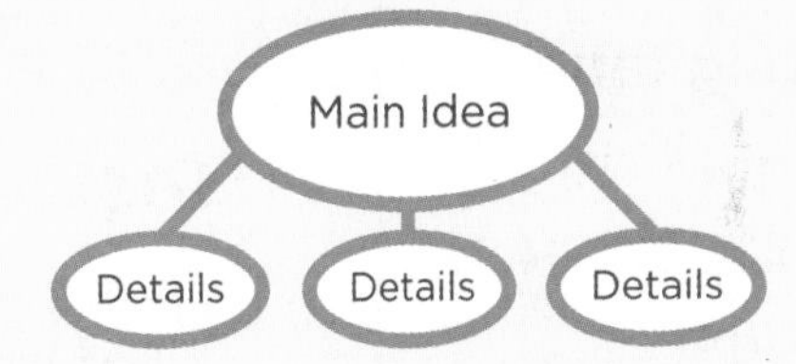

4. **Critical Thinking** Many of the fruits you eat come from tropical rain forests. What is it about tropical rain forests that allows fruits to grow?

5. **Test Prep** **All of the following are layers of the rain forest EXCEPT**
   - **A** emergent.
   - **B** submergent.
   - **C** canopy.
   - **D** understory.

Writing Link

Write a Paragraph
Rain forests are disappearing. Research and find out why. Look up ways we can help save rain forests. Then write a paragraph.

Math Link

Do Research
Find out about healthful products that come from the rain forest. Write a short paragraph about one of these natural wonders.

LOG ON e-Review Summaries and quizzes online at www.macmillanmh.com

Be a Scientist

Materials

brown and green construction paper

masking tape

ruler

scissors
△ **Be Careful.**

cardboard

lamp

Structured Inquiry

How do trees affect light in a rain forest?

Form a Hypothesis

Rain-forest trees can grow as high as 60 m (197 ft). The trees' branches spread wide to form the canopy. How does the thickness of the canopy affect the amount of light that reaches the forest floor? Write a hypothesis. Begin with "If the rain-forest canopy is thick, then . . ."

Test Your Hypothesis

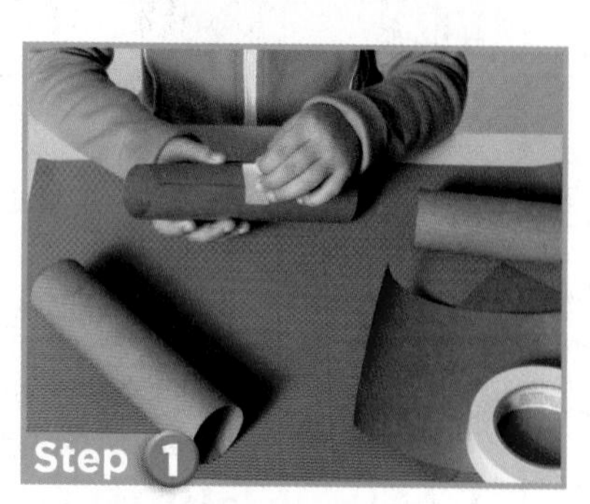

Step 1

1. **Make a Model** Use 6 sheets of brown paper to create 6 tubes of different heights. These model tree trunks.
2. Draw 3 circles with a diameter of about 8 cm on green paper. Draw 3 more circles with 4 cm diameters. Cut out the circles. These represent tree branches.
3. **Use Variables** Tape the circles to the tree trunks. Arrange the trees on a piece of cardboard so that the trees are close to each other and form a thick canopy.

Step 3

4. **Experiment** Shine a lamp down onto your forest. How much light reaches the forest floor? Record your observations.
5. **Use Variables** Repeat steps 3 and 4 several times. Vary the thickness of the canopy by placing the trees closer or farther apart.

Draw Conclusions

6. How does the thickness of the canopy affect the amount of light that reaches the forest floor?

7. **Infer** How do trees affect plants that grow on the forest floor?

Guided Inquiry

How do trees affect rainwater?

Form a Hypothesis

Does the canopy affect the amount of water that reaches the forest floor? Write a hypothesis.

Test Your Hypothesis

Design an experiment to see if the canopy affects the water that reaches the forest floor. Decide on the materials you will use. Then write the steps you will follow. Record your results and observations.

Draw Conclusions

Did your experiment support your hypothesis? Why or why not?

Open Inquiry

What else would you like to learn about rain forests? For example, what happens to plants in the understory if a tree is cut down? Design an experiment to find out about new questions you have.

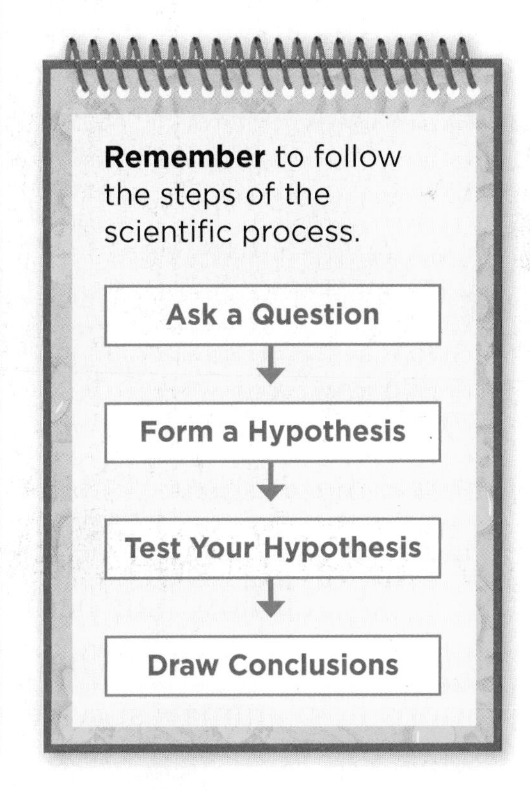

3-I.4. Predict the outcome of a simple investigation and compare the result with the prediction.

Lesson 4

Life in the Arctic Tundra

Look and Wonder

Did you know that a polar bear's hair is hollow? Hollow hair helps it absorb heat from the Sun. What other adaptations help animals survive in cold environments?

3-2.2. Explain how physical and behavioral adaptations allow organisms to survive.
3-2.3. Recall the characteristics of an organism's habitat that allow the organism to survive there.

Explore

Inquiry Activity

Does fat help animals survive in cold environments?

Form a Hypothesis

Does fat help animals stay warm? Does fat keep animals cool? Write a hypothesis. Start with "If an animal has extra fat, then . . ."

Test Your Hypothesis

1. Use a paper towel to spread vegetable fat over one of your index fingers. Try to coat your finger completely with fat.
2. **Predict** What will happen when you put both index fingers in a bowl of ice water?
3. **Experiment** Ask a partner to time how long you can keep each index finger in the ice water. Record the data in a chart.
4. Trade roles with your partner, and repeat steps 1 through 3.

Draw Conclusions

5. **Interpret Data** Did your observations match your prediction? What happened when you put both fingers in the ice water?
6. How does fat help animals survive in cold places?

Explore More

Experiment How does thick fur help animals survive in cold environments? Form a hypothesis. Then make a plan to test it.

Materials

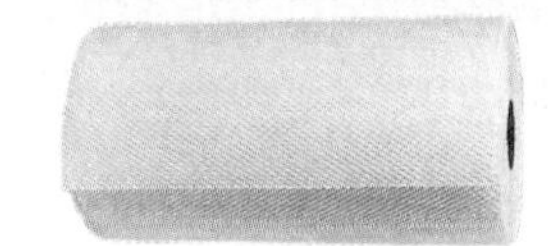

paper towel

vegetable fat

ice water

stopwatch

Step 1

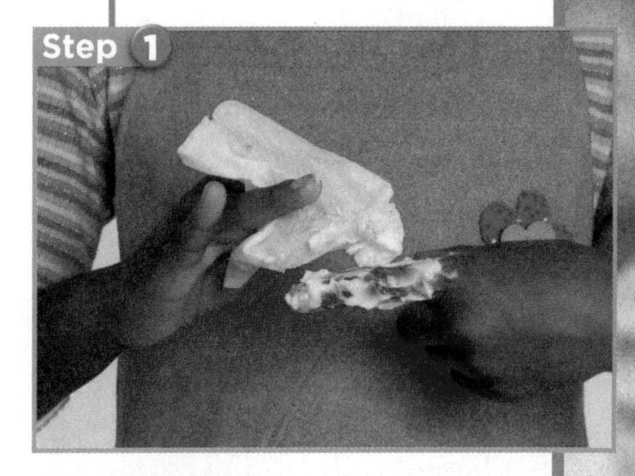

Step 3

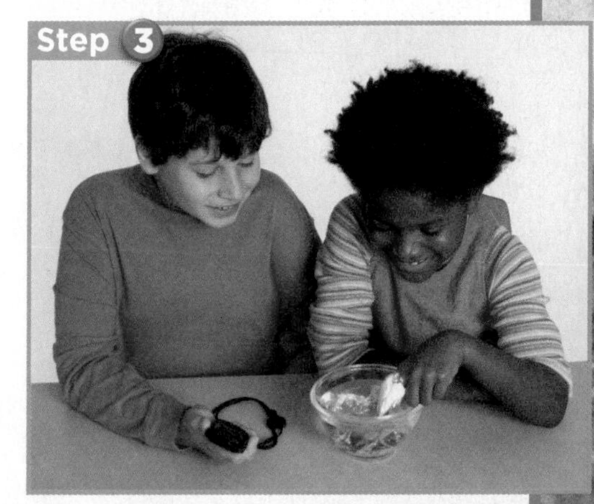

3-1.4. Predict the outcome of a simple investigation and compare the result with the prediction.

Read and Learn

Main Idea 3-2.2 3-2.3

The arctic tundra is a cold habitat with little rainfall. Tundra plants and animals have adaptations that help them survive.

Vocabulary

arctic tundra, p. 118

permafrost, p. 119

blubber, p. 122

migrate, p. 124

LOG ON e-Glossary at www.macmillanmh.com

Reading Skill

Draw Conclusions

Text Clues	Conclusions

What is an arctic tundra?

You have reached Denali National Park. The air is so cold it burns your lungs. A biting-cold wind whips across your face. The ground is frozen and hard beneath your feet. This is the arctic tundra.

The **arctic tundra** is the cold habitat above the Arctic Circle. Winters here are long and dark. In the middle of winter, the Sun never rises. Temperatures can drop to −60°F (−51°C), and several feet of snow fall. Few plants are able to survive here in winter. Many animals leave for warmer places.

In the six to ten weeks of summer, the Sun never sets. It is light during both the day and the night.

In winter, the arctic tundra is cold and dark. These caribou move south to find a warmer environment. ▼

With heat from the Sun, the snow melts. The melted snow cannot soak into the ground. A layer of permafrost keeps it from draining. **Permafrost** is soil that is always frozen. The land becomes soggy with pools of water.

As temperatures rise, the top few inches of soil thaw. Small plants grow in the wet ground. The arctic tundra comes to life as animals return to feed and nest.

Quick Check

Draw Conclusions Why is there permafrost in the arctic tundra?

Critical Thinking How is the arctic tundra similar to the desert? How is it different?

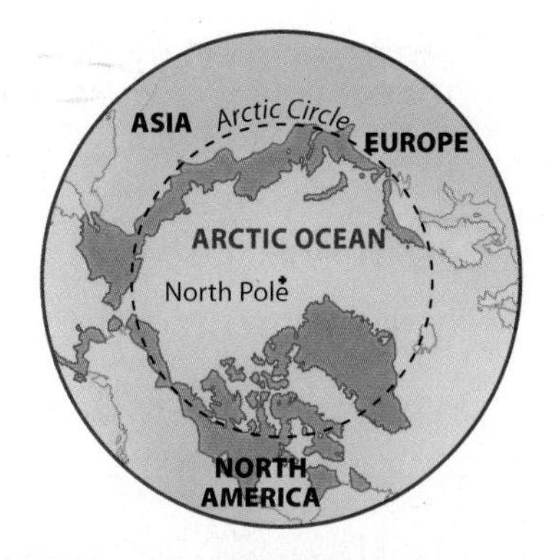

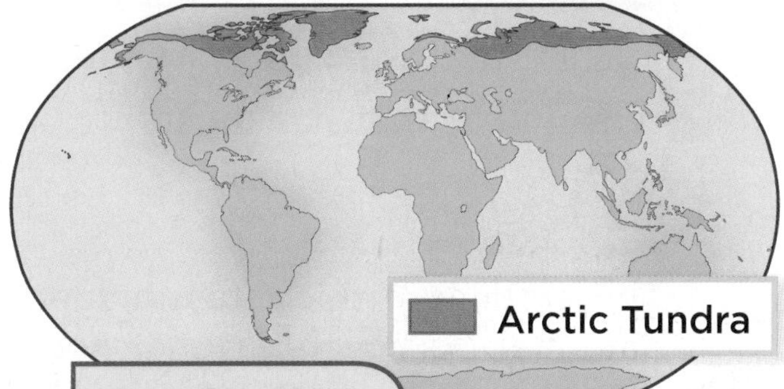

Read a Map

Where in the world is the arctic tundra?

Clue: A map key can help you understand the information on a map.

In summer, the arctic tundra becomes soggy with melted snow. ▼

What adaptations help arctic plants?

About 1,700 different kinds of plants can grow in the arctic tundra. Arctic plants have adaptations that help them survive in their cold, icy environment.

Shallow Roots

One adaptation that helps arctic plants survive is small, shallow roots. All of the plants that live in the arctic tundra have shallow roots or no roots at all. Shallow roots are necessary for surviving in an environment that has mostly frozen soil.

This arctic tern chick stays hidden among rocks covered with lichen. Lichen is similar to moss.

Short and Small

Small size is another adaptation that helps plants survive here. Most arctic plants grow close to the ground. They rarely reach more than 30 centimeters (1 foot) tall. This adaptation protects plants from the cold and wind.

Growing Together

Many arctic plants grow close together in tight clumps that look like cushions. Arctic forget-me-nots are an example. Growing together is an adaptation that protects plants from wind and freezing temperatures. Plants that grow this way are called *cushion plants*.

Dark Colors

A deep red or pink color helps many plants, such as dwarf fireweed, survive in the arctic tundra. Dark color is an adaptation that helps these plants absorb sunlight. It also helps attract birds and other animals that they depend on to spread their seeds and reproduce.

Quick Check

Draw Conclusions Could a banana tree live in the arctic tundra? Explain your answer.

Critical Thinking How does color help some plants survive in the arctic tundra?

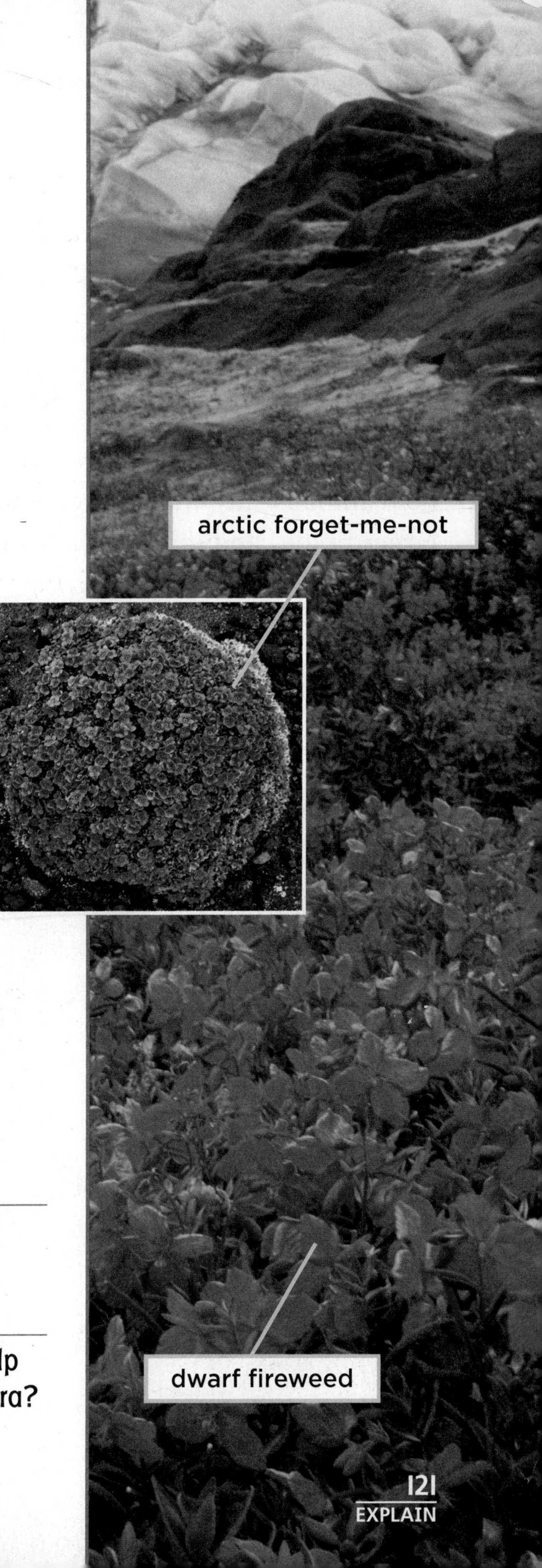

What adaptations help arctic animals?

A variety of animals make their home in the arctic tundra. Arctic animals have adaptations that help them survive in cold, snowy environments.

Staying Warm

Polar bears, musk oxen, and many other arctic animals have thick fur coats. They also have a thick layer of blubber. **Blubber** is fat. Thick coats and fat help animals stay warm. Arctic animals usually have larger bodies and thicker fur than their relatives in other habitats. They also have smaller ears and shorter legs. All these adaptations help them absorb and conserve heat.

A thick fur coat and layer of blubber help polar bears and musk oxen stay warm in the cold arctic tundra.

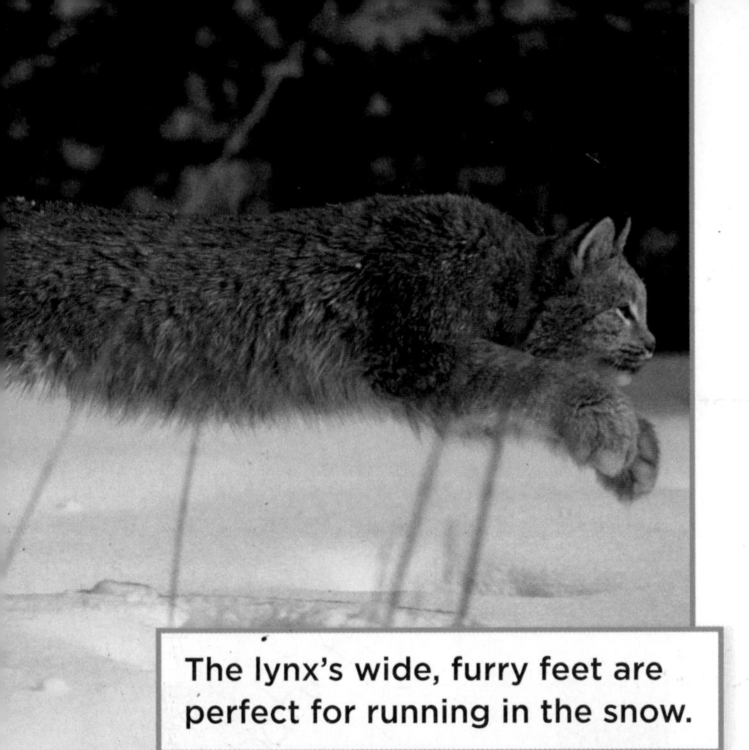

The lynx's wide, furry feet are perfect for running in the snow.

Wide Paws and Strong Claws

The lynx, snowshoe hare, and polar bear, among many tundra animals, all have wide, furry feet. This helps them run in the snow. Wide feet work like snowshoes. They keep animals from sinking into the snow. Long, strong claws give animals extra grip. They keep animals from sliding on slippery ice.

Quick Check

Draw Conclusions Why do most rain-forest animals have thinner fur coats than arctic animals?

Critical Thinking How do special feet help some animals survive in the tundra?

Quick Lab

Arctic Adaptations

1. **Observe** What do you notice about the arctic and desert foxes' features? What are their coats and bodies like?
2. **Compare** How are the animals alike? How are they different?
3. **Infer** How do the arctic fox's features help it survive in the arctic tundra?

arctic fox

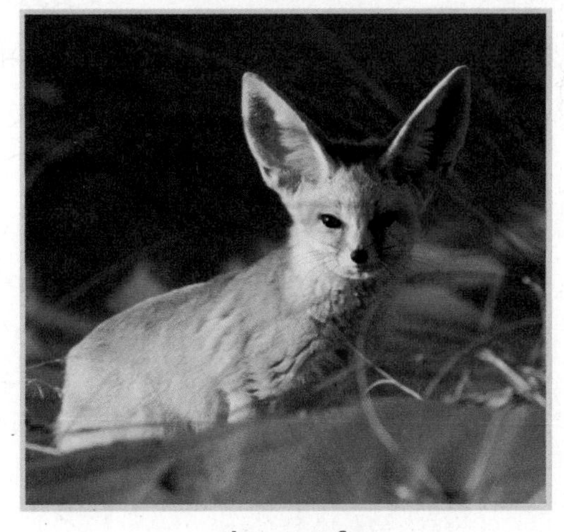

desert fox

What are some other arctic-animal adaptations?

Canada geese, tundra swans, and caribou are a few arctic animals that migrate (MIGH•grayt). To **migrate** means to move to another place. Animals migrate when their home environment can no longer meet their needs. In winter the arctic becomes too cold for plants to grow. Animals that eat plants move south where food is easier to find. When temperatures rise in the arctic in spring, plants begin to grow again. The animals can then return home.

The arctic hare and fox, among others, change color from season to season to stay camouflaged. Camouflage helps animals like the hare stay safe from animals that hunt them. It helps animals like the fox hunt without being seen.

Quick Check

Draw Conclusions How does color help some animals survive?

Critical Thinking Why do some animals migrate?

▲ Many Canada geese migrate south into parts of the United States.

▲ arctic fox in winter

arctic fox in summer ▶

Lesson Review

Visual Summary

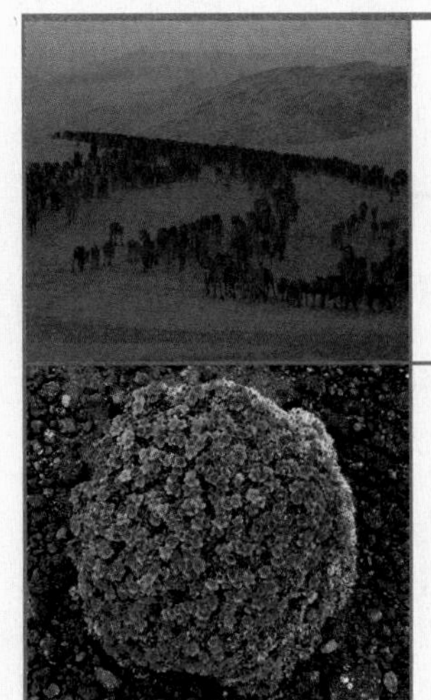

The **arctic tundra** is a cold, dry habitat above the Arctic Circle.

Arctic plants have adaptations that protect them from the cold and wind.

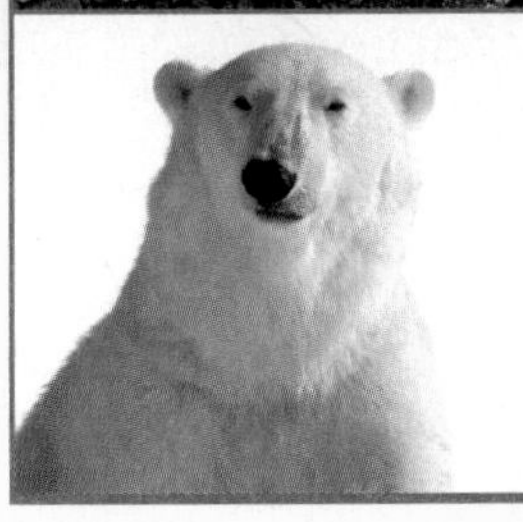

Arctic animals have adaptations that help them survive in cold, snowy environments.

Make a FOLDABLES™ Study Guide

Make a Pyramid Fold. Use it to summarize what you read about the arctic tundra.

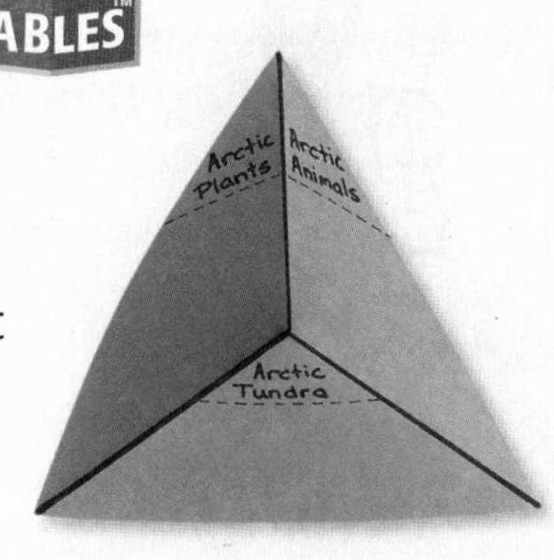

Think, Talk, and Write

1. **Main Idea** What adaptations help arctic plants and animals survive?
2. **Vocabulary** What is the arctic tundra like? Write about it.
3. **Draw Conclusions** Why can trees not grow in the arctic tundra?

Text Clues	Conclusions

4. **Critical Thinking** Could an arctic animal live in a hot desert? Explain your answer.
5. **Test Prep An arctic fox's white fur is an example of**
   A mimicry.
   B migration.
   C camouflage.
   D hibernation.

Writing Link

Writing That Compares

Describe your favorite arctic animal. What adaptations help it survive? Compare this animal to a forest animal. Write about how the animals are alike and how they are different.

Social Studies Link

Do Research

Few people live in the arctic tundra, but some Inuit live in areas where they can fish and hunt for food. Write a list of questions that you could ask someone who lives in the tundra. Research the Inuit to find the answers.

LOG ON e-Review Summaries and quizzes online at www.macmillanmh.com

Describe Where You Live

In this chapter, you went on a trip to different environments around the world. Now tell about where you live. Describe the sights and sounds of your community. What plants and animals live around you? What is the climate like?

Descriptive Writing

A good description

- includes describing words to tell how something looks, sounds, feels, smells, or tastes
- uses details to create a picture for the reader
- groups together details in an order that makes sense

Write About It

Descriptive Writing Write a description in your science journal about your environment. Use the first paragraph on page 118 as a model for your writing.

LOG ON e-Journal Research and write about it online at www.macmillanmh.com

Estimating the Area of Leaves

Most plants in the tundra are very small. This is an adaptation that helps them survive. What are plants like in your environment? Are they big and tall? What kind of leaves do they have?

Estimate Area

- First, trace a flat object on a piece of graph paper.
- Then, estimate the area by counting the number of squares it covers. Count any square that is more than half-covered.

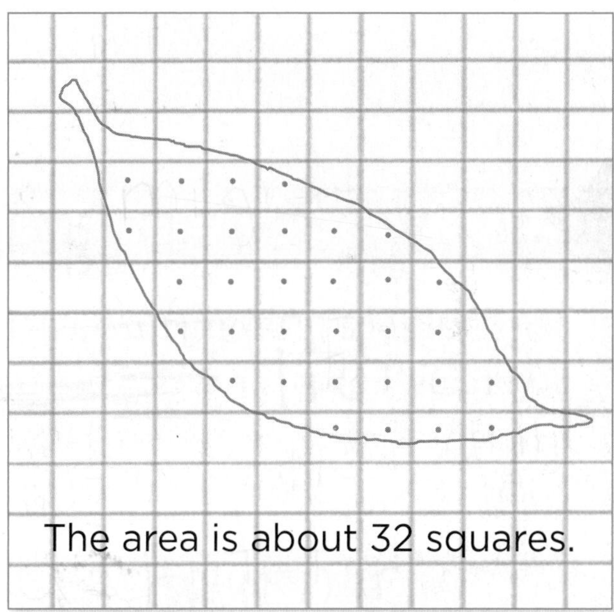

The area is about 32 squares.

Solve It

Collect the leaves of some plants from your environment. Compare their sizes. Estimate their areas.

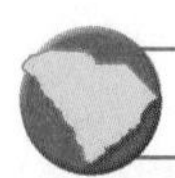

3-I.6. Infer meaning from data communicated in graphs, tables, and diagrams.

Lesson 5

Life in the Ocean

Look and Wonder

These strange life-forms are jellyfish. They have no brains, bones, or eyes. They have poisonous tentacles that capture food. How are their bodies adapted to move through water?

3-2.2. Explain how physical and behavioral adaptations allow organisms to survive.
3-2.3. Recall the characteristics of an organism's habitat that allow the organism to survive there.

How do jellyfish and some other water animals move?

Purpose

Model how jellyfish and some other ocean animals are adapted to move through water.

Procedure

1. **Make a Model** Blow up a balloon. Hold the end of the balloon tight so the air cannot escape. The balloon models the hollow, bell-shaped body of a jellyfish. The air is like water that fills the jellyfish's body.
2. **Predict** What do you think will happen when you let go of the balloon?
3. **Experiment** Let go of your balloon. What happens as "water" is pushed out of a "jellyfish's body"?

△ **Be Careful.** Make sure you do this away from other students.

Draw Conclusions

4. How does a jellyfish move through the ocean? How does this adaptation help a jellyfish survive in its water environment?

Explore More

How do other animals move through the ocean? Do research to find out.

Materials

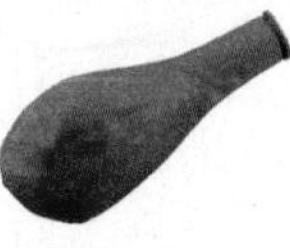

balloon

Step 1

Step 3

3-I.4. Predict the outcome of a simple investigation and compare the result with the prediction.

Read and Learn

Main Idea 3-2.2 3-2.3

The ocean is Earth's largest habitat. Ocean plants and animals have adaptations that help them survive in this environment.

Vocabulary

ocean, p. 131

algae, p. 132

gills, p. 134

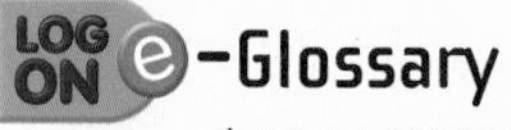

e-Glossary at www.macmillanmh.com

Reading Skills

Compare and Contrast

Different Alike Different

Coral reefs are found in the warm, shallow waters of tropical oceans.

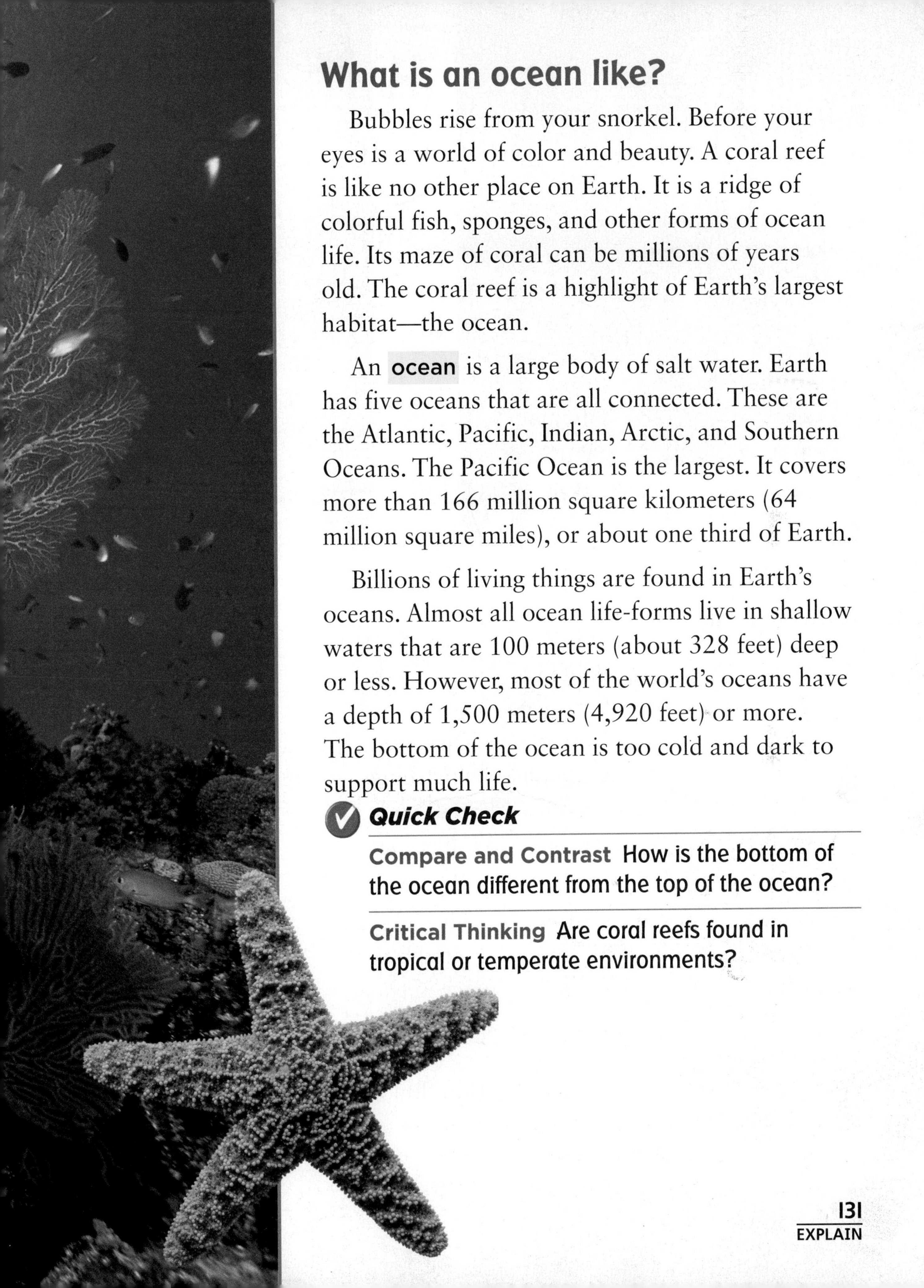

What is an ocean like?

Bubbles rise from your snorkel. Before your eyes is a world of color and beauty. A coral reef is like no other place on Earth. It is a ridge of colorful fish, sponges, and other forms of ocean life. Its maze of coral can be millions of years old. The coral reef is a highlight of Earth's largest habitat—the ocean.

An **ocean** is a large body of salt water. Earth has five oceans that are all connected. These are the Atlantic, Pacific, Indian, Arctic, and Southern Oceans. The Pacific Ocean is the largest. It covers more than 166 million square kilometers (64 million square miles), or about one third of Earth.

Billions of living things are found in Earth's oceans. Almost all ocean life-forms live in shallow waters that are 100 meters (about 328 feet) deep or less. However, most of the world's oceans have a depth of 1,500 meters (4,920 feet) or more. The bottom of the ocean is too cold and dark to support much life.

Quick Check

Compare and Contrast How is the bottom of the ocean different from the top of the ocean?

Critical Thinking Are coral reefs found in tropical or temperate environments?

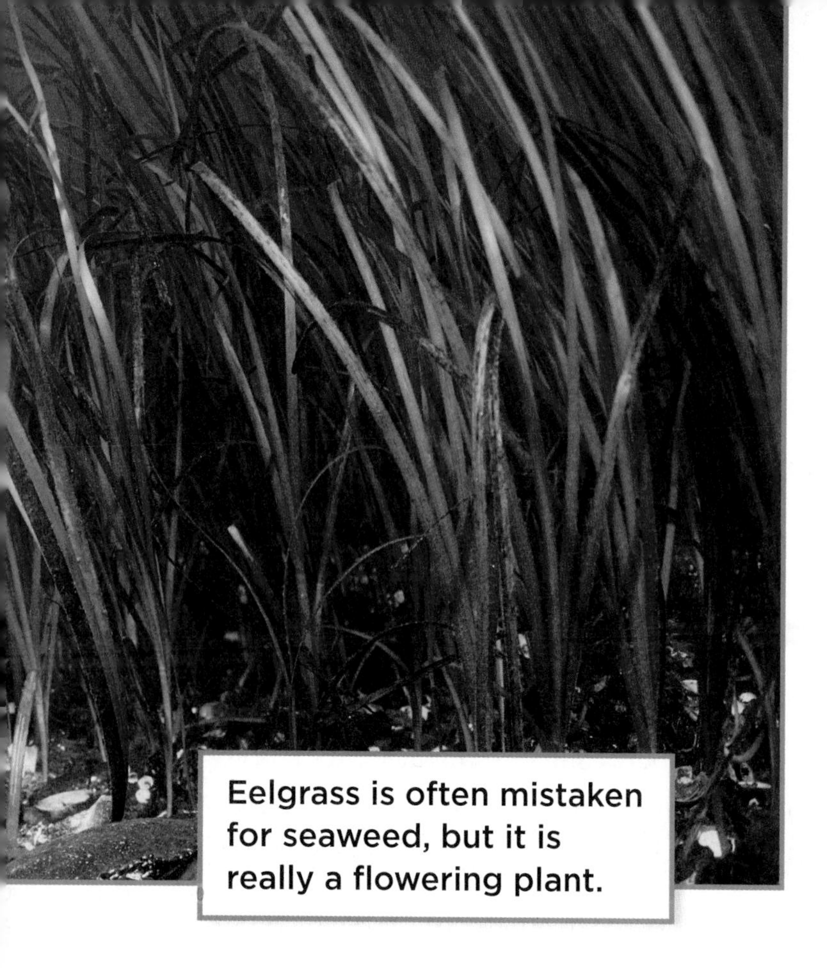

Eelgrass is often mistaken for seaweed, but it is really a flowering plant.

How do plants survive in the ocean?

Few true plants are adapted to survive in the ocean. Eelgrass is one of them. Most of the ocean's "plants" are not true plants. They are **algae** (AL•jee). Algae are plantlike living things. Just like plants, they use water, carbon dioxide gas, and sunlight to make their own food. Just like plants, they give off oxygen—the gas we breathe.

Two main kinds of algae are found in the ocean. One kind has rootlike structures that attach to the ocean bottom. These algae can only live in shallow water where they get enough sunlight to grow. The other kind does not have roots. These algae drift near the sunlit surface of the water. Both kinds of algae have adaptations that help them survive in the ocean's salty water.

Kelp forests grow tall toward the water's sunlit surface.

Kelp Forests

Algae grows very quickly. A type of algae called kelp can group together and grow to huge sizes. Kelp forests in the Pacific Ocean can reach heights of 30 meters (98 feet). Kelp has leaflike structures that take in sunlight. It also has balloonlike structures called *air bladders* that help it float. Kelp grows in clear, shallow water. Animals such as sea urchins and sea otters live in kelp forests.

◀ Kelp looks similar to a land plant, but it has adaptations that help it survive in water.

Quick Lab

Plant Growth

1. Get two self-sealing plastic bags. Place a paper towel in each plastic bag. Add 60 mL of water to one bag. Label it *Fresh Water*. Add 60 mL of water and 1 tsp of salt to the other bag. Label it *Salt Water*.
2. Punch a line of staples about 3 cm from the bottom of each bag. Drop 5 bean seeds into each bag. Hang the bags on a wall or a window.

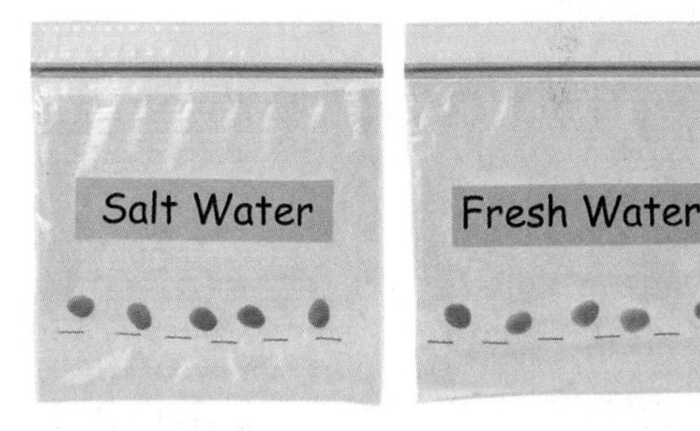

3. **Compare** Do plants grow in both water environments?
4. **Draw Conclusions** Do plants need special adaptations to survive in salt water?

Quick Check

Compare and Contrast How are ocean plants and land plants similar? How are they different?

Critical Thinking Where does some of the oxygen we breathe come from?

Breathing and Moving

1. Water enters the fish's mouth.
2. Structures in the gills then take in oxygen from the water.
3. Fins help the fish steer as it swims.
4. A fish moves forward by waving its muscular tail back and forth.

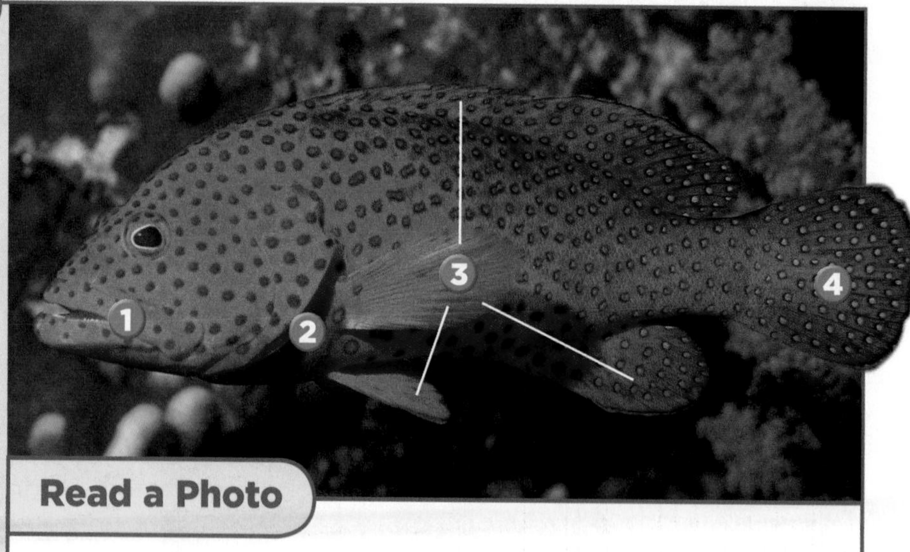

Read a Photo

How are fish specially adapted to life under water?

Clue: Match each body part with its numbered caption.

How do animals survive underwater?

Of all the animals in the ocean, fish are the most numerous. Ocean animals have adaptations that help them live in their environment.

Breathing

Like people, fish need oxygen to breathe. Fish use body parts called **gills** to get oxygen from water. The gills are located on both sides of the fish just behind its head. Water comes into the fish's mouth and then passes through the gills. The gills take in oxygen as the water passes out.

Moving

A fish's body is shaped to move easily through water. Fish have strong tails to help them move forward. Fins help them steer.

Crabs are related to spiders. Like spiders, they walk along the ground. ▼

Staying Safe

The ocean is a wild place. Many animals interact in this constantly changing environment. Small fish feed on plants, and large fish eat smaller fish. Still larger animals, such as sharks and whales, rule the underwater animal kingdom. How do animals stay safe in this environment?

The stingray has a sharp and poisonous tail. Waving its flat body, the stingray swims quickly along the ocean floor. If a stingray senses danger, in just a few seconds it will cover itself with some sand. Its skin is the same color as the sand. This camouflage is a way that the stingray and some other ocean animals stay safe underwater.

Quick Check

Compare and Contrast How are land animals different from ocean animals?

Critical Thinking How do ocean animals move through the water? Give some examples.

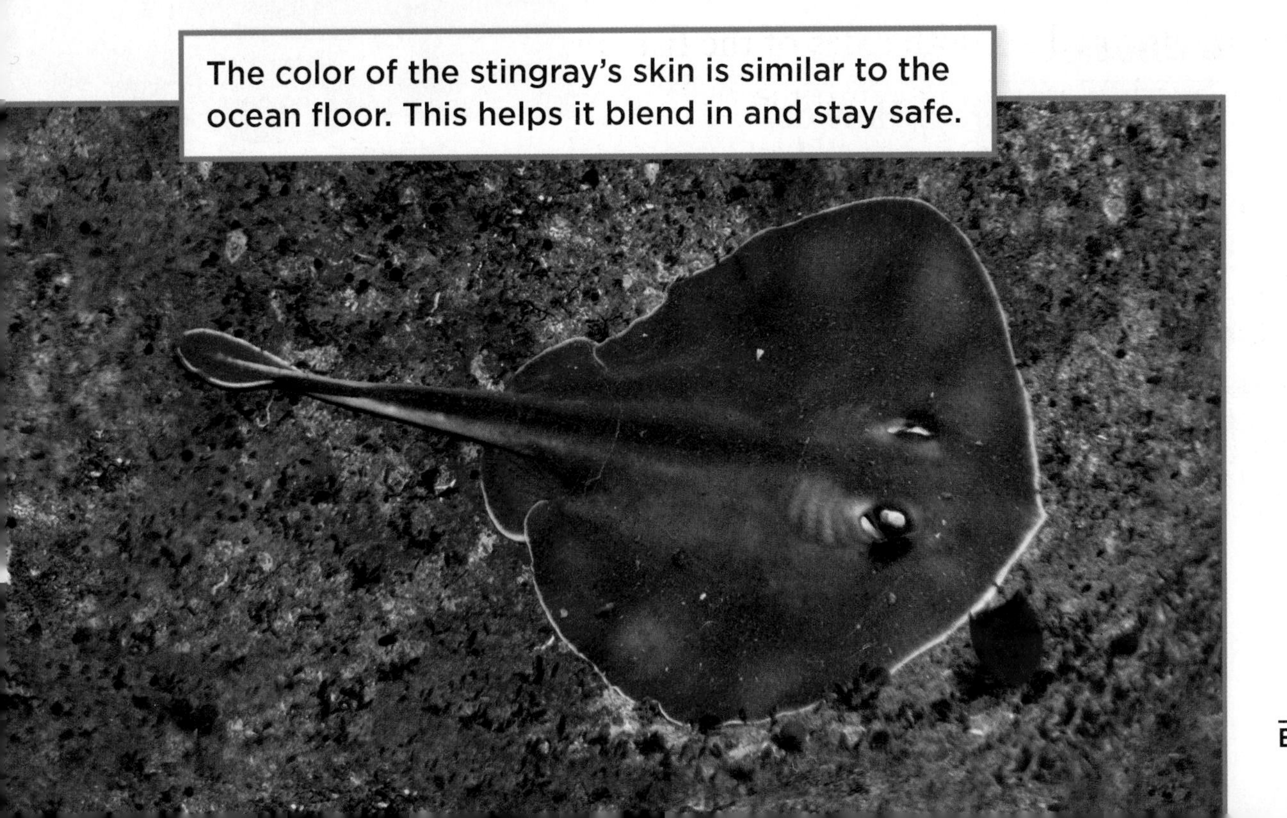

The color of the stingray's skin is similar to the ocean floor. This helps it blend in and stay safe.

How do animals survive in the very deep ocean?

Deep, deep down near the bottom of the ocean, it is extremely cold and dark. Only animals with special adaptations can live there. Look at the photo of the viperfish. Its giant eyes help it find food even in the dark. The giant squid, another deep-ocean animal, has eyes as big as volleyballs. On land, animals that hunt at night have big eyes, too. This adaptation is helpful in environments where there is little light.

The anglerfish, on the other hand, has small eyes. It has poor vision. It has a different adaptation that helps it get food. It has a growth on top of its head that lights up. Other animals are attracted to the light. When they swim close to the light, the anglerfish attacks. Both the viperfish and the anglerfish have very sharp teeth.

▲ The viperfish opens its jaws wide to capture fish swimming by.

▲ The anglerfish has a lighted "fishing pole" to attract prey.

Quick Check

Compare and Contrast How do animals that hunt at night compare with animals that hunt near the bottom of the ocean?

Critical Thinking Would large eyes be a necessary adaptation for animals that live near the surface of the water? Why?

Tube worms have hard-shelled tubes that protect them from predators. ▶

Lesson Review

Visual Summary

The **oceans** are Earth's largest habitat. The Pacific Ocean covers about one third of Earth's surface.

Ocean plants have special adaptations that help them survive in the ocean.

Ocean animals have body parts that help them live underwater. Some live in the very deep ocean.

Make a FOLDABLES Study Guide

Make a Four-Door Book. Use it to summarize what you learned about life in oceans.

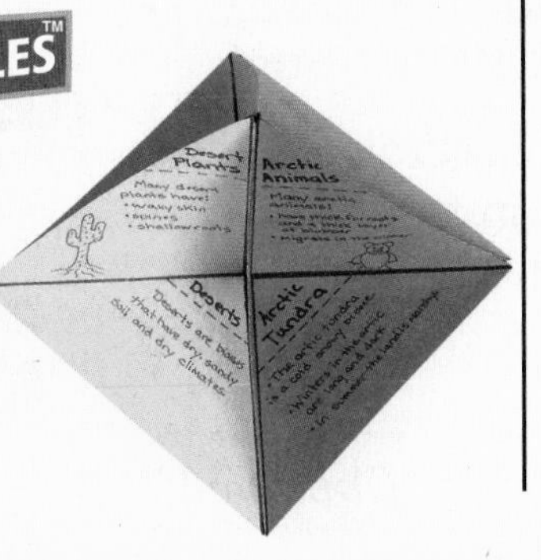

Think, Talk, and Write

1. **Main Idea** Why are most ocean plants found near the surface?

2. **Vocabulary** What is the main function of gills on a fish?

3. **Compare and Contrast** What are some differences between shallow-water and deep-water environments?

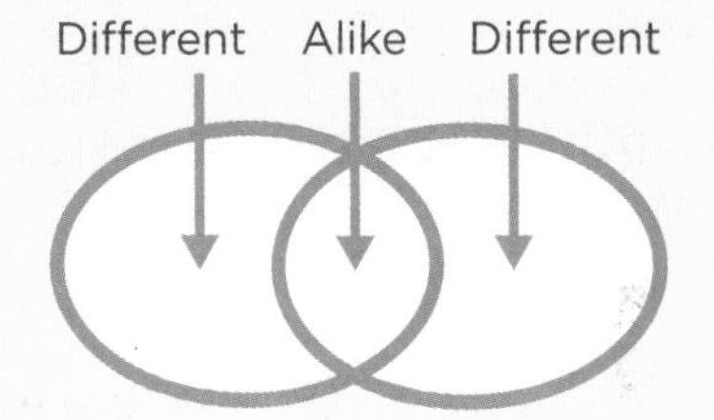

4. **Critical Thinking** Why is kelp important to animals such as sea urchins and sea otters?

5. **Test Prep** **Which of these is one way animals stay safe in the ocean?**
   - **A** waterproof skin
   - **B** camouflage
   - **C** hibernation
   - **D** breathing

Writing Link

Write a Summary
Write about an underwater environment in your own words. Be sure to mention plants and animals you learned about. Include important facts and details.

Math Link

Measure Volume
If you place an object in a container, the change in the water's measurement is the volume of the object. John puts a rock into a beaker, and the water level rises from 250 mL to 320 mL. What is the volume of the rock?

LOG ON e-Review Summaries and quizzes online at www.macmillanmh.com

Be a Scientist

Materials

2 mixing bowls

measuring cup and water

spoon

sea salt

1 fresh egg

Structured Inquiry

How does salt affect the way things float in water?

Form a Hypothesis

Animals that live in Earth's oceans move around easily. Does salt water affect the way things move or float? Form a hypothesis. Begin with "If water is salty, then . . ."

Test Your Hypothesis

1. **Measure** Label one bowl *Fresh Water* and the other bowl *Salt Water*. Pour 400 mL of water into each bowl.
2. **Measure** Pour $\frac{1}{8}$ cup of sea salt into the bowl labeled *Salt Water*. Stir.
3. **Observe** Carefully place a fresh egg in the *Fresh Water* bowl. Record what happens in a chart.

Bowl	What I Observed
Fresh Water	
Salt Water	

4. **Observe** Take the egg out, and gently place it in the *Salt Water* bowl. Record what you observe in your chart.

Step 1

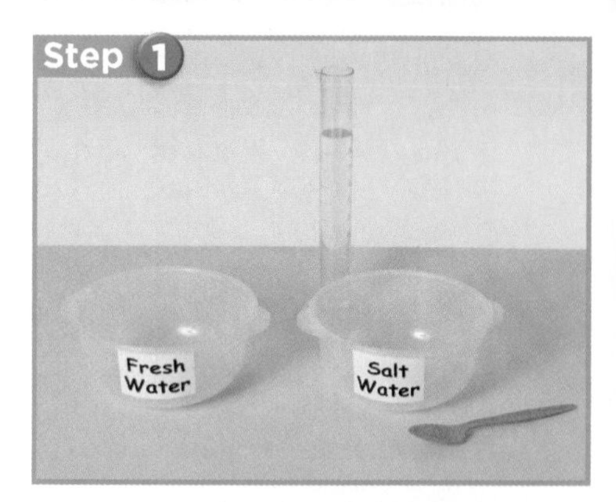

Step 2

Step 4

Draw Conclusions

5. **Interpret Data** Does the egg float in fresh water? In salt water?
6. **Infer** How does salt affect the way animals move in the oceans?

Guided Inquiry

Does salt water affect plants?

Form a Hypothesis

What effect does salt water have on some plants? Write your answer in the form "If water has salt, then . . ."

Test Your Hypothesis

Design an experiment to investigate what happens to lettuce when it absorbs fresh water and salt water. Write the steps you will follow.

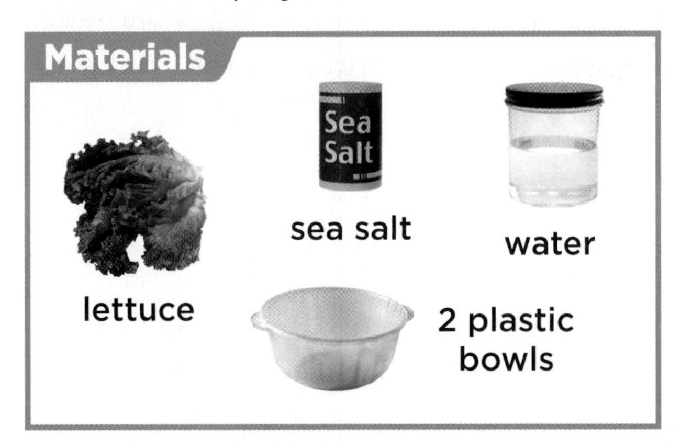

Draw Conclusions

Do your results support your hypothesis? Why or why not? Share your thoughts with your classmates.

Open Inquiry

What other questions do you have about animals and plants that live in the ocean? Talk with your classmates about questions you have. Make up the steps you will follow to answer your questions. Write a list of the materials you will use in your investigation.

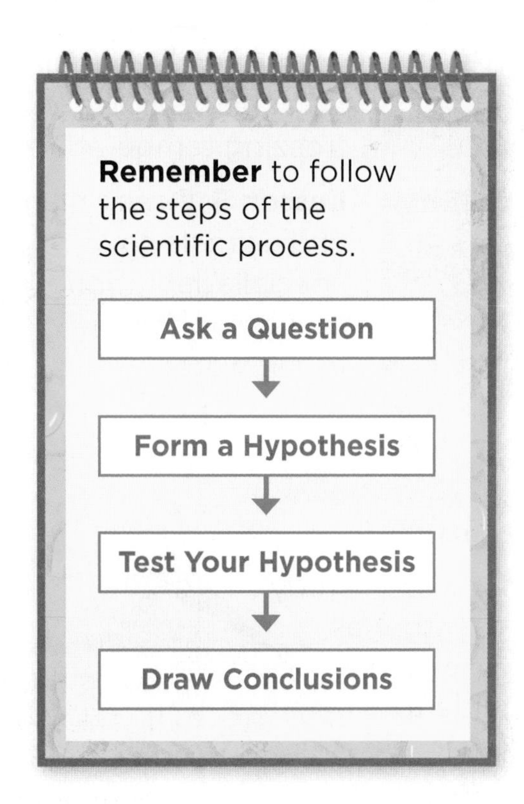

3-I.3. Generate questions about objects, organisms, and events in the environment and use those questions to conduct a scientific investigation.

CHAPTER 2 Review

Summarize the Main Ideas

Lesson 1 Desert plants and animals have adaptations that help them conserve water.

Lesson 2 Grassland plants and animals have adaptations that help them survive in grasslands.

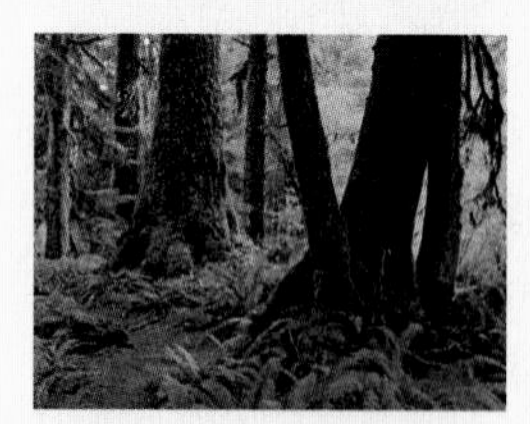

Lesson 3 Forest plants and animals have adaptations that help them survive in forests.

Lesson 4 Arctic plants and animals have adaptations that help them survive in freezing temperatures.

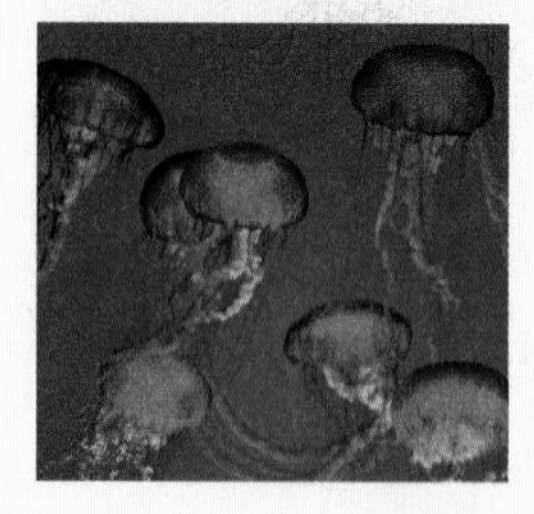

Lesson 5 Ocean plants and animals have special adaptations that help them survive in salt water.

Make a FOLDABLES™ Study Guide

Glue your lesson study guides together as shown. Use your study guide to review what you have learned in this chapter.

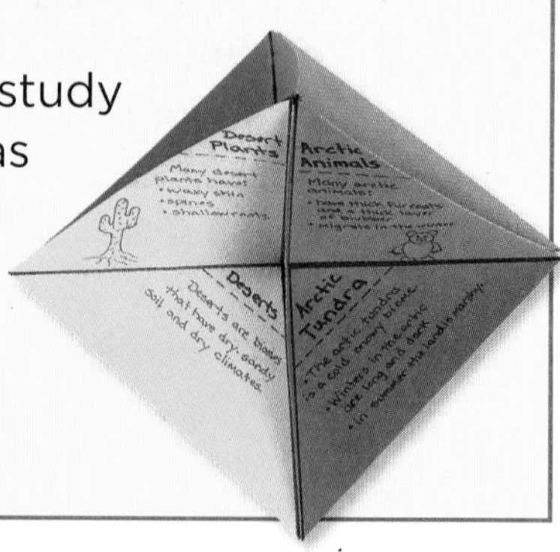

Vocabulary

Fill each blank with the best term from the list.

algae, p. 132	**gills**, p. 134
camouflage, p. 90	**grasslands**, p. 96
deciduous, p. 109	**migrate**, p. 124
desert, p. 86	**mimicry**, p. 110

1. Plantlike living things called __________ have adaptations that help them survive in salt water.
3-2.2
2. Animals use __________ to blend in with their environment.
3-2.2
3. A(n) __________ has a dry climate and sandy soil.
3-2.3
4. Trees that lose their leaves in fall are called __________.
3-2.2
5. Fish use special organs called __________ to get oxygen.
3-2.2
6. When animals __________ they leave their homes in winter for a warmer environment and then return home in summer.
3-2.2
7. Zebras, horses, and other grazing animals live mostly in __________.
3-2.3
8. An adaptation in which one kind of living thing looks like another is called __________.
3-2.2

Skills and Concepts

Answer each of the following in complete sentences.

9. Main Idea and Details How do adaptations protect animals from enemies?
3-2.2

10. Descriptive Writing Describe the arctic tundra.
3-2.3

11. Predict What might happen to some ocean animals if kelp forests disappeared?
3-2.3

12. Critical Thinking Why do trees in the rain forest not lose their leaves?
3-2.2

13. Compare the animals shown below. What special structures help them survive?
3-2.2

grasshopper

musk ox

14. How do adaptations help living things survive in different habitats?
3-2.2

Performance Assessment

Make a Habitat Book

grassland

desert

forest

- Make a book about a habitat you would like to visit. Include information about the climate and soil in this habitat.
- Tell about the plants and animals that live there. Explain what adaptations help the plants and animals survive in their environment.
- Compare and contrast the habitat in your book to another kind of habitat. How is it similar? How is it different?
- Make a cover for your book, and illustrate each page with pictures. Include a caption for each picture.

South Carolina Activity

Research an animal from South Carolina that uses camouflage. Draw a picture of that animal hidden in its environment. When you are finished, have a partner locate the animal. Discuss how the animal's camouflage helps it stay safe in its environment.

South Carolina Standards Practice

1 **Which feature allows kelp to float?**

A rootlike structures

B leaflike structures

C seedlike structures

D balloonlike structures

3-2.2

2 **This table shows the number of animals that are normally found in an arctic area during different seasons.**

Season	Year 1
summer	700
winter	60

What is the most likely reason for the difference between seasons?

F Most animals migrate south for the winter.

G Most animals are killed by predators in spring.

H Most animals drown when the ice melts in fall.

I Most animals die out when the weather gets cold.

3-1.6

3 **Many desert animals are nocturnal. This is because most deserts**

A have sandy soil.

B are cooler at night.

C get very little rain.

D are very dusty.

3-2.3

4 **Some plants in tropical rain forests have very large leaves. The large leaves help the plants**

F save their energy.

G lose extra rainwater.

H absorb more sunlight.

I support their tall trunks.

3-2.2

5 **The large ears of a desert jackrabbit help it**

A run fast.

B hear well.

C stay cool.

D blend in.

3-2.2

6 Which of the plants below would survive **best** in a desert habitat, and why?

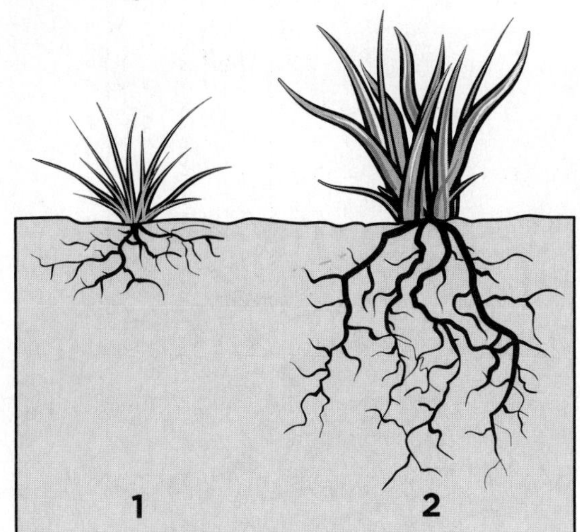

F plant 1, because of its shallow roots

G plant 1, because of its deep roots

H plant 2, because of its shallow roots

I plant 2, because of its deep roots

3-1.6

7 Where would you be **most likely** to find animals with thick fur and a lot of blubber?

A a desert

B a grassland

C a forest

D a tundra

3-2.2

8 Which **best** describes soil in a tropical rain forest?

F dry and rich in nutrients

G dry and not very rich in nutrients

H wet and rich in nutrients

I wet and not very rich in nutrients

3-1.1

9 What kinds of plants are found mainly in forests?

A grasses

B trees

C cushion plants

D cactuses

3-2.3

10 Two scientists studied different ocean animals. The first scientist found animals with very large eyes. The second scientist did not find animals with very large eyes. What is the **most likely** reason for this difference?

F The second scientist studied animals for a longer period of time.

G The second scientist studied animals when it was darker outside.

H The first scientist studied animals in saltier water.

I The first scientist studied animals in deeper water.

3-1.7

CHAPTER 3

Habitats Change

The Big Idea

How can changes affect living things and their environments?

A jack pine seedling sprouts after a wildfire.

Key Vocabulary

resource
something that helps an organism survive (p. 148)

competition
the struggle among living things for resources (p. 149)

pollution
what happens when harmful materials get into air, land, or water (p. 150)

endangered
when one kind of organism has very few of its kind left (p. 164)

fossil
the remains of organisms that lived long ago (p. 170)

extinct
when one kind of living thing has died out everywhere on Earth (p. 170)

More Vocabulary

reduce, p. 152
reuse, p. 152
recycle, p. 152
flood, p. 158
drought, p. 158
population, p. 162
community, p. 162

Lesson 1

Living Things Change Their Environments

Look and Wonder

Leaves fall from trees and cover the forest floor. Have you ever wondered what happens to fallen leaves? What makes them disappear?

3-2.4. Explain how changes in the habitats of plants and animals affect their survival.

How can worms change their environment?

Purpose

All living things change their environments as they get food, water, shelter, and other needs. In this activity, find out how worms change their environment.

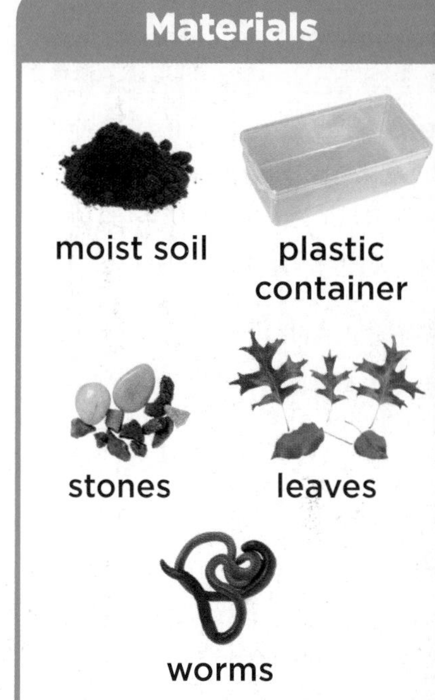

Procedure

1. **Make a Model** Put some soil in a plastic container. Then put small stones and leaves on top of the soil. This models a forest floor.
2. Place live worms on the "forest floor."
3. **Predict** What will the worms do? Make a short list of the things you might see the worms do.
4. **Observe** Check the worms, soil, leaves, and stones every three to four days. Keep the soil moist. Record your observations.

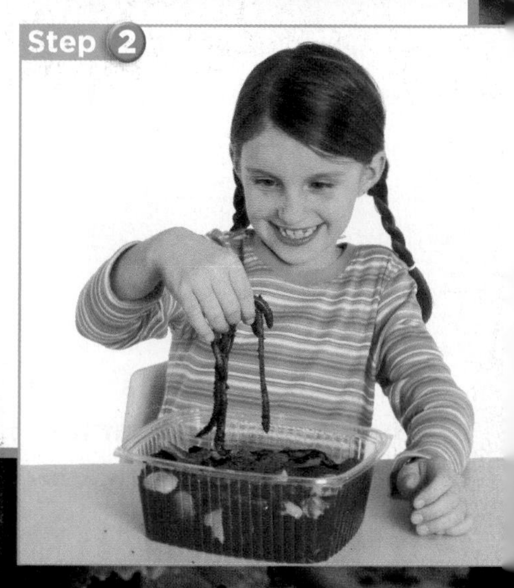

Draw Conclusions

5. **Infer** What happened to the leaves over time?
6. **Communicate** How do worms change the environment in which they live?

Explore More

Experiment How do other living things change their environments? Make a plan to test your ideas. Then try your plan.

3-I.3. Generate questions about objects, organisms, and events in the environment and use those questions to conduct a scientific investigation.

Read and Learn

Main Idea 3-2.4

Living things change their environments as they meet their needs. These changes can be helpful or harmful to their environments.

Vocabulary

resource, p.148

competition, p.149

pollution, p.150

reduce, p. 152

reuse, p.152

recycle, p.152

at www.macmillanmh.com

Reading Skill 

Predict

What I Predict	What Happens

How do living things change their environments?

Every living thing changes its environment as it meets its needs. A spider spins a web to catch insects for food. A bird builds a nest for shelter. A plant takes water from the soil. These actions change an environment in small ways.

Other living things make bigger changes to their environments. For example, bacteria, worms, and fungi break down leaves and other dead material. These decomposers return valuable nutrients to the soil. Later, plants can use those nutrients to grow.

All of these living things are trying to get resources. A **resource** is something that helps an organism survive. Food, water, air, space, sunlight, and shelter are some resources.

A Changing Environment

Seeds blow onto bare ground. The environment changes as plants take in water and nutrients.

As more plants grow, animals move to the environment. They use the plants for food and shelter.

Every environment has a limited amount of resources. As a result, living things must compete for them. **Competition** (kahm•pi•TISH•uhn) is the struggle among living things for resources. Competition can be a major cause of environmental change. The diagram below shows how one environment changes over time.

Quick Check

Predict How would a forest change if a big tree fell?

Critical Thinking How do you change your environment?

Read a Diagram

How has this environment changed over time?

Clue: Arrows help show a sequence.

LOG ON *Science in Motion* Watch environments change at www.macmillanmh.com

In time the plants grow larger. They compete for water, space, and sunlight. Animals compete for food and water.

Trees block sunlight from reaching smaller plants. These plants may die as trees grow larger.

How do people change their environments?

People change their environments more than any other organism. Changes, such as planting trees, are helpful. However, other changes can be harmful.

Pollution

People can harm their environments by creating pollution. **Pollution** happens when harmful materials get into the air, land, or water. Cars can pollute the air. Trash pollutes the water and land.

▲ The garbage on this beach is a form of land pollution.

Clearing Land

Sometimes, people change natural areas when they build shops and homes. In the past, people drained wetlands and built over them. Wetlands help filter water, so pollution increases without them.

People also cut down trees to make wood products. If forests are removed, living things can be left without a home. Soil can wear away without tree roots to hold it in place.

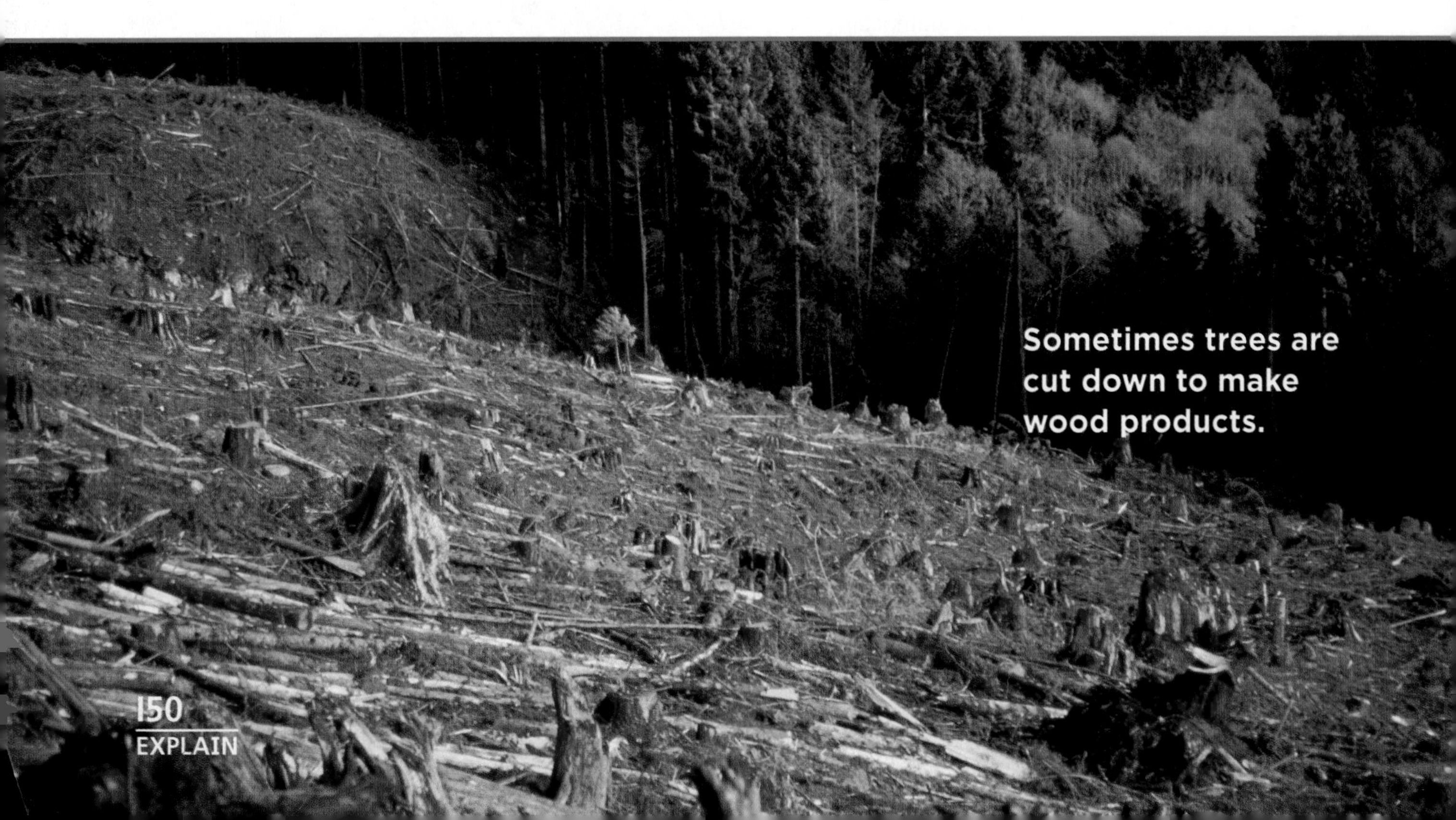

Sometimes trees are cut down to make wood products.

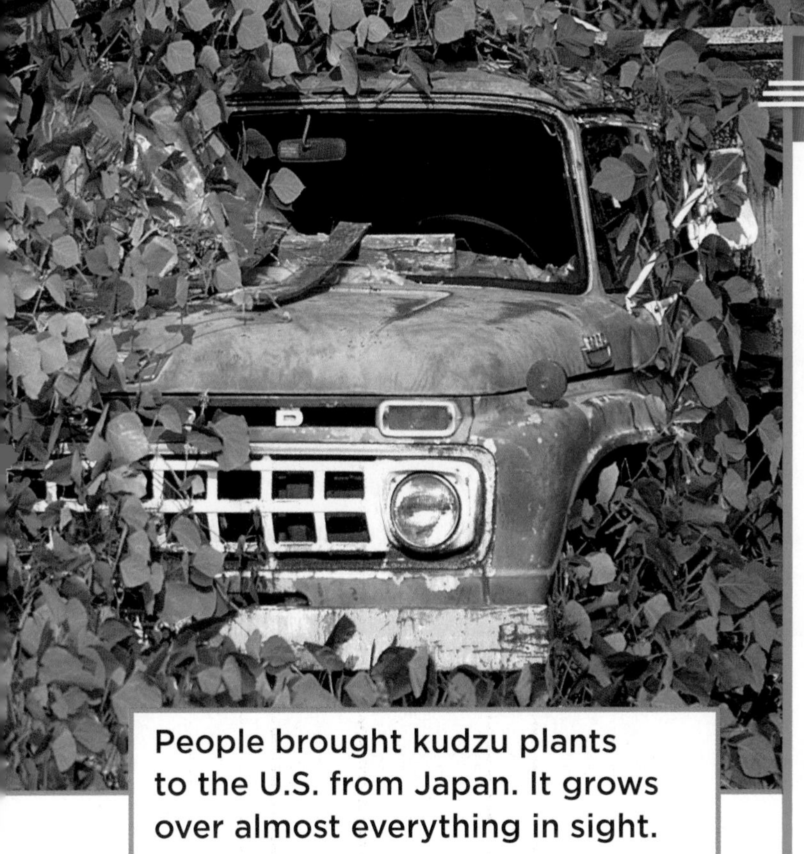

People brought kudzu plants to the U.S. from Japan. It grows over almost everything in sight.

Creating Competition

Sometimes people bring new organisms into an environment. These new organisms may harm the environment by competing for limited resources. For example, kudzu plants were brought to America from Japan. Kudzu can grow rapidly. It takes water and nutrients that other plants need.

The new organisms may not be eaten by many animals in their new environment. This lets them reproduce very quickly. If this happens, the new organisms can use up most of the limited resources in an environment.

Quick Lab

Model Pollution

1. **Observe** Look at the shell of a hard-boiled egg. Is it hard or soft? Why do you think the egg has this type of shell?
2. **Make a Model** Fill a large cup with vinegar. This models polluted land or water. Place your egg inside of the cup.

3. **Observe** Look at the egg throughout the day. Study the shell of the egg. Do you notice any differences in the egg or its shell?
4. **Infer** After being placed in vinegar, can the shell still protect the egg?
5. **Predict** What may happen to eggs near polluted land or water?

Quick Check

Predict What might happen to plants and animals if their environment is harmed?

Critical Thinking How does pollution affect people?

This house was built from reused bottles.

How can people protect their environments?

People can help protect their environments. One thing people can do is practice the 3 *Rs*—reduce, reuse, and recycle. To **reduce** means to use less of something. To **reuse** means to use something again. To **recycle** means to turn old things into new things. When you practice the 3 *Rs*, you produce less trash and cut down on pollution.

People can also help their environments by planting trees. Trees help environments in many ways. Trees clean the air and provide homes for animals. Their roots help keep soil from washing or blowing away. By planting a tree, you help keep your environment healthy.

Recycling is one way that people can help protect their environments.

Quick Check

Predict How might recycling paper protect your environment?

Critical Thinking List some things you can reuse.

Lesson Review

Visual Summary

Living things change their environments as they meet their needs.

People change their environments more than any other living thing.

People can help their environments by practicing the 3 *R*s.

Make a FOLDABLES™ Study Guide

Make a Trifold Book. Use it to summarize what you learned about environments and change.

Main Ideas	What I learned...	Examples
Living things change their environment...		
People change the environment...		
People help the environment...		

Think, Talk, and Write

1. **Main Idea** What are some ways in which plants and animals change their environments?

2. **Vocabulary** What is competition?

3. **Predict** What might happen if people don't practice the 3 *R*s?

What I Predict	What Happens

4. **Critical Thinking** What are some things you could reduce your use of?

5. **Test Prep People can do all of the following to help the environment EXCEPT**
   - **A** recycle.
   - **B** pollute.
   - **C** reuse.
   - **D** plant trees.

Math Link

Make a Bar Graph

Keep track of the paper, metal, plastic, and food scraps that you throw away in one week.
Make a bar graph that shows how many of each item you threw away during that week.

Art Link

Make a Poster

Make a poster about the things people can do to help the environment. Include things you learned from this lesson as well as things you already knew.

LOG ON e-Review Summaries and quizzes online at www.macmillanmh.com

Focus on Skills

Inquiry Skill: Use Numbers

The average American changes his or her environment by producing about 2 kilograms (4 pounds) of trash every day! We can never get rid of trash completely. However, we can cut down on the amount we create by practicing the 3 *Rs*. Do students in your school practice the 3 *Rs*? Find out the same way scientists do—**use numbers** to record data.

▶ Learn It

When you **use numbers**, you present data in a way that people can clearly understand. Basic math skills, such as counting and ordering numbers, help to collect and organize information. Often, scientists gather and record data by asking questions or by having people fill out surveys. Then they use numbers to put the data into a chart or graph. You can do it, too.

▶ Try It

In this activity, you will gather data and **use numbers** to find out how much trash is thrown out by students in your school. You cannot survey the whole school, but you can do a mini-survey.

1. Choose five students to survey in the lunchroom.
2. Ask each student questions about how many pieces of trash from lunch he or she threw away today. Ask about the containers used. Will anything be reused?

3-I.6. Infer meaning from data communicated in graphs, tables, and diagrams.

3 Use a table like the one shown below to organize your data.

Student's Name	Pieces Reused	Pieces Recycled	Pieces Thrown Away	Total Pieces of Trash
Total				

Now use numbers to answer the following questions.

- Did every student throw out some trash or packaging material?
- How many pieces of trash did the students recycle? How many pieces did they reuse?
- How many pieces of trash did these five people create altogether?

Apply It

Use numbers to combine your data with those of your classmates. Add to find the totals for each column. Then make a bar graph to show the results.

Do you predict these same students will throw out more or less trash tomorrow? Plan another survey. Then use numbers to compare the new results to your first results just as scientists do!

Lesson 2

Changes Affect Living Things

Look and Wonder

Plants need rain in order to grow. Can they get too much rain? How are living things affected when there is a flood?

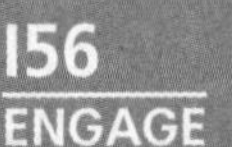

3-2.4. Explain how changes in the habitats of plants and animals affect their survival.

Explore

Inquiry Activity

How can a flood affect plants?

Form a Hypothesis

What happens to plants when they get too much water? Write a hypothesis.

Test Your Hypothesis

1. Label three plants *A*, *B*, and *C*. Water plant *A* once a week with 60 mL of water. Water plant *B* every day with 60 mL of water. Water plant *C* every day with 120 mL of water.
2. **Predict** Which plant will grow to be the tallest? Record your prediction.
3. **Observe** Monitor your plants every few days. Measure how tall they grow. Record how they look with words and pictures.

Draw Conclusions

4. **Interpret Data** How did the plants change over time? Which plant grew the tallest? Which do you think is the healthiest?
5. **Infer** What happens to some plants when there is a flood?

Explore More

Experiment Could your plant recover from a flood? Stop watering plant *C* for a week. How does the plant change?

Materials

3 identical plants

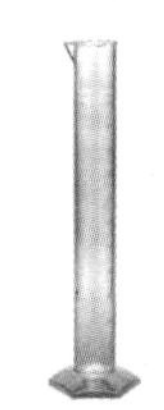

graduated cylinder and water

ruler

3-1.4. Predict the outcome of a simple investigation and compare the result with the prediction.

Read and Learn

Main Idea 3-2.4

Natural disasters and diseases can change environments. Living things respond to these changes in different ways.

Vocabulary

flood, p. 158

drought, p. 158

population, p. 162

community, p. 162

endangered, p. 164

e-Glossary at www.macmillanmh.com

Reading Skill

Cause and Effect

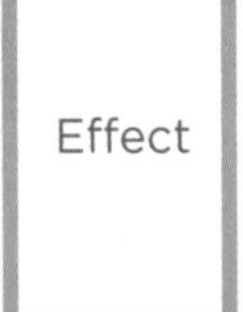

Technology SCIENCE QUEST

Explore how environments change with the Secret Agents.

What are some ways environments change?

You learned some ways that living things change their environments. Environments can be changed in other ways, too. Natural disasters and diseases can change an environment.

A flood is one type of natural disaster. A **flood** happens when dry land becomes covered with water. Heavy rains and other storms can cause a flood. Floods change an environment by washing away soil and plants. They can cause animals to lose their habitats.

A drought is the opposite of a flood. A **drought** (DROWT) happens when there is no rain for a long time. Without rain, rivers and lakes can dry up. Soil can also dry out. Living things need water to survive, so droughts can harm living things.

Before a drought set in, this area was a lake. Many living things once made their homes here.

Wildfires can destroy natural environments like this forest.

▲ New plants can grow after a fire.

Droughts can lead to wildfires. If a dry part of a forest or grassland is struck by lightning, a wildfire can start. Wildfires can harm plants and the habitats of many animals. Smoke from the fires pollutes the air.

Environments can also be changed by diseases. Many things, such as bacteria, mold, and mildew, can cause diseases. Some diseases spread easily and harm many living things. An entire forest, for example, may eventually be destroyed if one tree catches a disease.

The black spots on these rose leaves are a sign of a disease. ▼

Quick Check

Cause and Effect What can cause sudden changes in an environment?

Critical Thinking Can living things return to an environment after a natural disaster?

FACT Wildfires can help some plants.

How do organisms respond to changes?

Environmental changes can affect living things. For example, each year some grasslands in Africa go through a dry season. When this happens, plants and animals get less water. Watering holes can dry up. Tall grasses may dry out. Living things respond to these changes in different ways.

When an environment changes, some living things must move. They must find a new habitat in which to live. Elephants, for example, migrate in search of water and grasses.

▲ Animals, such as these springbok, depend on watering holes.

Some living things adjust in order to survive. Predators may hunt different prey or eat whatever is available. Some animals may hunt at night if it makes it easier to find food.

▲ Many frogs are adapted to burrow underground when their environment becomes dry.

Other living things have adaptations that help them survive changes. Some frogs and fish are adapted to burrow into mud when their environment becomes too dry. They go into a deep sleep and do not eat. They come out when the environment is wet again.

Living things that are not able to travel or change could die. Plants, such as savanna grasses, cannot move to new places. Without rain, these grasses begin to dry up. If the drought lasts for too long, they may die.

Quick Check

Cause and Effect What environmental changes might cause an animal to move to another place?

Critical Thinking What might happen to an elephant if its habitat suddenly becomes too cold?

◀ In a dry season, these African elephants migrate. They find a new habitat that can provide water, food, and shelter.

How do environmental changes affect an entire community?

Underneath the grasslands of the central United States lies an unseen world! Beneath the grasses is a complex system of tunnels. Prairie dogs build these tunnels and live in them. They come to the surface to eat grasses.

Prairie dogs are one population (pahp•yuh•LAY•shuhn) in a prairie. A **population** is all the members of one kind of organism in an ecosystem. All the coyotes are another population.

Populations in an ecosystem depend on each other. Burrowing owls and snakes make homes in the tunnels that prairie dogs leave behind. Eagles and coyotes feed on prairie dogs. If anything happens to prairie dogs, the whole community (kuh•MYEW•ni•tee) is affected. A **community** is all the populations in an ecosystem.

A Prairie Community

Sometimes, prairie dogs are harmed by disease. If the disease spreads, many prairie dogs could die. Animals that eat prairie dogs would lose a food source. Mice and snakes might not find homes.

The loss of prairie dogs could help some living things. Grasses may grow taller and thicker. Other animals may move into the area to feed on the new grasses.

Quick Check

Cause and Effect How could a disease that kills prairie dogs harm coyotes that live nearby?

Critical Thinking What might happen to prairie dogs if eagles left the ecosystem?

Quick Lab

A Changing Ecosystem

1. Make five character cards. Label the cards: prairie dog, snake, burrowing owl, eagle, and coyote.

2. Paste the cards onto a large sheet of paper.
3. Draw an arrow from each animal to the organisms it depends upon for food or shelter.
4. **Infer** What would happen if prairie dogs disappeared?
5. **Infer** What would happen if eagles disappeared?

after

Wild horses may join the community to feed on grasses.

If disease kills prairie dogs, eagles and coyotes lose a source of food.

Snakes and mice move into abandoned prairie dog holes.

Read a Diagram

What happens when prairie dogs leave a prairie ecosystem?

Clue: A before-and-after diagram shows change.

How does a living thing become endangered?

When an environment changes, organisms must migrate or adjust to their new surroundings in order to survive. Those organisms that cannot migrate or adjust may become endangered (en•DAYN•juhrd). An organism is **endangered** when there are only a few living members of its kind left.

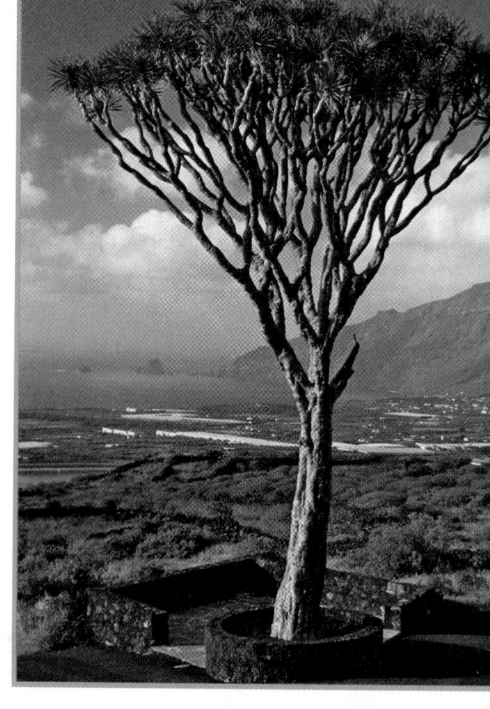

▲ Dragon trees may become endangered. Their environment is drying out.

Saharan cypress trees are endangered. They are found in the mountains of the Saharan Desert. Scientists think that Saharan cypress trees are adapted for a wet climate. Yet, their environment has become dry. Saharan cypress trees are endangered because they cannot adjust to the hot, dry weather.

Organisms can also become endangered as a result of people. Bengal tigers are endangered because hunters have killed many of them for their fur. Panda bears are also endangered, partly because people are destroying their forest habitat.

Quick Check

Cause and Effect What can cause an organism to become endangered?

Critical Thinking How can people help protect endangered organisms?

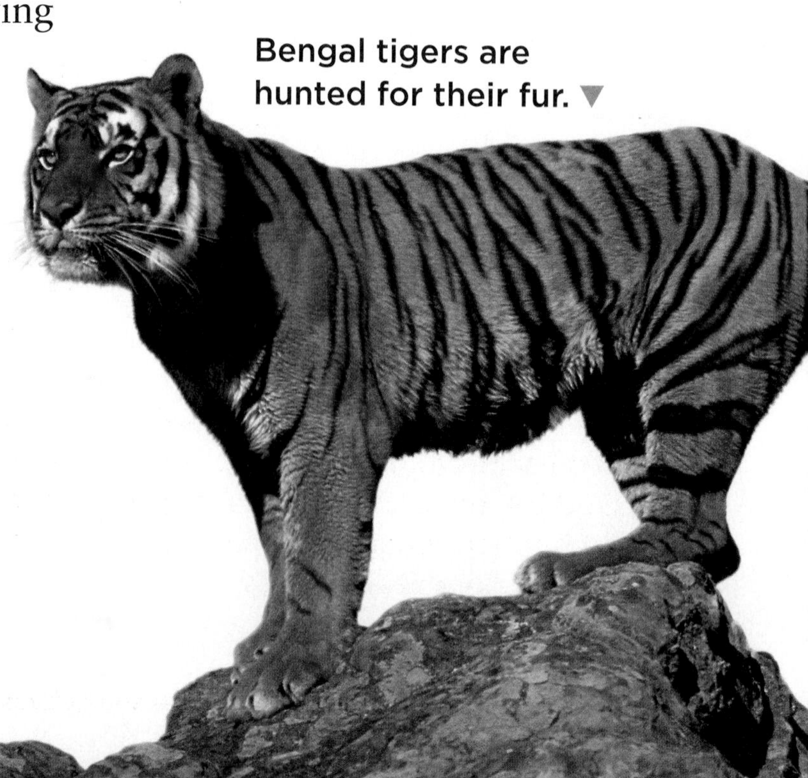

Bengal tigers are hunted for their fur. ▼

Lesson Review

Visual Summary

Natural disasters and disease can cause environments to change.

When environments change, living things may be harmed. Others may move or adjust.

Changes to one group of living things can affect other living things.

Make a FOLDABLES™ Study Guide

Make a Three-Tab Book. Use it to summarize what you learned about how changes affect organisms.

Think, Talk, and Write

1. **Main Idea** What are some ways in which living things respond to environmental changes?

2. **Vocabulary** What does the word endangered mean?

3. **Cause and Effect** What are some of the effects of a drought?

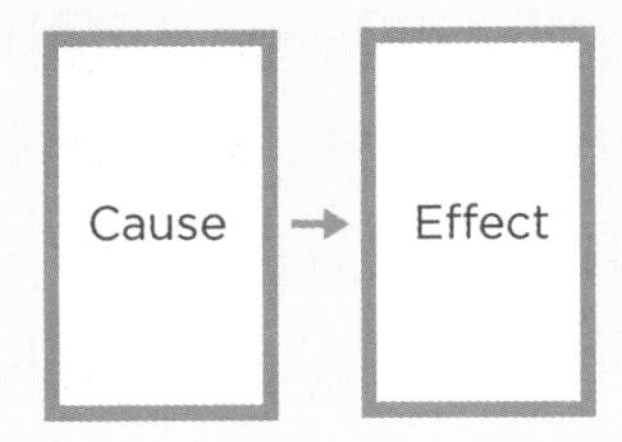

4. **Critical Thinking** Why should people take special care when they change a natural environment by building or farming? Explain.

5. **Test Prep** All of these are natural disasters EXCEPT

   A wildfires.
   B floods.
   C mold.
   D droughts.

Writing Link

Write an Essay
Learn about an environment that has recently changed. Then make a cause-and-effect chart. List what caused the environment to change and what happened as a result. Use your chart to write an essay.

Social Studies Link

Research Mount St. Helens
Use research materials to find out about Mount St. Helens. How did the eruption change the environment around Mount St. Helens? Make a poster or write a report.

LOG ON e-Review Summaries and quizzes online at www.macmillanmh.com

Save the Koala Bears

I believe it is very important to save the koala bears. We cannot let them die. Eucalyptus forests are where koala bears live and find food. People cut down these forests. They build new houses. Today, the forests are getting smaller. It is harder for koalas to find food. The death of one kind of animal can hurt other plants and animals around it. That is why it is important to save the koala bear.

Persuasive Writing

Good persuasive writing

- clearly states an opinion
- uses reasons to convince the reader to agree
- organizes the reasons in a logical order
- includes opinion words such as *I believe*

Koala bears live in Australia. They eat leaves from eucalyptus trees. ▶

Write About It

Persuasive Writing Choose an endangered animal you care about. Research to find out why this animal is in trouble. Write a paragraph to convince readers that this animal should be saved. Be sure to end with a strong argument.

Write about it online at www.macmillanmh.com

SUBTRACTING LARGE NUMBERS

Whooping cranes are endangered. There are very few of them left in the wild. Like many endangered animals, whooping cranes are protected. That means that people cannot hunt them or harm their habitat.

Look at the information in the chart. It shows how some living things grow in number when they are protected.

Subtract Multi-Digit Numbers

▶ First, subtract the ones. Regroup if necessary.

$$\begin{array}{r} {\scriptstyle 3\,11} \\ 3\not{4}\not{1} \\ -\;\;16 \\ \hline 5 \end{array}$$

▶ Then, subtract the tens. Regroup if necessary.

$$\begin{array}{r} {\scriptstyle 3\;\;} \\ 3\not{4}\not{1} \\ -\;\;16 \\ \hline 25 \end{array}$$

▶ Continue until you have subtracted the numbers in all the places.

$$\begin{array}{r} 3\not{4}\not{1} \\ -\;\;16 \\ \hline 325 \end{array}$$

Name of Animal	Year of Original Count	Original Count	2005 Count
whooping crane	1941	16	341
snow leopard	1960	1,000	6,105
California condor	1986	17	200
giant panda	1965	1,000	1,817
humpback whale	1966	20,000	35,105

whooping crane

Solve It

Use the chart above. Subtract the original count from the 2005 count for each kind of animal. This tells you how much each animal population grew.

Lesson 3

Living Things of the Past

Look and Wonder

These remains of a rhinoceros were found in Nebraska. It lived 10 million years ago. What could you learn about the past from looking at these remains?

3-2.4. Explain how changes in the habitats of plants and animals affect their survival. **3-3.4.** Infer ideas about Earth's early environments from fossils of plants and animals that lived long ago.

Explore

Inquiry Activity

How do fossils tell us about the past?

Purpose

Find out how fossils can teach about the past.

Procedure

1. Mix a little glue and water in a measuring cup.
2. **Make a Model** Pour a thin layer of colored sand into a paper cup. Add a "fossil" object. Cover the object with sand of the same color. Add a little water and glue to "set" this layer. This models a fossil in rock.
3. Repeat step 2 with different objects and different colors of sand. Make three layers in all. Allow the layers to dry.
4. **Observe** Trade cups with another group. Carefully peel the paper cup away. Use the brush to find the fossils. Start at the top layer. Work your way down.
5. **Communicate** Record in a table the order in which each fossil object was found.

Draw Conclusions

6. **Interpret Data** Which fossil was buried first? Last? Which fossil is oldest?
7. **Infer** What can layers of rock tell us about Earth's past?

Explore More

How else could you model a fossil? Make a plan and try it.

Materials

measuring cup and water

glue

colored sand

paper cup

"fossil" objects

brush

Step 4

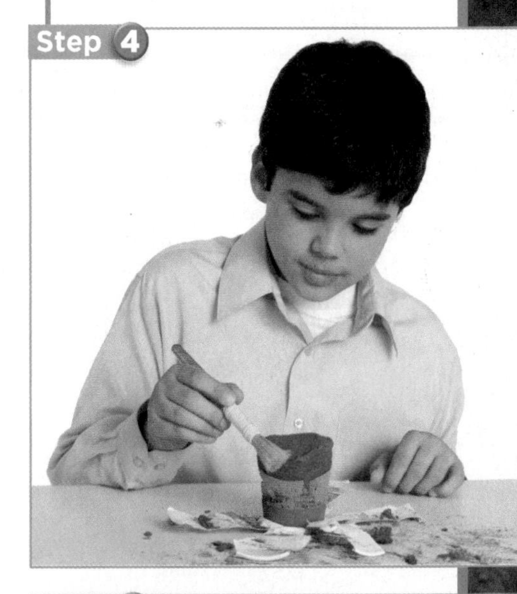

Step 5

Layer	Fossil
top	
middle	
bottom	

3-I.2. Classify objects or events in sequential order.

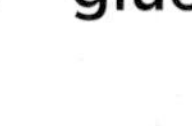

Read and Learn

Main Idea 3-2.4 3-3.4

We can study fossils to learn about ancient plants and animals and their environments.

Vocabulary

fossil, p.170

extinct, p.170

LOG ON e-Glossary at www.macmillanmh.com

Reading Skill

Draw Conclusions

Text Clues	Conclusions

What can happen if the environment suddenly changes?

Did you know that dinosaurs once lived in North America? Millions of years ago, dinosaurs may have been roaming through the land that is now your town! All that is left of dinosaurs today is their fossils (FOS•uhls). **Fossils** are the remains of organisms that lived long ago.

Many scientists think that dinosaurs became extinct (ek•STINGKT) after a meteor hit Earth a long time ago. A living thing is **extinct** when there are no more of its kind alive.

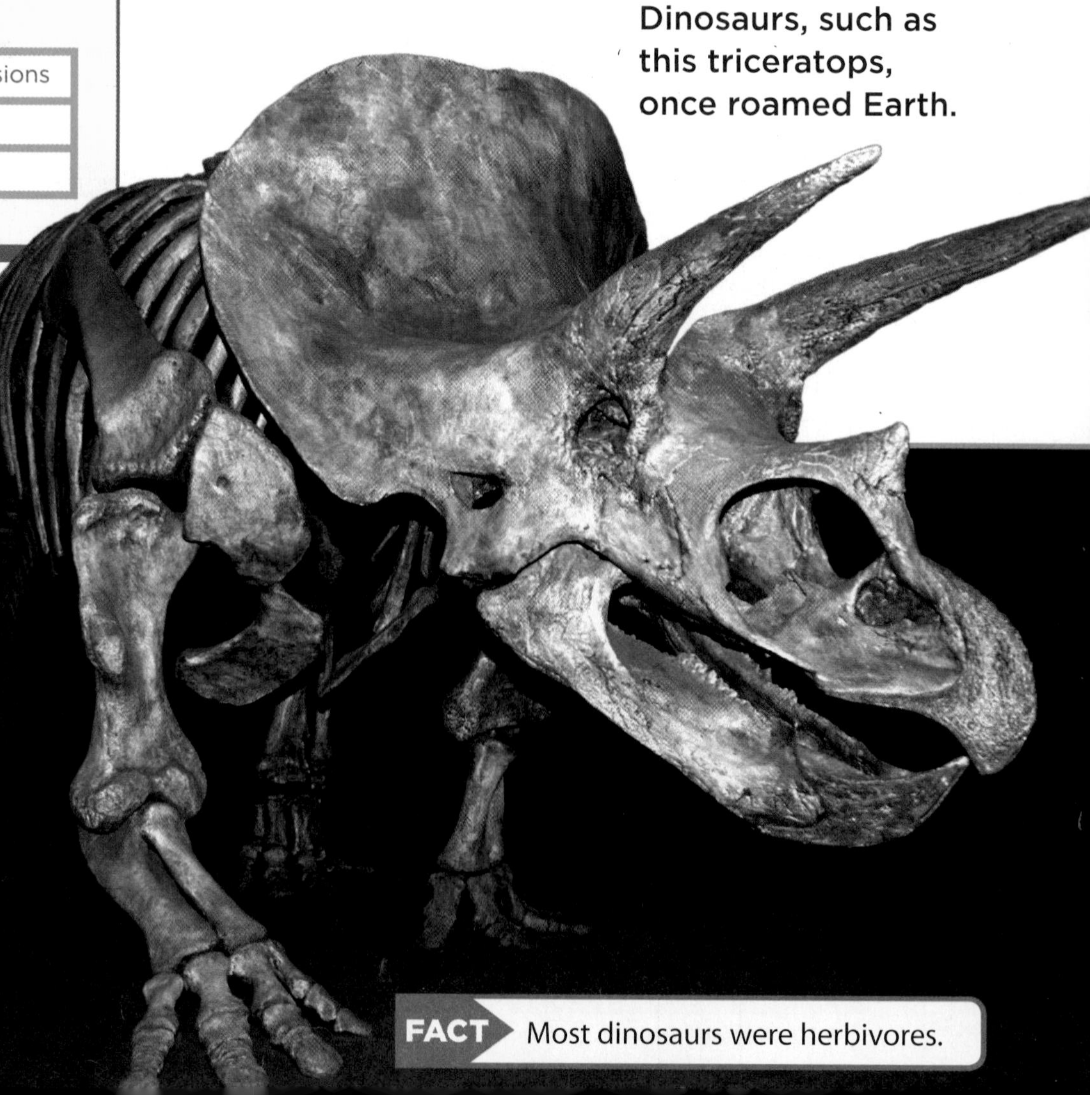

Dinosaurs, such as this triceratops, once roamed Earth.

FACT Most dinosaurs were herbivores.

After the dinosaurs, large animals such as saber-toothed cats made their homes in North America. These animals lived more than ten thousand years ago, during the Ice Age. Huge sheets of ice covered much of the land at that time. Then the climate changed. Temperatures began to rise, and the ice started to melt. The animals that the cats fed on could not survive. The cats lost their main food source. In time, the cats became extinct.

Saber-toothed cats had large front teeth. They used the teeth to pierce the thick skin of animals that they ate.

Some plants and animals are becoming extinct even today. Some scientists think that up to 100 kinds of organisms become extinct each day! In 1996 a type of mammal called the red gazelle became extinct. It was hunted too often by humans. The St. Helena Olive tree used to grow on an island off the coast of Africa. It became extinct in 2004 because of disease and dry weather.

Quick Check

Draw Conclusions What are some reasons that living things become extinct?

Critical Thinking If high temperatures cause polar ice to melt, what might happen to polar bears?

The St. Helena Olive tree, shown here, became extinct in 2004.

How can we learn about things that lived long ago?

You can learn about plants and animals that lived long ago by studying fossils. Some fossils give clues about a living thing's size and shape. The large skeleton of a *Tyrannosaurus rex* tells us that the animal was about 5 meters (16.4 feet) tall.

Fossils can also tell us what an animal ate. Animals with pointed teeth were probably meat eaters. Animals with flat teeth were probably plant eaters.

Other fossils can show how an animal moved. A fossil with fins shows that the animal could move through water. A fossil with wings shows that the animal could fly.

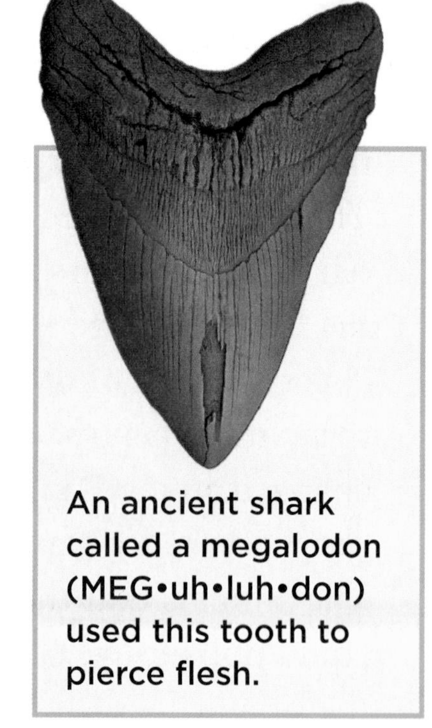

An ancient shark called a megalodon (MEG•uh•luh•don) used this tooth to pierce flesh.

The flat tooth of a woolly mammoth was used to grind leaves and grasses.

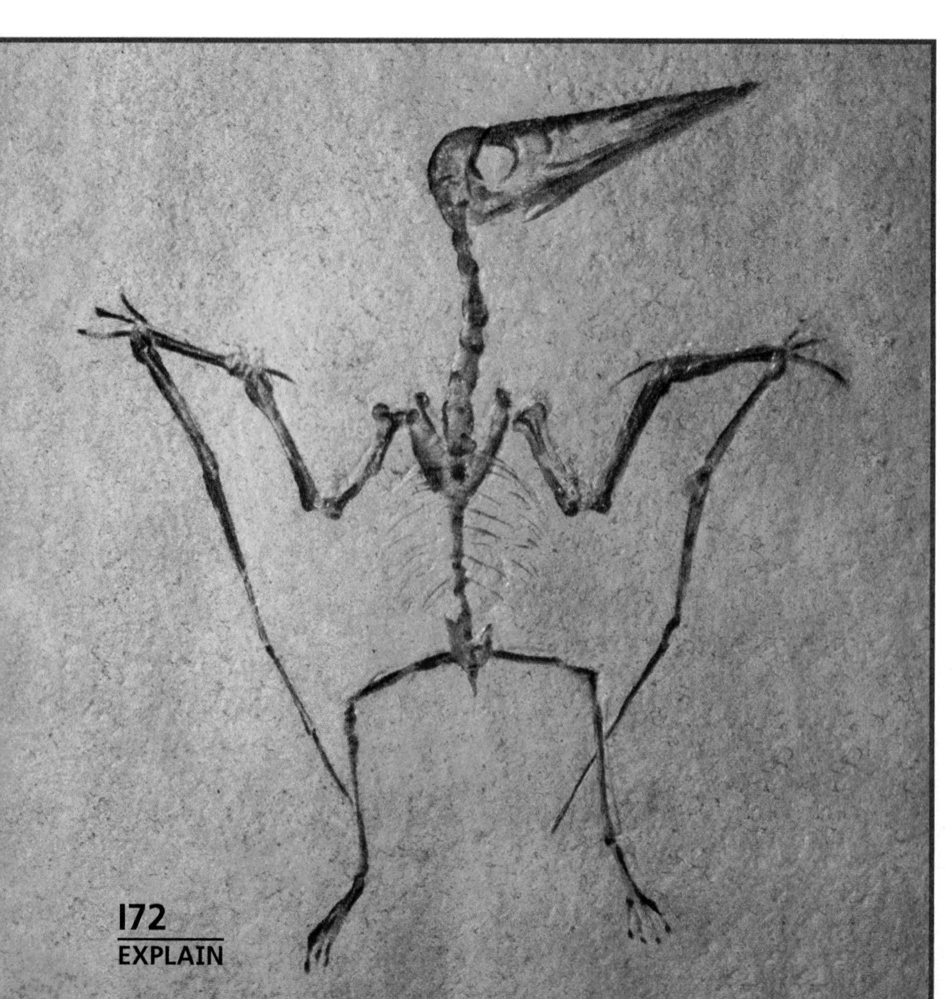

◀ This pterodactyl (ter•uh•DAK•tuhl) fossil shows that ancient reptiles may be related to modern birds.

Scientists also use fossils to find out how Earth and living things have changed over time. Many fish fossils are found on land. This means that millions of years ago, this land was covered with water. Over time, the land rose above the water. Fossils remained in the rock and soil that had been under water.

How deep a fossil is buried gives clues about when an organism lived. Fossils found closest to the surface are usually youngest. Fossils found in deeper layers are older.

Quick Check

Draw Conclusions What does a fossil with fins tell you about that animal?

Critical Thinking Why do you think scientists study fossils?

Plant fossils tell us where plants grew in the past.

Quick Lab

Fossil Mystery

1. **Make a Model** Choose a favorite animal. Then use the key below to make fossil marks for your animal on some modeling clay.

If your animal is a . . .	then shape the clay into a . . .
mammal	circle
bird	square
amphibian	rectangle
reptile	triangle
fish	ball

2. Use the key below to make more fossil marks.

If your animal . . .	then mark your clay with . . .
lives in water	fins
lives on land	feet
lives both in water and on land	fins and feet
is a carnivore	pointed teeth
is an herbivore	flat teeth
is an omnivore	pointed and flat teeth

3. Trade your model fossil with the person sitting to your right.

4. **Infer** What can you learn about the animal that your classmate chose? How do scientists use fossils to learn about extinct animals?

How are living things of today similar to those that lived long ago?

The woolly mammoth became extinct thousands of years ago. Fossils tell us that it had a large trunk and tusks. Yet, fossils cannot tell us how this animal used its body parts. Instead, scientists learn how ancient animals used their body parts by studying similar animals living today.

Elephants are similar to woolly mammoths. They use their trunks to grasp and smell. As a result, scientists think that the woolly mammoth used its trunk in similar ways.

Many organisms living today look similar to those that lived long ago. Some modern birds resemble ancient reptiles. Eagles look very similar to flying lizards called pterodactyls. Pterodactyls had long wingspans and large beaks. Scientists think pterodactyls used their beaks and claws to catch fish just like eagles!

Connecting with the Past

Read a Photo

What do the woolly mammoth and elephant have in common? What is different about them?

Clue: Compare the features of the animals in the photos above.

Quick Check

Draw Conclusions Why do scientists study elephants when they want to learn more about woolly mammoths?

Critical Thinking How are organisms of the past similar to organisms living today?

Lesson Review

Visual Summary

Living things can become extinct when their environment suddenly changes.

Fossils tell us about living things and environments of the past.

You can learn about extinct organisms by studying organisms of today.

Make a FOLDABLES™ Study Guide

Make a Layered-Look Book. Use it to summarize what you learned about living things of the past.

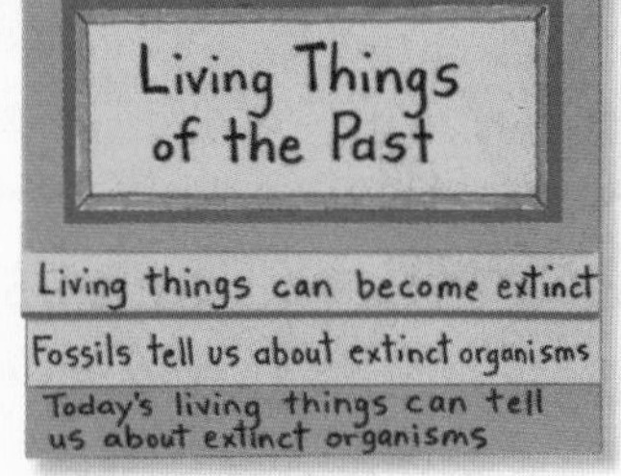

Think, Talk, and Write

1. **Main Idea** What can happen to living things when their environment suddenly changes?
2. **Vocabulary** What is a fossil?
3. **Draw Conclusions** What are some reasons an animal may become extinct?

Text Clues	Conclusions

4. **Critical Thinking** Why do people study fossils?
5. **Test Prep** All fossils
   - **A** are living things.
   - **B** are found only in cold places.
   - **C** are the remains of living things.
   - **D** were created millions of years ago.

Writing Link

Write a Report
Use research materials to learn about woolly mammoths. When did they live? What was their environment like? Write a report to share what you learn.

Math Link

Estimate
The bottom of a fossil bed has a fern plant that is 400 million years old. The top has a 300-million-year-old fern fossil. Between the two layers is a scorpion fossil. About how old do you think the scorpion fossil is?

LOG ON e-Review Summaries and quizzes online at www.macmillanmh.com

Looking at DINOSAURS

Dinosaurs were once common on Earth. Many dinosaurs became extinct millions of years ago. New evidence is helping scientists find out how dinosaurs lived and why they might have disappeared. Take a look at how ideas about dinosaurs have changed based on new evidence.

1842

1923

1995

Dinosaurs Are Named
In 1842 British scientist Richard Owen named the group of large, extinct reptiles "dinosauria." The name came from Greek words meaning "fearfully great lizard." People once thought dinosaurs' strange bones came from dragons or giants.

Dinosaur Nests Are Found
In 1923 American scientists Roy Chapman and Walter Granger found dinosaur nests in the Gobi desert in China. The nests prove that dinosaurs laid eggs.

Dinosaurs Don't Drag Their Tails
In 1995 the American Museum of Natural History changed its *T. rex* skeleton. Instead of standing upright, the new skeleton is displayed with its head low and its tail off the ground. This change was based on studies of fossils, dinosaur tracks, and how different animals move.

Fact and Opinion

- A fact is a true statement that you can prove.
- An opinion is how you feel about something.

Dinosaurs Have Feathers
In 2000 a team of Chinese and American scientists found a 130-million-year-old fossil dinosaur covered with feathers. Now most scientists agree that birds are living dinosaurs.

Today
Scientists continue to find new fossils. They use new tools to discover more about dinosaurs.

Write About It

Fact and Opinion What animal do scientists think are living dinosaurs? Why do scientists think this? What animal do you think dinosaurs are like?

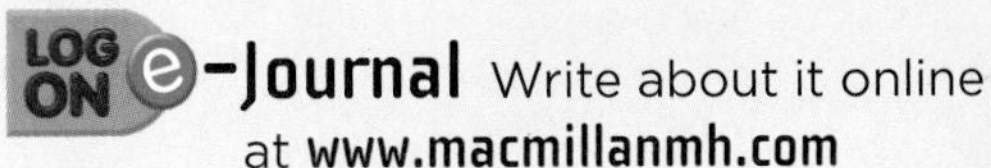

AMERICAN MUSEUM OF NATURAL HISTORY

CHAPTER 3 Review

Visual Summary

Lesson 1 Living things change their environments as they meet their needs. These changes can be helpful or harmful.

Lesson 2 Diseases and natural disasters can change environments. Living things respond to these changes in different ways.

Lesson 3 We can study fossils to learn about ancient plants and animals and their environments.

Make a FOLDABLES Study Guide

Glue your lesson study guides to a piece of paper as shown. Use your study guide to review what you have learned in this chapter.

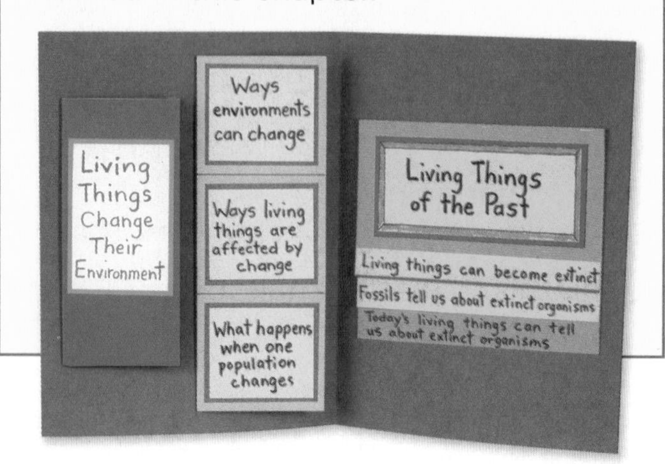

Vocabulary

Fill each blank with the best term from the list.

drought, p. 158	**fossil**, p. 170
endangered, p. 164	**pollution**, p. 150
extinct, p. 170	**recycle**, p. 152
flood, p. 158	**resource**, p. 148

1. If you _______ your old aluminum cans, companies can make them into new cans.
3-2.4

2. When there is little or no rain for a long time, a(n) _______ occurs.
3-2.4

3. Food is an example of a(n) _______ that living things need to survive.
3-2.4

4. Heavy rains can cause a(n) _______, in which water covers land that is usually dry.
3-2.4

5. A kind of organism is _______ when there are no more left alive.
3-2.4

6. When harmful materials are put into an environment, it is called _______.
3-2.4

7. A kind of organism is _______ when there are only a few left alive.
3-2.4

8. Scientists can use a(n) _______ to learn more about a living thing from the past.
3-3.4

LOG ON e-Review Summaries and quizzes online at www.macmillanmh.com

Skills and Concepts

Answer each of the following in complete sentences.

9. **Predict** How might cutting down trees in the rain forest affect people living there?

10. **Persuasive Writing** Write an advertisement that convinces people to visit a museum's new fossil exhibit. Include information about why fossils are important.

11. **Use Numbers** In 1963 there were only 417 pairs of bald eagles in the United States. In 2006 there were 7,066 pairs. How many more pairs were there in 2006?
3-2.4

12. **Critical Thinking** Cardinals live in forests. What may happen to a cardinal if a wildfire burns its forest habitat?
3-2.4

13. What modern animal does this fossil resemble? What traits do both animals have in common?
3-3.4

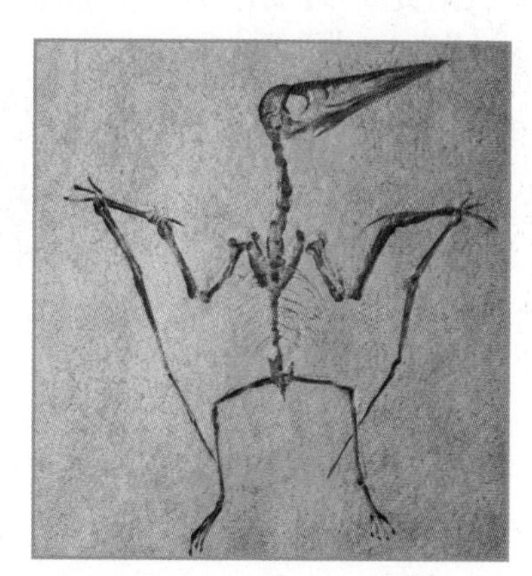

14. How can changes affect living things and their environments?
3-2.4

Performance Assessment

Conservation Cards

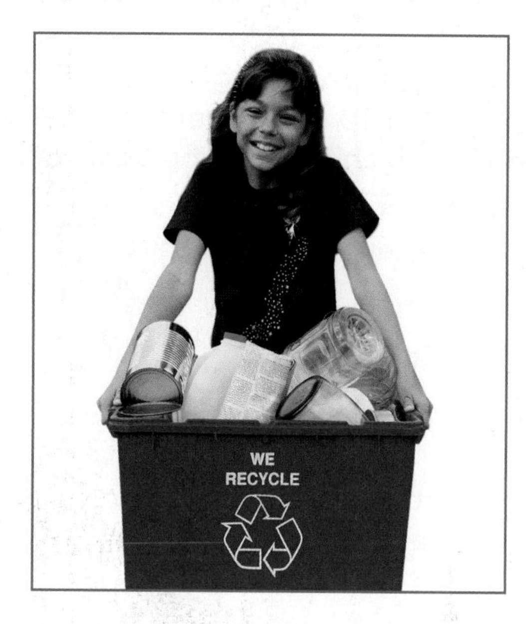

- Make three cards that show how people can protect the environment. Make one card for each of the 3 *Rs*.
- On the top of each card, write either *Reduce*, *Reuse*, or *Recycle*. Under each word, write a plan that helps people conserve resources. Then add a drawing to show how your plan works.
- On the back of each card, explain how your plan helps the environment.
- Share your cards with the class. Together, brainstorm ways to put your plans into action.

South Carolina Activity

Choose an area near your home, such as a park or a playground. Conduct research to learn how this habitat has changed. How have these changes affected the plants and animals that live there?

South Carolina Standards Practice

1 **Tara wants to know how drought affects corn plants. She will give one corn plant 200 mL of water each week. She will give another corn plant 10 mL of water each week. Which tool will be best for measuring the water?**

A a beaker

B forceps

C a meterstick

D a graduated cylinder

3-1.5

2 **The picture below shows a clearing in a forest.**

Which event will happen first?

F Animals move in.

G Plants compete for sunlight.

H Seeds blow onto bare ground.

I Animals compete for sunlight.

3-1.2

3 **Fossils found in deeper layers of rock are usually**

A older.

B younger.

C larger.

D smaller.

3-3.4

4 **Which of the following best explains how dinosaurs became extinct?**

F A meteor hit Earth.

G Ice sheets covered Earth.

H Ocean levels rose.

I Humans killed them.

3-2.3

5 **Which of these would most likely happen if prairie dogs were removed from a grassland?**

A Snakes would have more places to make their homes.

B Coyotes would have more food.

C Eagles would have less food.

D Owls would have less soil to make their burrows.

3-2.4

6 Which of the following is an example of a present-day animal and an ancient animal that look similar?

- **F** wolf and tiger
- **G** hummingbird and eagle
- **H** elephant and woolly mammoth
- **I** dragon and lizard

3-2.4

7 A student planted bean seeds in two containers. In container 1 he planted two seeds. In container 2 he planted five seeds. He placed the same amount of soil in each container, and he gave each the same amount of water. After 4 weeks he measured the height of the bean plants in both containers. The following chart shows his results.

Container	Number of Seeds Planted	Average Plant Height
1	2	25 centimeters
2	5	16 centimeters

According to his results, which **most likely** affected the growth of the plants in container 2?

- **A** predators
- **B** consumers
- **C** competition
- **D** pollution

3-1.6

8 Humans often cut down forests for wood. How does this affect forest animals?

- **F** It destroys their habitat.
- **G** It increases their numbers.
- **H** It gives them a larger habitat.
- **I** It increases their resources.

3-2.4

9 A new type of animal is brought into an area. It does not have any natural predators in the area. What will **most likely** happen to the new type of animal?

- **A** Its population will decrease.
- **B** Its population will increase.
- **C** It will become endangered.
- **D** It will become extinct.

3-2.4

10 Fossils show events that happened on Earth long ago. Which choice shows the correct order of events, from earliest to latest?

- **F** Dinosaurs lived on Earth; the Ice Age began; saber-toothed cats became extinct.
- **G** The Ice Age began; dinosaurs became extinct; saber-toothed cats lived on Earth.
- **H** The Ice Age ended; dinosaurs lived on Earth; saber-toothed cats became extinct.
- **I** Saber-toothed cats lived on Earth; the Ice Age ended; dinosaurs became extinct.

3-1.2

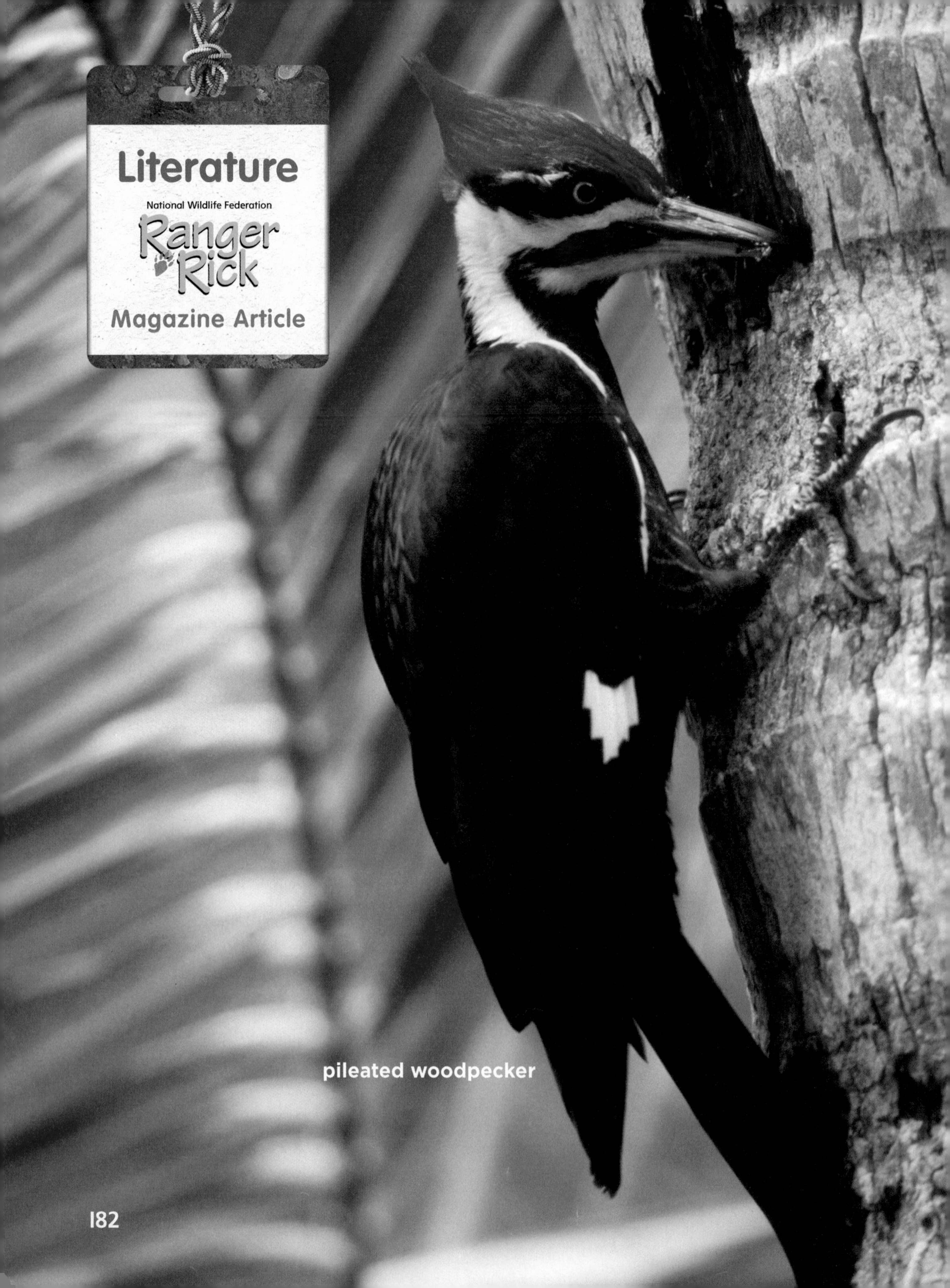

pileated woodpecker

from *Ranger Rick*

Once Upon a Woodpecker

Tap! Rap-tap-tap! Do you hear that drumming sound? Oh, look, there's a woodpecker tapping on that dead tree. Let's move closer for a better look. If we're quiet we can watch the woodpecker at work.

Woodpeckers have some amazing adaptations that help them survive. They hammer hard into tree trunks with their sharp beaks. Strong muscles in their necks put power behind each blow. These muscles also act as shock absorbers so woodpeckers don't get headaches!

Woodpeckers have extra long tongues for spearing insects they find inside tree trunks. A barb on the tip of their tongues works like a fishhook to reel in meals. Look out bugs! You can't hide from the well-adapted woodpecker!

Write About It

Response to Literature This article tells about special features of woodpeckers that help them survive. What are some special features you have that help you survive? Write about them.

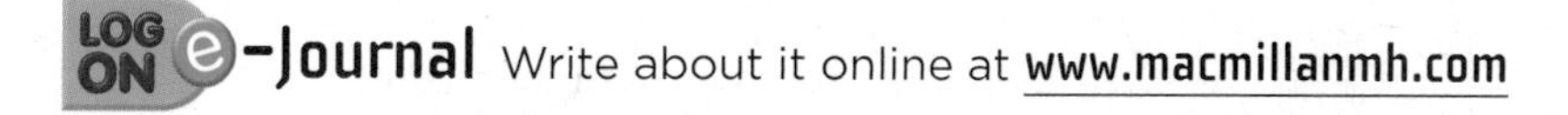

Wildlife Manager

Do you like to learn about plants and animals? Do you want to help keep environments clean and healthy? Then one day you might become a wildlife manager.

Wildlife managers help take care of animals and their environments. They keep track of the plants and animals in places such as wildlife parks. They look for ways to help living things. They also teach people about wildlife and why it is important to take care of environments.

To become a wildlife manager, you must care about environments and living things. Plan to study science in high school and college. You will also need a degree in a field such as biology or environmental science.

Here are some other Life Science careers:

- emergency medical technician
- animal rescue worker
- gardener
- park ranger

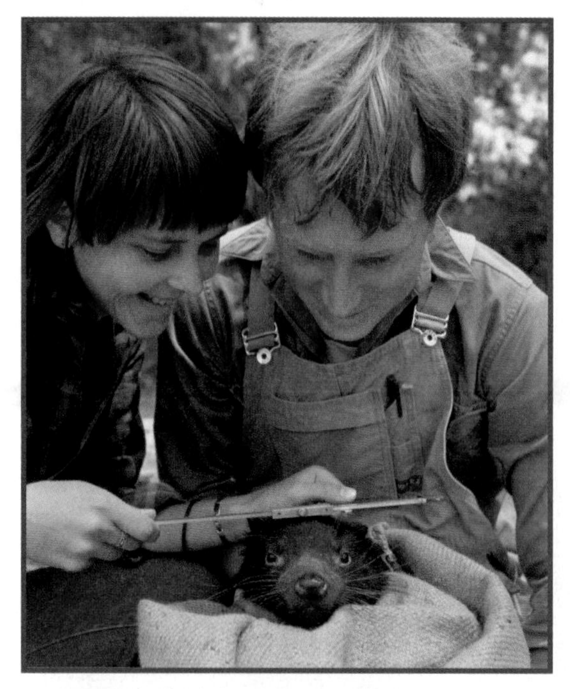

▲ Animal rescue workers measure a Tasmanian devil.

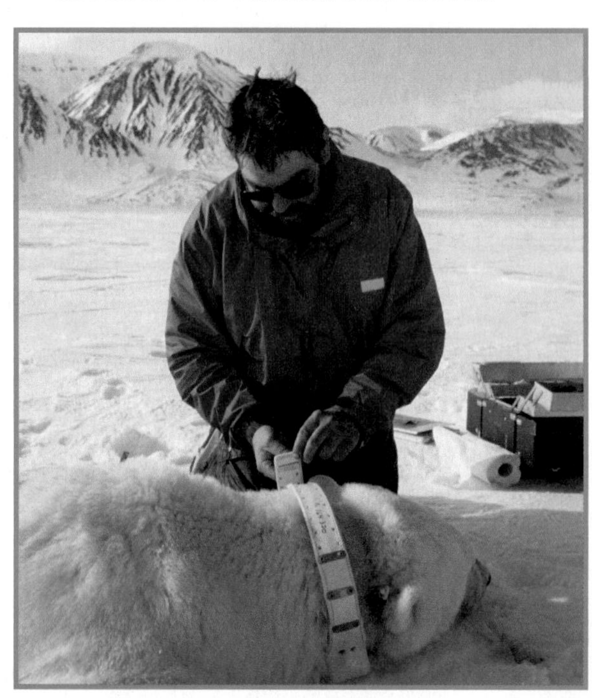

▲ A park ranger places a satellite collar on a polar bear to track its movements.

LOG ON e-Careers at www.macmillanmh.com

Earth Science

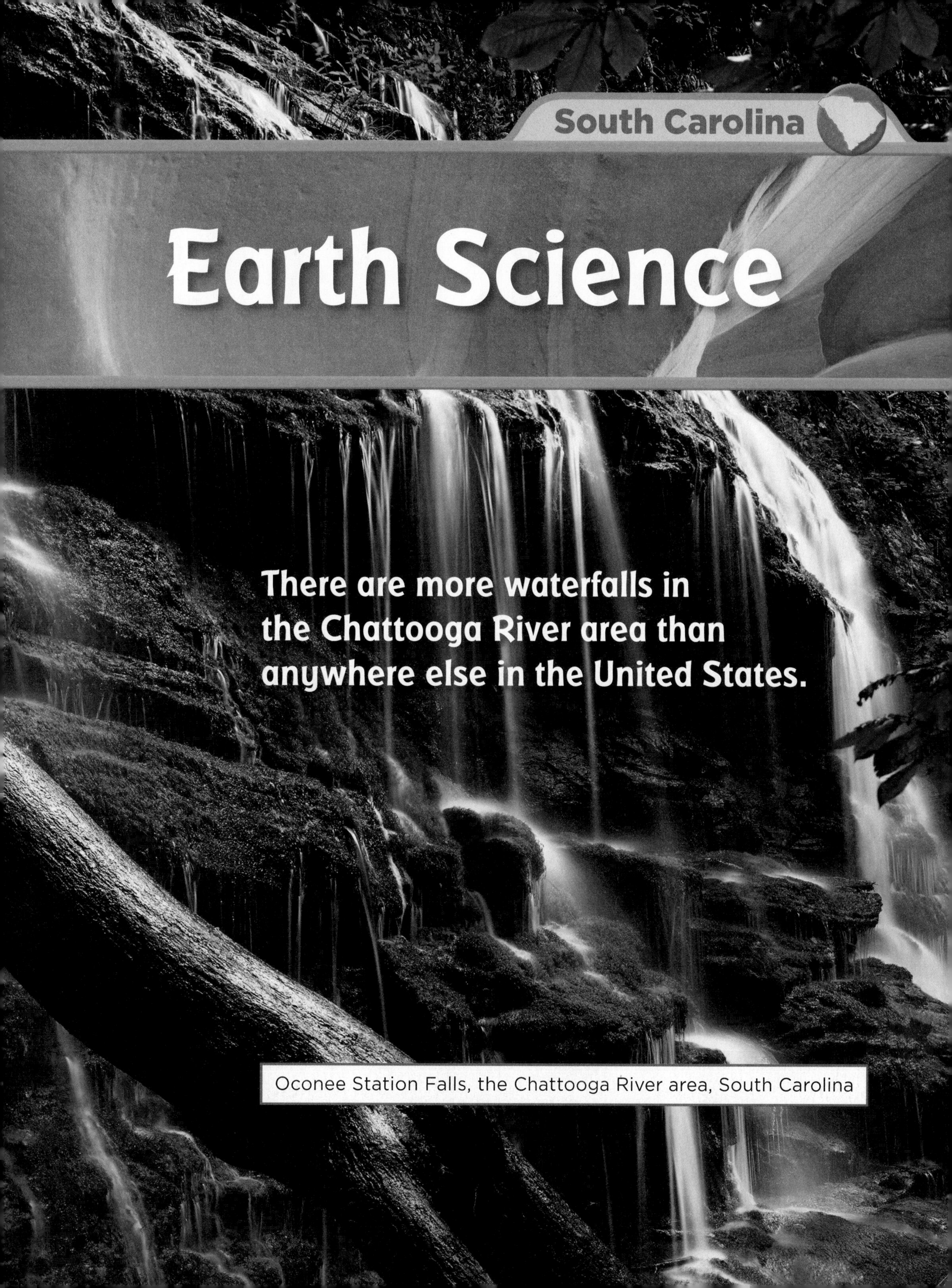

There are more waterfalls in the Chattooga River area than anywhere else in the United States.

Oconee Station Falls, the Chattooga River area, South Carolina

Sassafras MOUNTAIN

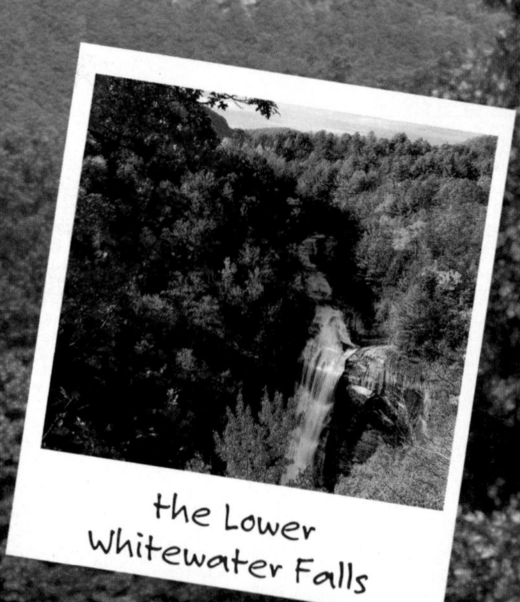
the Lower Whitewater Falls

The Blue Ridge Mountains

Can you name the highest point in South Carolina? It is the peak of Sassafras Mountain. If you hike to the top of this mountain, you will be 1,085 meters (3,560 feet) above sea level. Sassafras Mountain is part of the Blue Ridge mountain chain, which is part of the Appalachian Mountains. The Appalachian Mountains run along the eastern edge of North America.

The Appalachian Mountains

The Appalachians are the oldest mountains in the United States. Movements in Earth's crust formed the mountains about 342 million years ago. Layers of rock squeezed together. The layers buckled and folded. They pressed up to form a line of mountains, including Sassafras Mountain.

Trees and shrubs cover Sassafras Mountain. One of these is the sassafras tree. The bark and berries of this small tree contain a useful oil. It can be used as a perfume, as a medicine, and as a flavoring in foods.

Think, Talk, and Write

Critical Thinking Why do you think waterfalls are often found on mountains?

South Carolina

A CLOSER LOOK

Main Idea

Mountains such as Sassafras Mountain formed in a line about 342 million years ago.

Activity

Make a Model How do mountains form? In this activity you will make a model to find out.

- Gather two or three different colors of clay.
- Flatten each piece of clay.
- Stack the clay in layers.
- Press the ends of the stack. What happens to the clay in the middle? How is this similar to the way mountains form?

sassafras berries ▶

3-3.6. Illustrate Earth's land features (including volcanoes, mountains, valleys, canyons, caverns, and islands) by using models, pictures, diagrams, and maps.

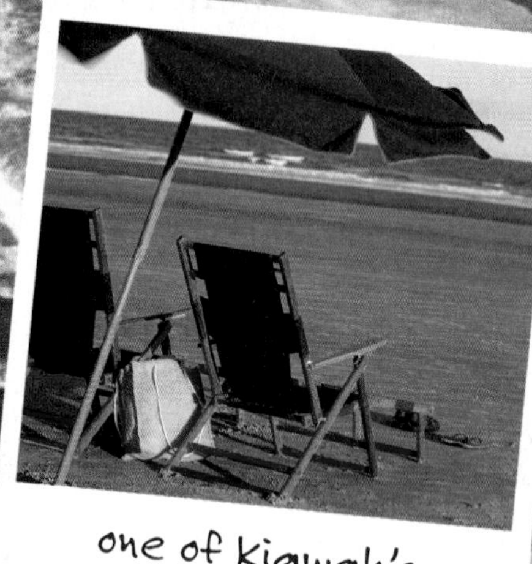
one of Kiawah's beaches

Kiawah Island

Sandy Beaches

The coast of South Carolina has several islands. One of these is Kiawah Island. Every year many people visit Kiawah's beaches.

Like all beaches, Kiawah's beaches lose sand in some places and gain sand in other places. Storms at the beach bring wind, rain, and high waves. The wind and waves wash sand away from one place. They carry the sand away and drop it farther down the shore. Some locations gain lots of sand, and others do not.

Replacing Lost Sand

Since 2000, the island's east end has lost more than 120 meters (400 feet) of sand dunes. To stop this, workers on Kiawah Island replace sand lost from wind and waves. The workers must take special care not to disturb the animals that live there. These animals include sea turtles, which nest on the beach.

Think, Talk, and Write

Critical Thinking How do storms affect beaches?

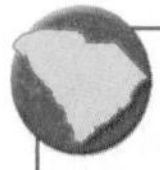

3-3.8. Illustrate changes in Earth's surface that are due to slow processes and changes that are due to rapid processes.

South Carolina

A CLOSER LOOK

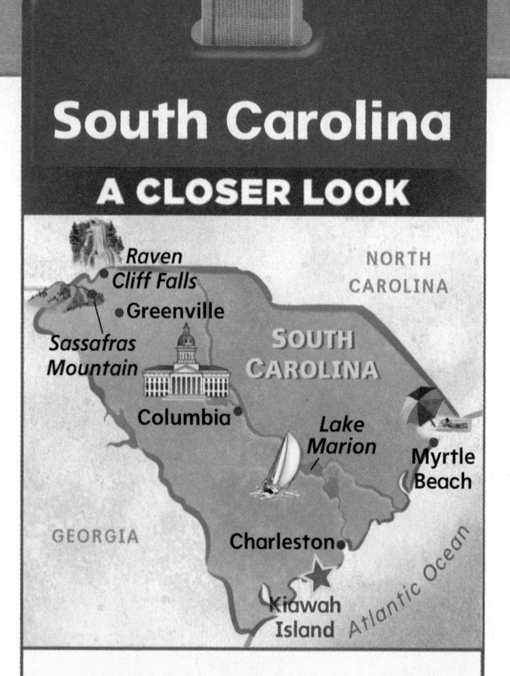

Main Idea

Wind and waves can change the shape of land at the shore.

Activity

Observe You can make a model to see how beaches lose sand.

- Place two cups of sand in a plastic box to make a "beach."
- Pour a cup of water over one edge of the sand. What happens?
- How is your model like a real beach? How is it different?

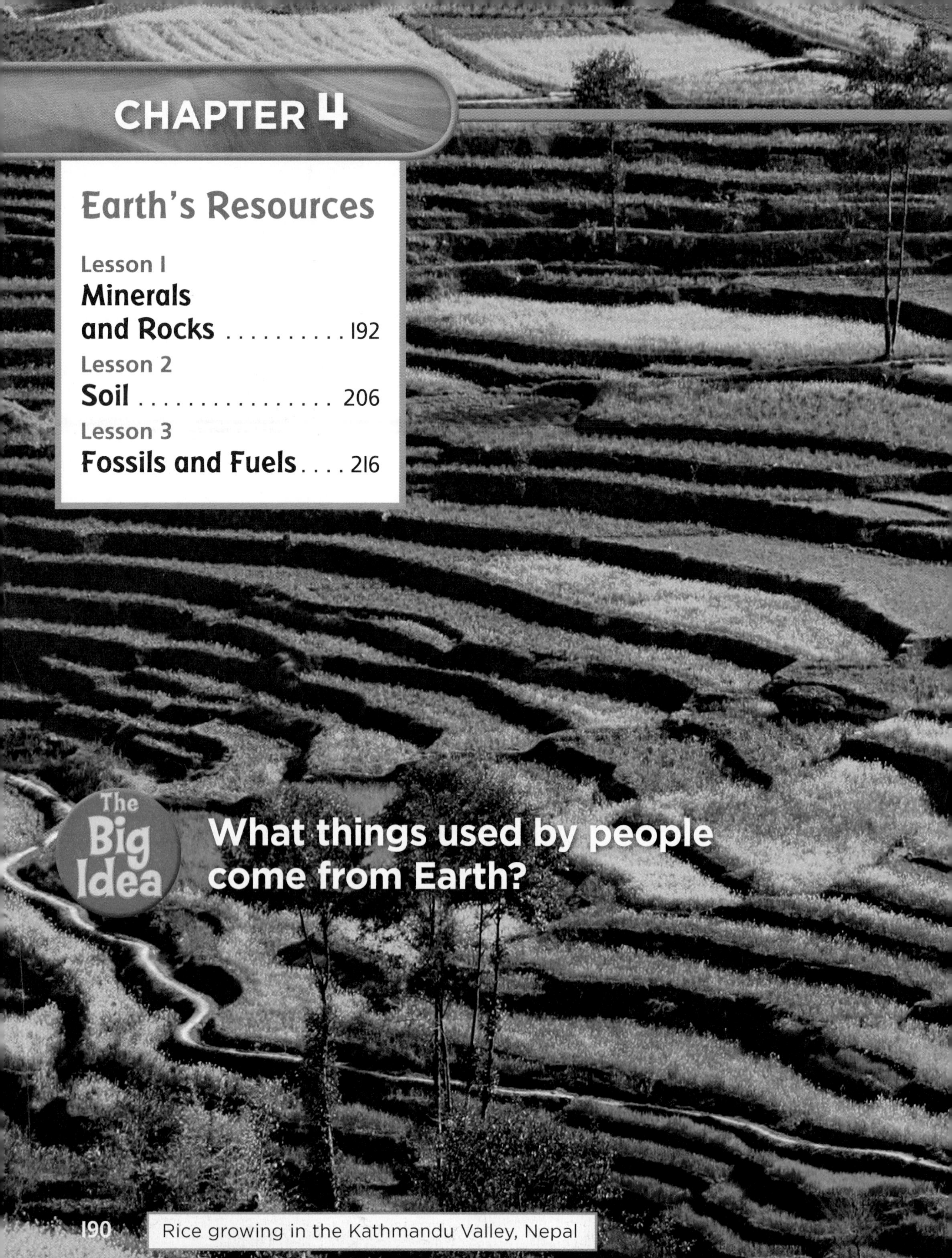

Earth's Resources

The Big Idea

What things used by people come from Earth?

Rice growing in the Kathmandu Valley, Nepal

Key Vocabulary

mineral
a solid, nonliving substance found in nature (p. 194)

soil
a mixture of minerals, weathered rocks, and other things (p. 208)

natural resource
a material on Earth that is necessary or useful to people (p. 212)

fossil
the trace or remains of something that lived long ago (p. 218)

fuel
a material that is burned for its energy (p. 220)

solar energy
energy from the Sun (p. 222)

More Vocabulary

rock, p. 198

igneous rock, p. 199

sediment, p. 200

sedimentary rock, p. 200

metamorphic rock, p. 201

humus, p. 208

renewable resource, p. 221

nonrenewable resource, p. 221

Lesson 1

Minerals and Rocks

Look and Wonder

This mineral looks like gold, but don't be fooled! It is really pyrite, or "fool's gold." How can you tell fool's gold from the real thing?

3-3.1. Classify rocks and soils on the basis of their properties. **3-3.2.** Identify common minerals on the basis of their properties by using a minerals identification key.

Explore

Inquiry Activity

How do a mineral's color and mark compare?

Make a Prediction

Some minerals leave a mark behind when you rub them on a white tile. Is the mark left behind always the same color as the mineral?

Test Your Prediction

1. Make a table like the one shown.

Mineral Color	Color Left Behind

2. **Observe** Look at one mineral. Record its color in the table.
3. **Experiment** Rub the mineral across the tile. What color is left behind? Record the color in the table.
4. Repeat steps 2 and 3 for each mineral.

Draw Conclusions

5. **Interpret Data** How did the colors and marks of the minerals compare?
6. **Infer** When might you use mineral marks to help you tell minerals apart?

Explore More

Experiment Are some minerals harder than others? Make a plan to find out. Then try it.

Materials

minerals

white tile

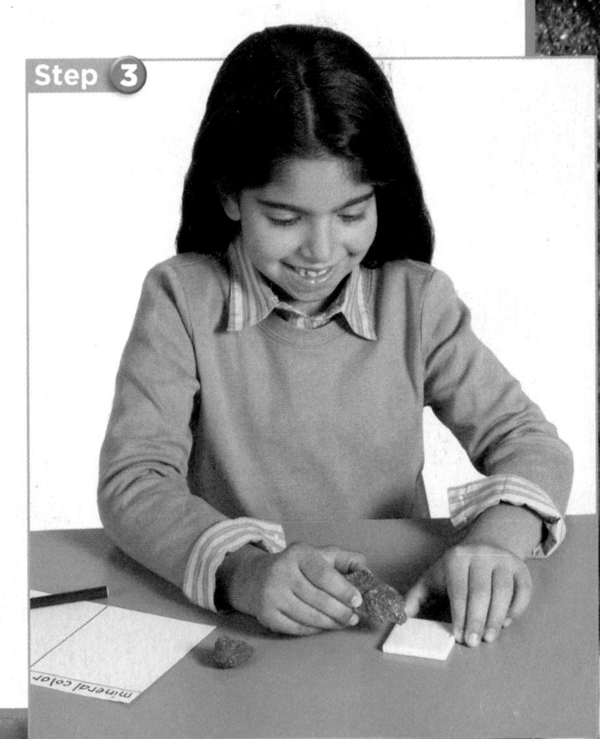

3-I.4. Predict the outcome of a simple investigation and compare the result with the prediction.

Read and Learn

Main Idea 3-3.1 3-3.2

Rocks are made of minerals. Rocks are classified as igneous, sedimentary, or metamorphic.

Vocabulary

at www.macmillanmh.com

Reading Skill

Classify

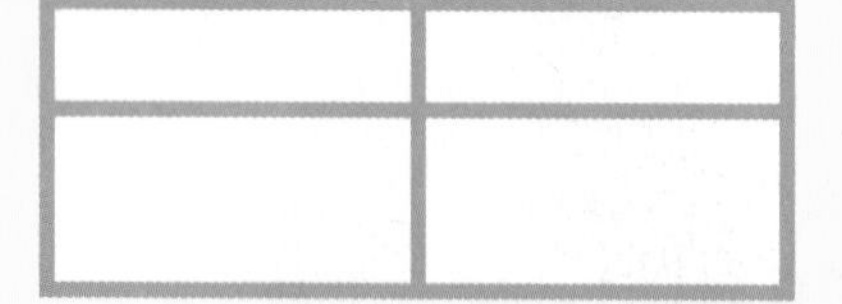

What are minerals?

Many common substances found on Earth are made of minerals (MIN•uhr•uhlz). A **mineral** is a solid, nonliving substance found in nature. Table salt, gold, and iron are minerals. The graphite in your pencil is a mineral, too. Minerals are the building blocks of rocks. They are found underground and in soil. They are even in the ocean and on the ocean floor.

There are more than 3,000 different kinds of minerals. Each mineral has its own properties. You can use the properties of minerals to tell them apart.

Color

It is easy to observe a mineral's color. Most minerals come in just one color. However, some, like quartz, come in many colors. Some, like gold and pyrite, are the same color. You cannot use color alone to identify a mineral.

▼ Minerals come in many colors.

turquoise

feldspar

quartz

Streak

Streak is another property used to identify minerals. *Streak* is the color of the powder left when a mineral is rubbed across a white tile. A mineral's streak may or may not be the same as the mineral's color.

Luster

Luster describes how light bounces off a mineral. Some minerals are shiny like metal. Others are not. Luster is another property used to identify a mineral.

Hardness

The *hardness* of a mineral describes how easily it can be scratched. Some minerals, like talc and gypsum, are soft. They can be scratched with a fingernail. Other minerals, like quartz, are much harder. Not even a steel file can scratch quartz.

▲ Pyrite may look like gold, but its streak is different. Pyrite's streak is greenish-black. Gold's streak is yellow.

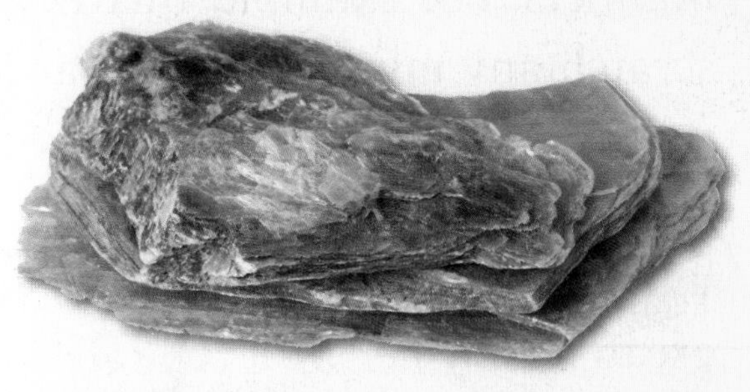

▲ Mica can have a pearly luster.

▲ Diamond is the hardest mineral. No other mineral or object can scratch it.

Quick Check

Classify What are some properties that help you identify a mineral?

Critical Thinking Is wood a mineral? Explain your answer.

How can hardness be used to identify minerals?

Mohs' hardness scale shows the hardness of a few common minerals. There are many more minerals for each level of hardness. Diamond, 10 on the scale, is the hardest mineral. Talc, 1 on the scale, is one of the softest minerals.

Minerals with higher numbers can scratch minerals with lower numbers. For example, quartz can scratch any mineral with a hardness that is less than 7. Quartz, however, can itself be scratched by a mineral with a hardness that is greater than 7.

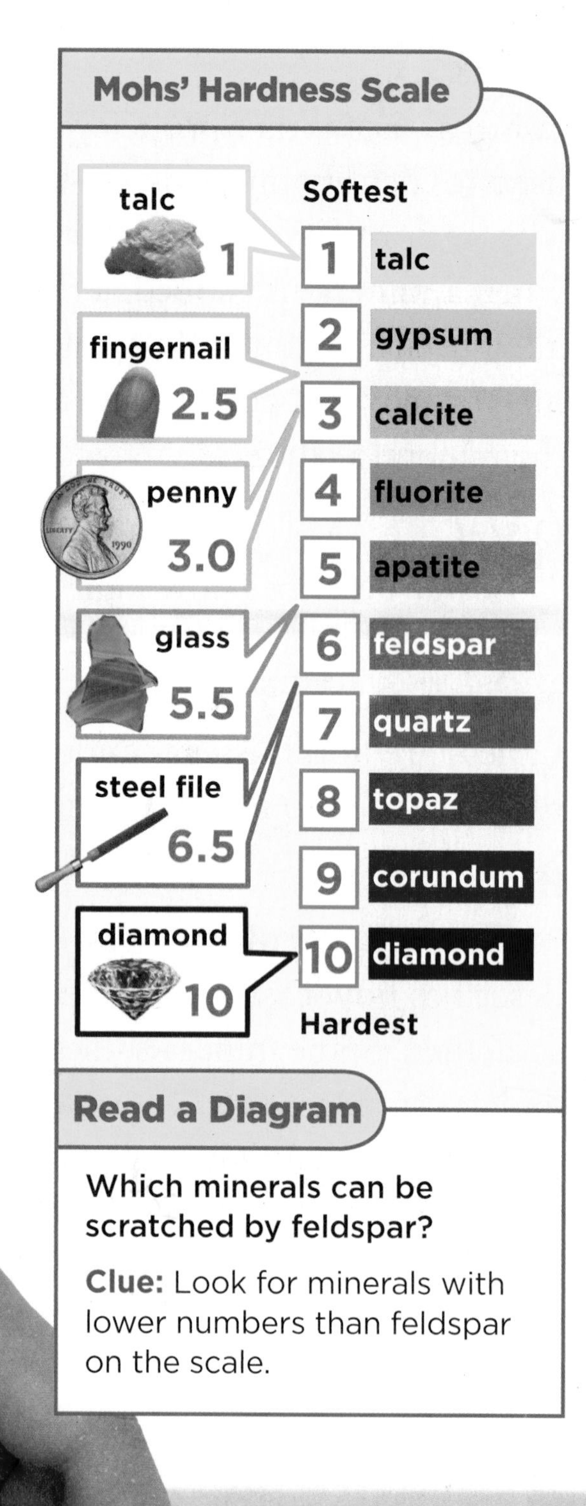

Read a Diagram

Which minerals can be scratched by feldspar?

Clue: Look for minerals with lower numbers than feldspar on the scale.

▼ Which mineral do you think is being scratched? How could you find out?

You can also tell the hardness of minerals by using some everyday items. Your fingernail can easily scratch gypsum and talc. A penny can scratch calcite, gypsum, and talc. Glass can scratch any mineral with a hardness that is less than 5.5. A steel file can scratch any mineral with a hardness that is less than 6.5.

Quick Check

Classify Which mineral on Mohs' hardness scale is harder than all other minerals?

Critical Thinking Why might people want to know the hardness of a mineral?

Quick Lab

Identifying Minerals

1. **Observe** Select a mineral sample. Scratch it with your fingernail, a penny, and a file or an iron nail to determine its hardness. Record your observations.
2. **Observe** Use a hand lens to observe the sample's other properties.
3. Draw a line with the mineral across a streak plate. Record the streak color.
4. Use the identification table below to name the mineral. Repeat steps 1–4 with other samples.
5. **Draw Conclusions** Which properties helped you most in identifying the minerals?

Mineral Identification Table

Mineral	Hardness	Luster	Streak	Color	Other
pyrite	6–6.5	metallic	greenish-black	brassy yellow	called "fool's gold"
quartz	7	nonmetallic	none	colorless, white, rose, smoky, purple, brown	
mica	2–2.5	nonmetallic	none	dark brown, black, or silver-white	flakes when peeled
feldspar	6	nonmetallic	none	colorless, beige, pink	
calcite	3	nonmetallic	white	colorless, white	bubbles when acid is placed on it

▲ A mineral identification table contains useful information about the properties of minerals.

What are rocks?

A **rock** is a nonliving material made of one or more minerals. There are hundreds of different types of rocks. Some rocks, like granite (GRAN•it), are made of several minerals. Some rocks, like limestone, are made mostly of one mineral. A rock's color gives clues about the minerals that make it up.

Grains

Rocks are made of mineral pieces called grains. To a person who studies rocks, a rock's *texture* (TEKS•chuhr) is how its grains look. Some rocks have large grains you can easily see. These rocks have a coarse texture. Some rocks have grains that are too small to see. These rocks have a fine texture.

Igneous-Rock Formation

Read a Diagram

Where does granite form?

Clue: A cutaway diagram can show what happens below the ground.

LOG ON *Science in Motion* Watch igneous rocks form at **www.macmillanmh.com**

Igneous Rocks

Rocks are classified by how they form. There are three kinds of rocks—igneous, sedimentary, and metamorphic.

An **igneous rock** (IG•nee•uhs) forms when melted rock cools and hardens. Inside Earth, melted rock called *magma* cools and hardens very slowly. A rock with large mineral grains forms. Granite is an example.

Melted rock that flows onto Earth's surface is called *lava*. Lava cools and hardens quickly. A rock with small mineral grains forms. Basalt is an example.

Quick Check

Classify What kind of rock is basalt?

Critical Thinking What is the difference between a mineral and a rock?

Basalt has a fine texture. It forms when lava cools quickly above Earth's surface.

Granite has a coarse texture. It forms when magma cools slowly beneath Earth's surface.

What are sedimentary and metamorphic rocks?

Some rocks are formed from sediment (SED•uh•muhnt). **Sediment** is tiny bits of weathered rock or once-living animals or plants. A **sedimentary rock** (sed•uh•MEN•tuh•ree) is a kind of rock that forms from layers of sediment. Sandstone, shale, and limestone are some kinds of sedimentary rocks.

▲ Shale is a sedimentary rock made up of bits of weathered materials.

Sedimentary rocks form where weathered and eroded materials are dropped. This often happens at the bottom of rivers, lakes, and oceans. Over time, sediment piles up. The top layers press on layers below. They squeeze the water and air from the lower layers and press the sediment together. In time the sediment becomes cemented together and forms rock.

▲ Fossils are often found in the sedimentary rock limestone. Limestone can form from the remains of once-living things.

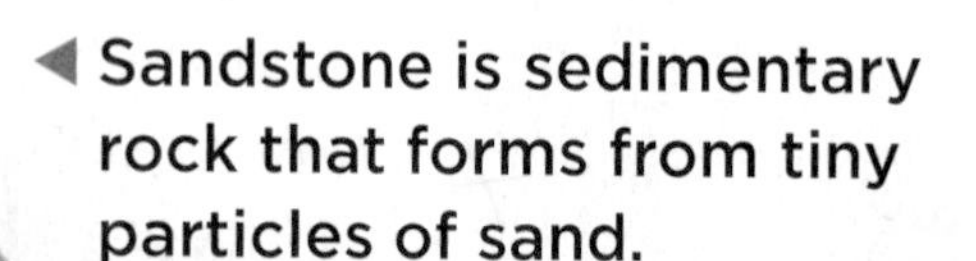

◀ Sandstone is sedimentary rock that forms from tiny particles of sand.

A third kind of rock is metamorphic (met•uh•MAWR•fik) rock. A rock that has been changed by heating and squeezing is a **metamorphic rock**.

Deep inside Earth, rocks heat up and "bake." They also get squeezed by the weight of the rocks above them. All this heating and squeezing can cause a rock's minerals to change into new minerals. A new rock forms with properties that are different from the original rock.

Quick Check

Classify What kinds of rocks are limestone and gneiss?

Critical Thinking What kinds of rocks can change into metamorphic rocks?

Metamorphic Rocks

▲ Gneiss is a metamorphic rock. It forms from granite.

▲ Slate is a metamorphic rock. It forms from shale.

▲ Phyllite is a metamorphic rock. It forms from the metamorphic rock slate.

How do we use minerals and rocks?

▲ Rubies and diamonds are gems.

Did you write with a pencil today? If so, you used the mineral graphite. Did you eat any food with salt? If so, you ate the mineral halite. Many of the things we use every day come from minerals. Telephone wires are made with the mineral copper. Some baseball bats are made with the mineral aluminum. Gold, silver, and iron are minerals we use for jewelry. In fact, most of the metals we use come from minerals. Minerals are even used to make glass, chalk, and toothpaste.

Other minerals, such as diamonds, topazes, and rubies, are *gems*. People value gems for their beauty.

Rocks are also useful. They are used for building roads, houses, and statues. Limestone is used to make cement. Coal is burned for heat.

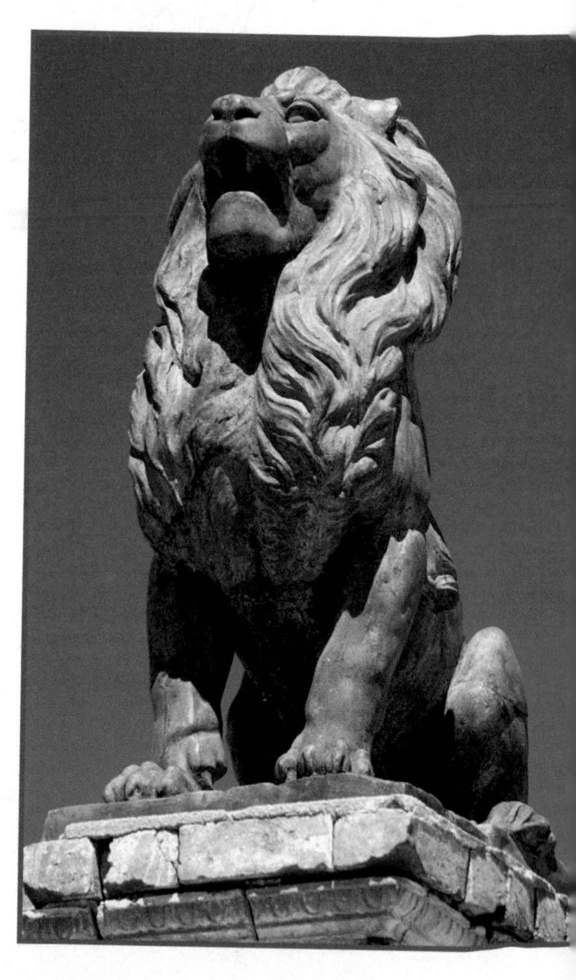

▲ Marble is a hard rock. It weathers very slowly.

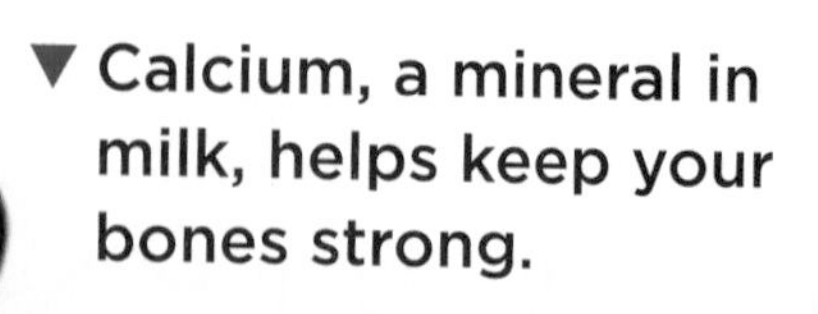

▼ Calcium, a mineral in milk, helps keep your bones strong.

Quick Check

Classify Is salt a gem?

Critical Thinking What minerals have you used today?

Lesson Review

Visual Summary

Properties such as color, hardness, luster, and streak are used to tell **minerals** apart.

Igneous, sedimentary, and metamorphic **rocks** form in different ways.

People **use** minerals and rocks for many things.

Make a FOLDABLES™ Study Guide

Make a Three-Tab Book. Use it to summarize what you learned about minerals and rocks.

Think, Talk, and Write

1. **Main Idea** What makes igneous, sedimentary, and metamorphic rocks different from each other?
2. **Vocabulary** What is a mineral?
3. **Classify** How could you classify granite, sandstone, basalt, and limestone?

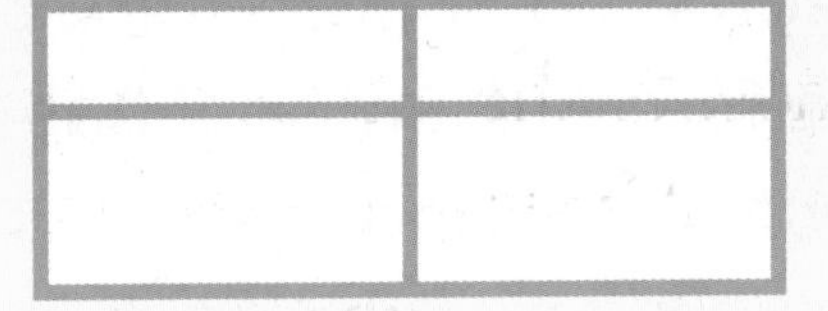

4. **Critical Thinking** Explain the relationship between rocks and minerals.
5. **Test Prep** **Which of the following is a sedimentary rock?**
   A sandstone
   B basalt
   C diamond
   D granite

Writing Link

Write a Poem
Write a poem about an igneous, sedimentary, or metamorphic rock. Tell how the rock formed or describe how it looks. Be sure to include a title.

Art Link

Make Rock Art
Find a box you can decorate with rocks. Collect small rocks of different colors and sizes. Glue the rocks to your box.

LOG ON e-Review Summaries and quizzes online at www.macmillanmh.com

Marble Memorials

The Lincoln Memorial and the Jefferson Memorial both honor a past American President. These two marble buildings are in Washington, D.C. Both have a statue of a President inside them.

The Lincoln Memorial has the shape of a rectangle. It has white columns. The Jefferson Memorial has columns, too, but it is round.

Descriptive Writing

A good description

- uses details to create a picture for the reader
- includes words that compare, such as *both, like,* and *too*
- includes words that contrast, such as *but* and *unlike*

Lincoln Memorial

Jefferson Memorial

Write About It

Descriptive Writing Choose two objects made from rock. Write a paragraph that describes and compares them.

e-Journal Write about it online at www.macmillanmh.com

Finding Fractions

This table shows the different rocks in a rock collection.

My Rock Collection		
Igneous	**Sedimentary**	**Metamorphic**
2 basalt	1 coquina	1 schist
3 granite	2 sandstone	1 slate

Fractions

- To find a fraction, use the total number of rocks as the denominator. Use the number of rocks for a particular kind of rock as the numerator.
- Example: What fraction of igneous rocks in the collection are granite?

  $\frac{3}{5}$ ← 3: granite rocks; 5: number of igneous rocks
- Example: What fraction of rocks in the collection are metamorphic?

  $\frac{2}{10}$ ← 2: metamorphic rocks; 10: total number of rocks

granite

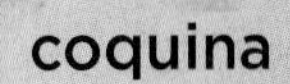
coquina

schist

sandstone

Solve It

What fraction of rocks in the collection are igneous rocks? What fraction of sedimentary rocks in the collection are sandstone?

Lesson 2

Soil

Prairie dogs in their burrow

Look and Wonder

Plants, animals, and people could not live without soil. What is in soil? Why is it important to many living things?

3-3.1. Classify rocks and soils on the basis of their properties. **3-3.7.** Exemplify Earth materials that are used as fuel, as a resource for building materials, and as a medium for growing plants.

Explore — Inquiry Activity

What makes up soil?

Purpose

Find out what soil is made of.

Procedure

1. Use a spoon to spread out the soil on the plate.

Step 1

2. **Observe** Use the hand lens to observe the soil. Is soil made of small bits of stuff? What is the shape and color of these small particles? Wash your hands. Record what you see.
3. **Communicate** Talk with others about what the tiny bits in soil may be.

Draw Conclusions

4. **Infer** What kinds of things make up this soil?

Explore More

Experiment Is all soil the same? Make a plan to find out. Then try out your plan.

Materials

plastic spoon

soil

paper plate

hand lens

Step 2

3-I.1. Classify objects by two of their properties (attributes). **3-I.7.** Explain why similar investigations might produce different results.

Read and Learn

Main Idea 3-3.1 3-3.7

Soil is made up of weathered rocks, minerals, and once-living things. Many living things need soil to survive.

Vocabulary

soil, p. 208

humus, p. 208

natural resource, p. 212

Reading Skill

Problem and Solution

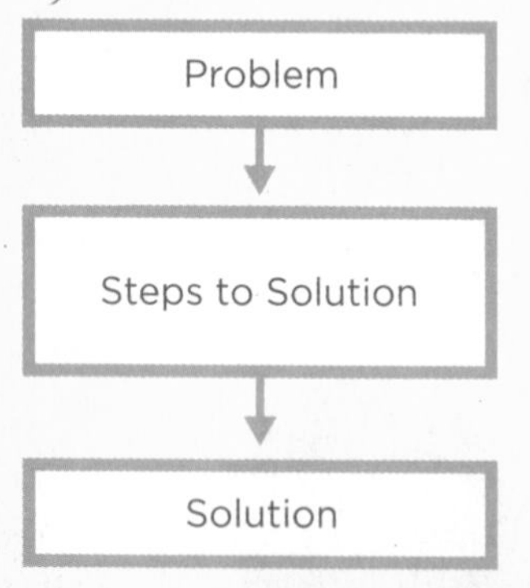

What is soil?

Soil is a mixture of minerals, weathered rocks, and other things. It has bits of decayed plants and animals called **humus** (HYEW•muhs). Humus looks dark. It adds nutrients to soil. Plants then use these nutrients. Humus works like a sponge to soak up rainwater and keep the soil moist. Water, air, and living things are also found in soil.

Living Things in Soil

If you dig away a chunk of soil, you might see roots. A plant's roots take in water and minerals from the soil. They also hold the soil in place and help slow erosion.

You might also see animals living in soil. Animals such as ants, earthworms, and moles break up soil. Their burrows help air and water get into the soil.

Ants and earthworms are just a few of the organisms that live in soil. ▼

FACT Most living things in soil are too small to see with just your eyes.

How Soil Forms

The making of soil starts with weathering. Weathering causes rocks to break down into smaller and smaller pieces. The tiny bits of weathered rock build up into layers. Living things die and decay in the weathered material and become humus. Over time, layers of soil form. The top layer is called *topsoil*. Topsoil is dark and has the most humus and minerals. Below the topsoil is *subsoil*. This layer is lighter in color and has less humus. Below the subsoil is *bedrock*, or solid rock.

Soil takes a long time to form—up to 1,000 years for just 1 centimeter! That is why people try to prevent soil erosion. They add minerals and humus to soil to keep it healthy.

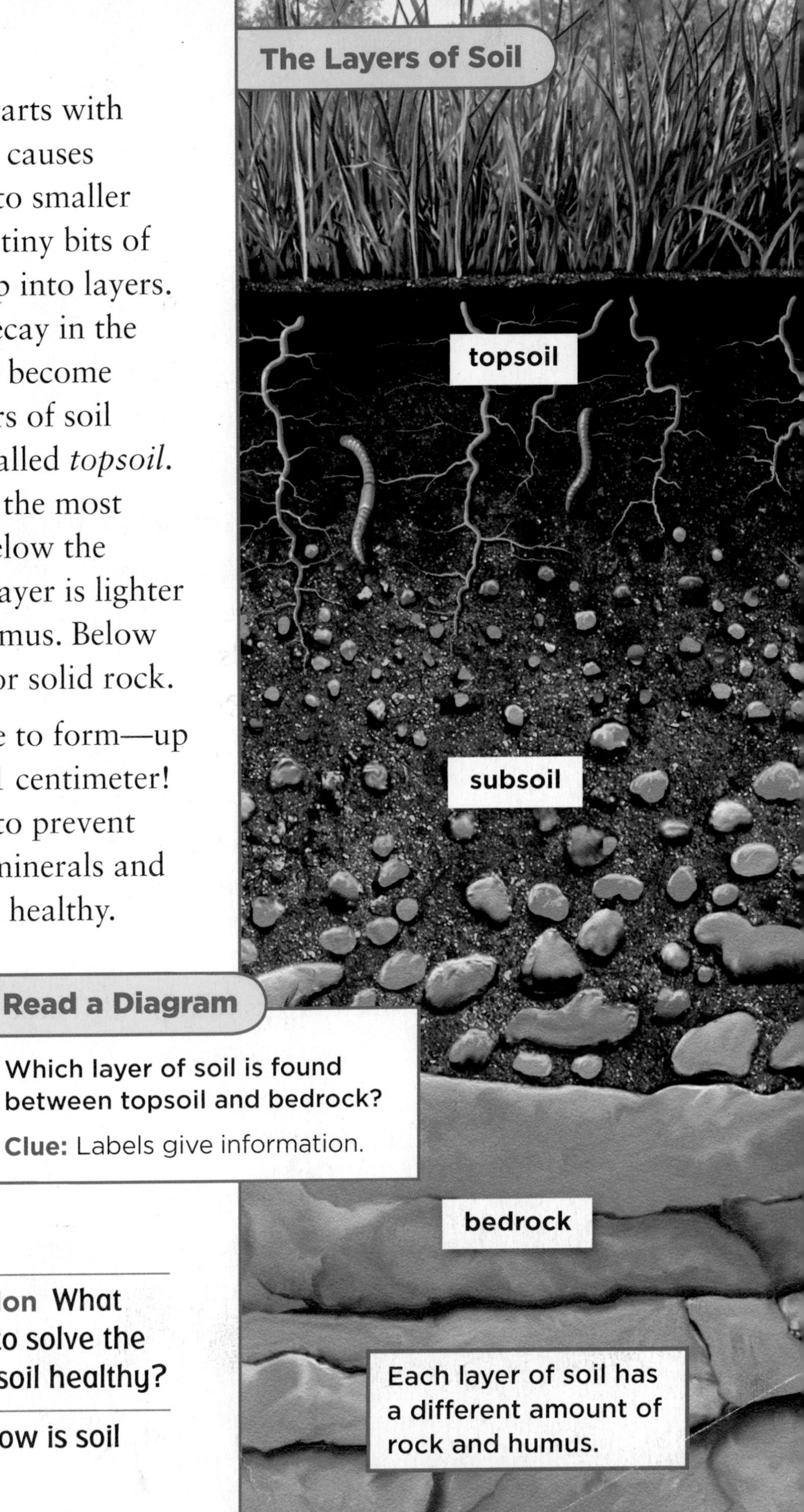

Each layer of soil has a different amount of rock and humus.

Read a Diagram

Which layer of soil is found between topsoil and bedrock?

Clue: Labels give information.

✓ Quick Check

Problem and Solution What do people do to try to solve the problem of keeping soil healthy?

Critical Thinking How is soil a habitat?

▲ This red soil is rich in iron.

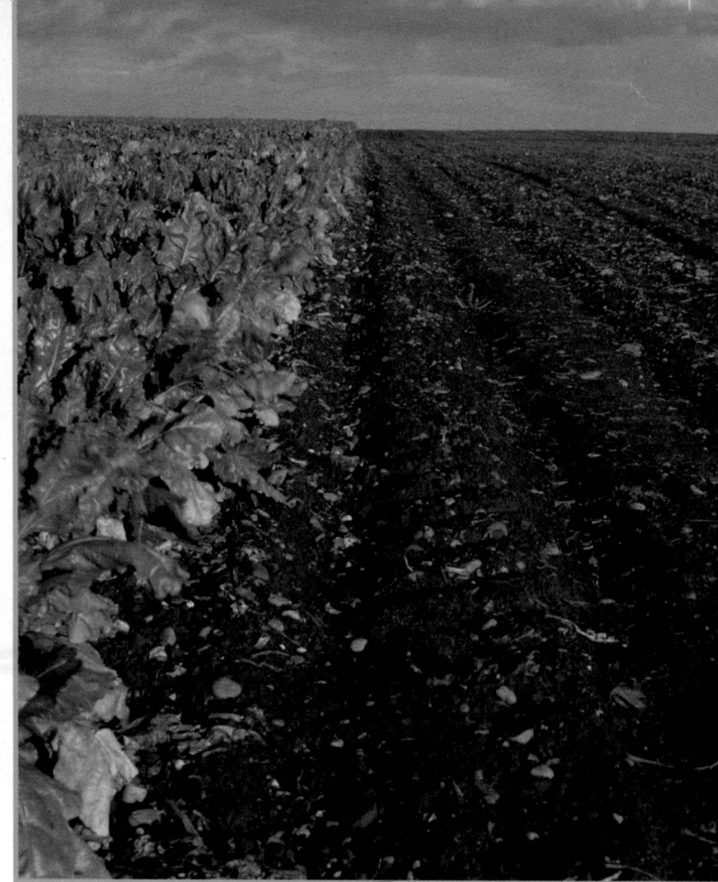

▲ This dark soil is rich in humus.

How are soils different?

Different soils are found in different places. They are made up of different rocks and minerals. They have different amounts of humus in them, too. Some soils have thick layers of topsoil. These soils are rich in humus. They are good for growing plants. Some soils have thin layers of topsoil. These soils have little humus. They are not as good for growing plants.

Soil Color

Like rocks, soils differ in color and texture. A soil's color depends on what is in it. Soil rich in humus looks dark brown or black. Soil with a lot of calcite (KAL•site) in it looks white. Soil with hematite (HEM•uh•tite) in it looks red. That is because hematite contains iron.

Soil Texture

Soil texture describes how big the pieces, or grains, of soil are. *Sandy soil* has a lot of small grains called sand. *Silty soil* has grains smaller than sand called silt. *Clay soil* has the smallest grains called clay. *Loam* is soil made up of a mixture of sand, silt, and clay.

Soil texture affects how much water soil can hold. Clay soil holds a lot of water. Sandy soil holds very little water. Many plants grow best in loam. It is neither too wet nor too dry.

Quick Lab

Classify Soils

1. **Observe** Look at the two soils in plastic bags. How are they alike? How are they different?
2. **Observe** Use a hand lens to look closely at each soil. Which soil has larger grains?
3. **Classify** Which soil is sandy soil? Which is clay soil? How do you know?

clay soil

sandy soil

loam

Quick Check

Problem and Solution What if plants could not grow well in your neighborhood? What might be the problem? How might you solve it?

Critical Thinking A cactus plant grows best in dry soil. Which soil would be best for a cactus?

Why is soil important?

Soil is a natural resource (NACH•uhr•uhl REE•sawrs). A **natural resource** is a material on Earth that is necessary or useful to people. Without soil, most plants could not grow. People and animals would not have food to eat. There would be no cotton to make clothes. There would be no wood to build houses or burn for heat. There would be fewer medicines.

It is important to keep soil healthy. It is also important to prevent soil erosion. We can farm in ways to help keep soil from eroding. We can keep soil healthy by keeping it clean. We can put nutrients into the soil for plants to use.

▲ The bark and leaves of the willow tree were once used to make aspirin.

 ***Quick Check***

Problem and Solution How can people keep soil healthy and prevent soil erosion?

Critical Thinking Are rocks and minerals natural resources? Why or why not?

Contour farming helps prevent soil erosion.

Lesson Review

Visual Summary

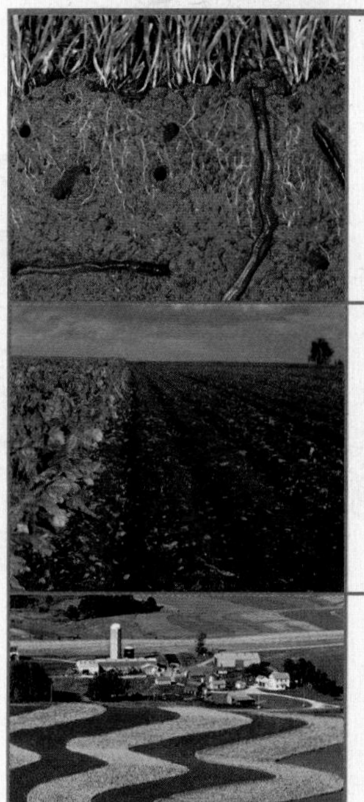

Soil is mostly made up of weathered rocks, minerals, and once-living things.

Soils have different colors and textures. They also hold different amounts of water.

Soil is a natural resource that is important to many living things.

Make a FOLDABLES™ Study Guide

Make a Trifold Book. Use it to summarize what you learned about soil.

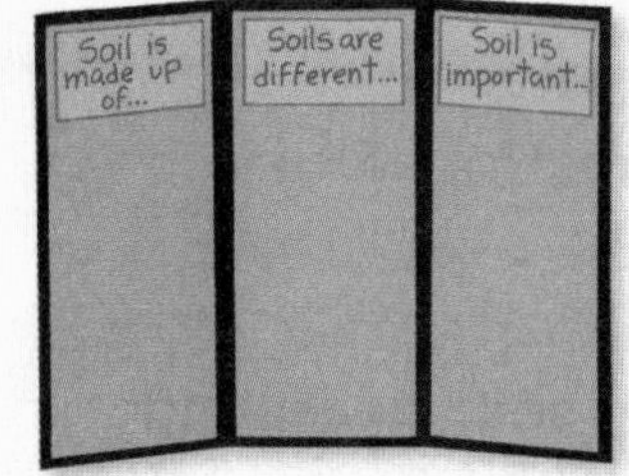

Think, Talk, and Write

1. **Main Idea** List some things that make up soil.
2. **Vocabulary** What is humus?
3. **Problem and Solution** What problems might occur if we do not protect soil?

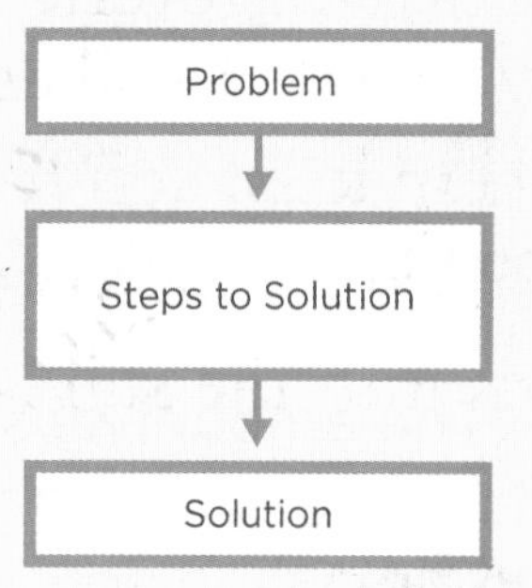

4. **Critical Thinking** Can soil form below Earth's surface? Explain your answer.
5. **Test Prep** **Which helps soil hold water?**
   - **A** humus
   - **B** air
   - **C** bedrock
   - **D** animals

Math Link

Solve a Problem
Suppose it takes 1,000 years for 1 centimeter of soil to form. How long would it take 5 centimeters of soil to form?

Health Link

Medicines from Plants
Research a medicine that people get from plants. If possible, find out what kind of soil the plant grows best in. Share your findings with the class.

LOG ON e-Review Summaries and quizzes online at www.macmillanmh.com

Focus on Skills

Inquiry Skill: Use Variables

Soils differ from place to place. They contain different amounts of humus and are made up of different kinds of rocks. Do all soils hold the same amount of water? To answer this question, you can **use variables** to test how water moves through different soils.

▶ Learn It

When you **use variables**, you identify things in an experiment that can be changed. Soil type is a variable, for example. The amount of soil you use in an experiment is also a variable. It is important that you change only one variable at a time when you experiment. You should keep all other variables the same. That way you can tell what caused the results.

▶ Try It

You will **use variables** to answer this question: Does sandy soil or potting soil hold more water?

Materials **pencil, 4 disposable cups, potting soil, measuring cup, water, sandy soil, watch or clock**

1. Use a pencil point to poke three tiny holes in the bottom of a cup.
2. Put 250 mL of potting soil into the cup. Pack the soil firmly.
3. Fill a measuring cup with 100 mL of water.

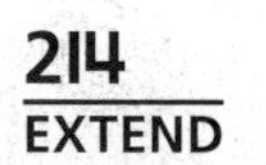

3-1.4. Predict the outcome of an investigation and compare the result with the prediction. **3-1.7.** Explain why similar investigations might produce different results.

4. Hold the cup of potting soil over an empty cup without holes. Slowly pour the water over the soil. Wait for two minutes. Write your observations in a table like the one shown.

5. Pour the water that drained out into the measuring cup. Record the volume in your table.

6. Repeat steps 1–5 using sandy soil in place of potting soil. Record the results.

7. Which soil held more water? How did changing the variable change the results?

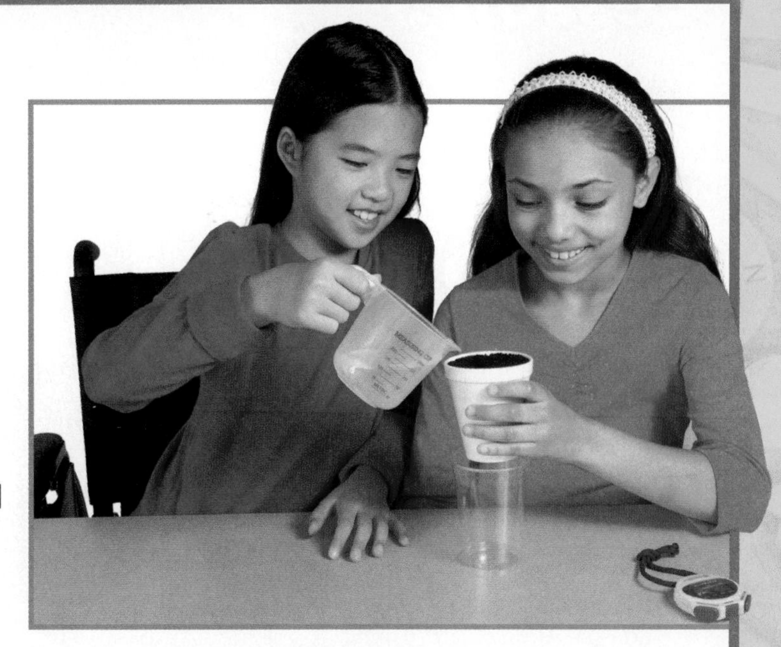

Variable	My Observations	Volume that Drained

▶ Apply It

Now **use variables** to experiment more. Choose one of the following variables to test. List the variable in a table and record the results of your experiment. Did changing the variable change the results? If so, how?

- Do not pack the potting soil firmly.
- Mix clay into the sandy soil.
- Mix larger rocks into the potting soil.
- Poke larger holes in the cups.

Lesson 3

Fossils and Fuels

Look and Wonder

This winged ant was trapped in amber millions of years ago. Now it is a fossil. It looks exactly as it did when it was alive. How do you think this fossil formed?

3-3.3. Recognize types of fossils (including molds, casts, and preserved parts of plants and animals). **3-3.7.** Exemplify Earth materials that are used as fuel, as a resource for building materials, and as a medium for growing plants.

Explore

Inquiry Activity

How do some fossils form?

Purpose

Find out how some living things of the past become fossils.

Procedure

1. **Make a Model** Hold a spoon over a paper towel. Squeeze a small amount of glue onto the spoon. Let the glue set for 10 minutes. This models sticky tree resin.
2. **Make a Model** Place a thin apple slice on top of the glue. This models an organism trapped in tree resin. Slowly add more glue until the apple slice is completely covered.
3. **Use Variables** Put the spoon on a paper towel. Place another apple slice next to the spoon.
4. **Observe** Look at the apple slices throughout the day. Record any changes you observe.

Draw Conclusions

5. **Interpret Data** Compare the two apple slices. What differences do you notice?
6. **Infer** What caused any differences you observed?
7. **Infer** How do some fossils form?

Explore More

Experiment Could an organism become a fossil in ice? Make a plan to find out.

Materials

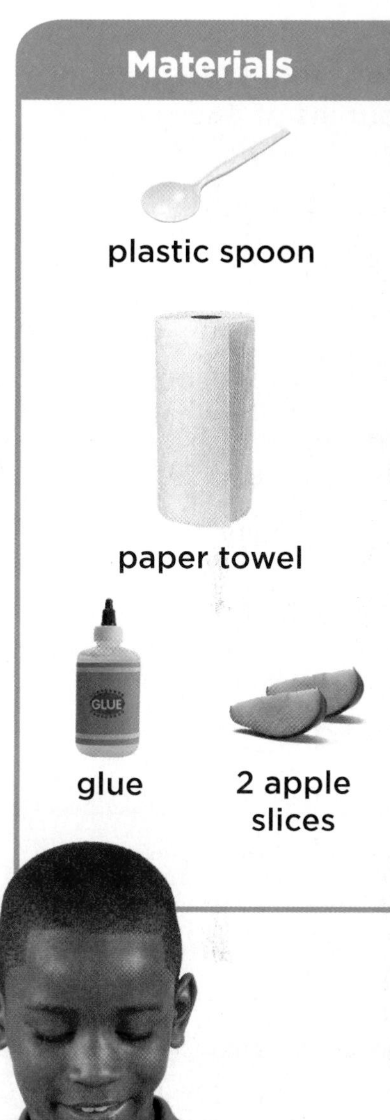

Step 2

3-I.8. Use appropriate safety procedures when conducting investigations.

These stone models of bones were once real dinosaur bones.

Read and Learn

Main Idea 3-3.3 3-3.7

Fossil fuels come from living things of long ago. They are nonrenewable sources of energy.

Vocabulary

fossil, p. 218

fuel, p. 220

renewable resource, p. 221

nonrenewable resource, p. 221

solar energy, p. 222

at www.macmillanmh.com

Reading Skill

Draw Conclusions

Text Clues	Conclusions

How are fossils formed?

A **fossil** (FOS•uhl) is the trace or remains of something that lived long ago. Shells, bones, skin, leaves, and footprints can become fossils.

Imprints

Sometimes living things leave marks, or *imprints*, in materials like mud. In time the materials may harden into rock. The imprints are saved in the rock.

Stony Models

Some fossils are actual organisms trapped in amber, tar, or ice. Others look like actual plant or animal remains but are not. They are only stony models in sedimentary rock.

◀ This imprint of a dinosaur's foot was left in mud. The mud turned to solid rock.

FACT People did not live when dinosaurs did.

Sometimes, sediment buries an organism that has died. The organism becomes a fossil as the sediment becomes rock. Slowly, water with minerals seeps into the hard parts of the organism. Minerals replace the hard parts of the organism. What is left is a stony model.

Molds and Casts

Shells often leave fossils called molds. A *mold* is an empty space in rock where something once was. A mold forms after a shell is buried in sand or mud. As water seeps in, it breaks down the shell. A shell-shaped space is left. Minerals may seep into this space and harden. They form a copy of the mold's shape called a *cast*.

Quick Check

Draw Conclusions What kinds of fossils show most what actual organisms were like?

Critical Thinking What can we learn from fossils?

Quick Lab

Model Imprints

1. Break a small chunk of clay into two pieces. Roll each piece to form a ball.
2. **Make a Model** Take one clay ball. Press the front of your thumb into it. Take the other clay ball. Press the back of your thumb into it.

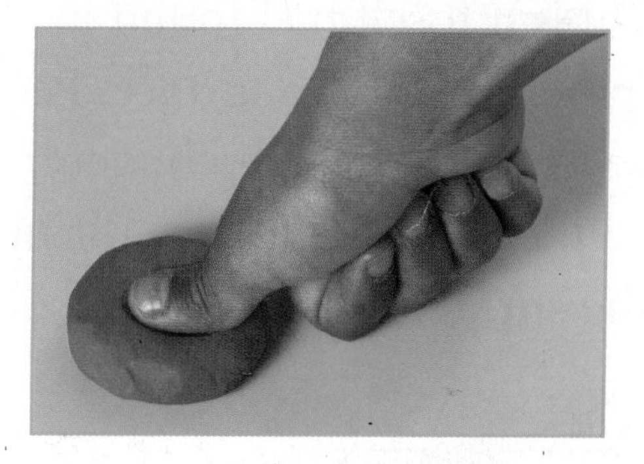

3. **Communicate** Switch clay balls with someone. How are the imprints like yours? How are they different?
4. **Infer** What can we learn by comparing fossil imprints?

The fossil on the right is the mold. The fossil on the left is the cast. ▶

What are fossil fuels?

The energy to heat homes and run cars and airplanes comes from fuels. A **fuel** is a material that is burned for its energy. Coal, oil, and natural gas are fossil fuels. A *fossil fuel* is a fuel that forms from the remains of ancient plants and animals. Fossil fuels can be used to make electricity.

Oil is a fossil fuel found in rocks deep below Earth's surface. People use huge drills to dig deep underground for oil. Pumps are used to bring oil to the surface.

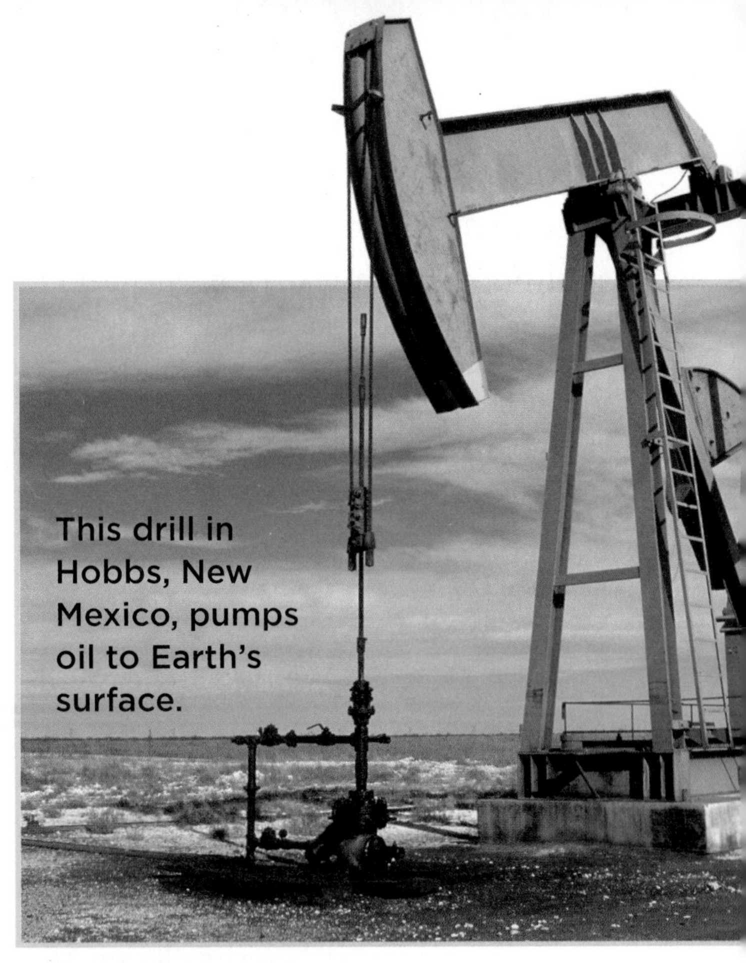

This drill in Hobbs, New Mexico, pumps oil to Earth's surface.

How Coal Forms

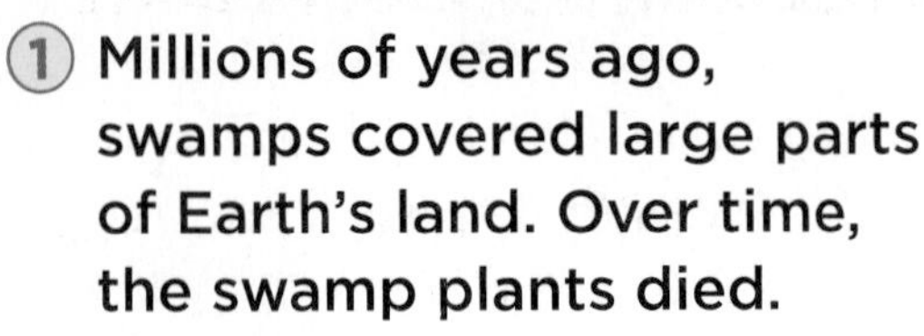

① Millions of years ago, swamps covered large parts of Earth's land. Over time, the swamp plants died.

② Layers of decayed plants formed a fuel called ***peat.*** Then the peat was buried under sediment.

Fossil fuels are natural resources. Plants, animals, water, and air are, too. Plants, animals, water, and air can be replaced. New plants are grown. New animals are born or hatched. Rain and snow bring more water. Plants put oxygen back into the air. Plants, animals, water, and air are renewable resources (ri•NEW•uh•buhl REE•sawr•ses). A **renewable resource** is a resource that can be replaced or used again and again.

Fossil fuels, however, are nonrenewable (non•ri•NEW•uh•buhl). A **nonrenewable resource** is a resource that cannot be replaced or reused easily. Fossil fuels take millions of years to form. Once they are used up, they are gone forever.

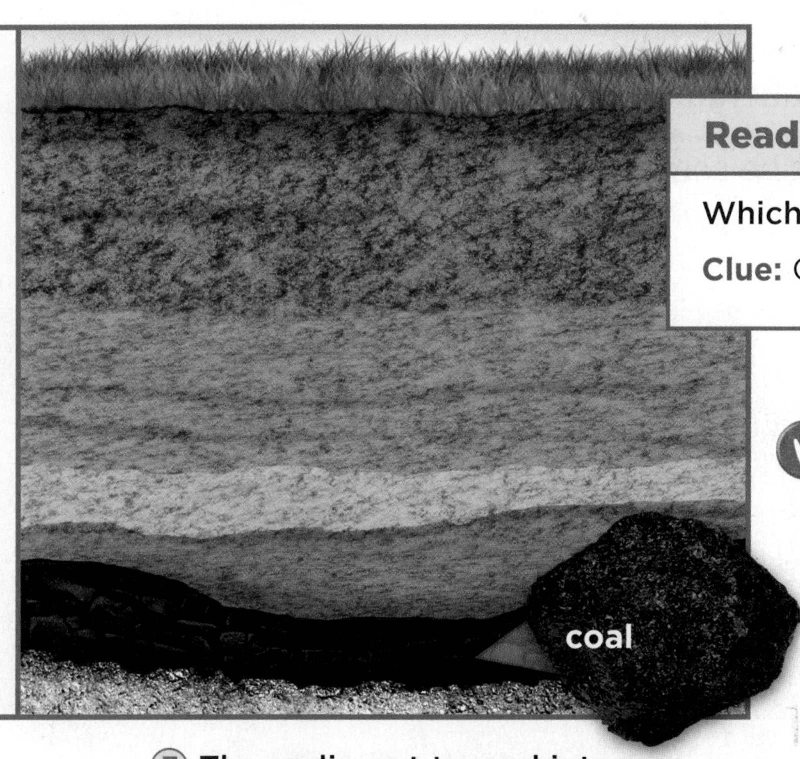

③ The sediment turned into sedimentary rock. Slowly the peat changed into the sedimentary rock ***coal***.

Read a Diagram

Which fuel forms before coal forms?

Clue: Captions give information.

Quick Check

Draw Conclusions Why should we be careful not to use up fossil fuels?

Critical Thinking What are other nonrenewable resources?

What are some other sources of energy?

Fossil fuels are just one source of energy. A *source* is where something comes from. Fossil fuels are nonrenewable. They can be used up. For this reason, we need to use renewable sources of energy.

Solar energy is a renewable source of energy. **Solar energy** is energy from the Sun. Moving water and wind are also renewable sources of energy. Underground heat is, too. Solar energy, moving water, wind, and underground heat can all be used to make electricity.

▲ Someday you may drive a car powered by solar energy.

Quick Check

Draw Conclusions Why are the Sun, wind, and moving water good sources of energy to use?

Critical Thinking Where might be some good places to use wind for making electricity?

Underground heat is used to make electricity in Iceland.

Lesson Review

Visual Summary

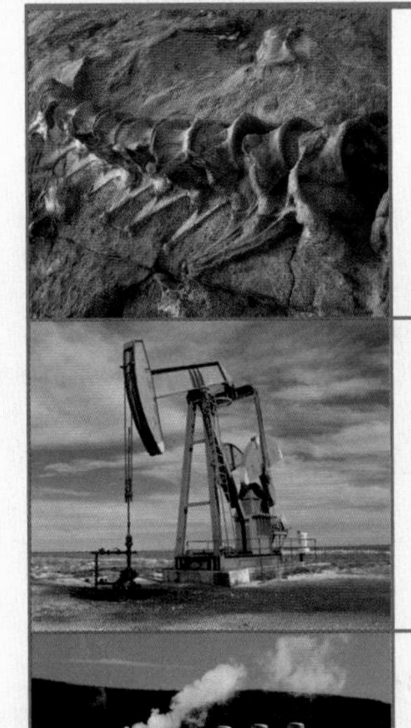

There are different **kinds of fossils**. Each forms in a different way.

Fossil fuels are nonrenewable sources of energy.

The Sun, wind, and moving water are some **renewable sources of energy**.

Make a FOLDABLES™ Study Guide

Make a Trifold Book. Use it to summarize what you learned about fossils and fuels.

Think, Talk, and Write

1. **Main Idea** What sources of energy do we use?

2. **Vocabulary** What is a fossil? Give two examples.

3. **Draw Conclusions** Is it possible to use up fossil fuels? Explain.

Text Clues	Conclusions

4. **Critical Thinking** How do you use fossil fuels?

5. **Test Prep** **Which one of the following is a nonrenewable resource?**
   A water
   B air
   C plants
   D coal

Math Link

Write a Number Sentence
Ultrasaurus was about 30 meters long. Triceratops was about 8 meters long. How much longer was Ultrasaurus than Triceratops? Write the number sentence that shows how you solved the problem.

Social Studies Link

Your State Fossil
Do research about your state fossil. Tell how the fossil formed. What was the organism like? Write this information in a report.

LOG ON e-Review Summaries and quizzes online at www.macmillanmh.com

Reading in Science

Turning the Power On

People use a lot of energy. We need it to power our cars, to heat our homes, and to run many of the machines we use each day. The energy sources we use most—coal and oil—are nonrenewable resources. They will be used up one day and will be gone forever. Other energy sources are renewable. The time line shows how people have developed renewable sources of energy.

Hydropower Energy The first plant in the U.S. opened in Wisconsin. River current was used to turn a turbine to produce electricity.

1890

Wind Energy Wind turbines were invented in Denmark. They used the energy of the wind to produce electricity.

1904

Geothermal Energy Heat energy from geysers was used in Italy. Steam from this hot water that shoots up from the ground was used to turn turbines to produce electricity.

3-3.7. Exemplify Earth materials that are used as fuel, as a resource for building materials, and as a medium for growing plants.

Renewable energy sources can be replaced in a short time. The renewable energy sources used most often are hydropower (water), wind, geothermal, solar, and biomass. No matter what energy source you use, it is important to conserve energy.

Draw Conclusions

When you draw conclusions,

- you explain the answer to a question
- you use what you already know
- you look for clues in the article

1985

Biomass Energy This energy source was first used in California. Materials such as dead trees, leftover crops, and animal waste were burned to produce heat, steam, and electricity.

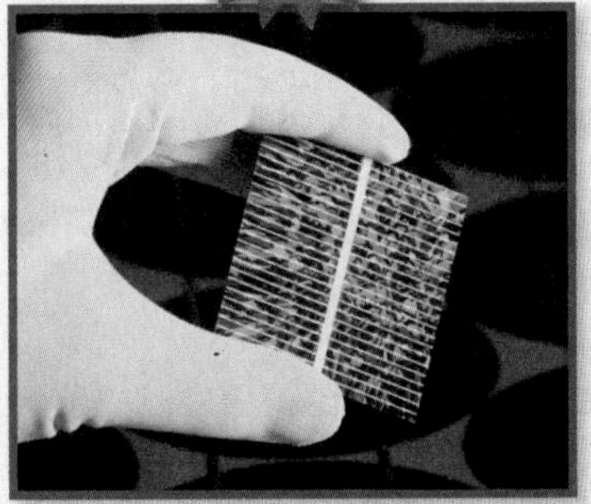

Solar Energy Russell Ohl invented a solar cell. It used light from the Sun to produce electricity.

Write About It

Draw Conclusions Why is it important for people to use renewable energy sources? Use what you already know and what you read in the article to draw a conclusion.

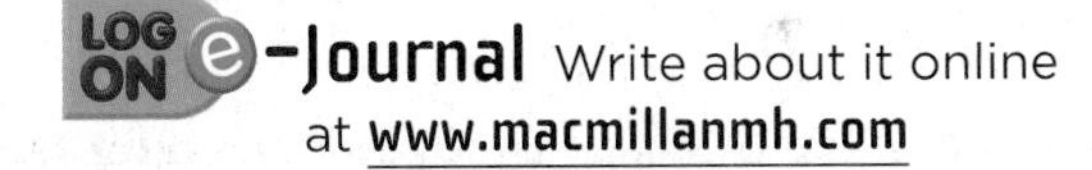

Write about it online at www.macmillanmh.com

CHAPTER 4 Review

Visual Summary

Lesson 1 Rocks are made of minerals. Rocks are classified as igneous, sedimentary, or metamorphic.

Lesson 2 Soil is made up of weathered rocks, minerals, and once-living things. Many living things need soil to survive.

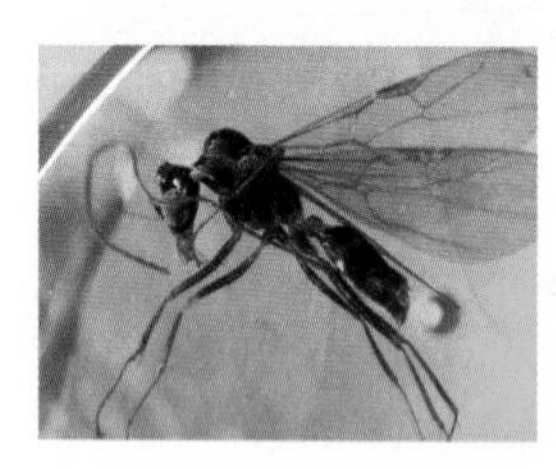

Lesson 3 Fossil fuels come from living things of long ago. They are nonrenewable sources of energy.

Make a FOLDABLES™ Study Guide

Glue your lesson study guides to a piece of paper as shown. Use your study guide to review what you have learned in this chapter.

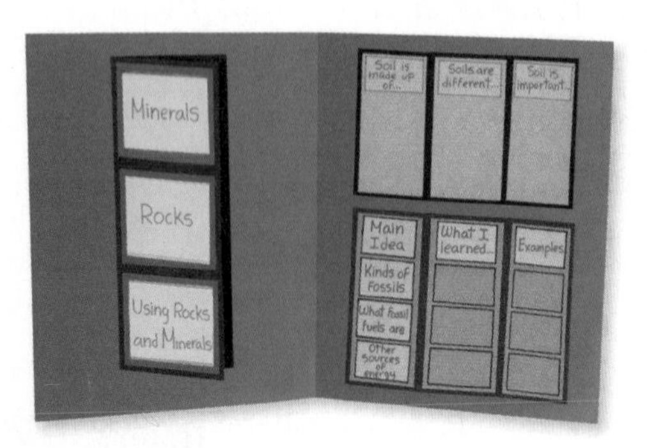

Vocabulary

Fill each blank with the best term from the list.

fossil, p. 218

humus, p. 208

igneous rock, p. 199

metamorphic rock, p. 201

minerals, p. 194

natural resource, p. 212

renewable resource, p. 221

sediment, p. 200

solar energy, p. 222

1. A rock that is changed by heating and squeezing is a(n) ________.
3-3.1

2. Imprints are one type of ________.
3-3.3

3. Rocks are made up of one or more ________.
3-3.2

4. Energy from the Sun is called ________.
3-3.7

5. Soil is an example of a(n) ________.
3-3.7

6. A fuel that can be replaced easily is a(n) ________.
3-3.7

7. Tiny bits of weathered rock or once-living animals or plants make up ________.
3-3.8

8. The decayed plants and animals in soil are known as ________.
3-3.1

9. Rock that forms when melted rock cools and hardens is ________.
3-3.1

LOG ON e-Review Summaries and quizzes online at www.macmillanmh.com

Skills and Concepts

Answer each of the following in complete sentences.

10. Draw Conclusions Scientists are developing fuels from plants such as corn. What kind of fuels would they be—renewable or nonrenewable? Explain.
3-3.7

11. Descriptive Writing Think of a sedimentary rock you learned about. Describe it.
3-3.1

12. Use Variables You want to find the best materials for filtering dirty water. You make one filter from paper and another from rocks and sand. You observe as you pour dirty water through them. Which variables changed? Which were the same?
3-1.7

13. Critical Thinking What can fossils tell us about early environments on Earth?
3-3.4

14. Which layer of soil has the most humus in it? Why?
3-3.1

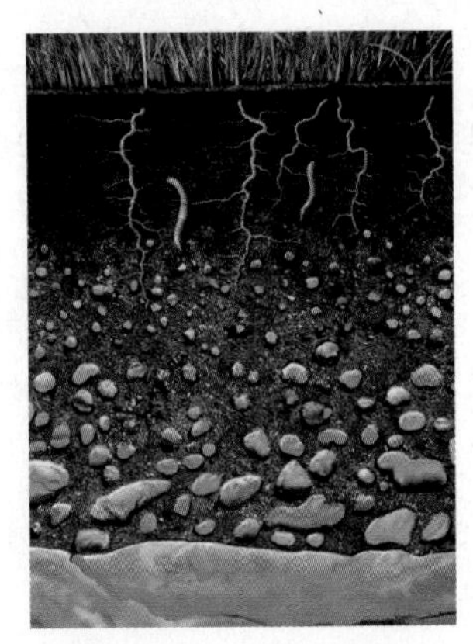

The Big Idea

15. What things used by people come from Earth?
3-3.7

Performance Assessment

Make a Poster

- Everyone can make natural resources last longer if they conserve. To conserve is to use resources wisely. Make a poster encouraging conservation of at least three different kinds of natural resources.
- Explain how people use each natural resource. Why do they need it?
- Suggest ways people can conserve each of these resources.

South Carolina Activity

Did you know that the "gold rush" started in the Carolinas? Many other natural resources are found in South Carolina besides gold. Find a map showing mines in South Carolina.

What other kinds of mines are in South Carolina? Write a report that summarizes your findings.

South Carolina Standards Practice

1 What kind of rock forms when sand is pressed together in layers?

A metamorphic rock

B igneous rock

C sedimentary rock

D weathered rock

3-3.1

2 This drawing shows a dinosaur footprint in rock.

Which type of fossil is the dinosaur footprint?

F cast

G mold

H model

I imprint

3-1.6

3 Which is an example of a fossil fuel?

A oil

B wind

C electricity

D moving water

3-3.7

4 Coal formed from swamp plants that lived millions of years ago. Which is the **best** explanation of how the plants turned into coal?

F The plants formed fossils, and the fossils changed into coal.

G The plants formed soil, and the soil changed into coal.

H The plants formed peat, and the peat changed into coal.

I The plants formed oil, and the oil changed into coal.

3-1.2

5 Soils differ in color depending on what they are made of. Black soils are rich in

A bedrock.

B humus.

C subsoil.

D sand.

3-3.1

6 **Which kind of rock forms when magma cools and hardens?**

F metamorphic rock

G igneous rock

H sedimentary rock

I weathered rock

3-3.1

7 **Which mineral is softest?**

Mohs' Hardness Scale	
Mineral	**Hardness**
gypsum	2
calcite	3
quartz	7
diamond	10

A gypsum

B calcite

C quartz

D diamond

3-1.6

8 **Kyla wants to know the texture of the soil in her garden. What should she do?**

F observe the color of the soil

G identify the minerals in the soil

H observe the size of the soil pieces

I measure how deep the soil is

3-1.3

9 **Limestone is used to make**

A telephone wires.

B diamonds.

C cement.

D coal.

3-3.7

10 **Which properties are most helpful for identifying minerals?**

F size and ability to float

G luster and streak

H weight and color

I crystal shape and width

3-3.2

CHAPTER 5

Earth Changes

The Big Idea What can cause Earth's features to change?

 Grand Canyon National Park, Arizona

Key Vocabulary

ocean
a large body of salt water (p. 234)

continent
a great area of land (p. 235)

earthquake
a sudden movement of rocks that make up Earth's crust (p. 246)

volcano
a mountain that builds up around an opening in Earth's crust (p. 248)

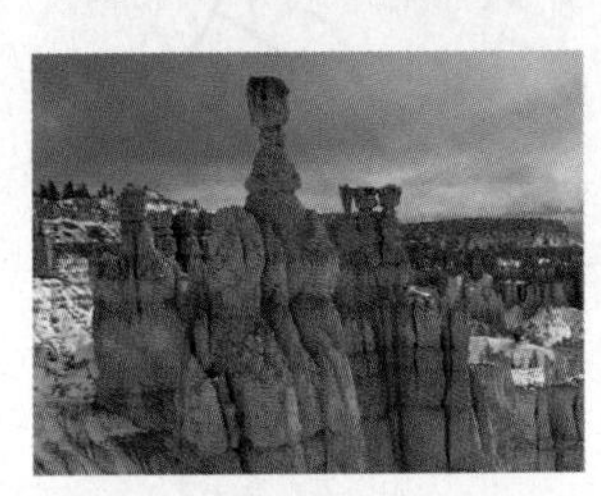

weathering
the breaking down of rocks into smaller pieces (p. 256)

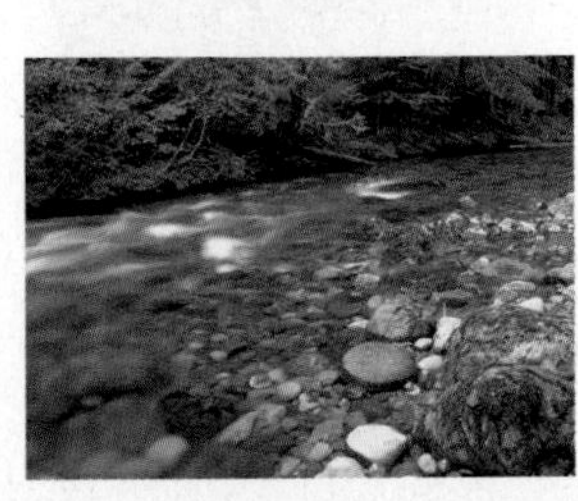

erosion
the movement of weathered rock (p. 258)

More Vocabulary

landform, p. 236

crust, p. 240

mantle, p. 240

core, p. 240

magma, p. 248

lava, p. 248

landslide, p. 250

flood, p. 250

glacier, p. 258

deposition, p. 258

Lesson 1

Earth's Features

Boardman State Park, along the Oregon coast

Look and Wonder

Both land and water cover Earth's surface. Which one covers more of Earth?

3-3.5. Illustrate Earth's saltwater and freshwater features. 3-3.6. Illustrate Earth's land features by using models, pictures, diagrams, and maps.

Explore

Inquiry Activity

Does land or water cover more of Earth's surface?

Make a Prediction

Do you think that there is more land or more water on Earth's surface? Write your prediction.

Test Your Prediction

1. Make a table like the one shown for 10 spins.
2. **Experiment** Slowly spin a globe. Do not look at it. Touch your finger to the globe to stop it.
3. **Observe** Did your finger stop on land or water? Record the information on the chart.
4. Repeat steps 2 and 3 nine more times.
5. **Use Numbers** How many times did you touch water? How many times did you touch land?

Draw Conclusions

6. **Infer** Is there more land or more water on Earth? How do your results compare with the results of others?

Explore More

Experiment Which covers more of Earth, rivers or oceans? Make a plan to find out.

Materials

globe

Step 1

Spin	Land	Water
1		
2		
3		
4		

3-I.4. Predict the outcome of a simple investigation and compare the result with the prediction.

Read and Learn

Main Idea 3-3.5 3-3.6

Earth's surface has many land and water features.

Vocabulary

ocean, p. 234

continent, p. 235

landform, p. 236

crust, p. 240

mantle, p. 240

core, p. 240

at www.macmillanmh.com

Reading Skill

Main Idea and Details

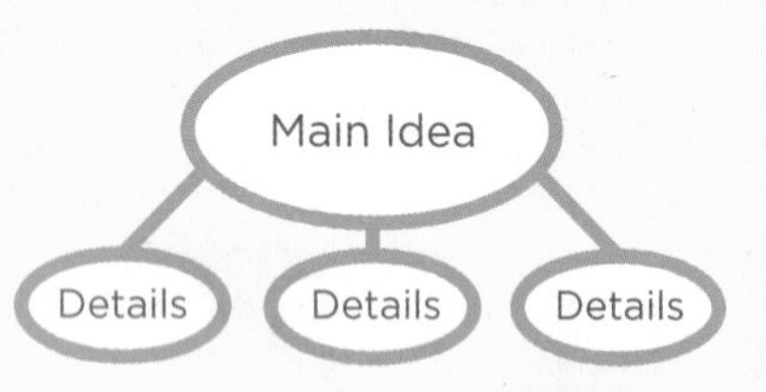

Technology

Explore Earth's features with the Secret Agents.

What covers Earth's surface?

If you could see Earth from space, it would look mostly blue. That is because almost three fourths of Earth is covered by water. Most of this water is in oceans (OH•shuhnz). **Oceans** are large bodies of salt water.

Rivers, streams, glaciers, and ponds are some other water features on Earth. These water features are made up of fresh water. *Fresh water* is water that is not salty. Lakes are another water feature. Most lakes are made up of fresh water. Some are made up of salt water.

Oceans and Continents

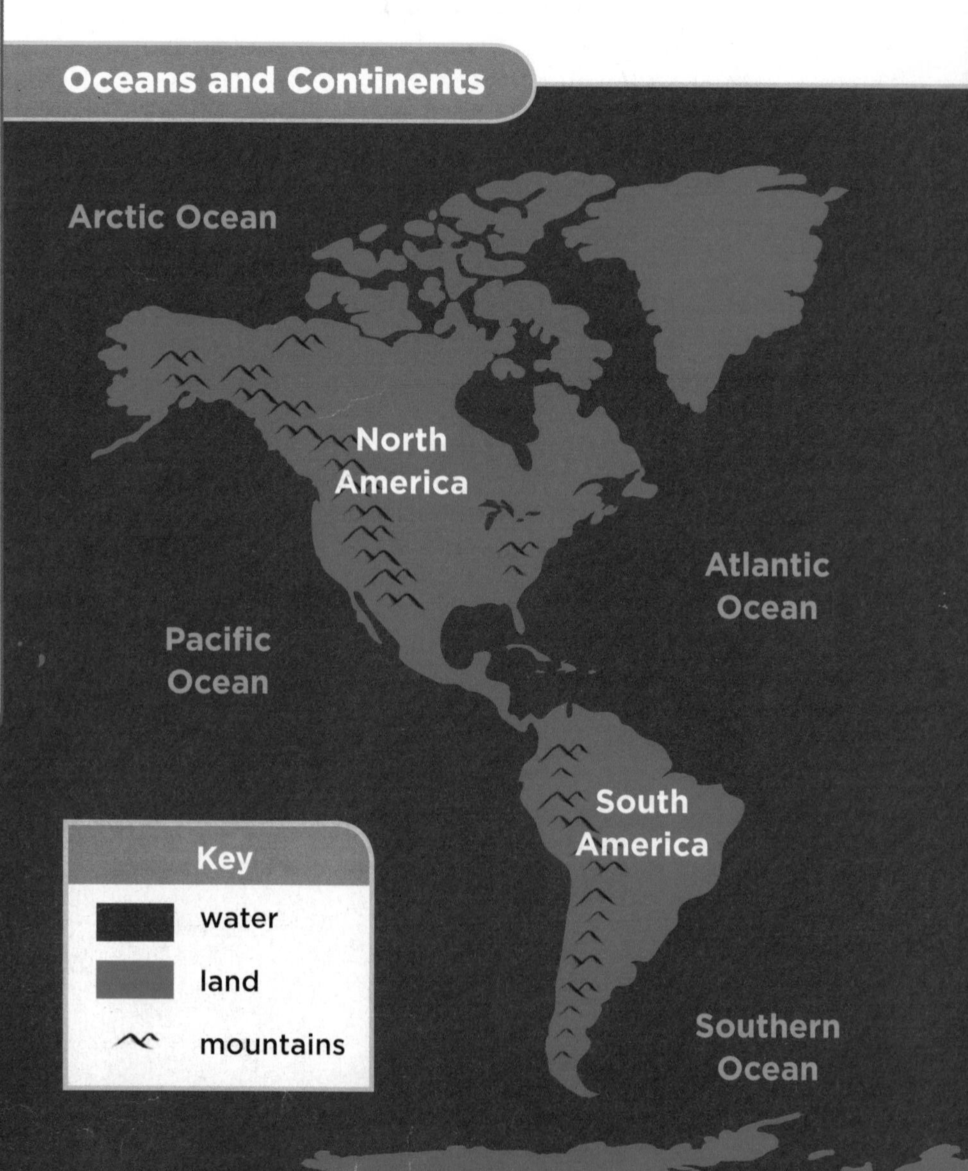

Earth also has seven great areas of land called **continents** (KON•tuh•nuhnts). North America is the continent you live on.

A map can show Earth's land and water features. To read a map, look at its key. A *key* shows what a map's colors and shapes mean. Can you find North America on the map below?

Quick Check

Main Idea and Details What covers Earth's surface?

Critical Thinking About how much of Earth is covered by land?

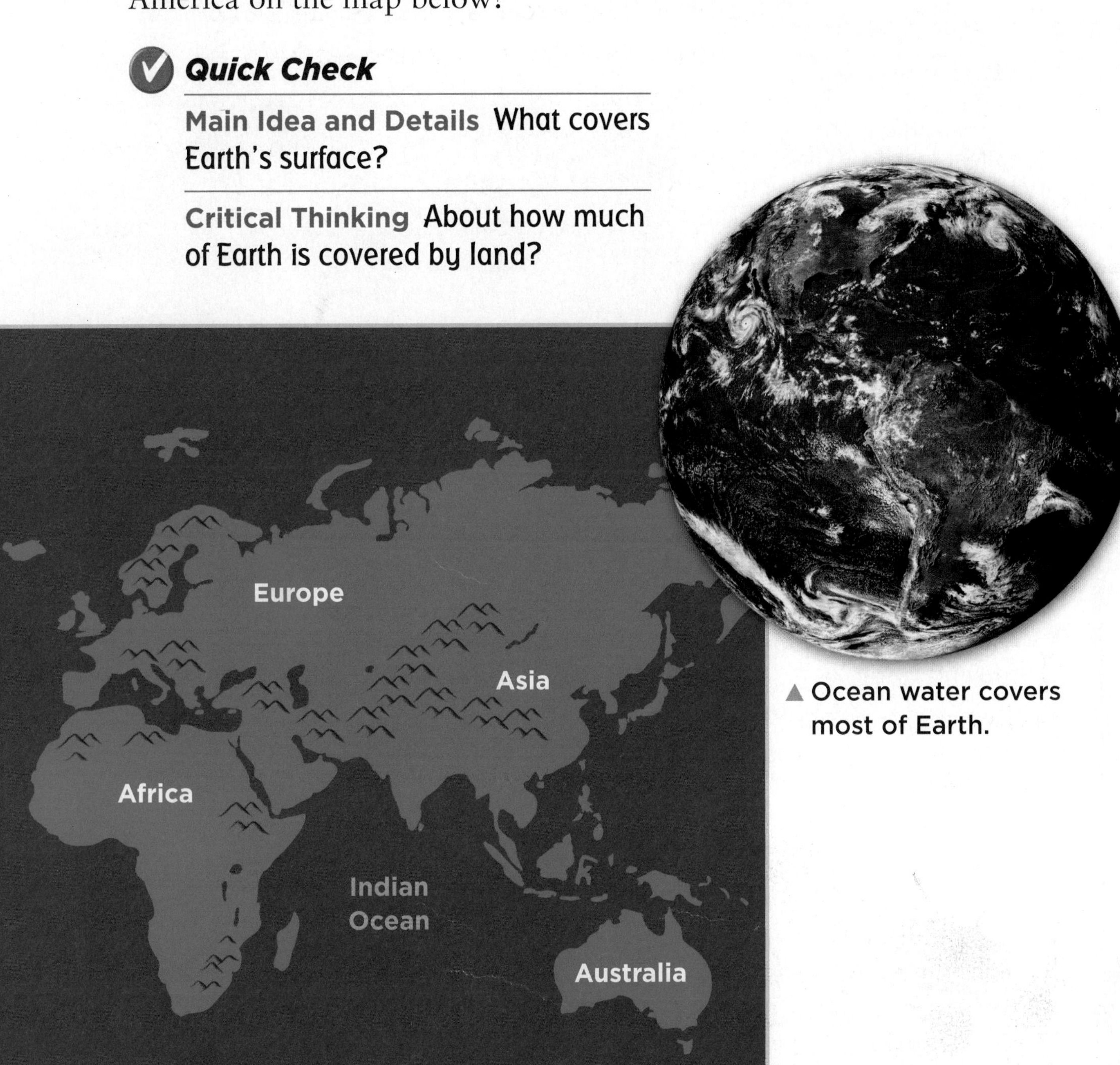

▲ Ocean water covers most of Earth.

FACT The oceans are really one big ocean.

What are some of Earth's land and water features?

There are many land and water features on Earth. Land features are called **landforms** (LAND•fawrmz). This diagram shows a few of Earth's features.

Features of Earth

1. A *mountain* is the tallest landform. It often has steep sides and a pointed top.
2. A *valley* is the low land between hills or mountains.
3. A *canyon* is a deep valley with steep sides. Rivers often flow through them.
4. A *plain* is land that is wide and flat.
5. A *lake* is water that is surrounded by land.
6. A *river* is a large body of moving water.
7. A *plateau* (pla•TOH) is land with steep sides and a flat top. It is higher than the land around it.
8. A *coast* is land that borders the ocean.
9. A *peninsula* is land surrounded by water on three sides.
10. An *island* is land with water all around it.

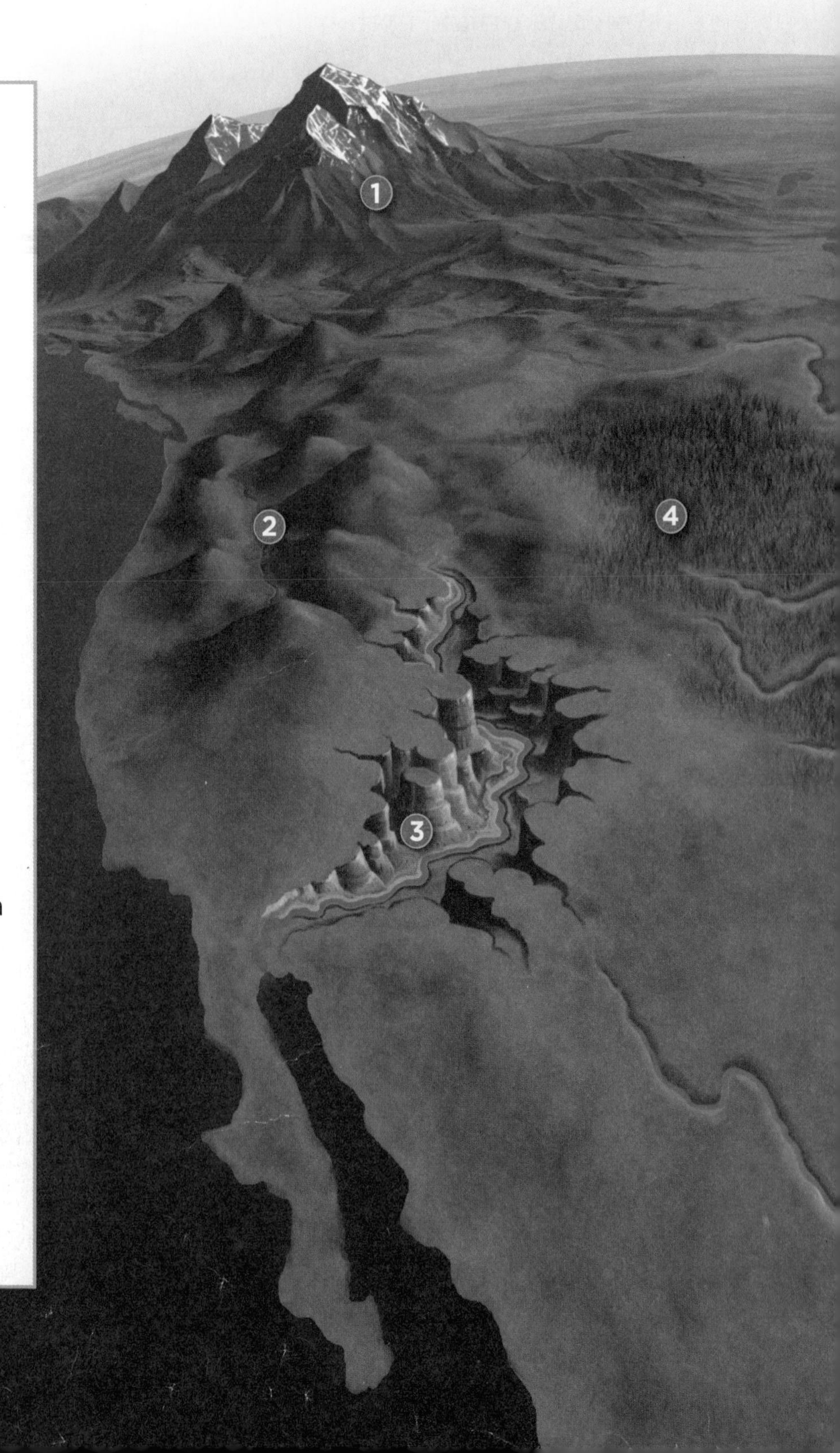

Main Idea and Details What are landforms?

Critical Thinking How could you tell a mountain from a plain?

Quick Lab

Your State's Features

1. **Make a Model** Draw a map of your state. Decide how to show your state's land and water features. Then make a key and complete the map.

2. **Observe** Where is your town or city located? Draw a large dot there. Which landforms and water features are found in your town or city? How do these features compare with those found in other parts of your state?

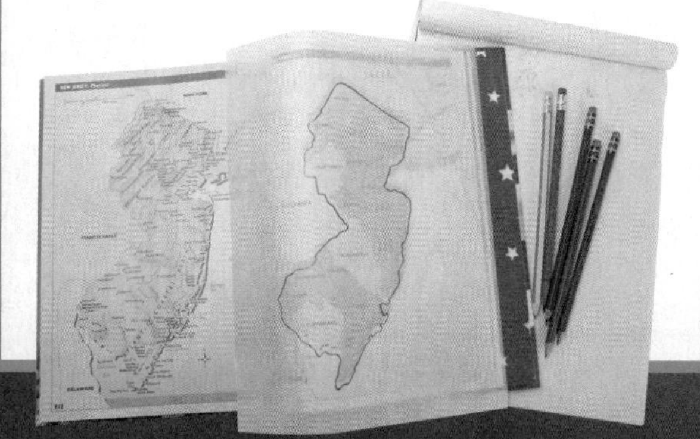

What land features are in the oceans?

Did you know that there is land below the ocean? The land below the ocean is called the *ocean floor*. If you could travel there, you would find mountains, valleys, and canyons. You would even see plains.

The ocean floor is a continuation of the continents. The ocean floor begins at a coast where dry land borders the water. Here you find a continental shelf. A *continental shelf* is like a huge plateau. It lies under the ocean at the edge of a continent. About 80 kilometers (50 miles) away from the coast, the continental shelf slopes down steeply.

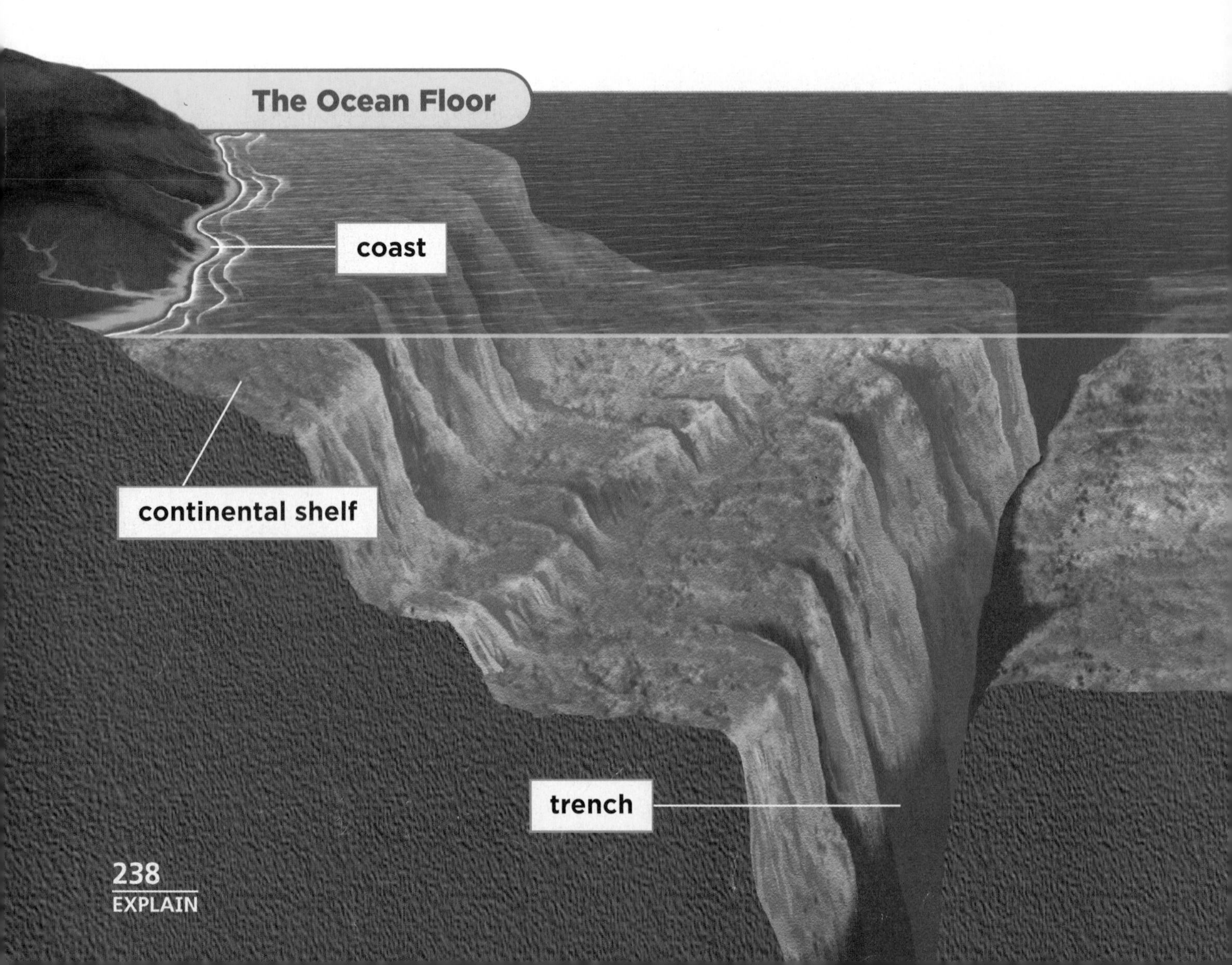

An abyssal plain (uh•BIS•uhl PLAYN) begins a little farther out. An *abyssal plain* is wide and flat. It stretches thousands of kilometers across the ocean.

A trench is another feature you might recognize. A *trench* is a canyon on the ocean floor. Trenches are the deepest parts of the ocean floor. The deepest trench is the Mariana Trench in the Pacific Ocean. It is almost 11 kilometers (7 miles) deep.

Quick Check

Main Idea and Details How is the ocean floor like the land of the continents?

Critical Thinking What do you think you would find on the abyssal plain? Hint: Think about what covers a river's bottom.

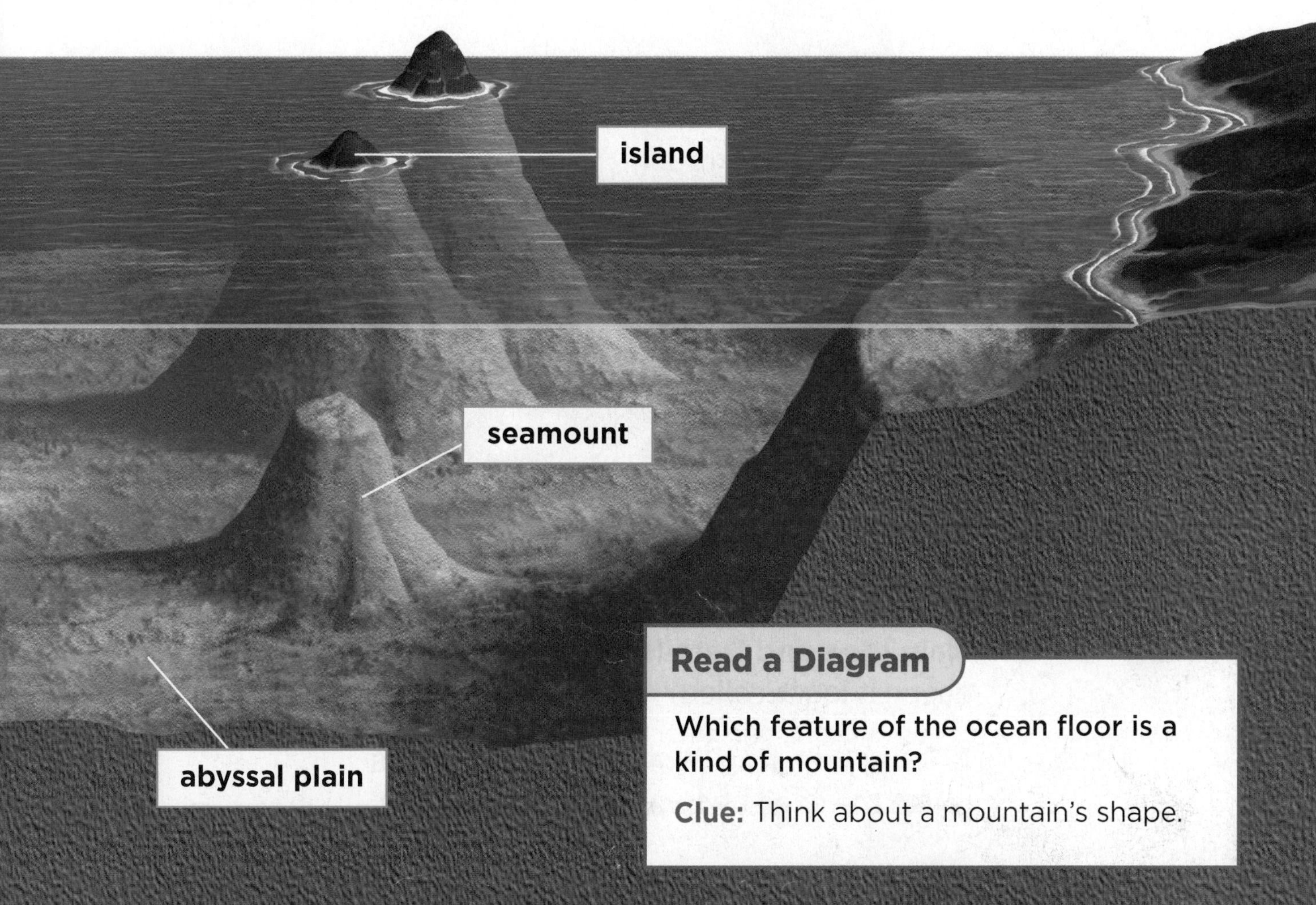

Read a Diagram

Which feature of the ocean floor is a kind of mountain?

Clue: Think about a mountain's shape.

What are the layers of Earth?

Have you ever eaten a hard-boiled egg? If so, you know that an egg has several layers. It has a thin shell, a white part, and a yolk.

Like an egg, Earth has several layers. The continents and ocean floor make up Earth's outermost layer, called the **crust**. The crust is Earth's thinnest and coolest layer.

The layer below the crust is the **mantle**. Part of the mantle is solid rock. Part is nearly melted rock that is soft and flows. It is a lot like putty.

At the center of Earth is the core. The **core** is the deepest and hottest layer of Earth. The *outer core* is melted rock. The *inner core* is solid rock.

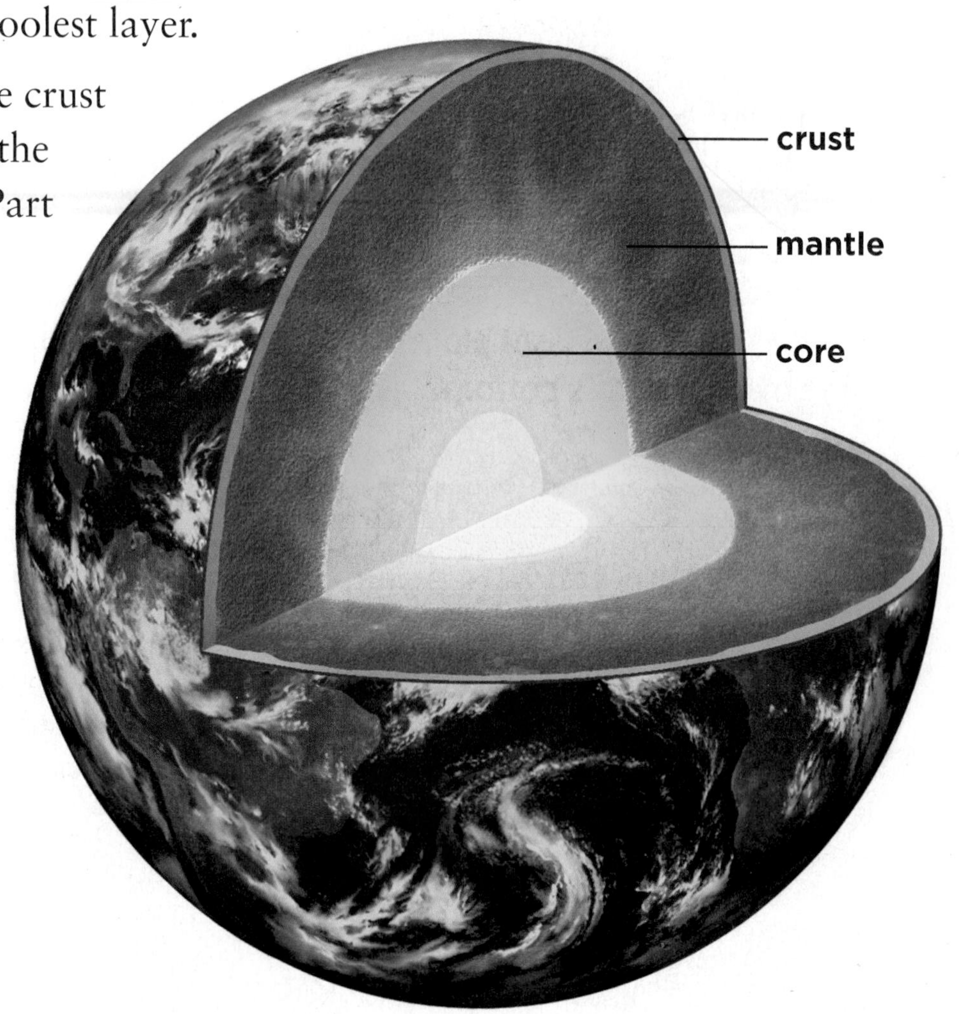

Quick Check

Main Idea and Details What is Earth's deepest layer called?

Critical Thinking Which of Earth's layers is like the shell of an egg? Why?

Lesson Review

Visual Summary

Earth has many **land features** and **water features**. Most of Earth is covered by water.

The ocean floor has features similar to Earth's land features.

Earth is made up of three main **layers**—the crust, the mantle, and the core.

Make a FOLDABLES™ Study Guide

Make a Layered-Look Book. Use it to summarize what you learned about Earth's features.

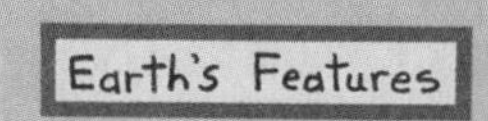

Think, Talk, and Write

1. **Main Idea** What do you find on Earth's surface?

2. **Vocabulary** Which landform is a deep, narrow valley with steep sides and a river flowing through it?

3. **Main Idea and Details** What are the layers of Earth?

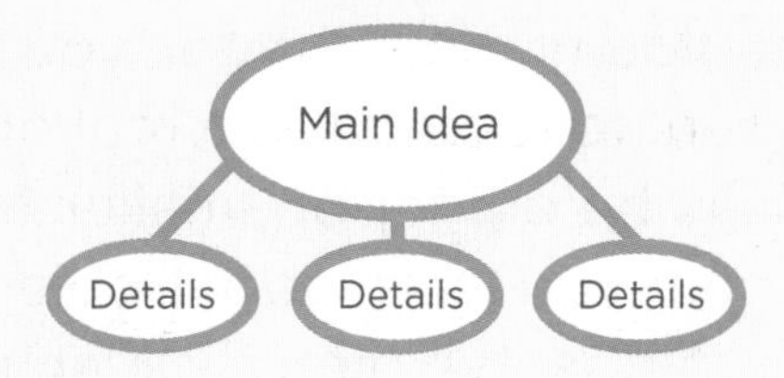

4. **Critical Thinking** Where would you be if you were at the deepest place on Earth's crust?

5. **Test Prep** **All of the following are landforms EXCEPT**

   A an island.
   B a canyon.
   C a plain.
   D a river.

Math Link

Compare Numbers
Here are the lengths of some coastlines in miles. Write the states in order from shortest coastline to longest coastline.

Oregon: 296
Georgia: 100
New Jersey: 130
South Carolina: 187
New York: 127
Maryland: 31

Social Studies Link

Do Research
Some people use stories, called *myths*, to explain how mountains formed. Research a myth that tells how mountains formed. Write a report about the myth.

LOG ON e-Review Summaries and quizzes online at www.macmillanmh.com

Focus on Skills

Inquiry Skill: Make a Model

You just learned about many landforms. Some of them are found on land. Some lie under the ocean. In some places a limestone cave forms below the ground. It forms when water seeps into the ground and changes rock. This can take millions of years. You can **make a model** to show a cave.

▶ Learn It

When you **make a model**, you build something to represent, or stand for, a real object or event. A model may be bigger or smaller than the real thing. Models help you learn about objects or events that are hard to observe directly. Maps and globes are two examples of models.

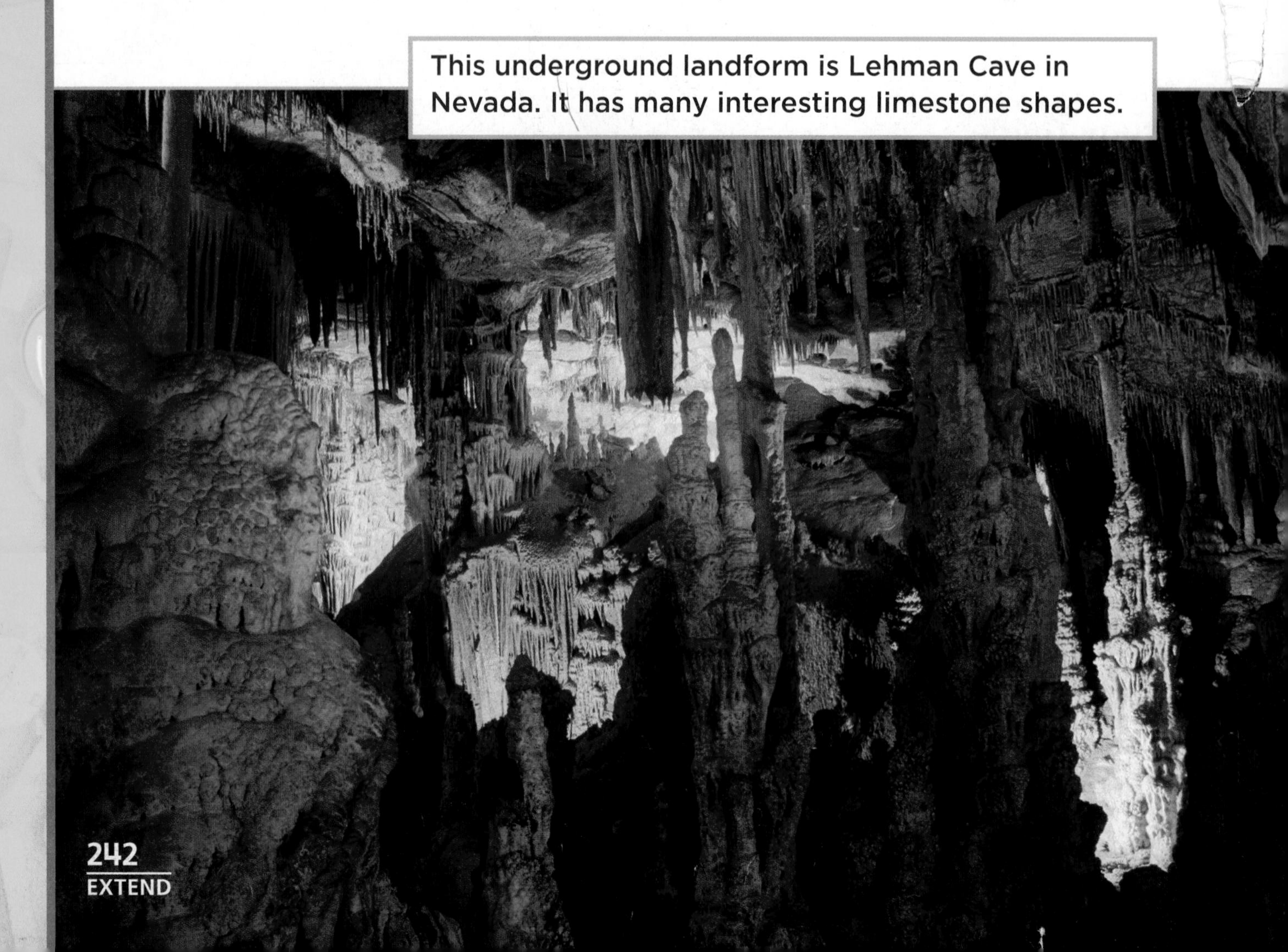

This underground landform is Lehman Cave in Nevada. It has many interesting limestone shapes.

▶ Try It

In this activity, you will **make a model** of a cave.

Materials **ruler, scissors, tan or white construction paper, crayon, shoe box or other small box, clear tape**

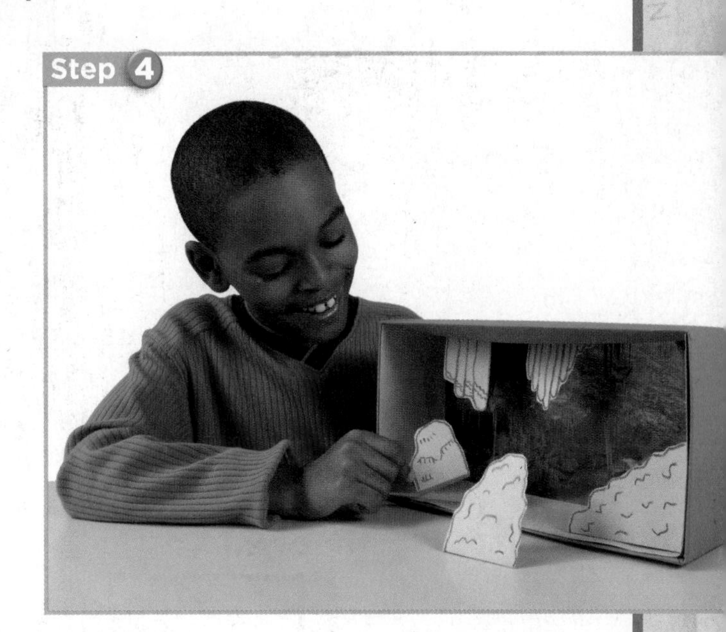
Step 4

1. Cut a piece of construction paper so that it is a little smaller than the size of the back wall of the box.
2. On the paper draw limestone rocks like the ones shown. Tape the paper to the box's back wall.

⚠ **Be Careful.**

3. Draw more limestone rocks on another piece of construction paper. Draw a flap for each rock.
4. Cut out each rock and its flap. Bend the flap for each rock. Tape each rock inside the box. Use the photo of the model to help you.

Now use your model to answer these questions:

- ▶ How would you describe the shapes of rocks in a limestone cave?
- ▶ Where do the rocks form?

▶ Apply It

Make a model of a landform that you learned about. It may be a landform on the ocean floor or one on land. What details do you want to show? Which materials will you use to help you model these details?

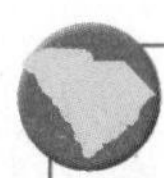

3-3.6. Illustrate Earth's land features (including volcanoes, mountains, valleys, canyons, caverns, and islands) by using models, pictures, diagrams, and maps.

Lesson 2

Sudden Changes to Earth

Look and Wonder

One minute, cars raced across this road in Oakland, California. Then the land shook. Part of the road collapsed. What might cause such a sudden change?

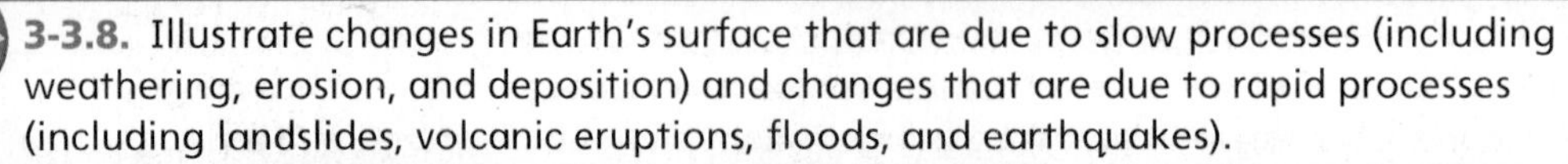

Explore

Inquiry Activity

How does sudden movement change the land?

Purpose

Model what happens when the land suddenly moves.

Procedure

1. **Make a Model** Fill a pan halfway with sand. Make a mountain with the sand.
2. Place blocks in the sand to model buildings. Add twigs to model trees.
3. **Communicate** Draw the land's surface.
4. **Experiment** What will happen if you tap the pan gently? Try it.
5. **Experiment** What will happen if you tap the pan harder? Try it.

Draw Conclusions

6. **Infer** How can the sudden movement of land change the land?

Materials

aluminum pan

sand

assorted blocks

twigs

Step 2

Explore More

Experiment Different rocks and soils make up land. Does sudden movement change all land the same way? Make a plan to find out. Try it.

3-I.3. Generate questions about objects, organisms, and events in the environment and use those questions to conduct a simple scientific investigation.

Read and Learn

Main Idea
3-3.8

Earthquakes, volcanoes, landslides, and floods cause Earth's surface to change quickly.

Vocabulary

earthquake, p. 246

volcano, p. 248

magma, p. 248

lava, p. 248

landslide, p. 250

flood, p. 250

at www.macmillanmh.com

Reading Skill

Cause and Effect

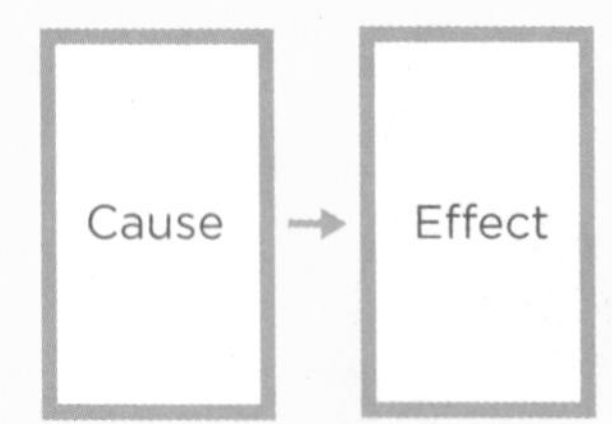

These rocks in Iceland are slowly pulling apart.

What are earthquakes?

Some events can change Earth's surface in less than a minute. One example is an earthquake (URTH•kwayk). What causes an earthquake? Why does it change the land? The answers are found under the ground.

Earth's Moving Crust

Earth's outside layer, the crust, is made up of huge slabs of rock. You may think that slabs of rock cannot move. They do move, however. Rocks deep below the ground can slowly slide past each other. They can press against each other. They can pull apart, too. These movements can cause rock to bend and snap back like a bent stick. This causes an earthquake. An **earthquake** is a sudden movement of the rocks that make up Earth's crust.

When an earthquake happens, the ground shakes, or vibrates. The vibrations travel out from the earthquake's center through the land. Some earthquakes are very weak. They are not even noticed. Some feel like a truck rumbling by. Others are very strong. Earthquakes may crack roads. They may cause buildings and bridges to fall. They may even cause parts of mountains to fall!

Quick Check

Cause and Effect What can happen when huge slabs of rock in Earth's crust move?

Critical Thinking You drop a pebble in water. How is what happens to the water similar to what happens to the crust during an earthquake?

Where Earthquakes Start

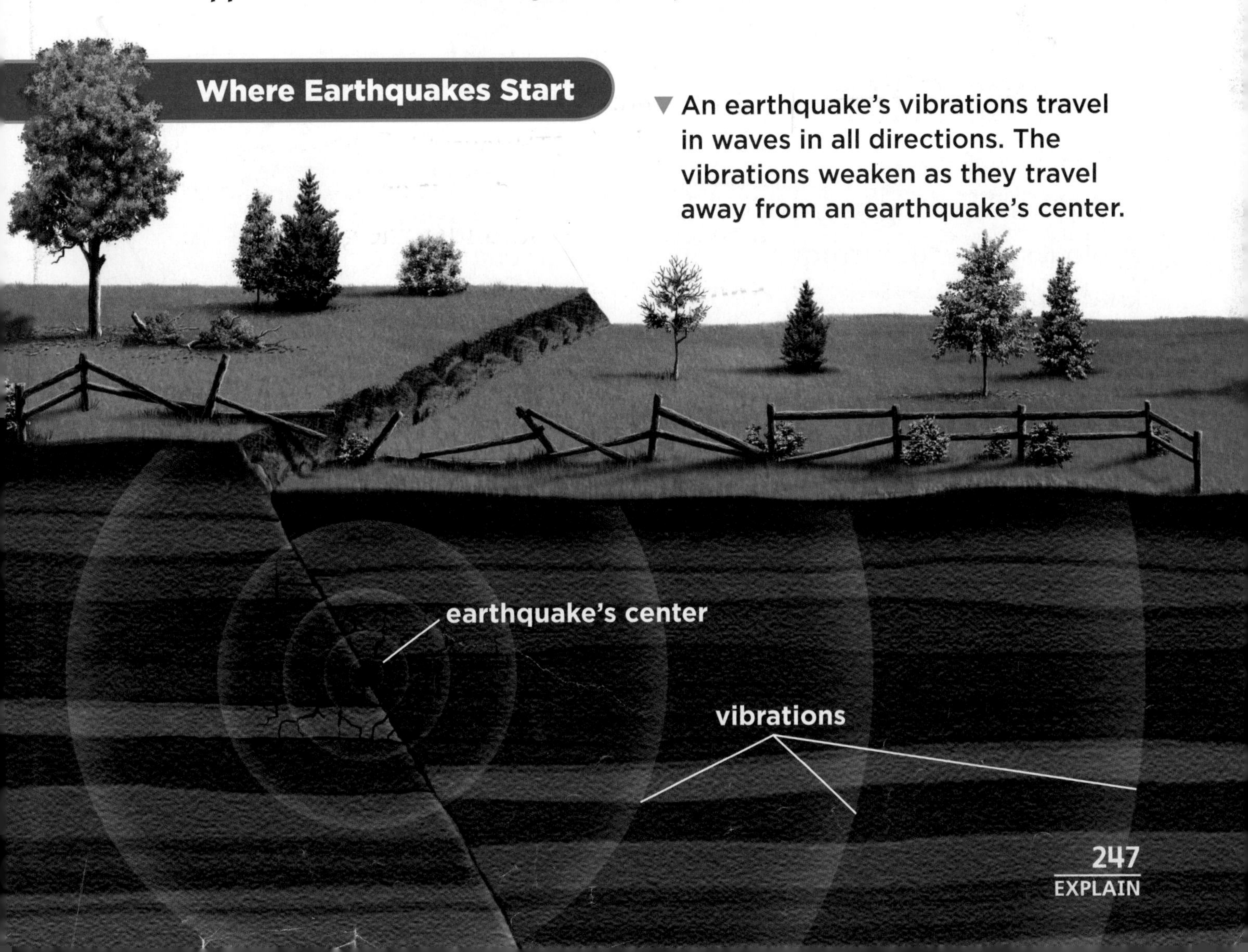

▼ An earthquake's vibrations travel in waves in all directions. The vibrations weaken as they travel away from an earthquake's center.

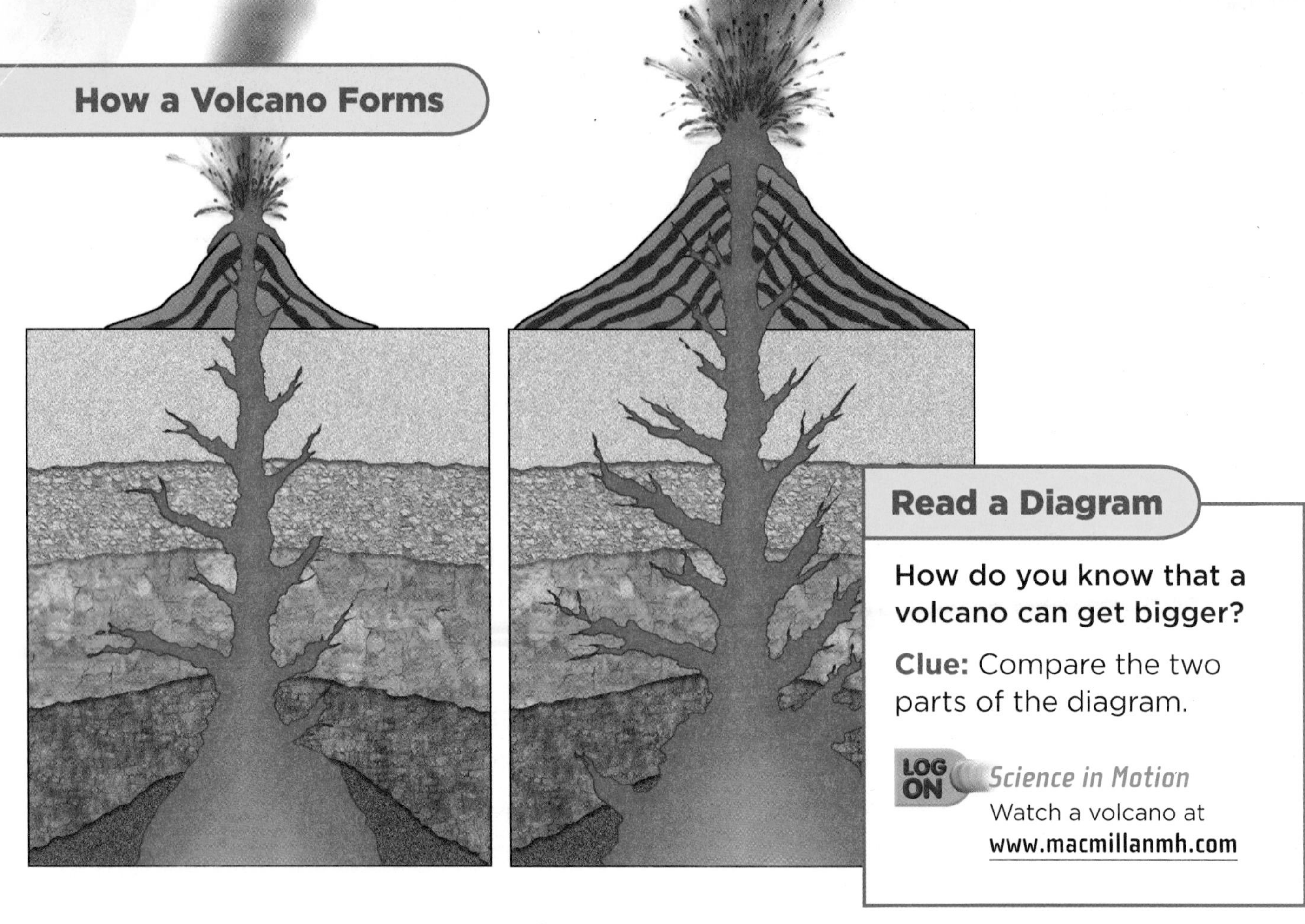

Read a Diagram

How do you know that a volcano can get bigger?

Clue: Compare the two parts of the diagram.

LOG ON *Science in Motion* Watch a volcano at **www.macmillanmh.com**

What are volcanoes?

A **volcano** (vol•KAY•noh) is a mountain that builds up around an opening in Earth's crust. Sometimes a volcano explodes. Like an earthquake, this event can change the land quickly.

Volcano Formation

In Lesson 1 you learned about Earth's layers, the crust, mantle, and core. Parts of the mantle and crust have melted rock called **magma**. Sometimes magma moves up through a large crack in the crust and flows onto land. Melted rock that flows onto land is called **lava**. Lava, rocks, and ash are forced out onto Earth's surface. They pile up in layers and form a mountain. Sometimes a volcanic mountain forms in just a few years.

FACT Volcanoes are not always active.

Effects of Volcanoes

Sometimes, lava oozes from a volcano slowly. The lava hardens and the mountain gets bigger. At other times, lava is forced out of a volcano in an explosion. When this happens, a large part of the mountain can be blown away. Materials from volcanoes can cause a lot of damage to buildings. They can harm living things, too.

Quick Check

Cause and Effect What happens when lava flows out of an opening in Earth's crust?

Critical Thinking Why are some volcanoes a danger to people?

Quick Lab

A Model Volcano

1. **Make a Model** Cover a desk with newspaper. Place a small tube of toothpaste on the desk to model Earth's surface.
2. Carefully make a hole in the tube on the side opposite the cap. This represents an opening in Earth's surface.
3. **Observe** Press on the tube near the cap. What happens by the hole? What do you think the toothpaste is a model of?
4. **Communicate** Did the same thing happen to everyone's tube? What was different? Why were there differences?

◀ Lava shoots out of this volcano in Hawaii.

What are landslides and floods?

Have you ever seen a pile of rocks at the bottom of a mountain? How did the rocks get there? Part of the answer is gravity. *Gravity* is a pulling force that acts on all objects. Gravity can cause a landslide. A **landslide** is the rapid movement of rocks and soil down a hill. A landslide can cause a hill or mountain to change quickly.

Heavy rains and melting snow can quickly fill a river. When water flows over a river's banks, or sides, there is a flood. A **flood** is water that flows over land that is usually dry. Flood waters are very strong. They can change land quickly by washing it away.

This mountain was quickly changed by a landslide.

Hurricane Wilma caused flooding in Florida in 2005.

Quick Check

Cause and Effect What effect do landslides have on land?

Critical Thinking Explain how an earthquake can cause a landslide to happen.

Lesson Review

Visual Summary

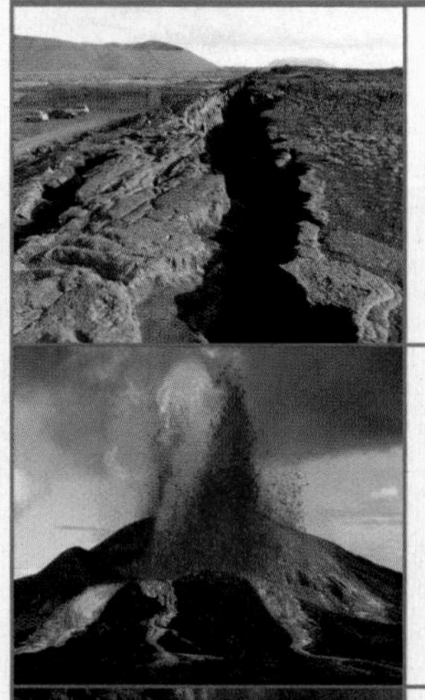

Earthquakes happen when rocks in the crust move. They can change the land quickly.

When lava, ash, and rock are forced from a **volcano**, the land can change quickly.

Landslides can quickly change the shape of a hill or mountain. **Floods** can wash land away.

Make a FOLDABLES™ Study Guide

Make a Three-Tab Book. Use it to summarize what you learned about how Earth changes quickly.

Think, Talk, and Write

1. **Main Idea** What are four events that can suddenly change the land?
2. **Vocabulary** What is a volcano?
3. **Cause and Effect** What causes earthquakes to happen?

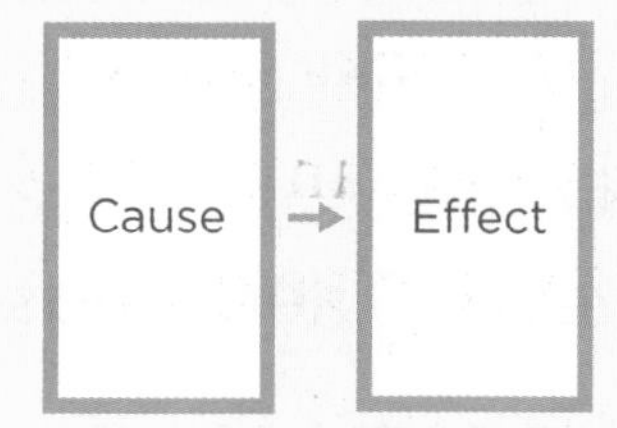

4. **Critical Thinking** What do earthquakes, volcanoes, landslides, and floods have in common?
5. **Test Prep** **Which event can be caused by heavy rains?**
   - **A** flood
   - **B** earthquake
   - **C** volcano
   - **D** drought

Writing Link

Write a Story
Think about what it must be like to experience an earthquake. Write a story about it. Be sure to mention what the earthquake does to land.

Math Link

Make a Bar Graph
The Richter scale rates earthquakes by how strong they are. Research the strengths of five major earthquakes in recent years. Make a bar graph to compare their strengths.

LOG ON e-Review Summaries and quizzes online at www.macmillanmh.com

SLIDE on the Shore

The western coast of the United States is a beautiful place to live. The views from its cliffs are awesome. Heavy rains, melting snow, and construction can weaken these cliffs, however. Then landslides may happen.

There are some things people can do to help prevent landslides. People can carve steps of land called *terraces* into the cliffs. Rocks and water stay on the terraces and do not flow to the bottom of the cliff.

People can also use drains and covers to keep the land dry. They can plant shrubs and other plants to help keep the soil in place.

People can build things to help keep the soil from moving down a hill. For example, walls of rock and concrete can support a cliff from below. Ditches can direct water around buildings. All of these things help keep people living on or around cliffs safe.

These ice plants help to control erosion on California's coast.

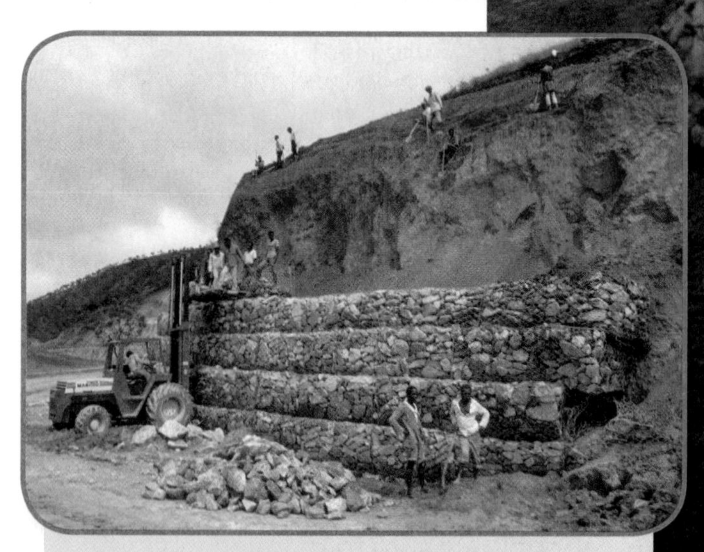

This rock wall will keep soil from moving down this hillside.

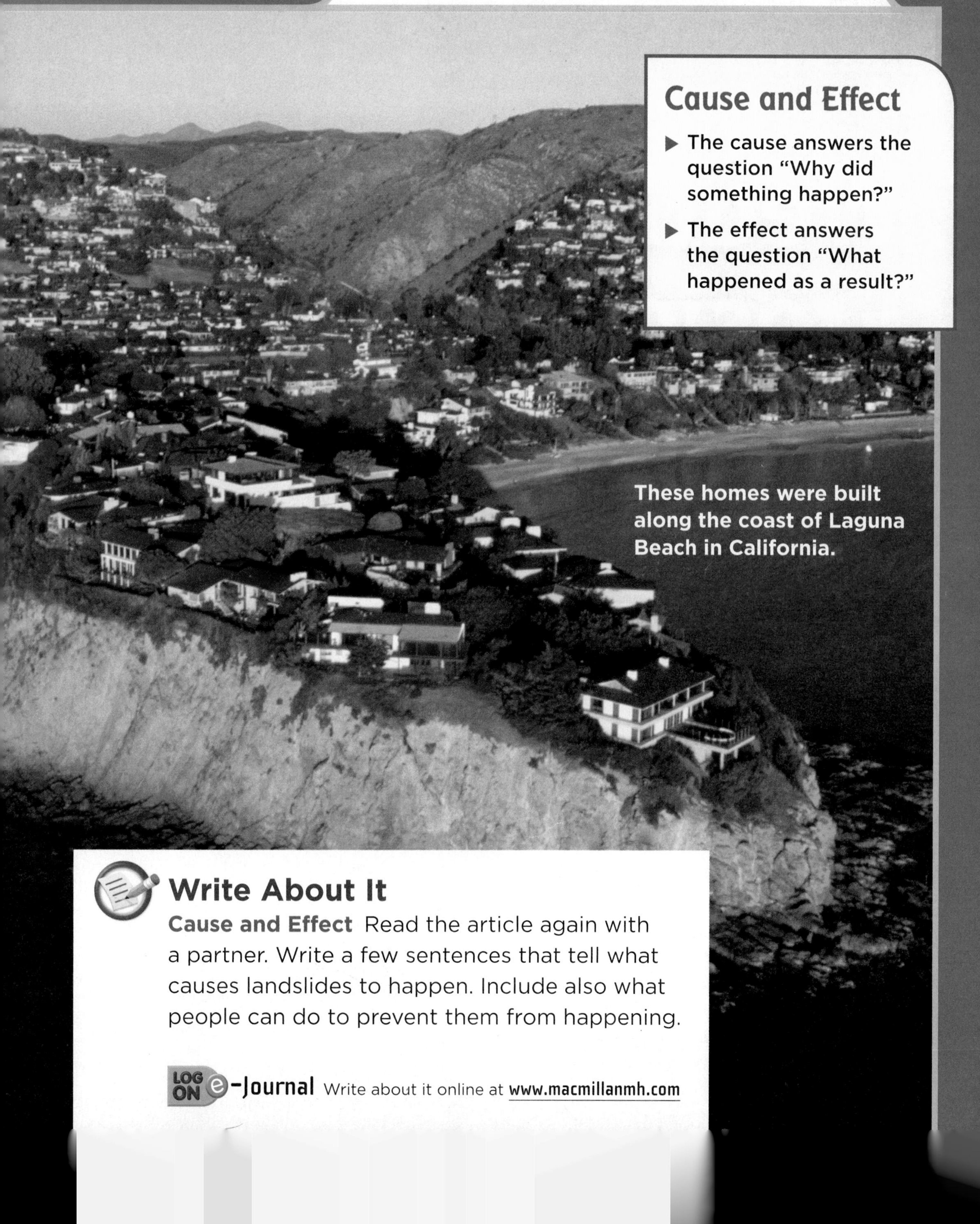

Cause and Effect

- The cause answers the question "Why did something happen?"
- The effect answers the question "What happened as a result?"

These homes were built along the coast of Laguna Beach in California.

Write About It

Cause and Effect Read the article again with a partner. Write a few sentences that tell what causes landslides to happen. Include also what people can do to prevent them from happening.

LOG ON e-Journal Write about it online at www.macmillanmh.com

Lesson 3

Weathering, Erosion, and Deposition

Look and Wonder

This canyon was once flat land. Today, parts of the Grand Canyon are nearly one mile deep. How do canyons form?

3-3.8. Illustrate changes in Earth's surface that are due to slow processes and changes that are due to rapid processes.

Explore

Inquiry Activity

How can rocks change in moving water?

Form a Hypothesis

What happens to rocks when they move around in water? Write a hypothesis in the form, "If I shake rocks in water, then . . ."

Test Your Hypothesis

1. **Measure** Label three jars *A*, *B*, and *C*. Put the same number of similar-sized rocks in each jar. Using the measuring cup, fill each jar with the same amount of water. Put a lid on each jar.
2. Let jar A sit. Do not shake it.
3. **Use Variables** Shake jar B hard for 2 minutes. Then let the jar sit.
4. **Use Variables** Shake jar C hard for 5 minutes. Then let the jar sit.
5. **Observe** Use a hand lens to observe the rocks in each jar. What happened? Did the results support your hypothesis?

Draw Conclusions

6. **Infer** How can rocks change in moving water?

Explore More

Experiment Would the results be the same if different rocks were used? Make a plan and try it.

Materials

- sandstone rocks
- measuring cup
- 3 plastic jars with lids
- stopwatch
- hand lens

Step 1

Step 3

3-I.4. Predict the outcome of a simple investigation and compare the result with the prediction.

Read and Learn

Main Idea 3-3.8
Weathering and erosion usually cause slow changes to Earth's surface.

Vocabulary

weathering, p. 256

erosion, p. 258

glacier, p. 258

deposition, p. 258

at www.macmillanmh.com

Reading Skill
Draw Conclusions

Text Clues	Conclusions

What is weathering?

You may think that hard rocks cannot change or break, but they do. Large rocks break into smaller rocks. Small rocks break down into sand and soil. The breaking down of rocks into smaller pieces is called **weathering** (WETH•uhr•ing). Weathering usually happens so slowly that you do not see it. The weathering of rocks can take millions of years.

What causes weathering? Running water, wind, rain, and temperature changes are some things that break down rocks.

Running water and wind pick up small rocks. These rocks scrape against other rocks. This scraping slowly wears away rocks.

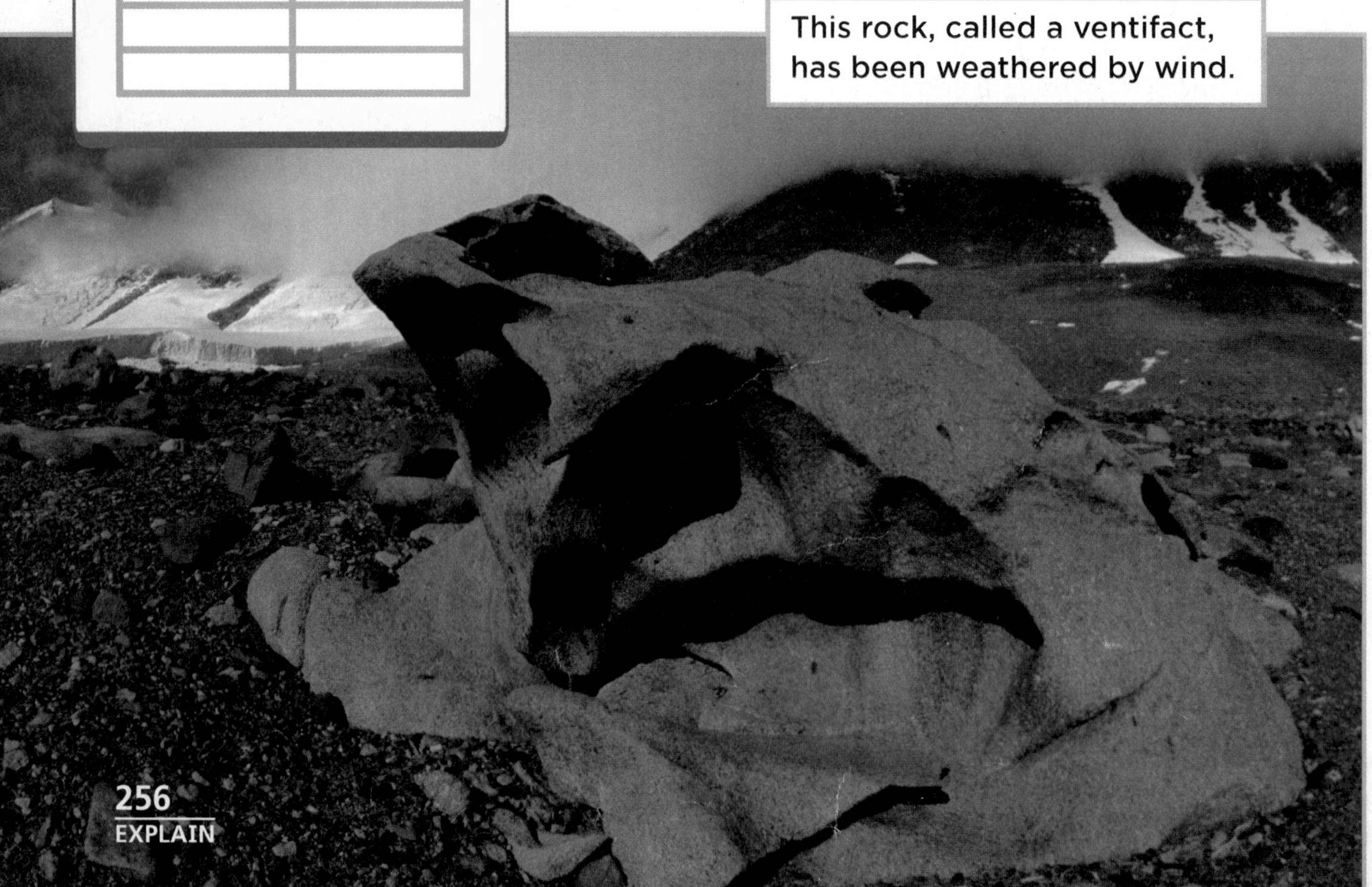
This rock, called a ventifact, has been weathered by wind.

▲ These hoodoos have been worn mostly by water that freezes and then thaws inside cracks in the rocks.

Rain and melting snow can enter the small cracks in rocks. When the water freezes, it *expands*, or takes up more space. This widens the cracks. Then the ice thaws and becomes liquid water again. Over time, repeated freezing and thawing breaks rocks apart.

This tree continues to break this rock apart. ▼

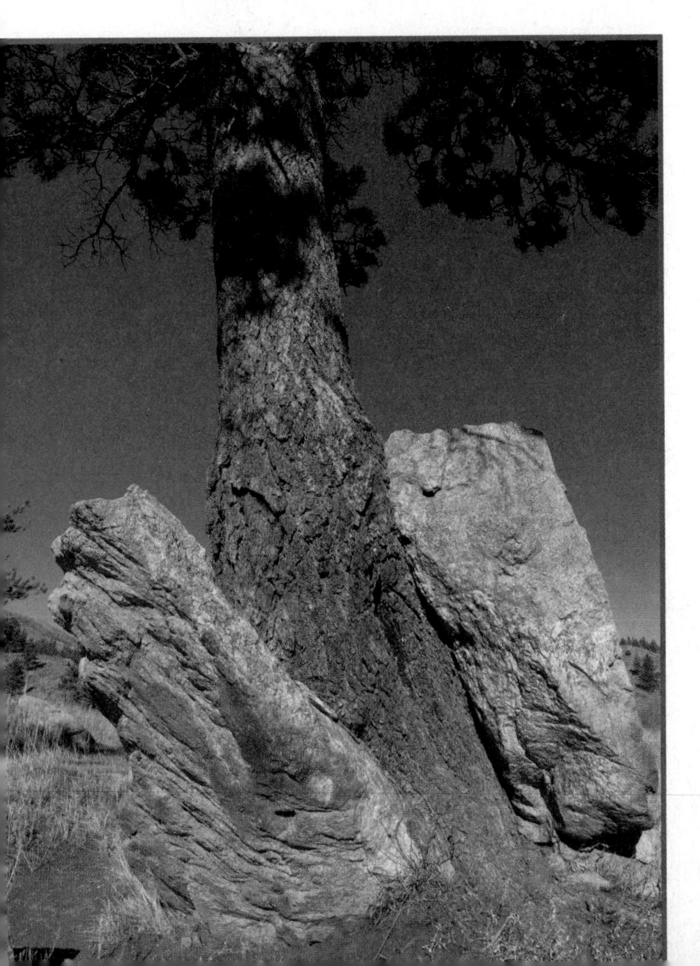

Living things can cause weathering. Plants may grow in the cracks of rocks. Their roots eventually split rocks apart. When animals dig in the ground, they can uncover buried rocks. The uncovered rocks can then begin to weather.

Quick Check

Draw Conclusions A sidewalk crack got wider during a cold winter. Why?

Critical Thinking Explain how people can cause weathering.

The rocks in this stream were carried here by moving water.

What is erosion?

Once rocks break apart, they are moved to other places. **Erosion** (i•ROH•zhuhn) is the movement of weathered rock. Moving water, wind, and glaciers (GLAY•shuhrz) all cause erosion. A **glacier** is a mass of ice that moves slowly across the land. Gravity also causes erosion. Gravity pulls weathered materials downhill.

Erosion usually happens very slowly. Weathering and erosion work together to change land. Weathering breaks rocks down. Erosion carries the weathered pieces away.

Moving Water and Wind

Moving water in rivers, streams, and ocean waves picks up rocks and sand. The rocks and sand may be carried far away. Then they are dropped in new places. **Deposition** (dep•uh•ZISH•uhn) is the dropping off of weathered rock.

Wind also picks up small bits of weathered rocks. When the wind slows down, they are deposited.

The rocks here were pulled down by gravity.

Glaciers

As it moves, a glacier picks up and carries away rocks of all sizes. The ice at the bottom of a glacier freezes onto rocks. As the glacier moves, it tears rocks out of the ground. A glacier can move rocks the size of a house. As a glacier melts, it drops off the rocks in a new place.

Quick Check

Draw Conclusions What causes erosion?

Critical Thinking When might erosion happen quickly?

Quick Lab

Materials Settle

1. **Make a Model** Pour one cup each of sand, soil, and pebbles into a jar. Fill the jar almost to the top with water. Seal the jar tightly.
2. Shake the jar 10 times. Then let it sit. Draw what you see.
3. **Interpret Data** In which order do the materials settle?
4. **Infer** What happens to eroded materials in a river as the river gradually slows down?

As a glacier moves across land, it forms a U-shaped valley.

uilding a Canal

▲ In 1913 the Culebra Mountain in Panama was carved out to build the Panama Canal.

Read a Photo

How did people change the land here?

Clue: Compare the "after" photo with the "before" photo.

How can people change the land?

People change the land, too. Some changes are very small, like digging a hole in your backyard. Other changes are much larger.

In some places trees are cut to build roads, stores, and homes. If trees are not replanted, soil can wash away. In other places ponds and swamps are drained. The dry soil left behind can blow away. In still other places, land is dug up to reach valuable rocks.

Quick Check

Draw Conclusions What effect might planting trees have on the land?

Critical Thinking How are people changing the land where you live?

Lesson Review

Visual Summary

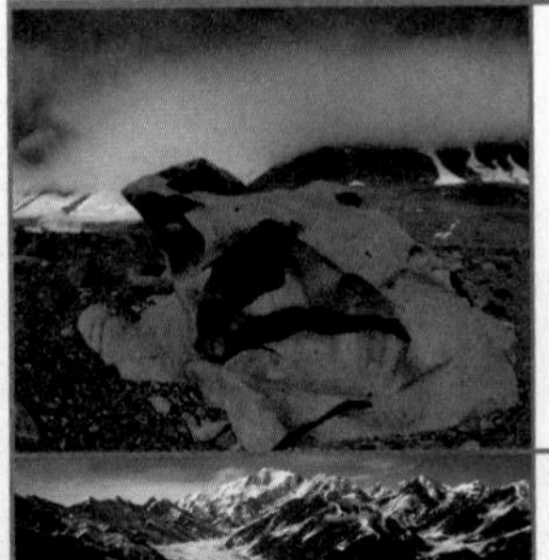

Weathering breaks down larger rocks into smaller rocks.

Erosion is the movement of weathered rock from one place to another.

People can cause **changes to land**.

Make a FOLDABLES™ Study Guide

Make a Trifold Book. Use it to summarize what you learned about weathering and erosion.

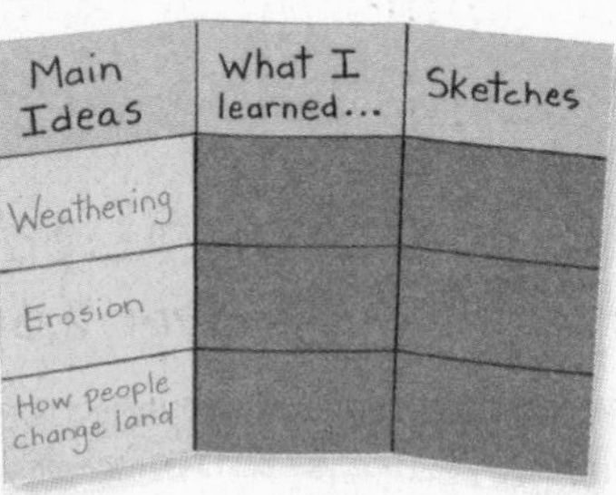

Think, Talk, and Write

1. **Main Idea** Which two things usually change the land very slowly?

2. **Vocabulary** What is erosion?

3. **Draw Conclusions** What happens to eroded rocks and soil once they are dropped off?

Text Clues	Conclusions

4. **Critical Thinking** How do weathering and erosion together change land?

5. **Test Prep** **All of the following may cause weathering to rocks EXCEPT**

   A ice.
   B light.
   C wind.
   D plants.

Writing Link

Write a Story

Suppose you are a small rock in a stream. Write a story about what happens to you due to weathering and erosion.

Social Studies Link

River Deltas

Do research about river deltas. Find out what they are and how they form. What are some famous deltas? Write your findings in a report.

LOG ON e-Review Summaries and quizzes online at www.macmillanmh.com

Missing Noses

Rocks are constantly changed by weathering and erosion. However, not all weathering happens the same way.

What happened to the noses on these statues? Did someone break them off? No, something else happened.

It all started when certain gases were released into the air. Many of these gases came from cars, trucks, and factories. The gases combined with rainwater. A weak acid formed. The acid rain chemically changed the minerals in the rock. This is called chemical weathering. The rock broke down. Then rain washed the changed minerals away.

One day, this ancient place could weather and erode completely. All it takes is rain, gases in air, and lots of time.

Expository Writing

Good expository writing

- has a topic sentence that tells the main idea
- supports the main idea with facts and details
- draws a conclusion based on the facts

Write About It

Expository Writing Write a paragraph to describe other causes of weathering. Remember to start with a topic sentence and to end with a conclusion.

Write about it online at www.macmillanmh.com

The Acropolis in Greece is over 2,500 years old. ▼

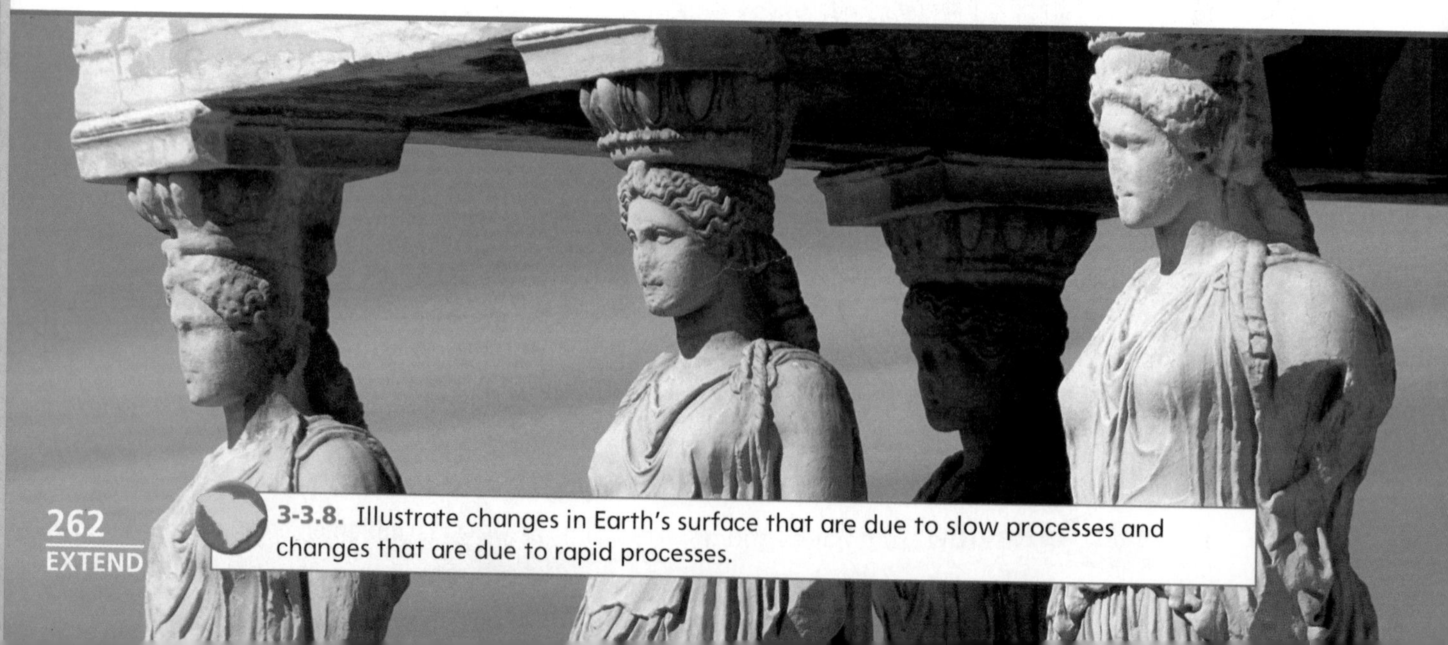

3-3.8. Illustrate changes in Earth's surface that are due to slow processes and changes that are due to rapid processes.

Estimate a Glacier's Change

Sometimes a glacier reaches the ocean and floats on top of it. This long, thin mass of floating ice is called an ice tongue.

The Mertz Glacier has a tongue. Since 1963, melting has caused the glacier's tongue to get longer. It "grows" about 0.9 kilometer each year. If this rate stays the same, about how much should the tongue grow over the next 5 years?

Make Estimations

- An estimate is a number that tells about how much or how many. To estimate the tongue's growth, first round 0.9 to the nearest whole number.
  0.9 kilometer (km) rounds to 1.0 kilometer (km).
- To estimate the change over 5 years, multiply the amount of change per year by the number of years.

  1 km per year x 5 years = 5 km

  The glacier's tongue will grow about 5 kilometers in 5 years.

▲ The Mertz Glacier's tongue is about 72 kilometers long.

Solve It

About how much should the glacier's tongue grow in 20 years? If the tongue grows longer than you estimated, what might this tell you about the rate with which the tongue is growing?

CHAPTER 5 Review

Visual Summary

Lesson 1 Earth's surface has many land and water features.

Lesson 2 Earthquakes, volcanoes, landslides, and floods cause Earth's surface to change quickly.

Lesson 3 Weathering and erosion usually cause slow changes to Earth's surface.

Make a FOLDABLES™ Study Guide

Glue your lesson study guides on a sheet of paper as shown. Use your study guide to review what you have learned in this chapter.

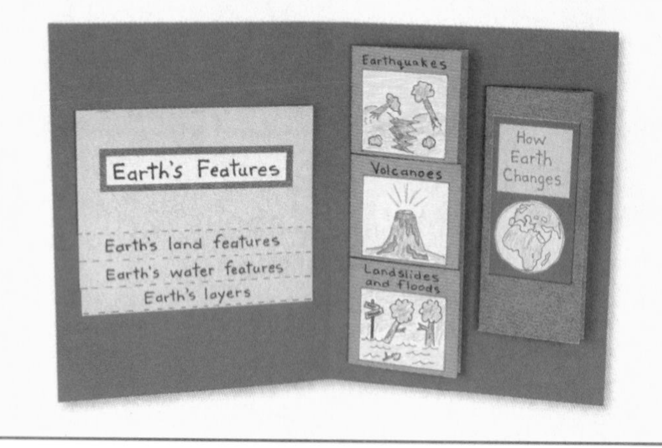

Vocabulary

Fill each blank with the best term from the list.

continent, p. 235
core, p. 240
crust, p. 240
earthquake, p. 246
erosion, p. 258
landform, p. 236
landslide, p. 250
magma, p. 248
volcano, p. 248
weathering, p. 256

1. Each of the seven great land areas on Earth is called a(n) ________.
3-3.6
2. The breaking down of rocks into smaller pieces is called ________.
3-3.8
3. A mountain is an example of a(n) ________.
3-3.6
4. A mountain that builds up around an opening in Earth's crust is a(n) ________.
3-3.8
5. The sudden movement of rocks in Earth's crust is called a(n) ________.
3-3.8
6. Melted rock below Earth's crust is called ________.
3-3.6.
7. The movement of weathered rock by such things as wind, moving water, and glaciers is known as ________.
3-3.8.
8. Earth's deepest, hottest layer is the ________.
3-3.6.
9. Earth's cool, thin top layer is called the ________.
3-3.6.
10. The rapid movement of rocks and soil downhill is a(n) ________.
3-3.8.

LOG ON e-Review Summaries and quizzes online at www.macmillanmh.com

Skills and Concepts

Answer each of the following in complete sentences.

11. Cause and Effect What causes landslides?
3-3.8

12. Expository Writing Describe what the ocean floor looks like.
3-3.5

13. Make a Model Suppose you wanted to show the difference between a plateau and a mountain. Explain how you could build a model to show the difference.
3-3.6

14. Critical Thinking What might cause a volcanic mountain to form quickly?
3-3.8

15. How can erosion be caused by a stream or a river?
3-3.8

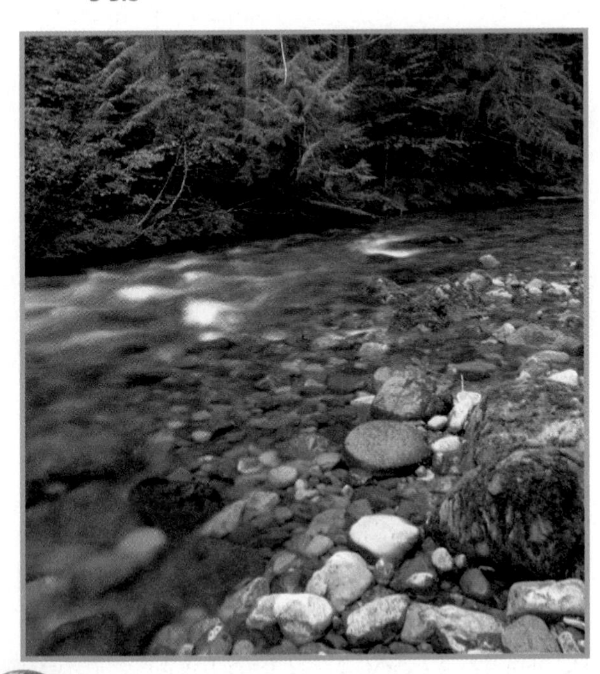

The Big Idea

16. What can cause Earth's features to change?
3-3.8

Performance Assessment

The Changing Earth

Find out how a recent event changed Earth's surface.

- Research a recent natural event that happened somewhere in the world. It could be an earthquake, a flood, a landslide, or a volcanic eruption.
- Find out when and where the event occurred. What caused the event to take place? Did it change the land? How did it affect the people, other living things, or buildings in the area?
- Write a short news report presenting the information you found.

NEWSPAPER

Rain Leads To Flooding

Twenty straight days of rain in Savannah, Georgia have led to severe flooding. Parts of the city are under as much as 6 feet of water.

South Carolina Activity

Earth scientists divide South Carolina into three regions: the Blue Ridge Mountains, the Piedmont Plateau, and the Coastal Plain. Find out where each region is located. On a blank map of South Carolina, color each region a different color. Label and describe the features of each region.

South Carolina Standards Practice

1 A student conducted an experiment to find out which type of soil eroded fastest. The soil types were in pans, each propped up at the same angle. She slowly poured water over each soil type. She poured until all of the soil had eroded. Then she recorded her findings in the chart below.

Soils	
Type of Soil	**Time to Erode**
sandy soil	20 seconds
topsoil	40 seconds
clay soil	60 seconds

Which one of the following **best** describes her results?

A Clay soil eroded the fastest.

B Sandy soil eroded the fastest.

C Topsoil eroded the slowest.

D Sandy soil eroded the slowest.

3-I.6

2 Which type of landform is formed when magma flows onto land?

F a peninsula

G a volcano

H a canyon

I a valley

3-3.8

3 Two scientists studied Earth's crust. One scientist found the mineral quartz. The other scientist found the mineral feldspar. The **most likely** reason for the different results is that the two scientists studied the crust

A in different places.

B during different seasons.

C using different instruments.

D for different amounts of time.

3-I.7

4 Which of the following is usually a slow process?

F beach erosion by a storm

G a volcanic eruption

H weathering of rocks

I an earthquake

3-3.8

5 The rapid movement of rocks and soil down a hill is called a

A flood.

B glacier.

C volcano.

D landslide.

3-3.8

6 **The rocks and sand along the side of this stream are an example of which process?**

F deposition

G transport

H erosion

I weathering

3-3.8

7 **A student completed an experiment only once. The results did not turn out as he expected. What should he do next?**

A do the experiment again

B change his prediction to fit the results

C change his results to fit the prediction

D conclude it was a good experiment

3-I.7

8 **A scientist recorded earthquake observations from three different locations. She recorded her data in a chart.**

Earthquake Observations	
Location 1	no vibrations
Location 2	ground shaking
Location 3	roads cracking

Which of the following inferences could she make from the data?

F Location 1 is closest to the earthquake.

G Location 1 is farthest from the earthquake.

H Location 2 is closest to the earthquake.

I Location 2 is farthest from the earthquake.

3-I.6

9 **Each of the following land features could be found in the ocean except**

A a trench.

B a plateau.

C a continental shelf.

D an abyssal plain.

3-3.6

10 **Each of the following is a freshwater feature except**

F a pond.

G a glacier.

H a river.

I an ocean.

3-3.5

Literature

Magazine Article

Liv and Ann each pulled a sled that weighed 267 pounds on their journey across Antarctica.

from *Time for Kids*

ONE COOL ADVENTURE

February 23, 2001

▲ Liv Arnesen and Ann Bancroft

Whew! They made it! On February 11, former teachers Ann Bancroft of the U.S. and Liv Arnesen of Norway reached the Ross Ice Shelf in Antarctica. They became the first women to cross Antarctica's land mass on skis! It took the explorers 90 days to ski and parasail across 1,688 miles of ice. They kept going despite bitter cold, injuries, ripped sails and broken sleds.

The pair had hoped to cross the Ross Ice Shelf, but lack of wind forced them to shorten their trek. They flew back to McMurdo Station to catch a ship before icy waters made the trip home dangerous.

Write About It

Response to Literature This article tells about the first women to cross Antarctica on skis. What do you know about Antarctica or other places on Earth? Suppose you took a trip around the world. What kinds of things might you see? Write about it.

LOG ON e-Journal Write about it online at www.macmillanmh.com

Mapmaker

Do you like working on puzzles with small pieces? Are you good at giving directions or describing places? You might think about becoming a mapmaker.

Scientists who make maps have many different skills. Some gather data about the geography of an area. Others make three-dimensional models of landforms. Still others use data and models to draw the maps with computerized mapping programs.

There are things you can do right now to prepare for this job. Learn about Earth's land and water. Play games that require you to solve a problem. In high school take math, science, and computer classes. Then, get a college degree.

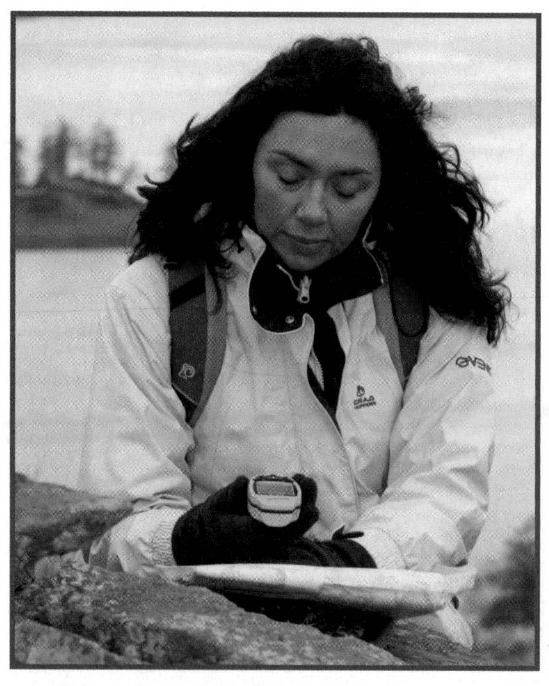

▲ This scientist is gathering data about landforms.

Here are some other Earth Science careers:

- oceanographer
- miner
- jewelry designer
- geologist

This surveyor is using a *transit*. The information he records will help him map an area.

LOG ON e-Careers at www.macmillanmh.com

South Carolina

Physical Science

Only about one tenth of an iceberg can be seen above water.

FALL FOR GREENVILLE

Bluegrass Instruments

Have you ever listened to a bluegrass band? You might hear banjos, violins, guitars, mandolins, and a bass fiddle. Each instrument in the band has its own sound.

One place to hear bluegrass music is Fall for Greenville. You will find a stringed instrument in most musical groups that play there.

How Strings Make Sound

When you play a stringed instrument, the strings move back and forth. This back-and-forth motion is called a vibration. Vibrations produce the sounds you hear as notes. Fast vibrations produce high notes. Slow vibrations produce low notes.

Musicians control the sound of stringed instruments by making the strings tighter or looser. They use knobs on the necks of the instruments to tighten or loosen the strings. A tighter string vibrates faster than a looser string.

Think, Talk, and Write

Critical Thinking **How could you make a violin string play a higher note? How could you make it play a lower note?**

3-5.5. Recall that vibrating objects produce sound and that vibrations can be transferred from one material to another.
3-5.8. Explain how the vibration of an object affects pitch.

South Carolina

A CLOSER LOOK

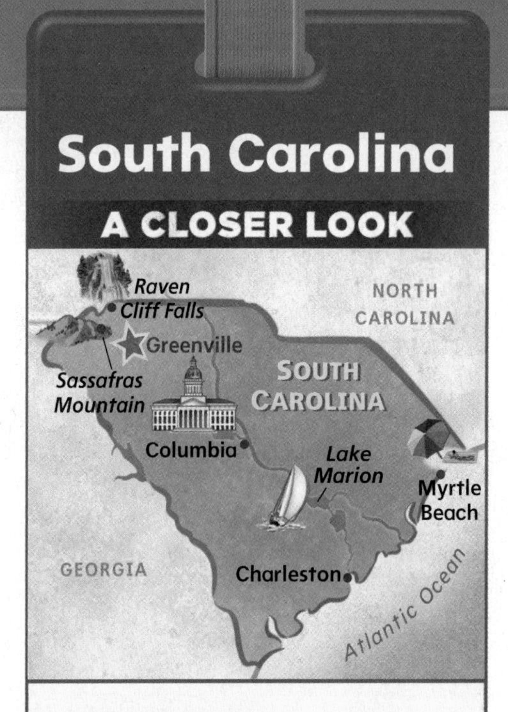

Main Idea

The vibrations of strings make different kinds of sounds.

Activity

Form a Hypothesis

How will changing the thickness of a guitar string affect its sound? Write a hypothesis.

- Make a "guitar" by stretching rubber bands of different sizes around a shoe box.
- Pluck the strings. Do thicker rubber bands produce higher or lower notes? Why do you think this is so?

South Carolina
Philharmonic
a woodwind instrument

Woodwind Instruments

Some musicians in the South Carolina Philharmonic make music using air. They play woodwind instruments.

Woodwinds are made from metal or wooden tubes. Examples include flutes and clarinets. The musician blows into or across the top of the tube. The air in the tube starts to vibrate. The vibration travels down the tube and back again, making sound. Short tubes produce high notes. Long tubes produce low notes.

Making Different Notes

Woodwind players open and close the holes along the length of the tube. Closing all the holes produces the lowest note. As the player opens holes from the bottom up, the notes become higher.

Some woodwind instruments have reeds. A reed closes the mouth of the tube. Clarinets have a single reed. Other woodwinds, such as oboes, have double reeds. Reeds vibrate and change the sound of the instrument.

Think, Talk, and Write

Critical Thinking Which can make higher notes: the piccolo or the bassoon? Explain.

South Carolina

A CLOSER LOOK

Raven Cliff Falls
Greenville
Sassafras Mountain
Columbia
Lake Marion
Myrtle Beach
Charleston
NORTH CAROLINA
SOUTH CAROLINA
GEORGIA
Atlantic Ocean

Main Idea

Vibrating air gives woodwinds their sounds.

Activity

Use Variables How does changing the size of an instrument affect its sound?

- Blow across the top of an empty bottle.
- Blow across the top of a smaller bottle. Then try a larger bottle. Describe how the sound changes.
- Add water to one of the bottles. Does this make the tube shorter or longer? Explain how this changes the sound.

3-5.5. Recall that vibrating objects produce sound and that vibrations can be transferred from one material to another.
3-5.8. Explain how the vibration of an object affects pitch.

CHAPTER 6

Matter and Heat

The Big Idea

What are some ways you can describe matter?

Castle Geyser in Yellowstone National Park

Key Vocabulary

matter
anything that takes up space and has mass (p. 280)

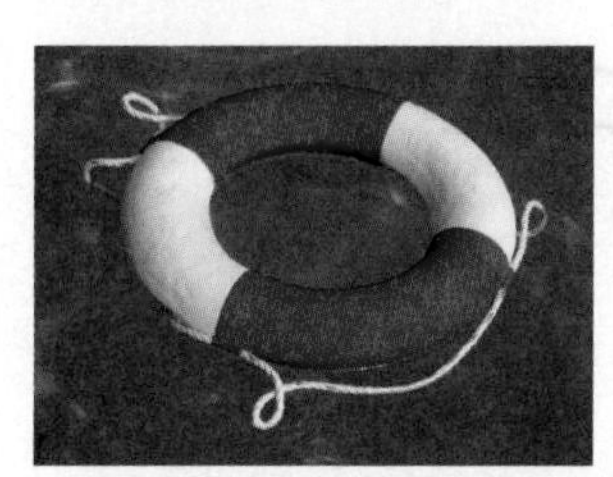

property
a characteristic of something (p. 281)

states of matter
the three forms of matter—solid, liquid, and gas—that exist on Earth (p. 300)

solid
matter in a state that has a definite shape and volume (p. 300)

liquid
matter in a state that has a definite volume but not a definite shape (p. 302)

gas
matter in a state that has no definite shape or volume (p. 303)

More Vocabulary

volume, p. 281
mass, p. 281
element, p. 284
metric system, p. 290
pan balance, p. 292
gravity, p. 294
weight, p. 294
heat, p. 310
thermal energy, p. 312
temperature, p. 312
thermometer, p. 313
conductor, p. 314
insulator, p. 314
melt, p. 320
boil, p. 321
evaporate, p. 321
condense, p. 322
freeze, p. 323

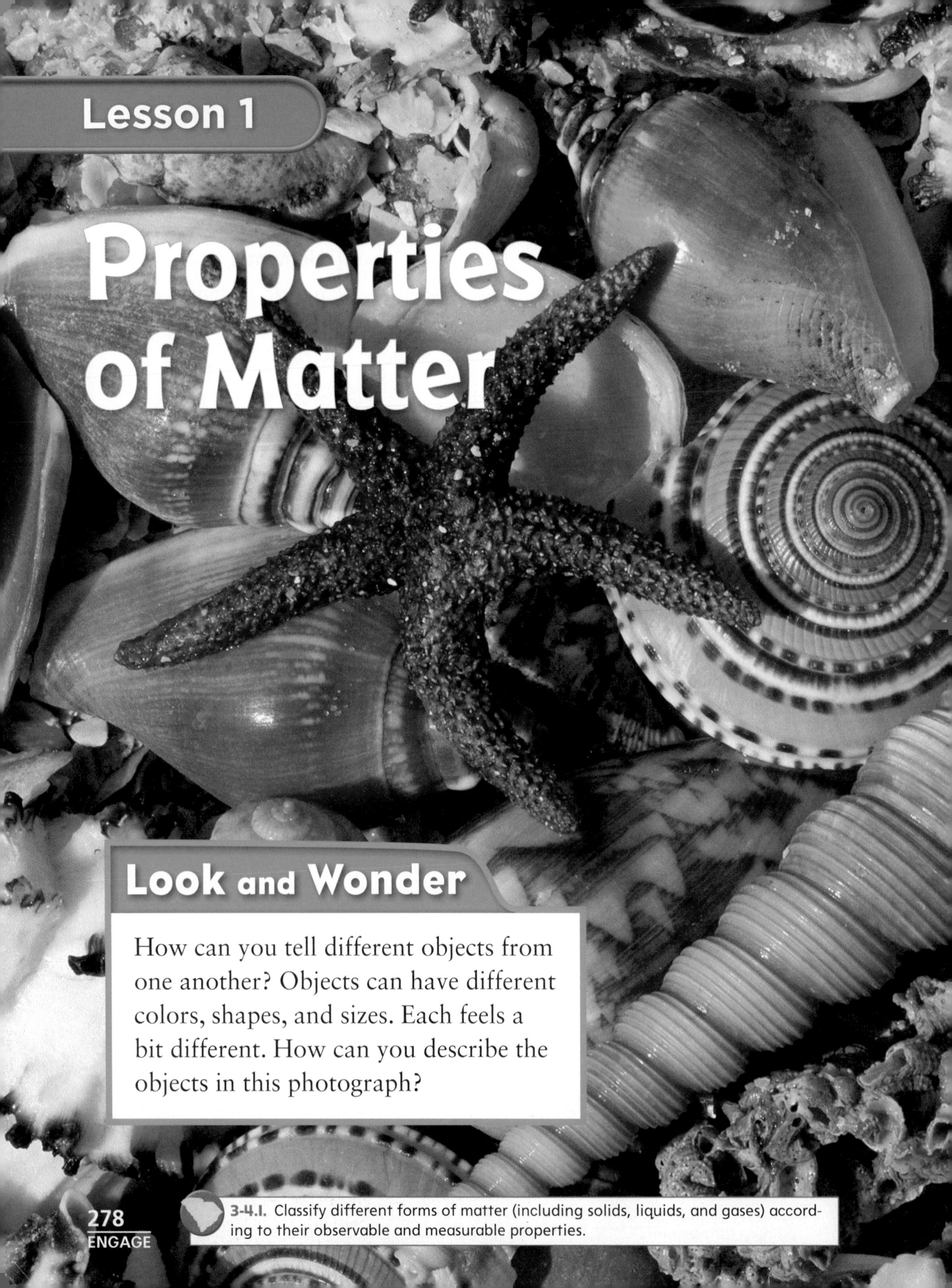

Lesson 1

Properties of Matter

Look and Wonder

How can you tell different objects from one another? Objects can have different colors, shapes, and sizes. Each feels a bit different. How can you describe the objects in this photograph?

3-4.1. Classify different forms of matter (including solids, liquids, and gases) according to their observable and measurable properties.

Explore

Inquiry Activity

How do you describe objects?

Purpose

Explore ways to describe objects.

Procedure

1. **Observe** Select a "mystery object" in your classroom. Observe the object. What color is it? How does it feel? What is the object's shape and size?
2. **Communicate** Record your observations in a word web like the one shown. Label each line with a word that describes your mystery object. Leave the circle blank.
3. **Infer** Trade webs with a partner. Think about the descriptive words on your partner's web. What classroom object do the words describe? Label the circle with the name of your partner's mystery object.

Draw Conclusions

4. Were you able to guess your partner's mystery object? Was your classmate able to guess your mystery object?
5. What helped you most in figuring out your partner's object?

Explore More

Experiment How might your web be different if you were blindfolded and could only touch the mystery object? Try it to find out.

Materials

classroom objects

hand lens

Step 1

Step 2

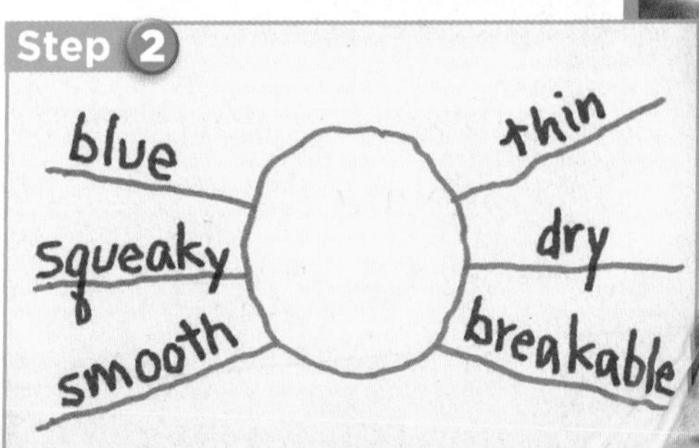

3-I.7. Explain why similar investigations might produce different results.

Read and Learn

Main Idea 3-4.1

Matter is anything that has volume and mass. You can use properties to describe and identify matter.

Vocabulary

matter, p. 280

volume, p. 281

mass, p. 281

property, p. 281

element, p. 284

at www.macmillanmh.com

Reading Skill

Main Idea and Details

Main Idea

Details | Details | Details

What is matter?

Look around. Do you see things with different colors, sizes, and shapes? Things differ in the way they look, feel, sound, and smell. All the things around you are alike in one way, however. All are made of matter (MAT•uhr).

Matter is anything that takes up space. You are matter. This book is matter. Even the air you breathe is matter. All of these things take up space.

What can you see, hear, and touch at the beach?

Volume

Volume (VOL•yewm) describes how much space an object takes up. It tells how big or small an object is. This beach ball takes up more space than this bowling ball. The beach ball has more volume.

Mass

All objects have mass. **Mass** is a measure of the amount of matter in an object. An object with a large mass feels heavy. An object with a small mass feels light. This bowling ball feels heavier than this beach ball. This is because the bowling ball contains more matter. The bowling ball has more mass.

▲ This beach ball has more volume but less mass than this bowling ball.

Volume and mass are properties (PROP•uhr•teez) of matter. A **property** is a characteristic of something. The way an object looks, tastes, smells, sounds, and feels are other properties that you can observe.

Properties of a Pineapple

Property	Description
Color(s)	brown, green
Shape	round and spiky
Feel	rough
Taste	sweet

Read a Table

How does a pineapple taste?

Clue: Headings help you find information.

✓ *Quick Check*

Main Idea and Details What are two properties of all types of matter?

Critical Thinking Why is sound not matter?

What are some properties of matter?

The world is full of many kinds of matter. We use properties to tell them apart. An object may be hot or cold. It could feel smooth or rough, wet or dry. Here are some properties that help us describe and identify matter.

Sinking and Floating

Some matter sinks in water. Some matter floats. For example, a rock sinks in water and an apple floats. Metal objects usually sink, while wooden objects often float. Objects sink or float because of their mass and volume. Objects with a lot of mass and little volume tend to sink. Objects with little mass and a lot of volume tend to float.

A life preserver floats on water. ▼

An anchor sinks in water.

Magnetism

Magnets have a special property. Magnets pull on, or *attract*, certain metals, such as iron. They do not attract wood, plastic, or water. Put a magnet near an object made of iron. What happens? The magnet pulls on the object, and then the object "sticks" to the magnet.

Conducting Heat

Some matter *conducts* heat. This means that some kinds of matter let heat move through them easily. For example, heat moves easily through metals such as iron and copper. This is why these materials make good cooking pots. Heat moves from the stove through the metal pot. The pot gets warm. Wood does not heat up quickly. This is why wood makes good pot handles and cooking spoons.

Quick Lab

Classify Matter

1. Look at ten objects.
2. **Communicate** List the properties of each object in a table like the one shown.
3. **Classify** Sort the objects into groups that have similar properties. Give each group a name that describes how its items are alike.

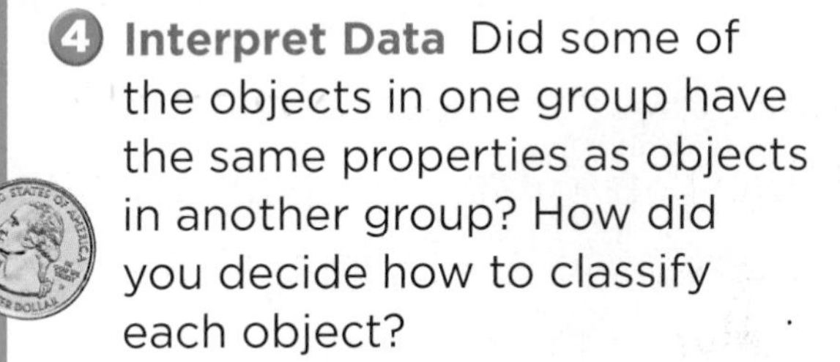

4. **Interpret Data** Did some of the objects in one group have the same properties as objects in another group? How did you decide how to classify each object?
5. **Communicate** Is there more than one way to classify these objects? Explain your answer.

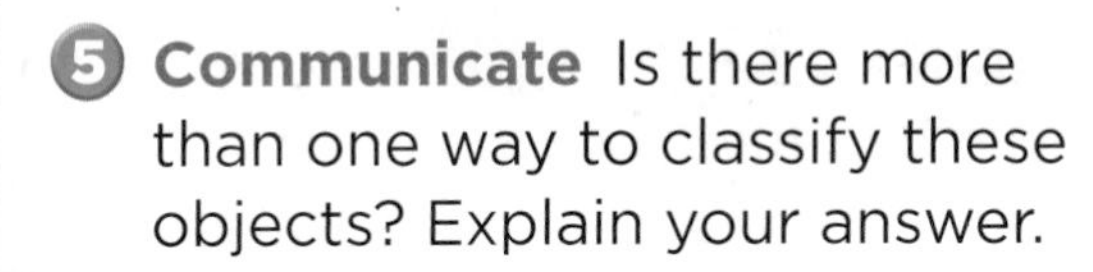

Object	Properties

Quick Check

Main Idea and Details Name three properties of matter.

Critical Thinking What properties of plastic make it useful as a bowl but not as a cooking pan?

FACT Only some metals are attracted to magnets.

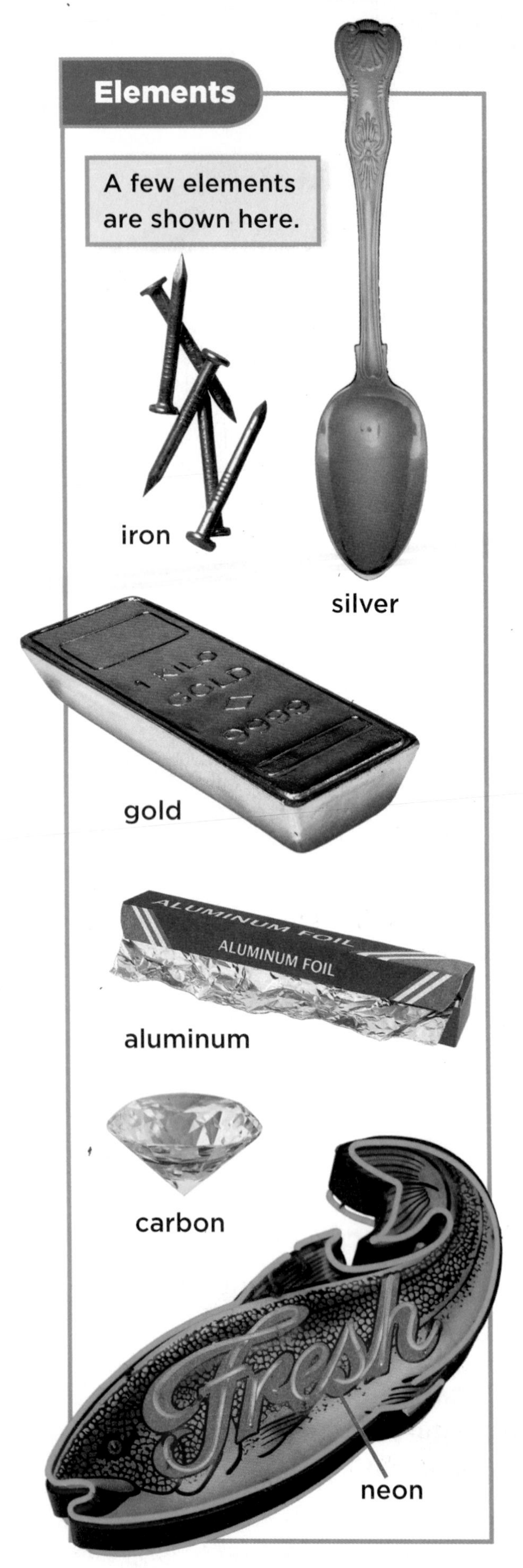

What is matter made of?

People once thought that all matter was made up of combinations of water, air, earth, and fire. We now know that all matter is made up of elements (EL•uh•muhnts). **Elements** are the building blocks of matter. There are more than 100 different elements. They make up all the matter in the world.

Some matter is made up of mostly one element. An iron nail contains mostly the element iron. Aluminum (uh•LEW•muh•nuhm) foil contains mostly the element aluminum.

Most matter on Earth is made up of more than one element. Water is made up of the elements hydrogen and oxygen. Sugar is made up of hydrogen, oxygen, and a third element called carbon. Elements join in different ways and in different amounts to form everything in our world.

Quick Check

Main Idea and Details Why are elements called the building blocks of matter?

Critical Thinking How is an iron nail different from water?

Lesson Review

Visual Summary

Matter is anything that has **volume** and **mass**.

Matter can be described and identified by its **properties**.

All matter is made up of **elements**.

Make a FOLDABLES™ Study Guide

Make a Trifold Book. Use it to summarize what you learned about matter and its properties.

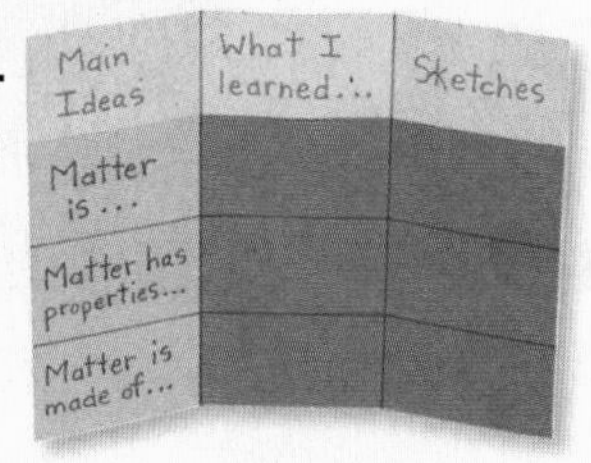

Think, Talk, and Write

1. **Main Idea** What are some properties of matter?
2. **Vocabulary** What is matter?
3. **Main Idea and Details** Choose two objects. List all the properties you can to describe each one.

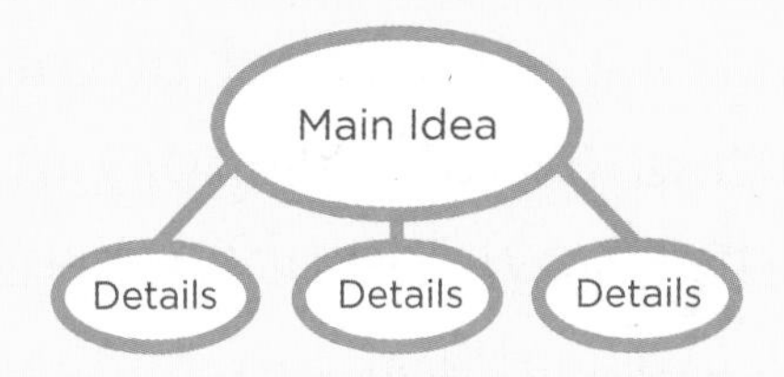

4. **Critical Thinking** What property of glass makes it a good material for windows?
5. **Test Prep** **What are the building blocks of matter?**
   - **A** liquids
   - **B** elements
   - **C** wood
   - **D** water

Writing Link

Writing That Describes
Suppose you brought your favorite toy to school and lost it. Write a notice to hang on your classroom bulletin board. What properties of the toy will you describe?

Math Link

Make a Table
Collect five small objects. Predict which ones will sink and which ones will float. Then put the objects in a tank of water. Record your results in a table.

LOG ON e-Review Summaries and quizzes online at www.macmillanmh.com

Meet Neil deGrasse TYSON

Did you know that you are "star dust"? Neil deGrasse Tyson can tell you what that means. He is a scientist at the American Museum of Natural History in New York. He studies how the universe works.

Your body is full of hydrogen, carbon, and many other elements. All these elements were first formed in stars a long time ago. How did these elements make their way from the stars to your body?

Most elements form inside the dense and fiery centers of stars. Hydrogen combines to form all of the other elements in these conditions. Throughout their lives, stars scatter elements into space. Over millions of years, these elements combine to form new stars, planets, or even living things like you!

Neil is an astrophysicist. An astrophysicist is a scientist who studies how the universe works.

Main Idea and Details

- A main idea tells what the article is about.
- Details, such as facts and examples, support the main idea.

A nebula is a cloud of gas and star dust in space. The Horsehead Nebula shown here gets its name from its horselike shape.

Write About It

Main Idea and Details Read the article with a partner. What is the main idea? What details add to the main idea? Fill in a main-idea chart. Then write a few sentences to explain the main idea.

LOG ON e-Journal Write about it online at www.macmillanmh.com

Lesson 2

Measuring Matter

Look and Wonder

This diver is measuring the length of a grass plant on the sea floor. Why is it important to know how to measure matter?

3-4.1. Classify different forms of matter (including solids, liquids, and gases) according to their observable and measurable properties.

Explore

Inquiry Activity

How can you measure length?

Make a Prediction

How wide is your classroom? Write a prediction.

Test Your Prediction

1. **Measure** Work with a partner. Stand with your back against one wall. Slowly walk across the room, placing one foot in front of the other. The heel of your front foot should meet the toe of your back foot. Your partner will count the number of steps it takes to cross the room.
2. Trade roles with your partner and repeat step 1.
3. **Communicate** Compare your data with the class's data. Make a table listing the data for the entire class.

Draw Conclusions

4. **Interpret Data** What is the highest measurement? What is the lowest measurement? Did anyone get the same measurement?
5. **Infer** Why were there different measurements? Why is it useful to use measuring tools, such as a ruler?

Explore More

Measure Scientists use the metric system to measure matter. Predict how wide your classroom is in meters and centimeters. Then use a metric ruler to measure the width of your classroom. How do your measurements compare with your predictions?

3-I.4. Predict the outcome of a simple investigation and compare the result with the prediction.

Read and Learn

Main Idea 3-4.1

Matter can be measured using tools that record standard units.

Vocabulary

metric system, p. 290

pan balance, p. 292

gravity, p. 294

weight, p. 294

at www.macmillanmh.com

Reading Skill 

Summarize

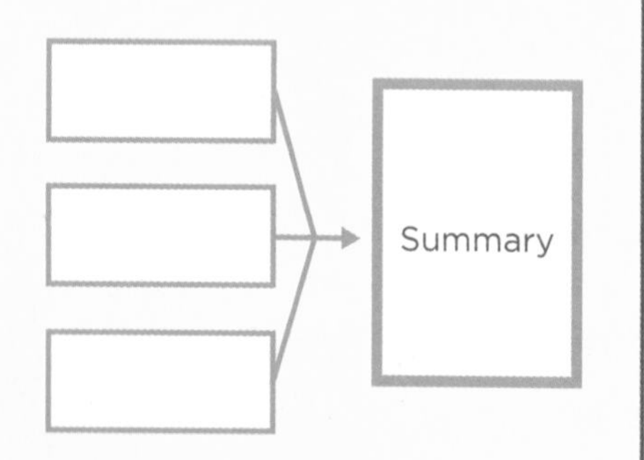

How is matter measured?

Many properties of matter can be observed or measured with tools. You can look closely at an object with a hand lens. You can measure its length and width with a ruler. You can use a thermometer to measure its temperature.

Measuring is a way to compare sizes or amounts. People use tools marked with standard units to measure matter. A *standard unit* is a unit of measurement that people agree to use, such as feet or miles. A common system of standard units is the **metric system** (MET•rik SIS•tuhm). Scientists use the metric system.

Length

You measure length to find out how long something is. You have probably used rulers to measure how tall you are. In the metric system, length is measured in units called meters.

Measuring helps this man build a bookcase that fits together. ▶

Measuring the Volume of a Solid

Read a Photo

How can you measure the volume of this rock?

Clue: Look how the water level changes.

▲ The volume of a liquid may be measured using a graduated cylinder, beaker, or measuring cup.

Volume

Volume describes how much space an object takes up. You probably have used measuring cups to measure the volume of liquids. You can also use beakers or graduated cylinders. In the metric system a liquid's volume is measured in units called liters.

You can measure the volume of a solid, too. First, measure some water. Then place a solid object completely under the water. Subtract the original water level from the new water level. The difference is the solid's volume.

Quick Check

Summarize What are three measurements you could make to describe matter?

Critical Thinking Why is it important to use standard units?

How do we measure mass?

You can use a **pan balance** to measure mass. Remember that mass is a measure of the amount of matter in an object. To find an object's mass, you balance it with objects whose masses you know. First, place the object on one end of a pan balance. Then add the known masses to the other side until both sides are level. When the two sides are level, you know the mass of the object.

▲ Gram masses can be used to find the mass of an object.

In the metric system, mass is measured in grams. A gram is close to the amount of mass in two small paper clips. A kilogram is the same as 1,000 grams.

Objects with the same volume do not always have the same mass. A marble is about the same size as a piece of popcorn. However the marble has a greater mass. How is that possible?

Matter is made up of tiny particles. In some objects the particles are close together. In other objects they are farther apart. The particles inside a marble are packed together more tightly than those inside a piece of popcorn. A marble has more particles than a piece of popcorn. It has more mass.

Quick Check

Summarize How can you measure mass using a pan balance?

Critical Thinking How could you measure the mass of a liquid with a balance?

Quick Lab

Measure Mass and Volume

1. **Predict** Look at a toy car, golf ball, and marble. Predict which object has the most mass. Which has the greatest volume?
2. **Measure** Find the mass of each object. List the objects from most mass to least mass.
3. **Measure** Fill a measuring cup with 250 mL of water. Add one object at a time to the measuring cup. Record the water level for each object.
4. **Interpret Data** List the objects from greatest to least volume.
5. **Interpret Data** Which object has the most mass? Which object has the greatest volume? How did the results compare with your prediction?

bag of popcorn

bag of marbles

◀ The bag of marbles has more mass than the bag of popcorn.

FACT Air has mass.

How are mass and weight different?

What happens when you leap into the air? Do you float away? No, you come back to the ground. This happens because of gravity (GRAV•i•tee). **Gravity** is a pulling force that holds you on Earth. Gravity keeps you and everything on Earth from floating into space.

You can measure how much Earth's gravity pulls on you. This measurement is your weight (WAYT). **Weight** is a measure of the pull of gravity on you. Weight can be measured with a spring scale. Weight is different from mass. If you visited the Moon, your mass would stay the same. The matter inside you would not change. However your weight would change. This is because the pull of the Moon's gravity is weaker than the pull of Earth's gravity. Your weight on the Moon would be less than your weight on Earth. Your mass would be the same.

Spring scales are used to measure weight.

◀ The pull of gravity is weaker on the Moon than on Earth.

Quick Check

Summarize How is weight different from mass?

Critical Thinking Do you think you could jump higher on the Moon? Explain.

Lesson Review

Visual Summary

	Properties of matter, such as **length** and **volume**, can be measured and observed with tools.
	**Mass** can be measured with a pan balance.
	Mass stays the same. The **weight** of an object depends on the force of gravity.

Make a FOLDABLES™ Study Guide

Make a Layered-Look Book. Use it to summarize what you learned about measuring.

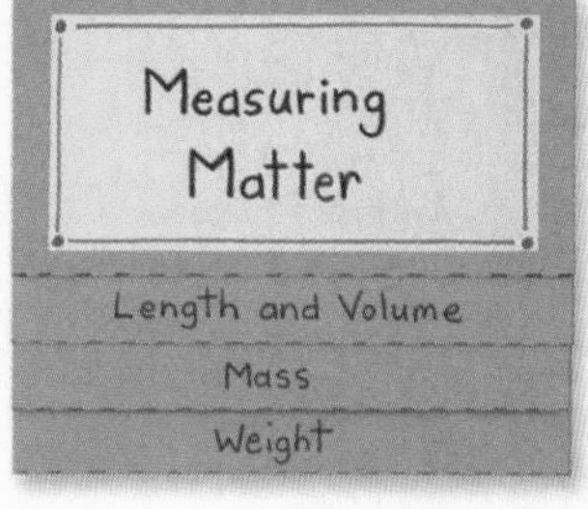

Think, Talk, and Write

1. **Main Idea** How is matter measured?
2. **Vocabulary** What is gravity?
3. **Summarize** Does a large object always have a lot of mass? Explain your answer.

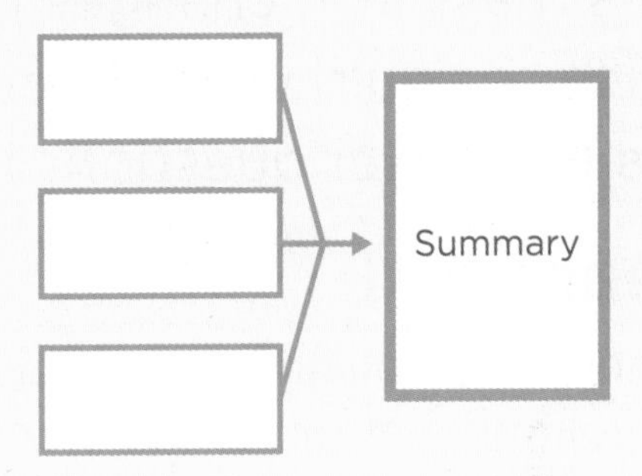

4. **Critical Thinking** Why is it important to measure accurately?
5. **Test Prep What tool would you use to measure weight?**

   A thermometer
   B hand lens
   C spring scale
   D ruler

Math Link

Metric Measurements
What tool would you use to measure the length of a pencil in centimeters? Use this tool to measure the length of four objects. List them in order from shortest to longest.

Social Studies Link

Do Research
About 5,000 years ago people began using standard weights. Some early weights were the shekel (SHEK•uhl) and the mina (MYE•nuh). Find out more about early systems of measurement.

LOG ON e-Review Summaries and quizzes online at www.macmillanmh.com

Focus on Skills

Inquiry Skill: Measure

You have learned that matter is anything that takes up space and has mass. Water is matter that is important to life on Earth. It is found on Earth as solid ice and liquid water. It is even found in the air. What happens to water's mass as it changes from a chunk of solid ice to liquid water? Scientists **measure** things to answer questions like this.

measuring cup

▶ Learn It

When you **measure**, you find such things as the mass, volume, length, or temperature of an object. You can also measure distances and time. Scientists use many tools to measure things. Some of these tools are shown on this page. Scientists use measurements to describe and compare objects or events.

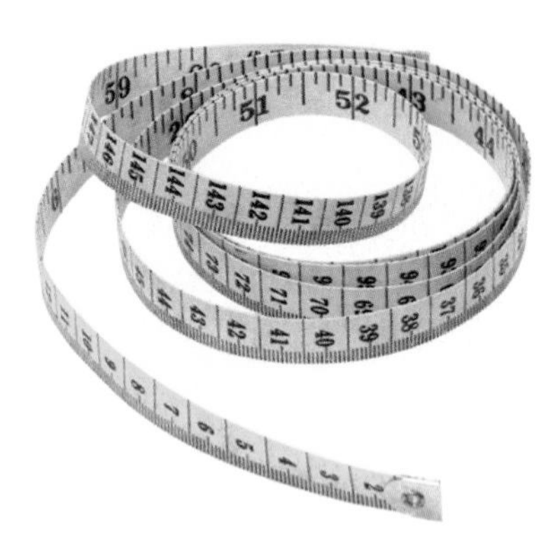

tape measure

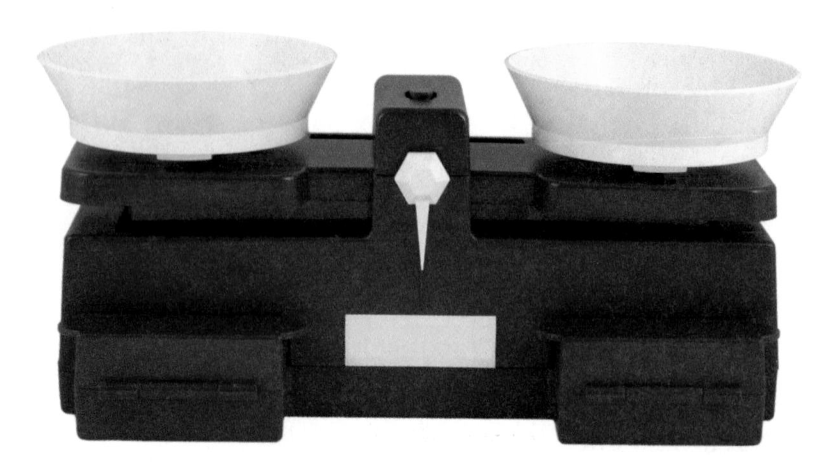

pan balance

thermometer

3-1.4. Predict the outcome of a simple investigation and compare the result with the prediction.

▶ Try It

You know that scientists **measure** things to answer questions. You can measure, too. Answer this question. Do ice cubes have the same mass after they melt?

1. To start, place several ice cubes in a cup. Then cover the cup with plastic wrap so the water stays inside the cup.
2. Measure mass by placing the cup on one end of a pan balance. Add masses to the other side of the pan balance until both sides are level. Record the mass on a chart.

Time	Mass

3. Measure the mass every $\frac{1}{2}$ hour until the ice is completely melted.
4. Now use your measurements to answer the question. Do ice cubes have the same mass after they melt?

▶ Apply It

Now **measure** to answer this question: Does ice cream have the same mass after it melts? How do you know?

Lesson 3

Solids, Liquids, and Gases

Look and Wonder

This person is soaring through the air. What do you think you could see from up high? How would you describe the land and water?

3-4.1. Classify different forms of matter (including solids, liquids, and gases) according to their observable and measurable properties.

Explore

Inquiry Activity

How are solids different from liquids?

Make a Prediction

How do you know if something is solid? How do you know when something is a liquid?

Test Your Prediction

1. **Observe** Touch the block. Does it feel more like a solid or more like a liquid? Why?
2. **Experiment** Put the block into the beaker. Record your observations.
3. **Experiment** Use the spoon to stir the block. What happens? Record your observations. Empty the beaker.
4. Repeat steps 1–3. Instead of the block, use the water, salt, hand soap, and clay. Test each object one at a time.

Draw Conclusions

5. Which objects did not change shape? Which objects were easy to stir?
6. **Classify** Which objects are solids? Which are liquids?
7. Explain how solids are different from liquids.

Explore More

Experiment What would happen if you put each object in the freezer? What would happen if you put each object in a warm place? Form a hypothesis and test it.

Materials

block

beaker

plastic spoon

water

salt

hand soap

safety goggles

clay

Step 2

Step 4

3-I.1. Classify objects by two of their properties (attributes).

Read and Learn

Main Idea 3-4.1

Solids, liquids, and gases are three forms of matter.

Vocabulary

states of matter, p. 300

solid, p. 300

liquid, p. 302

gas, p. 303

at www.macmillanmh.com

Reading Skill

Classify

What are three forms of matter?

Matter comes in many forms. Look at the picture below. The canoe is a solid. The river is made up of water, a liquid. The air is made of gases. Solids, liquids, and gases make up three forms of matter. Scientists call these forms **states of matter**. Each of these states of matter has certain properties.

Solids

Most of the things you see around you are solids (SOL•idz). A **solid** is matter that takes up a definite amount of space and has its own shape. Definite means "it stays the same." This book is a solid. Pencils, desks, and pillows are solids, too. If you put a pencil into a jar or box, it stays the same. It has a definite size and shape.

How are these boys using three states of matter?

Remember that matter is made up of tiny particles. These particles are too small to see. In a solid these particles are packed closely together. They do not have a lot of room to move around. The particles stay in place so the solid keeps its shape.

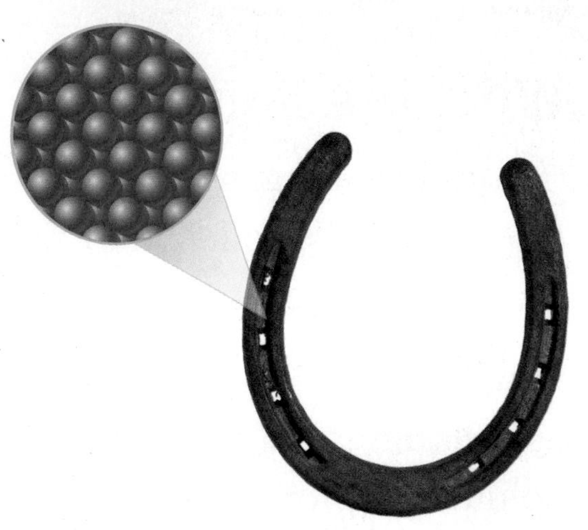

The particles in this solid horseshoe cannot move much.

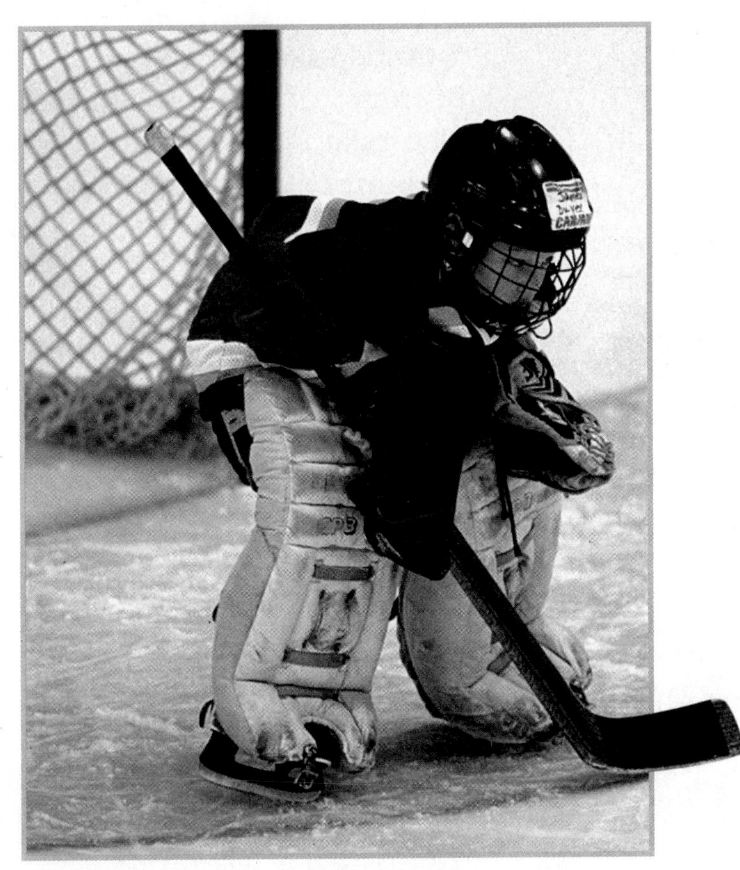

▲ Solids can be hard or soft. This goalie's helmet is hard, but his leg pads are soft.

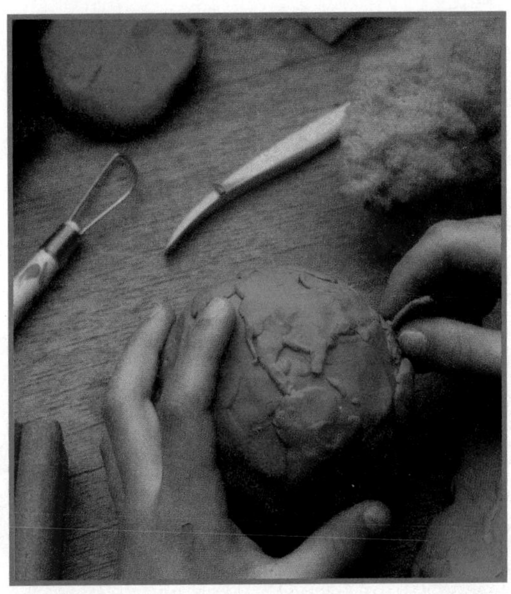

▲ Even though you can change the shape of clay, it is still a solid.

Quick Check

Classify What are three solids you use every day?

Critical Thinking A rubber band can change its shape when it is stretched. Do you think a rubber band is a solid or a liquid? Explain your answer.

What are liquids and gases?

Liquids and gases are two other states of matter. Like solids, they take up space and have mass.

Liquids

A **liquid** is matter that has a definite volume but not a definite shape. A liquid takes the shape of its container. Water, shampoo, and milk are some liquids. When milk is inside a carton, it takes the shape of the carton. When you pour milk into a glass, it takes the shape of the glass. If you spill the milk, it will spread out over the floor. If you were able to mop up the milk and put it back into the carton, it would still be the same amount of milk. The volume of the milk stays the same. Only its shape changes.

▲ Liquids take the shape of their containers. Liquids also take up a definite amount of space inside their containers.

Liquid Particles

◀ The particles in a liquid are able to slide past one another. That is why liquids can change shape.

Read a Diagram

How would you describe the particles in a liquid?

Clue: Illustrations can help show things that are hard to see.

LOG ON *Science in Motion* Watch how the particles of a liquid move at www.macmillanmh.com

Gases

You cannot always see gases, but they are all around you. A **gas** is matter that has no definite shape or volume. A gas takes the shape and volume of its container.

Think about balloons being blown up with a helium tank. Helium is a gas. When it is in the tank, it has a small volume. It has the shape of the tank. When the gas is used to fill balloons, it spreads out. It then has a much greater volume. It also changes shape. It takes the shape of the balloons.

▲ The particles in a gas have more energy than the particles in a liquid. In a gas, the particles of matter can move about freely.

Quick Lab

Compare Solids, Liquids, and Gases

gas

1. Blow into an empty bag. Then quickly seal the bag.

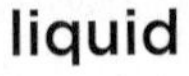

liquid

2. Fill a second bag with water and seal this bag. Put a rock in a third bag and seal it.

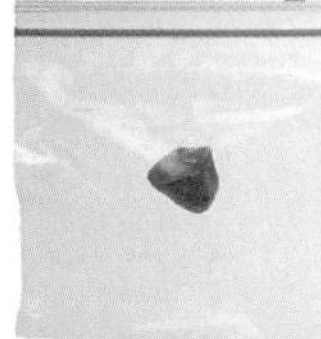

solid

3. **Observe** Each bag contains matter in a different state. How does each bag look and feel? Record your observations.

5. **Observe** Open each bag. What happens?
   △ **Be Careful.** Hold the bag filled with water over a container.

6. **Communicate** Describe the properties of a solid, a liquid, and a gas. Tell how these three states of matter are different from one another.

✓ *Quick Check*

Classify List three liquids you drink every day.

Critical Thinking Suppose a balloon filled with helium bursts. What would happen to the gas?

How do you use all the states of matter?

Solids, liquids, and gases are all around you. You use them in many ways. Many of the foods you eat are solids. Your body needs water, a liquid. You need oxygen, a gas from the air. Oxygen helps you get the energy you need from the food you eat.

You use the states of matter in other ways, too. You can find three states of matter on a bicycle, for example. Many parts of the bicycle are made of solids. The handlebars, seat, and the rubber of the tires are solids. The tires are filled with air, a gas. The oil on the bicycle chain is a liquid.

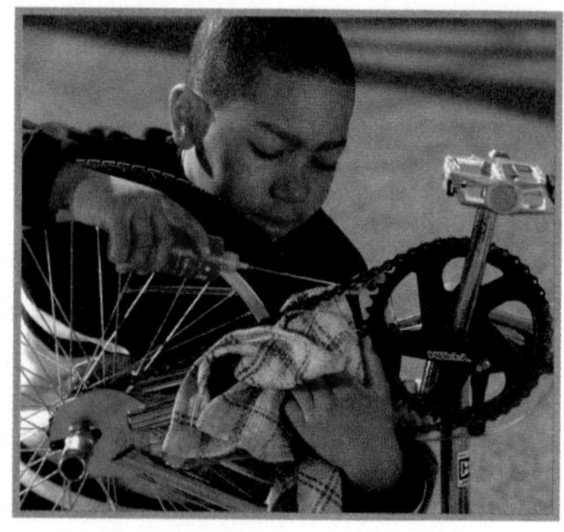

▲ Oil, a liquid, helps a bicycle chain move smoothly.

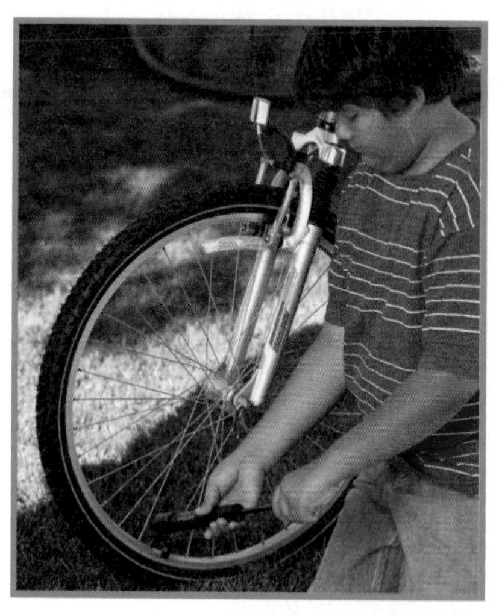

▲ You pump air into the tires to inflate them.

 ***Quick Check***

Classify What are three states of matter found on a bicycle?

Critical Thinking How do you use the different states of matter?

The bicycle frame is solid. It has to be solid to keep the bicycle together. ▶

Lesson Review

Visual Summary

	A **solid** is matter that has a definite volume and shape.
	A **liquid** is matter that has a definite volume but no definite shape.
	A **gas** is matter that has no definite volume or shape.

Make a FOLDABLES™ Study Guide

Make a Layered-Look Book. Use it to summarize what you learned about states of matter.

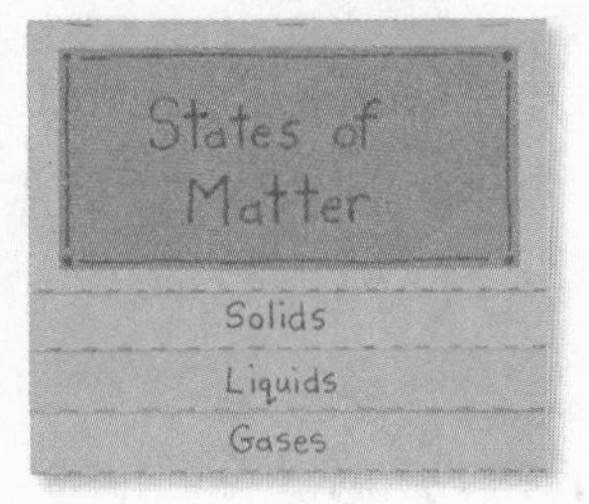

Think, Talk, and Write

1. **Main Idea** What are the properties of a solid, liquid, and gas?

2. **Vocabulary** What is matter that has no definite shape or size?

3. **Classify** What kind of matter is this book? What kind of matter is water? What kind of matter is air?

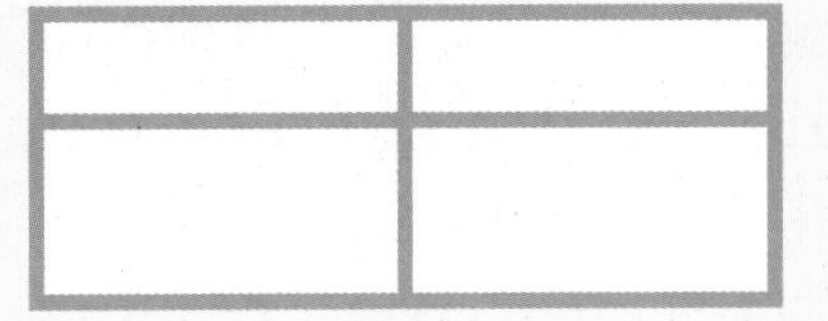

4. **Critical Thinking** Compare solids, liquids, and gases. How are they alike? How do they differ?

5. **Test Prep** **Matter that spreads out to fill its container is a**
   - **A** gas.
   - **B** liquid.
   - **C** mass.
   - **D** solid.

Math Link

Solve a Problem
A helium tank can inflate 126 large balloons. It can inflate three times as many small balloons. How many small balloons can the tank inflate?

Art Link

Make a Poster
Draw diagrams that show the differences among solids, liquids, and gases. Write a brief explanation of each diagram.

LOG ON e-Review Summaries and quizzes online at www.macmillanmh.com

Describe Matter

You can describe matter in many ways. How would you describe a pizza to someone who has never seen one? How does it look? How does it smell? These are some of the pizza's observable properties. How big is the pizza? What is its mass? These are some of its measurable properties. Is it a solid or a liquid? This is its state of matter.

Descriptive Writing

A good description

- includes describing words to tell how something looks, sounds, feels, smells or tastes
- uses details to create a picture for the reader
- groups together details in an order that makes sense

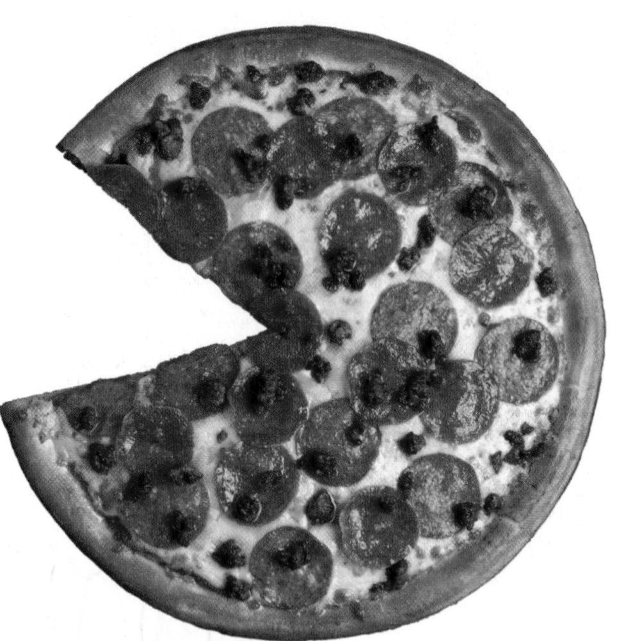

Write About It

Descriptive Writing Think of an object you use every day, such as your book bag. How would you describe it to someone who has never seen it before? Use the object's properties to write a description of the object.

Write about it online at www.macmillanmh.com

Measuring Perimeter

Solids come in many shapes and sizes. They can be round like a ball or square like a brick. They can be huge like a skyscraper or tiny like a grain of sand. You can measure the distance around a solid. The distance around a solid object is called the *perimeter*.

Find the Perimeter

▶ To find the perimeter of an object, add the lengths of all of its sides.

6 + 2 + 6 +2 = 16
This rectangle's perimeter is 16.

6

2 2

6

Solve It

Find the perimeter of the red square. Find the perimeter of the blue triangle. How can you find the perimeter of the entire house? Try it.

Lesson 4

Heat

Look and Wonder

Hot air causes these balloons to rise into the sky. What happens to air as it is heated?

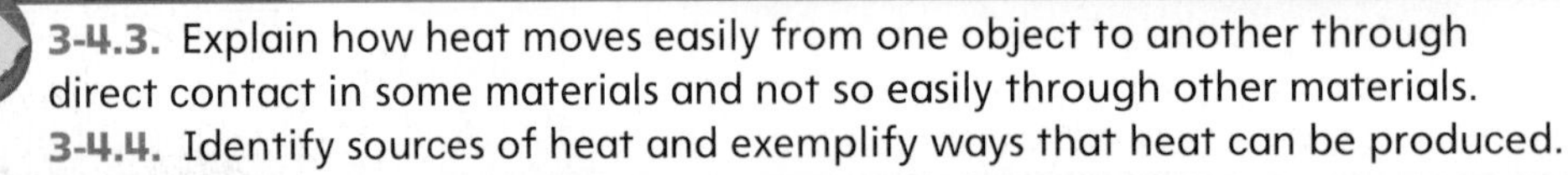

3-4.3. Explain how heat moves easily from one object to another through direct contact in some materials and not so easily through other materials.
3-4.4. Identify sources of heat and exemplify ways that heat can be produced.

Explore

Inquiry Activity

What happens to air when it is heated?

Form a Hypothesis

How does heat affect air? Does it make air get bigger or smaller? Write a hypothesis.

Test Your Hypothesis

1. Use a dropper to place five drops of water along the edge of a bottle's opening. Place a plastic disk on top of the opening. Then put the bottle in a refrigerator for several hours.
2. **Predict** What will happen to the disk if the temperature of the air in the bottle increases?
3. **Observe** Remove the bottle from the refrigerator. Rub your hands together quickly. When your hands feel warm, place them on the bottle. Look at the disk.

Draw Conclusions

4. **Communicate** What happened to the disk? Was your prediction correct?
5. **Infer** Think about what happened to the disk. What happens to air when it is heated?

Explore More

Experiment Place an empty plastic bottle in the refrigerator for several hours. Remove the bottle from the refrigerator and immediately stretch a balloon over the opening. What happens to the balloon?

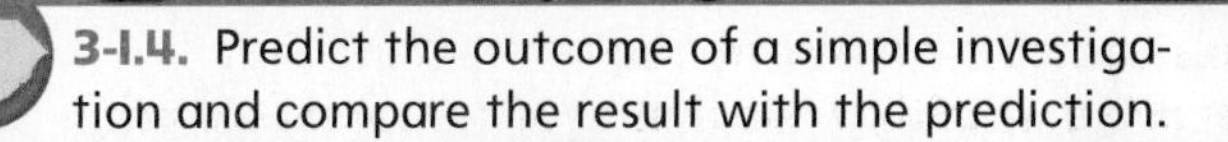

3-1.4. Predict the outcome of a simple investigation and compare the result with the prediction.

Read and Learn

Main Idea 3-4.3 3-4.4

Heat affects matter in many ways. Heat always moves from warmer objects to cooler objects.

Vocabulary

heat, p. 310

thermal energy, p. 312

temperature, p. 312

thermometer, p. 313

conductor, p. 314

insulator, p. 314

at www.macmillanmh.com

Reading Skill

Main Idea and Details

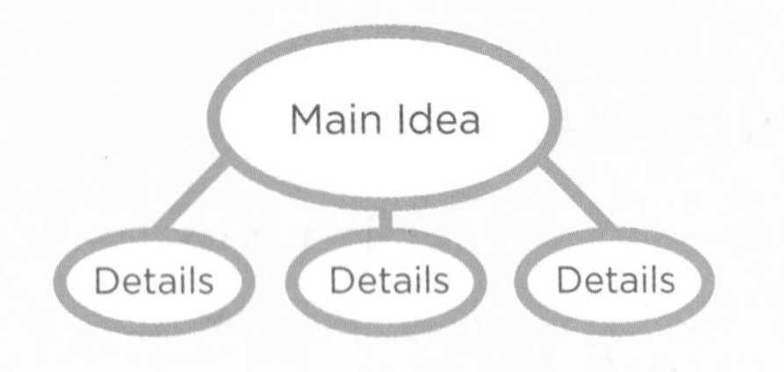

The Sun's energy warms the air, land, and water.

What is heat?

Have you ever put your hands on a bowl of hot soup? What happened? Your hands got warm. Heat moved from the hot bowl to your cool hands. **Heat** is a form of energy that moves between objects. Heat can travel through solids, liquids, and gases. It can even travel through space. No matter what it travels through, heat always flows from a warmer object to a cooler one.

Sources of Heat

The Sun is Earth's main source of heat. A *source* is where something comes from. The Sun's heat warms the air, land, and water. Without the Sun's heat, it would be too cold on Earth for most living things to survive.

Quick Lab

Heating Water and Soil

1. **Predict** Which heats up faster, a cup of water or a cup of soil?
2. **Use Variables** Fill one cup with 150 mL of water. Fill another cup with 150 mL of soil.
3. **Measure** Put a thermometer in each cup and measure the temperature of the water and soil. Record the data.
4. **Experiment** Put the cups in a warm place. Record the temperature in each after 15 minutes.

5. **Use Numbers** Find the difference between the first and last readings of each thermometer.
6. **Interpret Data** Which cup warmed up more? How do you know?

Fires, light bulbs, and stoves are some other sources of heat. Fires use chemical changes to produce heat. Light bulbs and some stoves use electricity to produce heat. Rubbing two objects together can also produce heat. This is why your hands get warm when you rub them together.

Heating Objects

Some objects heat up faster than others. For example, at the beach you will find sand and water. Both are warmed by the Sun. The sand gets very hot, but the water stays much cooler.

Quick Check

Main Idea and Details Describe how heat flows.

Critical Thinking What are some ways people use heat?

How does heat affect matter?

Remember that all matter is made of tiny particles. These particles are always moving. The energy that makes them move is called **thermal energy** (THUR•muhl EN•uhr•jee). Heating matter increases how much thermal energy the particles have. A hot object, such as hot soup, has a lot of thermal energy. Its particles move quickly. A cold object, such as an ice cube, has much less thermal energy. Its particles move slowly.

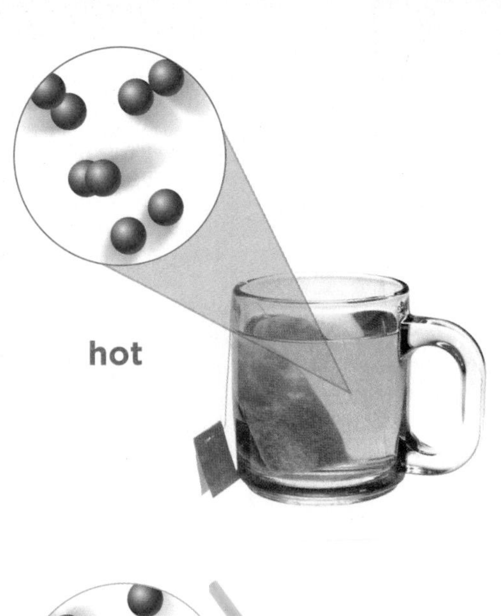

Thermal energy is what makes objects feel hot or cold. In fact, when you measure an object's temperature (TEM•puhr•uh•chuhr), you are really measuring its thermal energy. **Temperature** is a measure of how hot or cold something is. It describes how much thermal energy an object has. The more thermal energy an object has, the higher its temperature will be.

Measuring Temperature

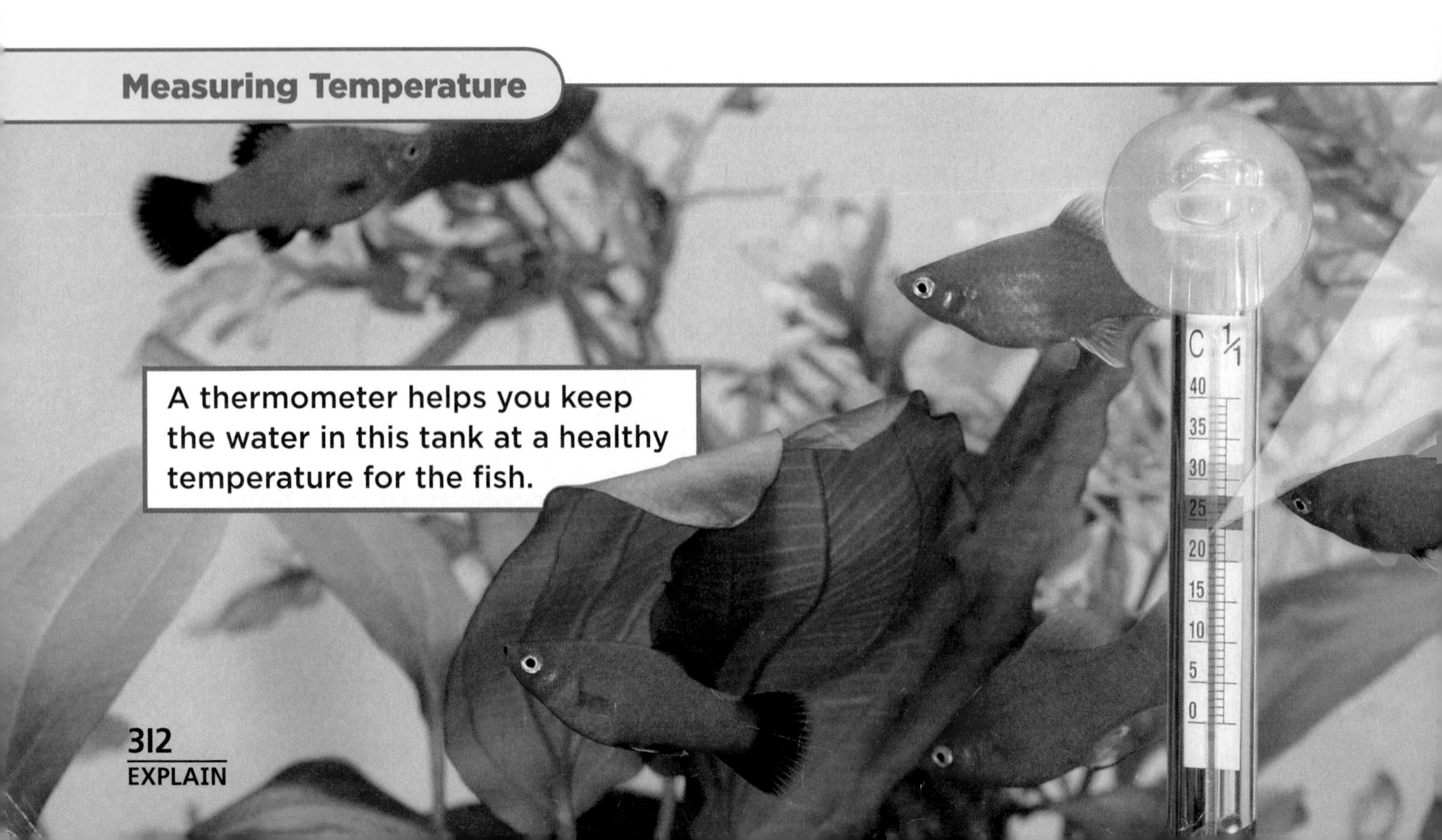

A thermometer helps you keep the water in this tank at a healthy temperature for the fish.

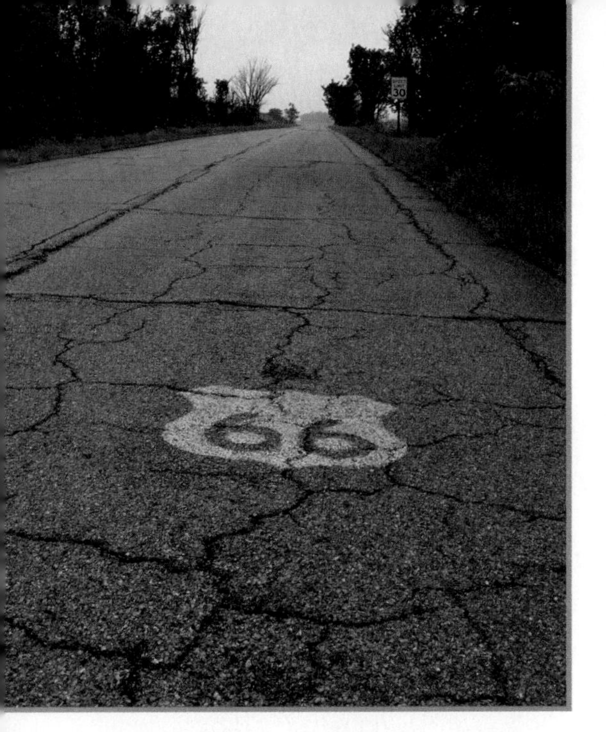

▲ Roads can crack as they expand and contract with changing temperatures.

Expanding and Contracting

When heat flows into an object, the object gains thermal energy. Its temperature increases. Its particles move faster and farther apart. The object gets bigger, or *expands*. When heat flows away from an object, the object loses thermal energy. Its temperature decreases. Its particles move more slowly. The object gets smaller, or *contracts*.

You can see matter expand or contract in a thermometer (thuhr•MOM•i•tuhr). A **thermometer** is a tool used to measure temperature. Some thermometers are made up of a clear tube filled with a liquid. When the temperature of the liquid increases, the liquid expands. It rises and fills more of the tube. When the temperature of the liquid decreases, the liquid contracts. It fills less of the tube.

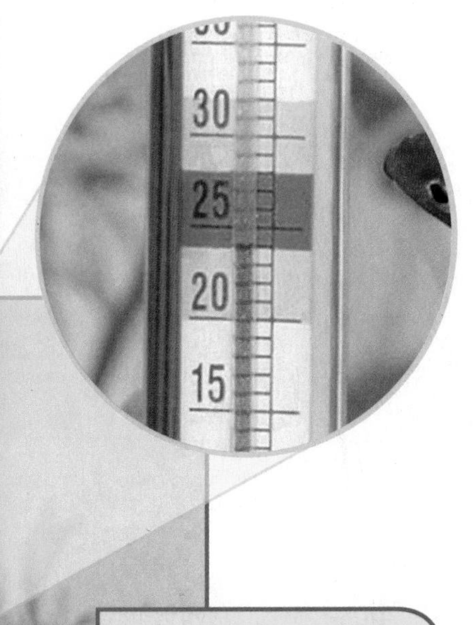

Read a Photo

What is the temperature shown on the thermometer? Give your answer in °C.

Clue: Line up the top of the red liquid with the black markings on the thermometer.

Changing State

Heat can cause matter to change state. Solids, such as ice cream, can melt when they are heated. Liquids, such as water, can evaporate when they are heated. They can freeze when heat flows from them.

Quick Check

Main Idea and Details List some ways heat affects matter.

Critical Thinking What happens to an ice pop when it is out of the freezer?

How can you control the flow of heat?

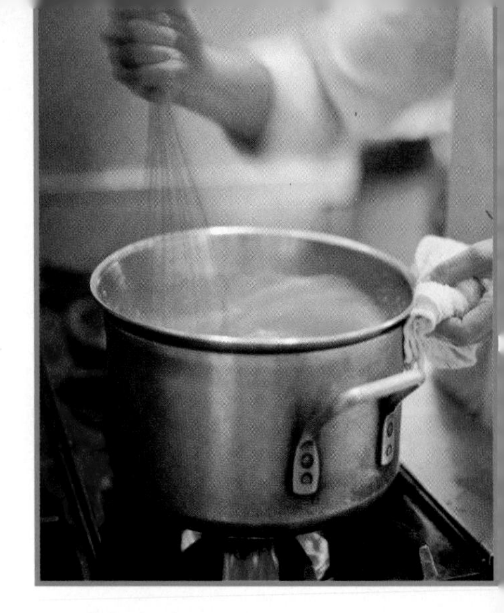

▲ Metal pots are conductors.

Heat moves more easily through some materials than others. That is why pots are often made of metal. Heat moves easily through metals. Heat moves from the stove to the metal pot. The whole pot gets warm. Materials such as metals are good conductors (kuhn•DUK•tuhrz). A **conductor** is a material that heat moves through easily.

When you are cold, you wrap yourself in a blanket to keep warm. A blanket is an insulator (IN•suh•lay•tuhr). An **insulator** is a material that heat does not move through easily. Wool, cotton, and fur are examples of insulators.

Quick Check

Main Idea and Details What is a conductor? What is an insulator? Give an example of each.

Critical Thinking Why do people use foam cups when drinking hot chocolate?

Snow can be an insulator. Heat cannot flow easily through the walls of this igloo.

Lesson Review

Visual Summary

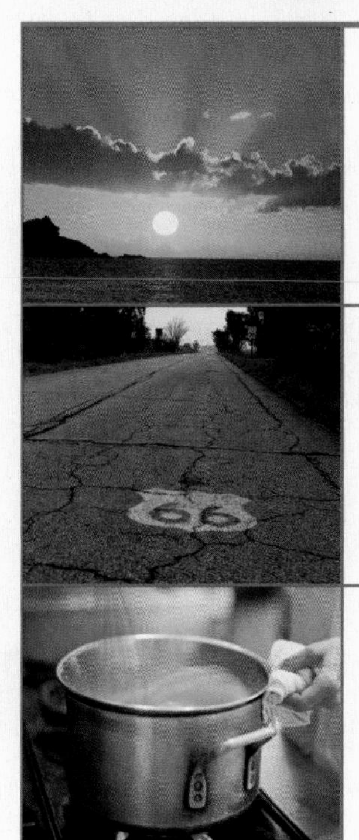

Energy that moves from a warmer object to a colder object is called heat.

Heat affects matter in many ways.

Heat moves easily through **conductors**. Heat does not move easily through **insulators.**

Make a FOLDABLES™ Study Guide

Make a Three-Tab Book. Use it to summarize what you learned about heat.

Think, Talk, and Write

1. **Main Idea** How does heat move?

2. **Vocabulary** How is temperature different from heat?

3. **Main Idea and Details** How does matter change when heat flows into it?

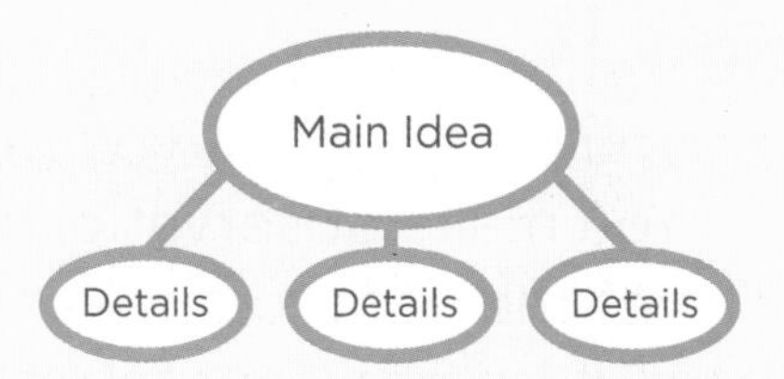

4. **Critical Thinking** Sometimes when people have a fever, they put a cold wet cloth on their forehead. How does this cool them off?

5. **Test Prep** **Most of Earth's heat comes from**
   - **A** the Sun.
   - **B** water.
   - **C** batteries.
   - **D** electricity.

Math Link

Solve a Problem
Yesterday the temperature outside was 21°C. Overnight the temperature dropped 8 degrees. What is the new temperature?

Health Link

Do Research
Fires are a source of heat. However, fires can be dangerous. Find out ways to prevent fires. Make a pamphlet to share this information.

Focus on Skills

Inquiry Skill: Experiment

You just learned about heat. You read that an insulator is a material that does not allow heat to pass through it easily. How can you find out if something is an insulator? You can **experiment** to answer a question like this.

▶ Learn It

When you **experiment**, you perform tests to answer a question. You make observations and collect data. Then you interpret the data to answer a question. When you experiment, it is important to test only one thing at a time. This helps you know what caused your results.

▶ Try It

Experiment to find out which is the best insulator: paper, plastic, or foam.

Materials **paper cup, plastic cup, foam cup, 6 ice cubes, plastic wrap, 3 rubber bands**

1. Which material do you think will keep the ice cubes solid the longest: paper, plastic, or foam? Write a hypothesis.
2. Put two ice cubes into each cup.
3. Cover each cup with plastic wrap. Use a rubber band to seal the wrap to the cup.

3-I.3. Generate questions about objects, organisms, and events in the environment and use those questions to conduct a scientific investigation.

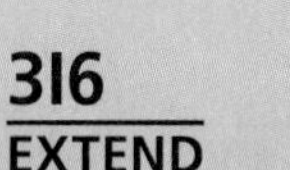

4. Place the cups in a warm place.
5. Observe the ice in the cups every ten minutes for one hour. Record the changes that you observe.

Now use your results to draw conclusions.

- In which cup did the ice cubes melt the slowest?
- Which cup is the best insulator?

Apply It

Now **experiment** to find out which is the best conductor of heat: aluminum, plastic, or wax paper. Remember that a conductor is a material that lets heat pass through it easily.

Repeat this experiment using three different types of wraps and three paper cups. Wrap aluminum foil around one cup, plastic wrap around the second cup, and wax paper around the third cup. Remember to record your observations.

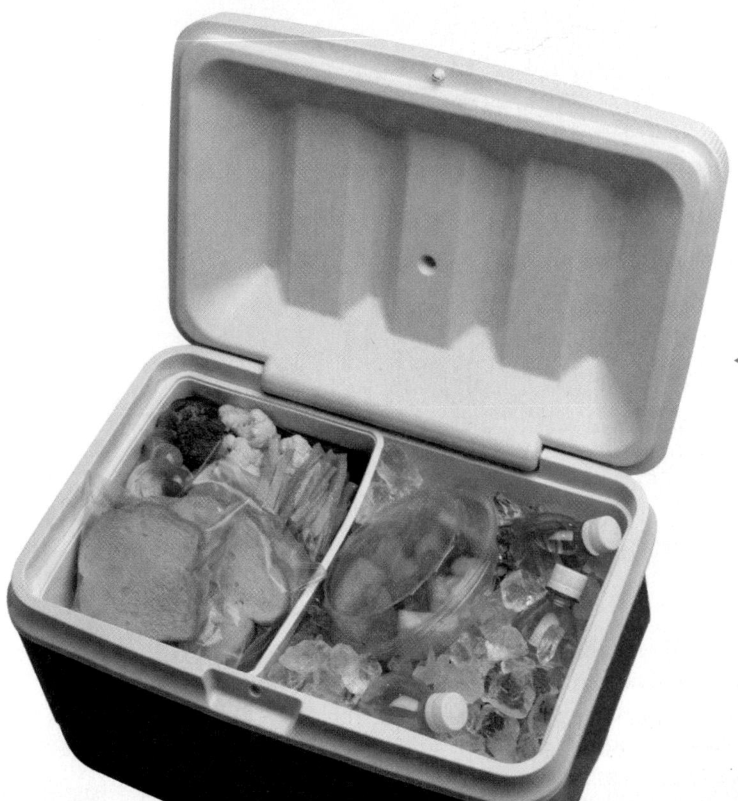

A cooler is an insulator. It keeps your food from getting warm.

Lesson 5

Changes of State

Look and Wonder

A winter storm can bring snow and ice. What happens to snow on a warm, sunny day? What causes this change?

3-4.2. Explain how water and other substances change from one state to another (including melting, freezing, condensing, boiling, and evaporating).

What happens when ice is heated?

Make a Prediction

How does ice change as it is heated? Write a prediction.

Test Your Prediction

1. **Measure** Place a thermometer in a cup of ice. Measure the temperature of the ice. Record the temperature in a table like the one shown.
2. Place the cup in a warm place, such as on a sunny windowsill.
3. **Measure** Stir the ice and measure its temperature every 10 minutes for the next hour. Record the temperature in the table.
4. Describe how the ice changes.

Draw Conclusions

5. **Communicate** How did the ice change as it was heated? Was your prediction correct?
6. **Infer** What happened to the temperature of the water as the ice melted? At what temperature does ice melt?

Explore More

Predict What will happen to the water as it continues to sit in the warm place after the ice has melted? Test your prediction and find out.

Materials

thermometer

plastic cup of ice

spoon

Step 1

Time	Temperature

Step 3

3-I.4. Predict the outcome of a simple investigation and compare the result with the prediction.

Read and Learn

Main Idea 3-4.2

Adding or removing heat can cause matter to change state.

Vocabulary

at www.macmillanmh.com

Reading Skill 

Predict

What I Predict	What Happens

Technology 

Explore how matter changes with the Secret Agents.

What happens when matter is heated?

When matter is heated, it gains energy. Its temperature rises. At certain temperatures, matter will change state.

Changing from a Solid to a Liquid

If you heat most solids to a high enough temperature, they will melt. To **melt** is to change from a solid to a liquid. Different kinds of matter melt at different temperatures. Ice melts at a lower temperature than rocks. Ice melts at 32°F (0°C). Rocks melt at over 1,100°F (593°C)!

Remember that all matter is made up of tiny particles. In solids these particles are held closely together. When a solid is heated and gains energy, its particles begin to move away from each other. They flow around each other and are no longer held tightly together. This causes the solid to lose its shape. It becomes a liquid.

The lava flowing from this volcano is rock that melted deep beneath Earth's surface.

▲ These clothes will dry when the liquid water changes into a gas.

Changing from a Liquid to a Gas

If you heat a liquid to a high enough temperature, it will boil. To **boil** is to change from a liquid to a gas. Energy from heat causes the particles in a liquid to move faster. They spread apart. The liquid turns into a gas.

Liquids can also **evaporate**, or change into a gas, slowly. When wet clothes are placed in the Sun, the water in the clothes evaporates. The Sun heats water droplets in the clothes. The water turns into a gas and your clothes dry. The gas state of water is called *water vapor.* You cannot see water vapor, but it is part of the air.

Heating Water

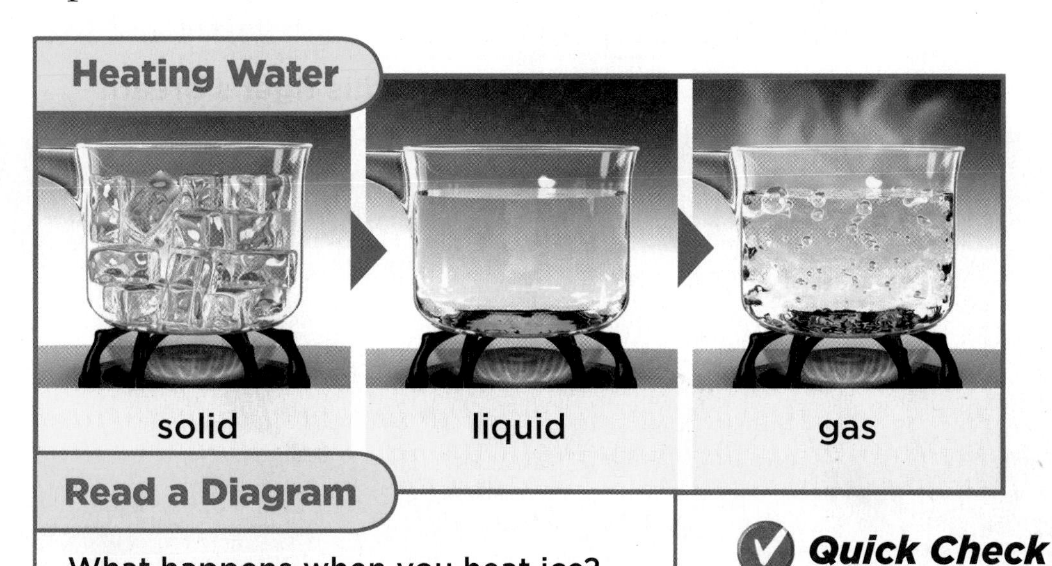

Read a Diagram

What happens when you heat ice?

Clue: Arrows show a sequence.

LOG ON *Science in Motion* Watch how matter changes at **www.macmillanmh.com**

Quick Check

Predict What will happen to cheese when it is heated?

Critical Thinking How does a blow dryer get your hair dry?

What happens when matter is cooled?

When matter is cooled, it loses energy. Its temperature drops. At certain temperatures, matter will change state.

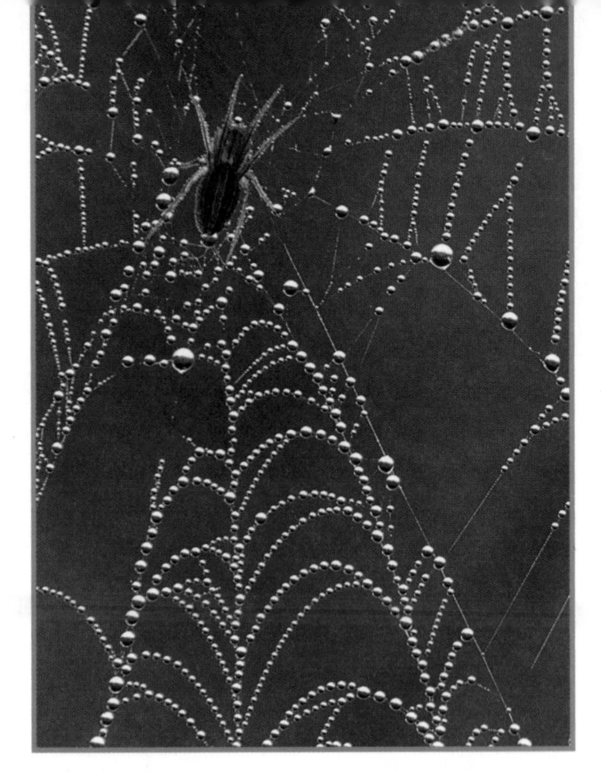

Dew forms when water vapor in the air cools and condenses.

Changing from a Gas to a Liquid

If you cool a gas to the right temperature, it will condense (kuhn•DENS). To **condense** is to change from a gas to a liquid. For example, on cool mornings, small droplets of water called dew can appear on grass and windows. This happens when water vapor in the air touches cool objects and loses energy. Particles of water vapor come closer together. They change into drops of liquid water.

Water vapor in this tiger's breath condenses on a cold day.

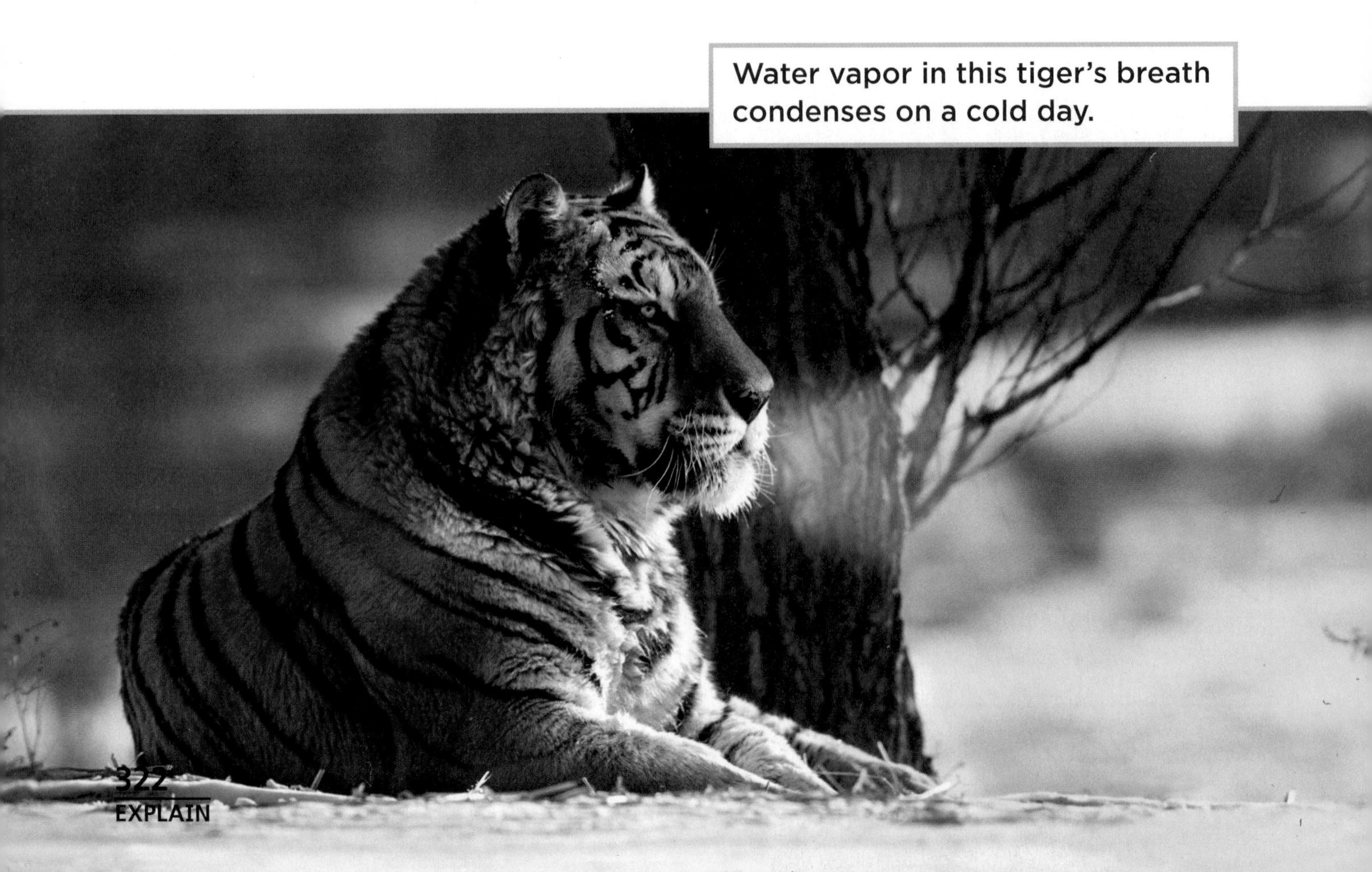

Changing from a Liquid to a Solid

If you cool a liquid to the right temperature, it will freeze. To **freeze** is to change from a liquid to a solid. The particles in the liquid lose energy and move slower and closer together. They get locked into position and form a solid. For example, when you put liquid water into the freezer, it loses energy. It cools to a certain temperature and turns into ice.

Quick Lab

Condense Water Vapor

1. **Observe** Feel an empty plastic cup. Does it feel wet or dry? Does it feel hot or cold? Record your observations.
2. Fill your cup with ice cubes. Next add cold water to the cup.
3. **Observe** Feel your cup again. Does the cup feel wet or dry? Does the cup feel hot or cold? Record your observations.
4. **Observe** Look at your cup after five minutes. What do you notice about the outside of the cup? Is it wet or dry?
5. **Infer** Where did the water on the cup come from?

When juice is cooled enough, it will freeze and become a solid.

Quick Check

Predict What will happen to water vapor when it is cooled?

Critical Thinking How could you make an ice pop?

How is water different from other kinds of matter?

Most kinds of matter shrink as they freeze. Their particles get packed more closely together. They take up less space. Yet water gets larger when it freezes.

As water freezes, its particles rearrange themselves. They make a special pattern. Empty spaces form between the particles. The frozen water takes up more space than the liquid water. This is why freezing a glass of water cracks the glass.

Ice floats in liquid water. This keeps lakes and ponds from freezing from the bottom up. Living things can survive under the ice.

Quick Check

Predict What would happen if you put a plastic bottle filled with liquid water in the freezer? Why does this happen?

Critical Thinking Describe how water changes when it melts.

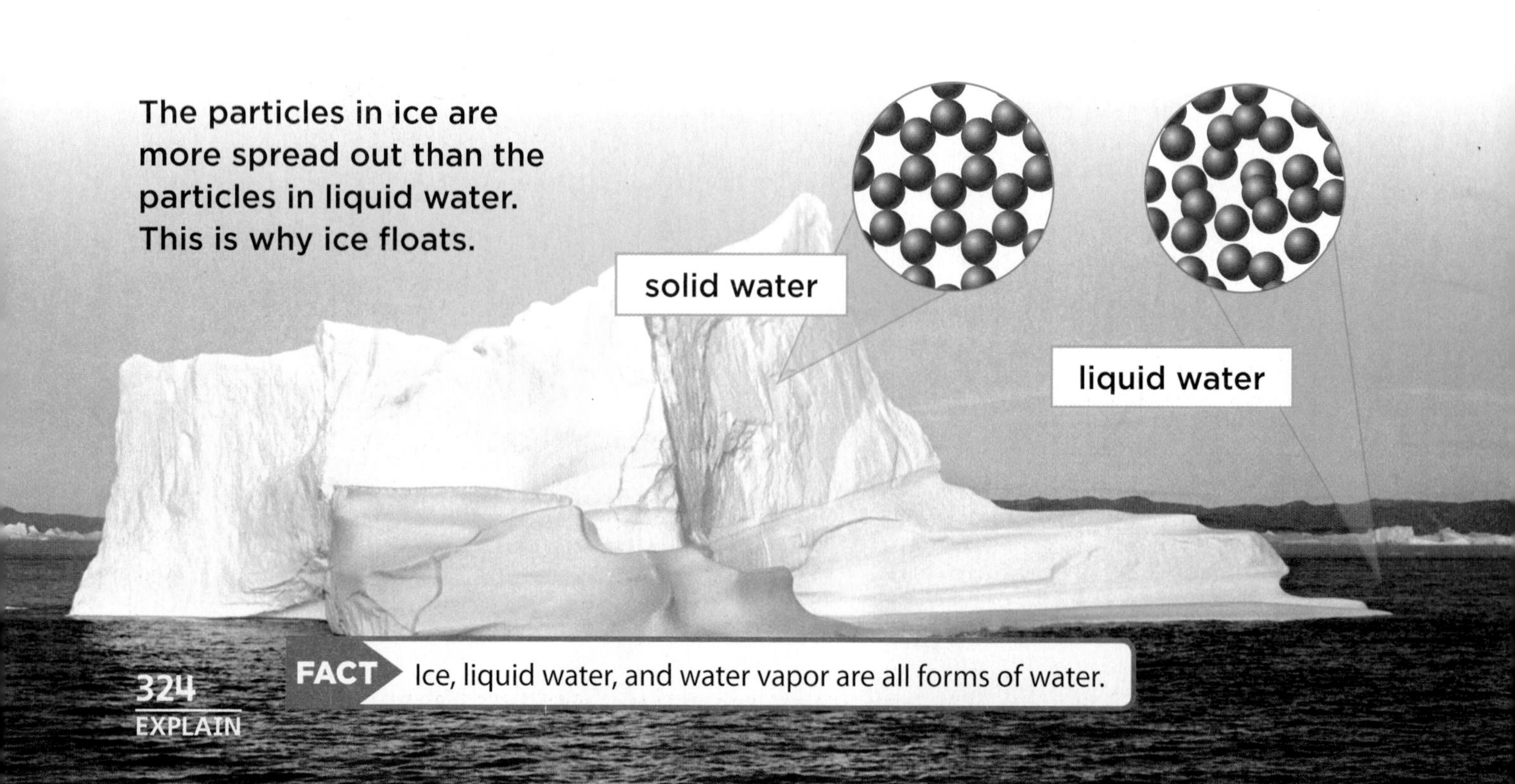

The particles in ice are more spread out than the particles in liquid water. This is why ice floats.

FACT Ice, liquid water, and water vapor are all forms of water.

Lesson Review

Visual Summary

When most **solids** are heated, they melt into **liquids**. When a **liquid** is heated, it changes into a **gas**.

When a **gas** cools it usually condenses into a **liquid**. When a **liquid** cools it freezes into a **solid**.

Water is a special kind of matter. It gets larger when it freezes.

Make a FOLDABLES™ Study Guide

Make a Layered-Look Book. Use it to summarize what you learned about changes of state.

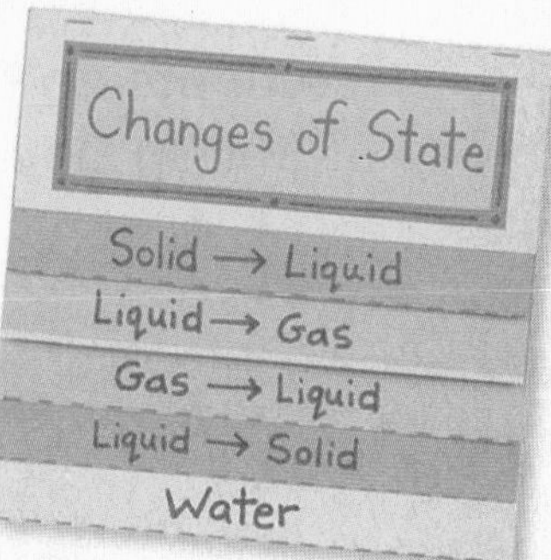

Think, Talk, and Write

1. **Main Idea** How can heat change matter?
2. **Vocabulary** What happens when a gas condenses?
3. **Predict** After a rainstorm the Sun comes out and shines brightly. What will happen to puddles of rainwater?

What I Predict	What Happens

4. **Critical Thinking** You see drops of water on the bathroom mirror after a shower. What caused the water drops to form?
5. **Test Prep** **How is water different from other liquids?**
   A Water gets larger as it freezes.
   B Water gets smaller as it freezes.
   C Water stays the same as it freezes.
   D Water never freezes.

Writing Link

Write a Story
Describe how your life would be different if liquids changed into solids when heated. For example, it could snow when the temperature outside was very hot.

Math Link

Find the Difference
Ice melts at 32°F. Water boils at 212°F. How many degrees are there between water's melting and boiling temperatures?

LOG ON e-Review Summaries and quizzes online at www.macmillanmh.com

Focus on Skills

Inquiry Skill: Predict

You just learned about how liquids change to solids. Which do you think freezes faster, salt water or fresh water? To find answers to questions like this, scientists first **predict** what they think will happen. Next, they experiment to find out what does happen. Then, they compare their results with their prediction.

▶ Learn It

When you **predict**, you state the possible results of an event or experiment. It is important to record your prediction before you do an experiment. Next, you record your observations as you experiment and record the final results. Then you have enough data to figure out if your prediction was correct.

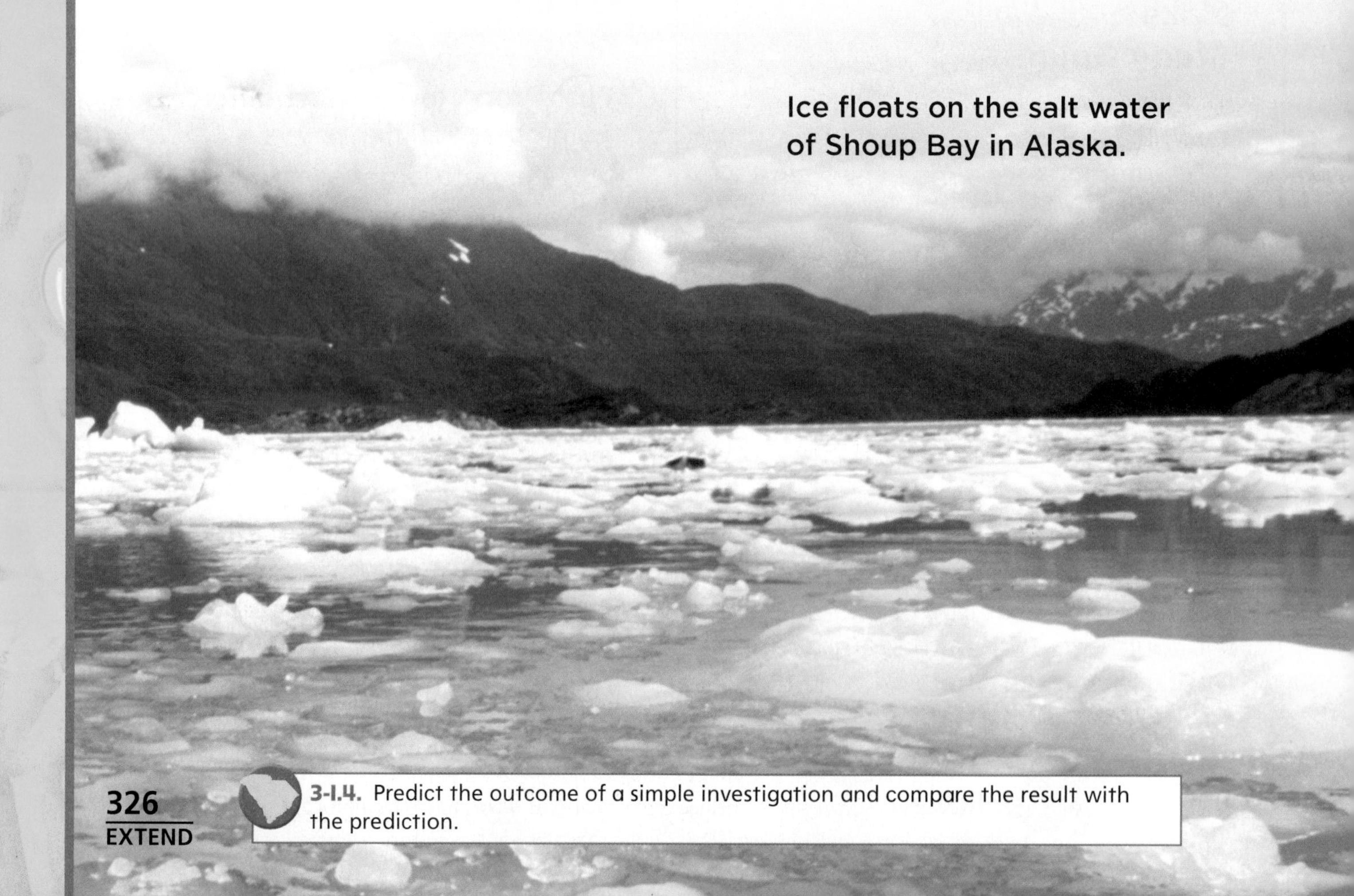

Ice floats on the salt water of Shoup Bay in Alaska.

3-I.4. Predict the outcome of a simple investigation and compare the result with the prediction.

▶ Try It

Which do you think freezes faster, salt water or fresh water? **Predict** what will happen when you freeze fresh water and salt water. Write your prediction on a chart like the one shown. Then do an experiment to test your prediction.

Materials **measuring cup, water, two plastic cups, salt, measuring spoon**

1. Pour 125 mL of water into a plastic cup. Label this cup *Fresh Water.*
2. Pour 125 mL of water into another plastic cup. Add 1 tablespoon of salt and stir with a spoon. Label this cup *Salt Water.*
3. Place both cups into the freezer. Check them every 15 minutes. Draw or write your observations.

Now answer these questions. Which freezes faster, fresh water or salt water? Was your prediction correct?

Which Freezes Faster?	
My Predictions	
Observations of fresh water	
Observations of salt water	
Results	

▶ Apply It

Now that you have learned to think like a scientist, make another prediction. Do you **predict** that salt water or fresh water will evaporate faster? Plan an experiment to find out if your prediction is correct.

CHAPTER 6 Review

Visual Summary

Lesson 1 Matter is anything that has volume and mass.

Lesson 2 Matter can be measured using tools that record standard units.

Lesson 3 Solids, liquids, and gases are three forms of matter.

Lesson 4 Heat affects matter in many ways. Heat always moves from warmer objects to cooler objects.

Lesson 5 Adding or removing heat can cause matter to change state.

Make a FOLDABLES™ Study Guide

Glue your lesson study guides to a piece of paper as shown. Use your study guide to review what you have learned in this chapter.

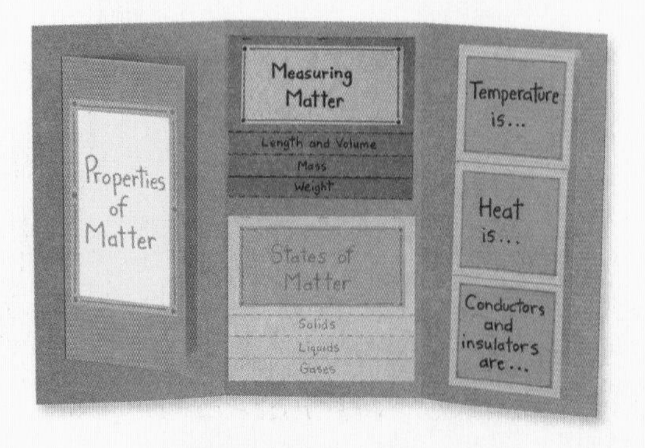

Vocabulary

Fill each blank with the best term from the list.

gas, p. 303	**mass**, p. 281
gravity, p. 294	**matter**, p. 280
heat, p. 310	**melt**, p. 320
insulator, p. 314	**metric system**, p. 290
liquid, p. 302	**volume**, p. 281

1. Matter with no definite shape or volume is a(n) ________. 3-4.1
2. The amount of space an object takes up is its ________. 3-4.1
3. Scientists make measurements using the ________. 3-4.1
4. If matter has a definite volume but not a definite shape, it is in a(n) ________ state. 3-4.1
5. The pulling force that holds you on Earth is called ________. 3-5.4
6. A material that heat does not move through easily is a(n) ________. 3-4.3
7. The amount of matter in an object is its ________. 3-4.1
8. Thermal energy that moves between objects is called ________. 3-4.4
9. To change from a solid to a liquid is to ________. 3-4.2
10. Anything that has mass and volume is ________. 3-4.1

Skills and Concepts

Answer each of the following in complete sentences.

11. Summarize Name three properties of an object that you can measure using the metric system. What standard units would you use for each?
3-4.1

12. Expository Writing Describe what happens to water as it freezes.
3-4.2

13. Predict It is a warm and sunny day. You leave a bar of chocolate on the window sill. How do you think it will change? Can you change it back?
3-4.2

14. Critical Thinking Where can you find the three states of matter in a car?
3-4.1

15. What properties might the two objects shown below have in common? How do you think their properties might be different?
3-4.1

gold

aluminum

The Big Idea

16. What are some ways you can describe matter?
3-4.1

Performance Assessment

What Is It Made Of?

▶ Make a book about some of the matter that surrounds you every day—the clothes you wear.

▶ Choose some of your favorite articles of clothing. Then describe their physical properties. What materials are they made of? What colors are they? What other properties do they have?

▶ Put a picture or drawing of each piece of clothing on a page in your book. Include a description of the properties of the clothing next to each item.

▶ Choose two pieces of clothing. How are they the same? How are they different? Use their properties to describe their similarities and differences.

South Carolina Activity

In the morning, place a cup of water near a window that gets direct sunlight. Use a thermometer to measure the water's temperature. Continue measuring it every hour during the day. Make a line graph to show how the temperature changes.

South Carolina Standards Practice

1 If you leave a shallow dish of water on a windowsill for one week, what will **most likely** happen?

A The water will boil.

B The water will freeze.

C The water will melt.

D The water will evaporate.

3-4.2

2 The drawing shows a spring scale measuring a property of matter.

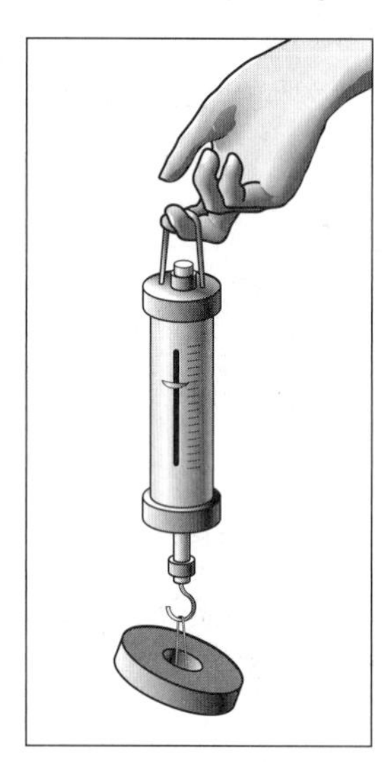

What property of matter does the spring scale measure?

F mass

G weight

H volume

I magnetism

3-1.5

3 A student wrote about matter in her lab book. Which of her following notes is correct?

A Matter is too small to be seen with the unaided eye.

B Matter is too large to be seen with the unaided eye.

C Matter comes from the Sun.

D Matter takes up space.

3-4.1

4 Which **best** explains why cooking pots are often made of metal?

F Metal conducts heat well.

G Metal cools down slowly.

H Metal takes a long time to heat up.

I Metal is a good insulator.

3-4.3

5 How do **most** types of matter change as they are heated?

A They lose mass.

B They gain mass.

C They take up less space.

D They take up more space.

3-4.2

6 The amount of space something takes up is its

F volume.

G length.

H weight.

I mass.

3-4.1

7 Fredo heated a pot of water to 40°C. He poured equal amounts of the water into each of 4 cups. After 30 minutes, he measured the temperature of the water in each cup. The table summarizes his results.

Cup	Temperature (in degrees Celsius)
1	22
2	28
3	33
4	36

Which cup is the **best** insulator?

A cup 1

B cup 2

C cup 3

D cup 4

3-1.6

8 One form of matter has a definite volume but no definite shape. This form of matter is classified as a

F gas.

G solid.

H particle.

I liquid.

3-1.1

9 How can you find out whether a certain kind of matter is a good conductor?

A measure how long it takes for it to heat up when it touches a hot object

B measure the thermal energy of the matter when it is cold and again when it is hot

C heat the matter and see whether it boils or melts

D freeze the matter and then measure its temperature

3-1.3

10 What form of matter is the helium in a balloon?

F air

G gas

H solid

I liquid

3-4.1

CHAPTER 7

Forces and Motion

The Big Idea

What makes something move?

Grand prix race car

Key Vocabulary

position
the location of an object (p. 336)

motion
a change in position (p. 338)

force
a push or pull; what makes an object move (p. 346)

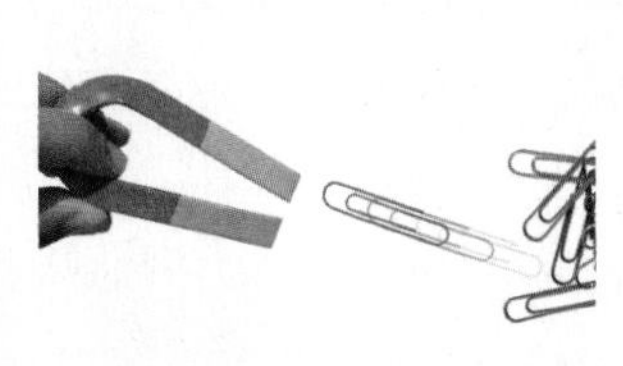

magnet
any object with a magnetic force (p. 348)

vibrate
to move back and forth quickly (p. 356)

sound
a form of energy that comes from objects that vibrate (p. 356)

More Vocabulary

distance, p. 337

speed, p. 340

friction, p. 350

volume, p. 358

pitch, p. 359

Lesson 1

Position and Motion

Look and Wonder

Snowboarding is like skateboarding on snow. How does this snowboarder's position change as she travels down the mountain?

3-5.1. Identify the position of an object relative to a reference point by using position terms and a distance scale or measurement. **3-5.2.** Compare the motion of common objects in terms of speed and direction.

Explore

Inquiry Activity

How can you describe an object's position?

Purpose

Find out ways to describe a block's position.

Procedure

1. Sit opposite a partner at a table. Prop up a notebook between the two of you.
2. One partner, "the builder," uses the blocks to make a building. Make sure the other partner, "the copier," cannot see the building.
3. **Communicate** The builder tells the copier how to make the same building. Make a list of the words you use.
4. **Observe** Remove the notebook. Are the buildings the same? Switch roles and try the activity again.

Draw Conclusions

5. What words did you use to describe your building?
6. **Infer** Could you describe the position of each block without comparing it to other blocks around it?

Materials

notebook

two sets of 10 colored blocks

Step 2

Explore More

Communicate
How could you direct someone from your home to your school?

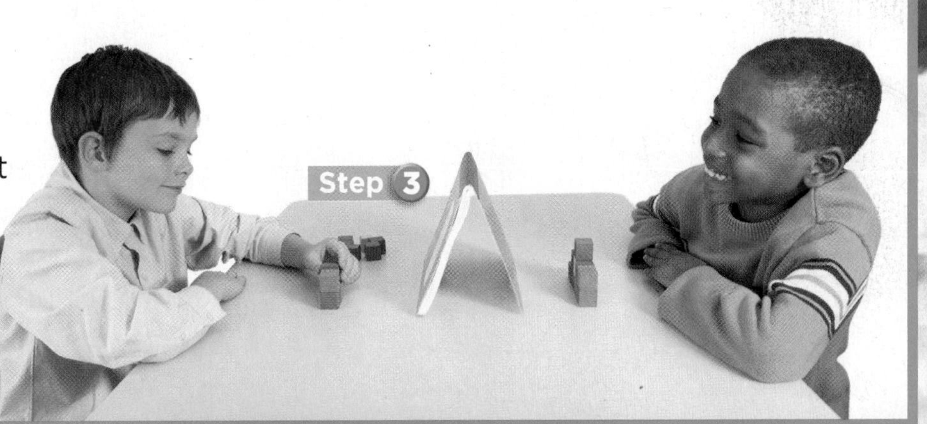

Step 3

Read and Learn

Main Idea 3-5.1 3-5.2

An object is in motion when its position changes.

Vocabulary

position, p. 336

distance, p. 337

motion, p. 338

speed, p. 340

at www.macmillanmh.com

Reading Skill

Compare and Contrast

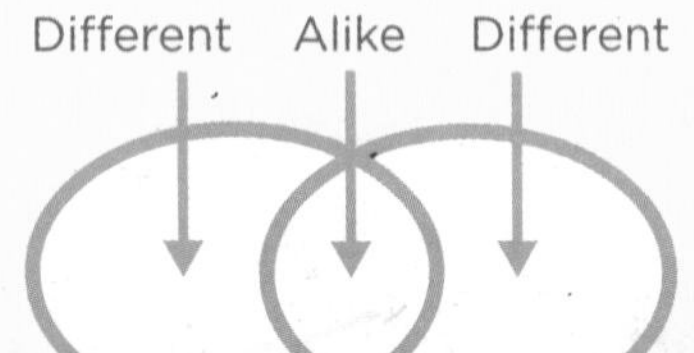

How can you describe position?

Look at the children below. Where is the boy in the red shirt? He is next to the girl in the pink shirt. He is under the girl wearing the blue overalls. When you describe where something is, you describe its position (puh•ZISH•uhn). **Position** is the location of an object.

You can describe something's position by comparing it to the position of other things. Words such as *over*, *under*, *left*, *right*, *on top of*, *beneath*, and *next to* give clues about position. You could say that a mouse is under a table or that a cat is on top of a shelf. When we describe the position of something, we compare it with objects around it.

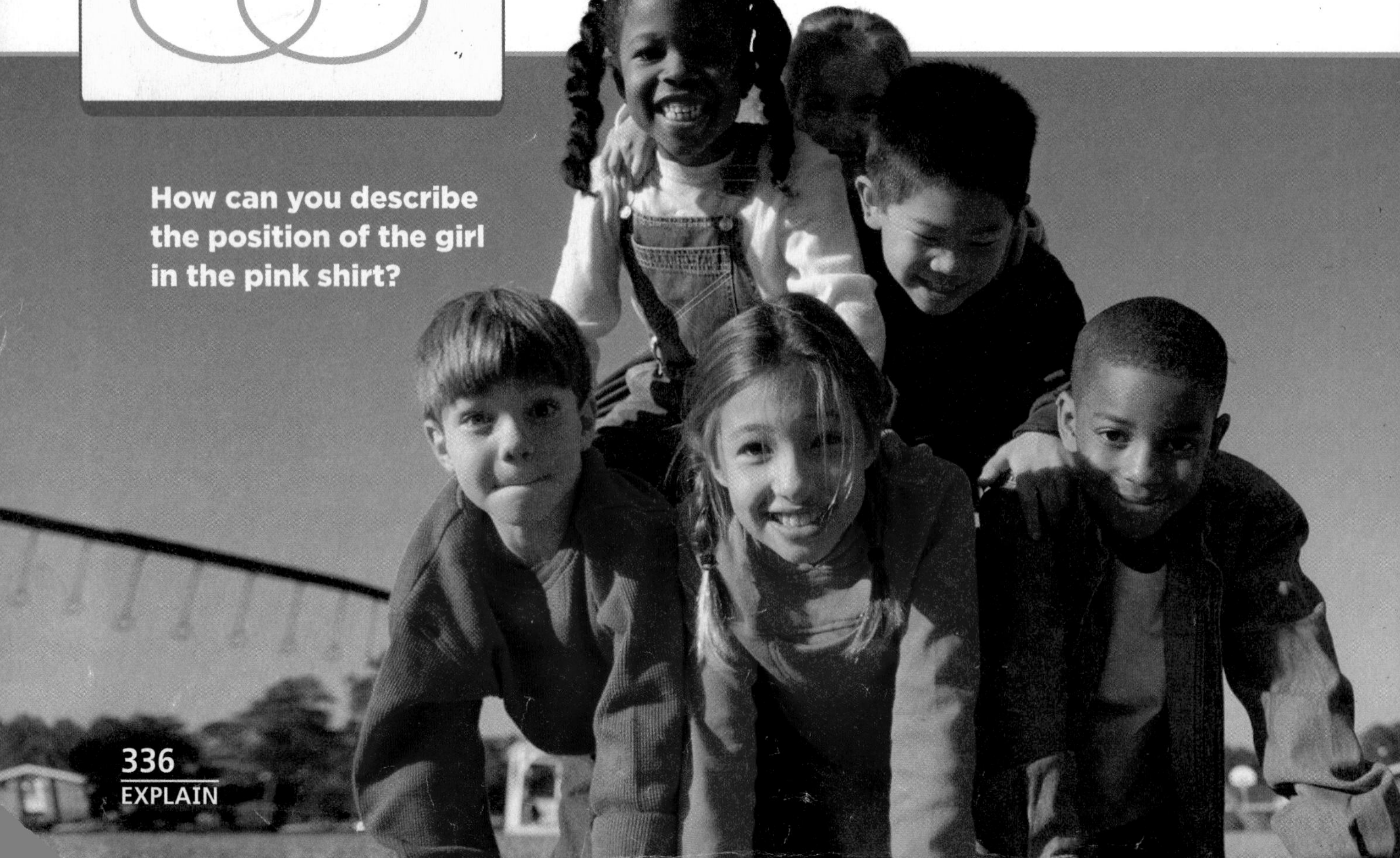

How can you describe the position of the girl in the pink shirt?

Distance

You can also describe something's position by measuring its distance (DIS•tuhns) from other objects. **Distance** is the amount of space between two objects or places. Distance can be measured in inches, yards, or miles. In the metric system, distance is often measured in centimeters, meters, or kilometers. You can use a ruler or meterstick to measure distances. The distance between the two toys shown below is 10 centimeters.

Quick Check

Compare and Contrast What must you compare an object to in order to describe its position?

Critical Thinking Use position words to describe the location of your classroom.

How can you measure the distance between these two toys?

What is motion?

Look at the pictures of the mouse below. In the first box, the mouse is on a rock. In the second box, it is between the two rocks. What happened to the mouse? It moved. You know that the mouse moved because its position changed. While an object is changing position, it is in motion (MOH•shuhn). **Motion** is a change in position.

▲ A swing moves back and forth.

Objects can move in different ways. Look at the chart on the next page. The runner moves forward in a straight line. The figure skater spins round and round on the ice. The snowboarder moves down the hill in a zigzag. A zigzag is a path with short, sharp turns from one side to another. The skateboarder moves back and forth in the pipe. Straight line, round and round, zigzag, and back and forth are types of motion.

▼ How can you tell that the mouse has moved?

Quick Check

Compare and Contrast How are zigzag and back and forth motions similar?

Critical Thinking List some objects that move round and round.

Types of Motion

Read a Chart

What are some ways objects can move?

Clue: Arrows can show directions.

Quick Lab

Measure Speed

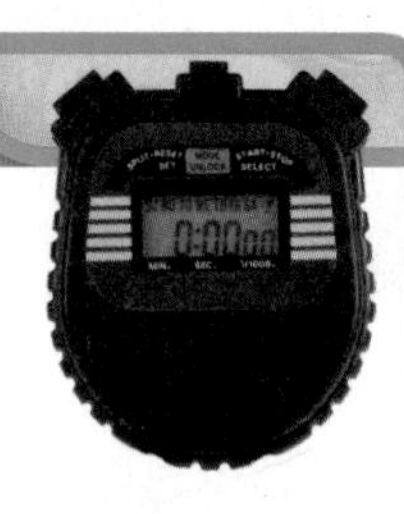

1. Set up a racetrack as shown below.

2. **Measure** Wind up a wind-up toy. Place it at the starting line and let it go. Have a partner use a stopwatch to time the toy's trip. Measure how far the toy travels. Record your measurements.
3. **Communicate** Make a drawing to show how the toy moved.
4. **Use Numbers** How far did the toy travel? How fast did it travel? What two measurements do you need to find the toy's speed?

What is speed?

Some things move faster than others. A cheetah moves faster than a snail. **Speed** describes how quickly an object moves. An object's speed tells how far it will move in a certain amount of time.

You can measure the speed of an object. You need to know how far the object traveled. You also need to know how much time it took for the object to travel that distance. If a car traveled 50 kilometers in an hour, its speed was 50 kilometers per hour.

Quick Check

Compare and Contrast Which is faster, a plane or car? Explain.

Critical Thinking A red car moves faster than a green car. Both move for three seconds. Which car moves farther? Why?

Slow-moving objects take longer to travel a distance than fast-moving objects.

Lesson Review

Visual Summary

Position is the location of an object.

When an object's position changes, the object is in **motion**. Objects can move in different ways.

Speed describes how quickly an object moves.

Make a FOLDABLES Study Guide

Make a Three-Tab Book. Use it to summarize what you learned about position and motion.

Think, Talk, and Write

1. **Main Idea** How can you tell if an object has moved?

2. **Vocabulary** What is the position of an object?

3. **Compare and Contrast** How is zigzag motion like back and forth motion? How are they different?

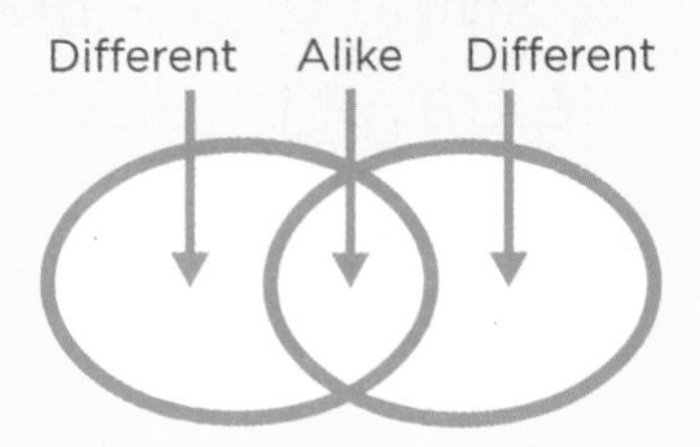

4. **Critical Thinking** Suppose you rode a bike at 10 kilometers per hour for three hours. How far would you travel?

5. **Test Prep** **Which tool measures distance?**
   - **A** stopwatch
   - **B** thermometer
   - **C** pan balance
   - **D** meterstick

Writing Link

Write a Description

Hold a ball in your hand. Drop it. How does the ball move? Then toss the ball to a friend. How does the ball move? Describe the different ways the ball moves.

Math Link

Make a Graph

Use research materials to find the speed of five objects. Organize this information into a chart. Then make a bar graph. Is it easier to compare data using a chart or a bar graph? Explain your answer.

LOG ON e-Review Summaries and quizzes online at www.macmillanmh.com

Travel Through Time

People have always wanted to travel. They found ways to travel within their state, across the country, and throughout the world. People have even traveled into space. The time line below shows some of the first machines that helped people travel to distant places.

1804

In England Richard Trevithick built the first steam engine for a train. The steam engine helped people travel great distances. It also helped them get to their destinations more quickly.

1884

In Germany Karl Friedrich Benz built the first car to run on gasoline. It worked similarly to the cars you see on the road today. However, his car had only three wheels!

American Museum of Natural History

1903

Wilbur and Orville Wright constructed the first motorized airplane that flew and landed safely. Their airplane's engine ran on gasoline. It flew for 12 seconds over 36 meters (120 feet).

1961

Russian astronaut Yuri Gagarin was the first person in space. His spaceship had special engines. They produced a force that was stronger than the pull of Earth's gravity. These engines helped the spaceship leave Earth's surface and orbit the planet.

Problem and Solution

A problem and solution

- gives a problem
- tells how to solve the problem

Write About It

Problem and Solution How have machines helped people learn about distant places? Read the article again. Then write about ways machines have helped people solve problems.

e-Journal Write about it online at www.macmillanmh.com

Lesson 2

Forces

Look and Wonder

Wind can push sailboats to move great distances. What would happen to these sailboats if the wind blew harder?

3-5.3. Explain how the motion of an object is affected by the strength of a push or pull and the mass of the object. **3-5.4.** Explain the relationship between the motion of an object and the pull of gravity.

Explore

Inquiry Activity

How can pushes affect the way objects move?

Form a Hypothesis

What will happen to an object if you increase the force you use to push it? Write a hypothesis. Start with "If I push an object with more force, then . . ."

Test Your Hypothesis

1. Stack three books on the floor. Then lean a piece of cardboard against the top book to make a ramp. Tape down the edge along the floor.
2. **Observe** Place a toy car at the bottom of the ramp. Hold a tennis ball at the top of the ramp. Then let the ball go so that it pushes the toy car. What happens?
3. **Measure** Find out how far the car travels.
4. **Use Variables** Add three more books to the stack. The ball pushes the car with more force when you increase the height of the ramp. Repeat steps 2 and 3.

Draw Conclusions

5. **Infer** What caused the car to move?
6. **Interpret Data** When did the car travel farthest?
7. **Infer** How does the amount of force you use to push an object affect how far the object travels?

Explore More

What would happen if you added a weight to the toy car and repeated the activity?

Materials

- 6 books
- cardboard
- masking tape
- toy car
- tennis ball
- ruler

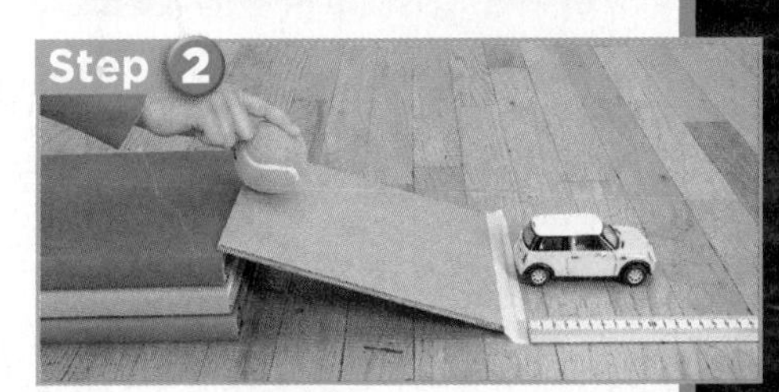

3-I.3. Generate questions and use questions to conduct a scientific investigation.

Read and Learn

Main Idea 3-5.3 3-5.4

Forces change an object's motion.

Vocabulary

force, p. 346

magnet, p. 348

friction, p. 350

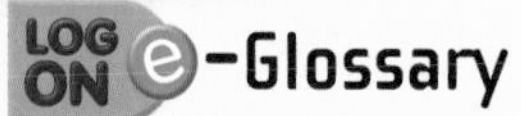

at www.macmillanmh.com

Reading Skill

Cause and Effect

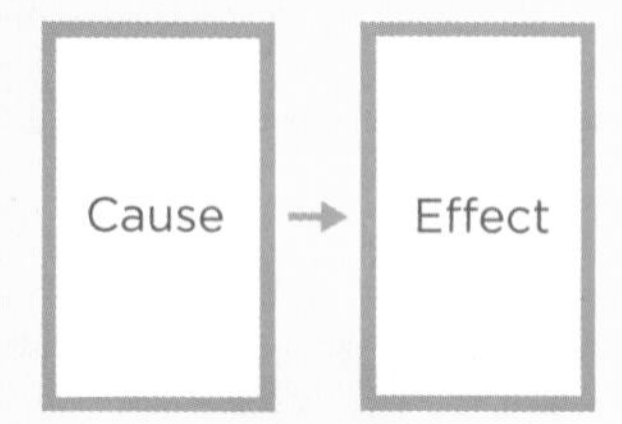

What are forces?

Objects do not move by themselves. Something must apply a force (FAWRS) to make them start moving. A **force** is a push or a pull. You use forces to move things all the time. When you pull on a door handle or push a wagon, you apply a force to make something move.

Forces can be large or small. The force a crane uses to lift a truck is huge. The force your hand uses to lift a feather is tiny. It takes more force to move heavy objects than light objects. Forces also affect an object's speed. The more force you use, the faster an object will move.

A push and a pull make this red wagon move.

Changes in Motion

Forces can change the motion of objects. They can make objects start moving, speed up, slow down, or stop moving. They can make objects change direction, too.

Forces can change a soccer ball's motion. A goalie applies a force to throw the ball to a teammate. The ball starts to move. The teammate applies another force when he kicks the ball. The ball changes direction. Each time a force is applied the motion of the ball changes. When a goalie catches the ball, the ball's motion is stopped.

A change in an object's motion is the result of all the forces that are acting on the object. Think of the game tug of war. When both sides pull equally on the rope, the forces are balanced. Nothing moves. If one side pulls harder, the forces become unbalanced. Now the rope moves. There is a change of motion.

Quick Check

Cause and Effect How can forces affect an object's motion?

Critical Thinking
What happens when you kick a moving soccer ball?

Changes in Motion

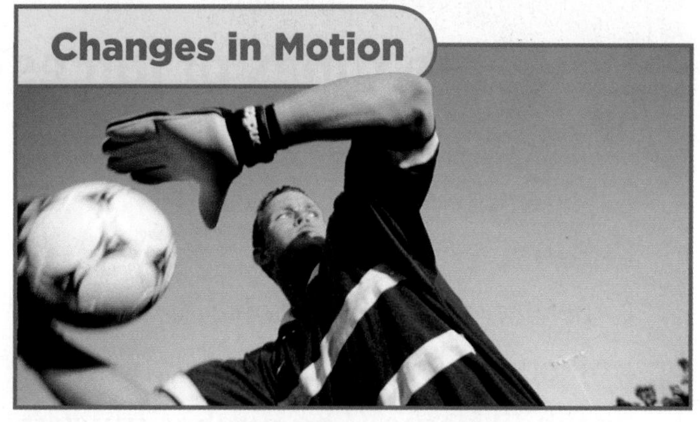

① The goalie throws the ball to start its motion.

② This player kicks the ball, changing its speed and direction.

③ The other goalie catches the soccer ball, stopping its motion.

Read a Photo

How have forces changed the motion of this soccer ball?

Clue: Captions give information.

What are types of forces?

There are many types of forces. The forces you are probably most familiar with are contact forces. *Contact forces* happen between objects that touch. Think about a baseball game. The pitcher must touch the ball to throw it to home plate. A bat must touch the ball to change its direction. Some forces can act on an object without touching the object. Magnetism and gravity are examples.

When the bat hits the ball, the ball changes direction.

Magnetism

Have you ever used magnets? What did you notice? When you bring two magnets together, they may *attract*, or pull on, each other. They may also *repel*, or push away from, each other. Magnets can attract or repel each other without touching. The force that causes this to happen is called a *magnetic force*. A **magnet** is any object with a magnetic force.

Magnets can attract or repel each other. They can also attract things made of certain metals like iron. They cannot attract things made of wood, glass, plastic, or rubber. Magnets can attract or repel objects through solids, liquids, or gases.

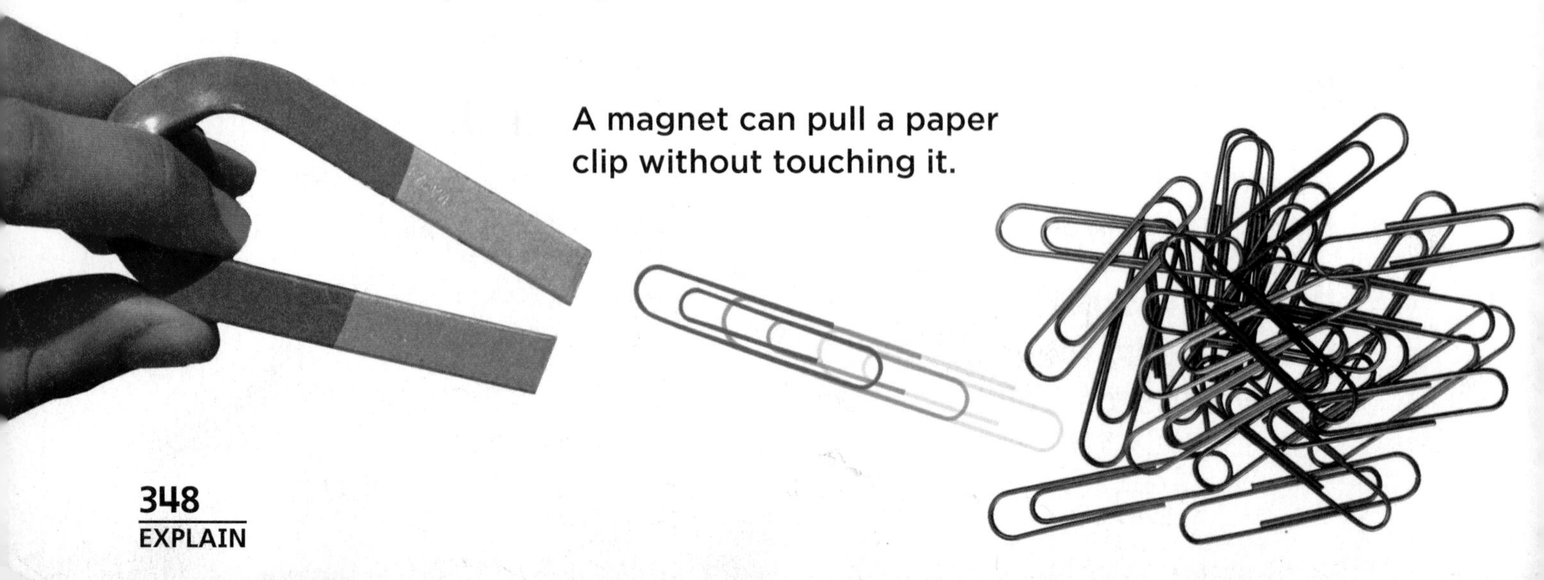

A magnet can pull a paper clip without touching it.

Gravity

You cannot see gravity, but it is what keeps you on Earth. Gravity is a pulling force between two objects, such as you and Earth. Gravity pulls objects together. When you jump up, Earth's gravity pulls you down. Gravity pulls through solids, liquids, or gases.

How much gravity does it take to keep you on Earth? The answer is your weight. An object's weight is a measure of the pull of gravity on it. The more mass an object has, the more gravity pulls on it.

Quick Check

Cause and Effect What effect does gravity have on objects?

Critical Thinking How can you pick up metal paper clips without touching them?

Quick Lab

Observe Gravity

1. **Predict** Does gravity act the same on all objects? Would it act the same on two plastic bottles that have the same volume but different mass?
2. Hold an empty plastic bottle in one hand. Hold an identical bottle full of water in the other hand. Hold each arm away from your body.

3. **Observe** Describe what you feel. Is each bottle pulled toward Earth with the same force?
4. **Infer** Is the amount of gravity on the two bottles the same? How could you tell?

Gravity is pulling these skydivers to Earth.

What is friction?

A block slides on the floor. It then slows down and stops. Why does this happen? A force called friction (FRIK•shuhn) is acting on the block. **Friction** is a force that occurs when one object rubs against another. It pushes against moving objects and causes them to slow down.

Different surfaces produce different amounts of friction. Rough surfaces, such as sandpaper, usually produce a lot of friction. Smooth surfaces, such as ice, usually produce less friction.

People use slippery things to reduce friction. Oil is often put on moving parts of machines to reduce friction. People use rough or sticky things to increase friction. The brakes on a bike use rubber pads to increase friction. When you squeeze the brake handles, the brake pads press against the rim of the wheel. The friction between the pads and rim cause the bike to stop.

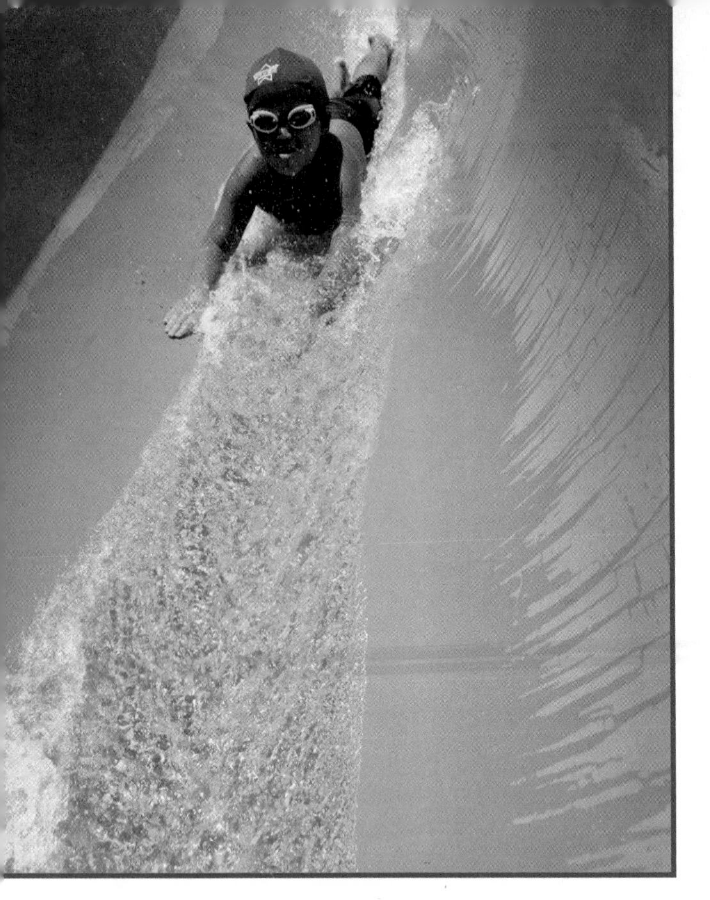

▲ This water slide is smooth and has little friction.

Friction between the brake pad and the bike rim stops the bike. ▼

Quick Check

Cause and Effect What happens when you squeeze a hand brake on a bicycle?

Critical Thinking How can you tell that friction is a force?

Lesson Review

Visual Summary

A force is a push or a pull. Forces can change the motion of objects.

Contact, magnetism, and gravity are different types of forces.

Friction is a force that occurs when one object rubs against another.

Make a FOLDABLES™ Study Guide

Make a Trifold Book. Use it to summarize what you learned about forces.

Think, Talk, and Write

1. **Main Idea** How can forces affect an object?
2. **Vocabulary** What is friction? Talk about it.
3. **Cause and Effect** You are swinging on a swing. What force causes you to slow down as you go up?

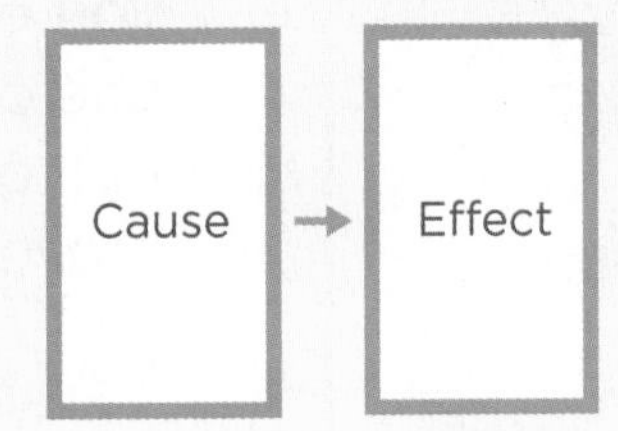

4. **Critical Thinking** How can friction help keep you safe?
5. **Test Prep** **Which is an example of a contact force?**

A a magnet attracting a paper clip
B two magnets repelling each other
C a bat hitting a ball
D gravity pulling on a leaf

Math Link

Put Numbers in Order
Weigh five objects on a spring scale. Measure their weight in newtons, the unit of force in the metric system. Organize your data in a bar graph from least weight to greatest weight.

Health Link

Use Your Muscles
You use your muscles when you push or pull things. Find out about some of the muscles in your body. What do your muscles do? How do your muscles help you move?

Be a Scientist

Materials

magnet

paper clips

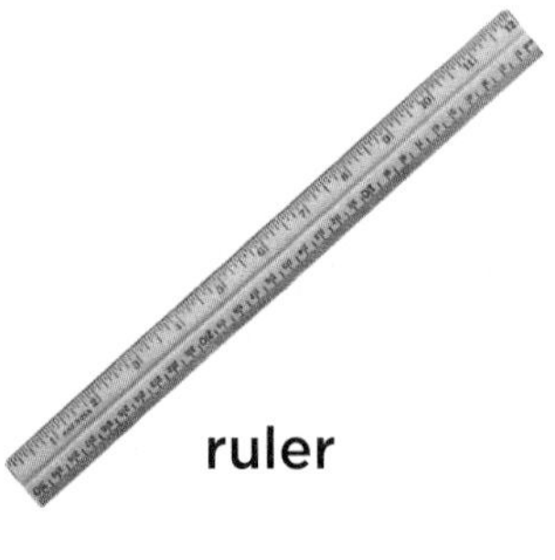

ruler

Structured Inquiry

How does distance affect the pull of a magnet on metal objects?

Form a Hypothesis

You know that some metal objects, such as paper clips, are attracted to magnets. What happens when you change the distance between a magnet and a pile of paper clips? How does this affect the magnet's pull on the paper clips? Write a hypothesis. "If you move a magnet closer to a pile of paper clips, then . . ."

Test Your Hypothesis

1. Gather a pile of paper clips on your desk. Stand up a ruler near the paper clips.
2. **Experiment** Hold a magnet as shown below. Slowly lower the magnet until it is only 1 cm above the pile.

3. **Measure** Move the magnet away from the pile. Remove the paper clips and count how many stuck to the magnet. Record the data in a table.
4. Repeat steps 1–3, holding the magnet 2 cm and 3 cm away from the pile of paper clips. Record your data.

Step 3

Distance	Number of Paper Clips
1 cm	
2 cm	
3 cm	

Draw Conclusions

5. **Use Numbers** At what distance did the magnet pick up the most paper clips?
6. **Interpret Data** Does a magnet's pull on objects get greater or smaller as the magnet moves away from the objects?

Guided Inquiry

Can magnetic force pass through an object?

Form a Hypothesis

Can a magnetic force pass through different objects, such as wood, plastic, paper, or foil? Write a hypothesis.

Test Your Hypothesis

Design a plan to test your hypothesis. List the materials you will use. Write down the steps you plan to follow.

Draw Conclusions

Did any of the objects block magnetic force? Did any of the objects make the magnetic force stronger or weaker? Share your results with your classmates.

Open Inquiry

What other questions do you have about magnets? For example, what common objects are attracted to magnets? Design an experiment to find out.

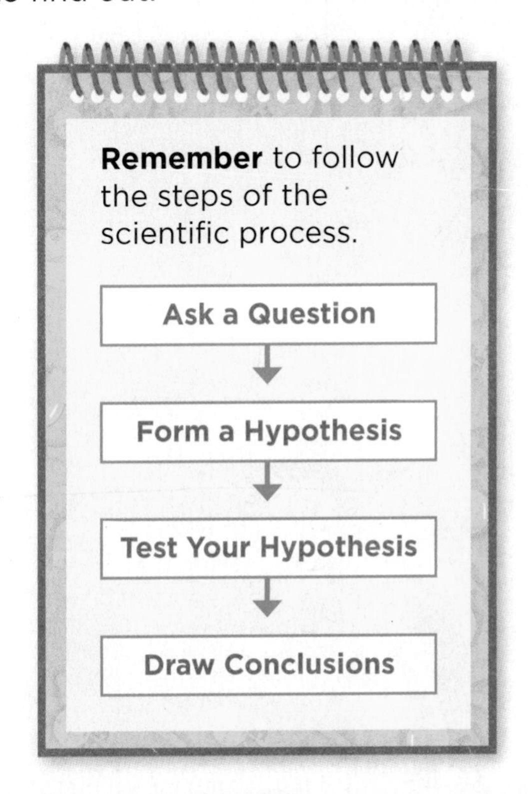

3-I.4. Predict the outcome of a simple investigation and compare the result with the prediction.

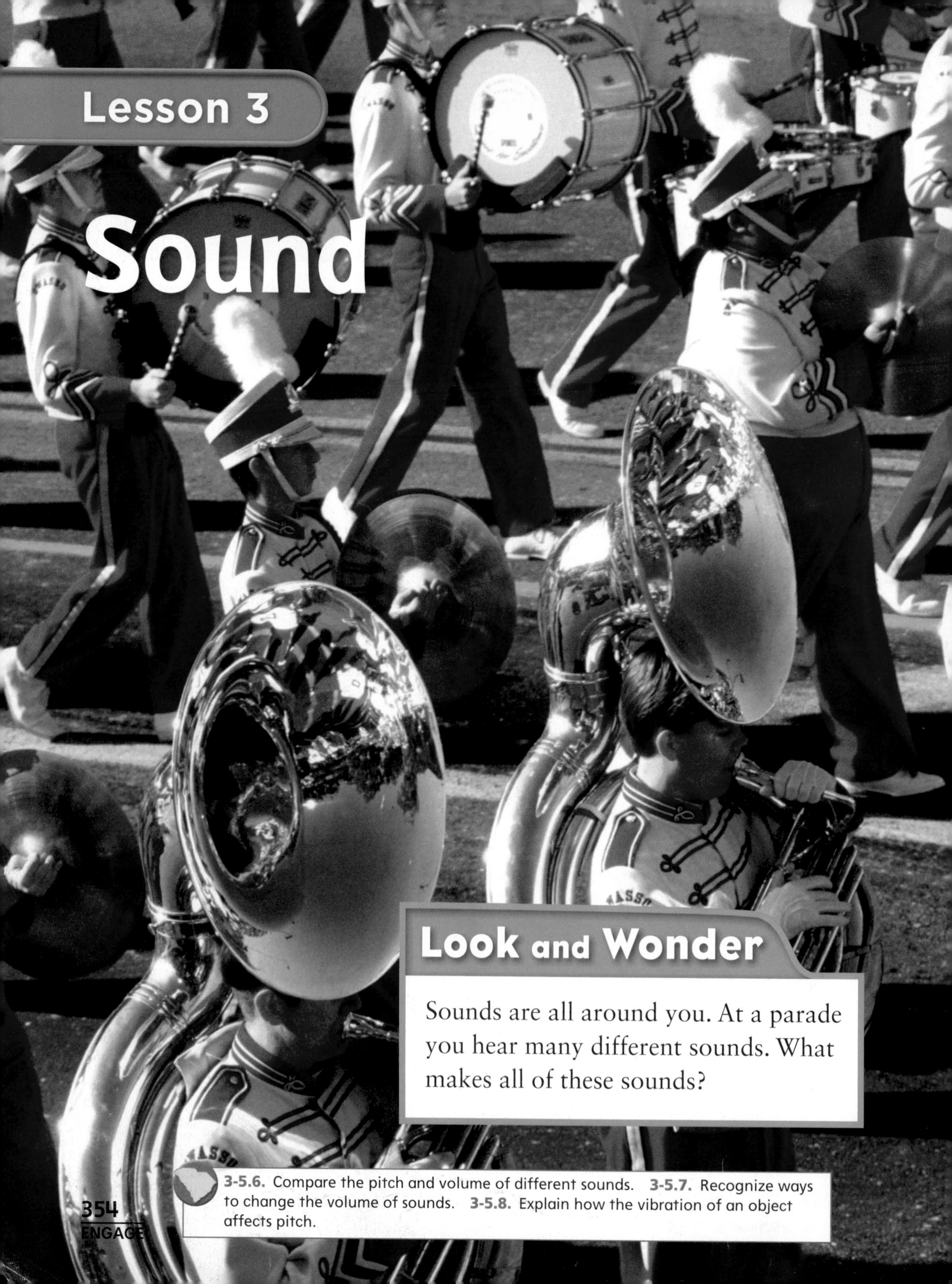

Lesson 3

Sound

Look and Wonder

Sounds are all around you. At a parade you hear many different sounds. What makes all of these sounds?

3-5.6. Compare the pitch and volume of different sounds. **3-5.7.** Recognize ways to change the volume of sounds. **3-5.8.** Explain how the vibration of an object affects pitch.

Explore

Inquiry Activity

How can you make sounds?

Make a Prediction

Look at the paper, ruler, and rubber band. What must you do to make a sound with each object?

Test Your Prediction

⚠ **Be Careful.** Wear goggles.

1. **Observe** Hold a piece of paper by one corner. Wave it around. What happens?
2. **Observe** Place a ruler on a desk. Extend half of it over the edge of the desk. Hold one end of the ruler down, and tap the other end. What happens?
3. **Observe** Wrap a rubber band around a box. Pluck the rubber band. What happens?

Draw Conclusions

4. What happened when you moved the paper, ruler, and rubber band?
5. **Infer** Can you make a sound with the paper, ruler, or rubber band without making it move? Explain your answer.
6. **Infer** How are sounds made?

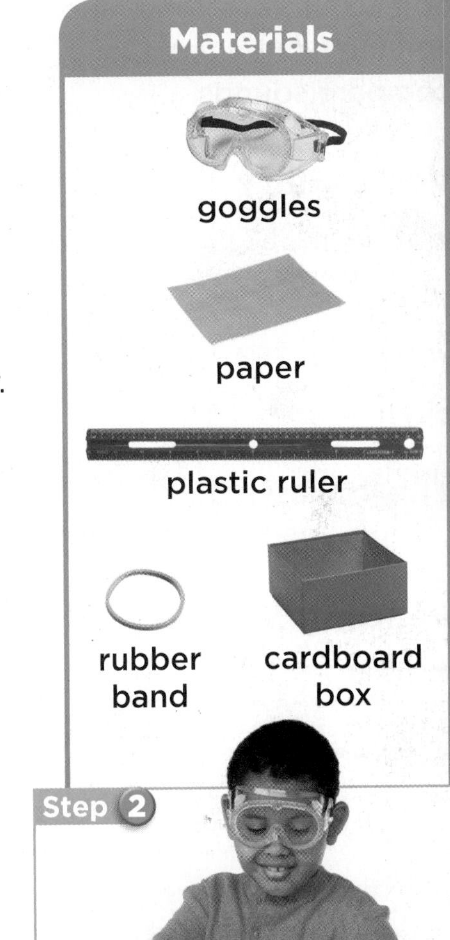

Explore More

Experiment Test ways to change the sound you made with each object. Try to make the sounds louder or softer, higher or lower. For example, try pulling the rubber band tighter and then plucking it. Record your results and the steps you follow.

3-5.5. Recall that vibrating objects produce sound and that vibrations can be transferred from one material to another.

Read and Learn

Main Idea 3-5.6, 3-5.7 3-5.8

Sounds are made when objects vibrate. Pitch and volume can be used to compare sounds.

Vocabulary

vibrate, p. 356

sound, p. 356

volume, p. 358

pitch, p. 359

at www.macmillanmh.com

Reading Skill

Predict

What I Predict	What Happens

What is sound?

Think about the many sounds you hear. Some sounds are musical, such as the notes on a guitar. Other sounds are harsh, such as chickens squawking. All sounds begin when something vibrates (VYE•brayts). To **vibrate** is to move back and forth quickly. You cannot make a sound without making something move. **Sound** is a form of energy that comes from objects that vibrate.

How Sound Travels

Have you ever dropped a stone into a pond? The stone makes waves in the water that move out in all directions. Sound travels in waves, too. When you pluck a guitar string, it vibrates. This creates a sound wave. The sound wave moves through the air. You hear the sound when the sound wave reaches your ear.

You can make sound when you pluck, tap, or blow on an object.

Orca whales use sounds to communicate.

Sound waves can travel through air, a gas. Sound waves can also travel through liquids and solids. Some sea animals communicate by making sounds underwater. You hear a knock on the door because sound travels through the door. Sound waves travel through matter. Sound cannot travel in space.

Sound does not travel at the same speed through all materials. Sound travels slowest through a gas. It travels faster through a liquid. It travels fastest through a solid.

Quick Check

Predict You hit a drum with a stick. What happens?

Critical Thinking Do you think that you can hear sound in outer space?

Tie a piece of string to two cups. Then talk in one end while a friend listens in the other. Why can you hear your friend?

The sounds of jets roaring through the sky are louder than the chirps of a bird.

How are sounds different?

Close your eyes and listen. What sounds do you hear? What makes different sounds different?

Volume

Sounds can have different volumes. **Volume** describes how loud a sound is. A plane flying overhead is louder than a bird's song. A plane has a greater volume.

Loud sounds are made by objects that vibrate with a lot of energy. The more energy an object vibrates with, the louder the sound it makes. Tap your foot on the floor. Then stomp your foot. You use more energy to stomp your foot than to tap it. Stomping makes a high-energy vibration, so you hear a loud sound. Tapping makes a low-energy vibration, so you hear a soft sound.

Pitch

Some sounds are high, such as the squeaking of a mouse. Other sounds are low, such as the croaking of a bullfrog. A sound's **pitch** (PICH) is how high or low it is. An object that vibrates quickly has a high pitch. An object that vibrates slowly has a low pitch.

An object's length can affect pitch. Look at the marimba below. When hit, the shorter keys vibrate faster than the longer ones. The shorter a key is, the faster it vibrates and the higher its pitch.

The thickness of an object can also affect pitch. A guitar has both thin and thick strings. Thin strings vibrate faster than thick strings, so they have higher pitches.

Quick Check

Predict How does tightening a rubber band affect its pitch?

Critical Thinking Compare the sound of a bicycle horn to a car horn.

Quick Lab

Changing Sounds

1. **Predict** How can you change the sound a straw makes?
2. Flatten one end of a straw. Then cut across the tip of this end as shown.

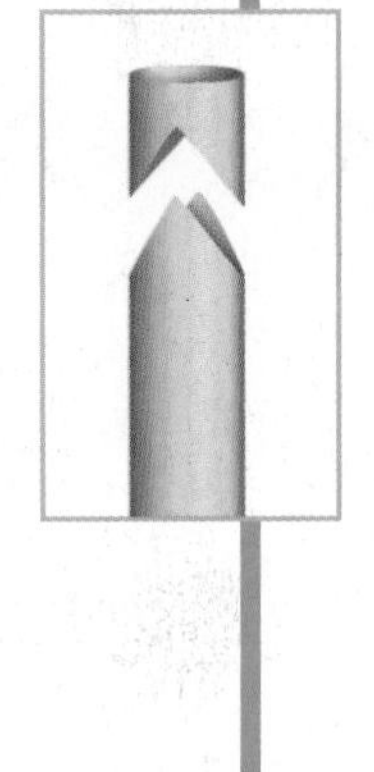

3. **Experiment** Cover your teeth with your lips and then blow hard through the cut end of the straw. Describe what you hear. Now blow softer. How does the sound change?
4. **Experiment** Now try using straws of different lengths. Remember to cut the tip before you blow into the straw. Describe what you hear. How does the sound change?

A marimba can make sounds with a high or a low pitch.

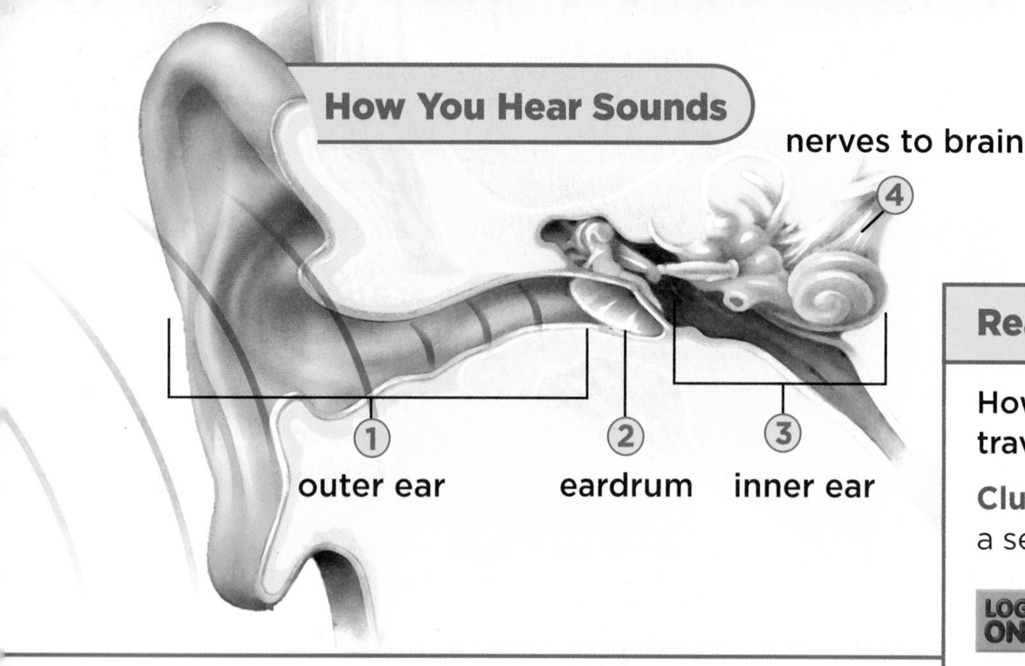

Read a Diagram

How does a sound wave travel through your ear?

Clue: Numbers help show a sequence.

Science in Motion Watch how sound moves at www.macmillanmh.com

How do you hear sounds?

What happens to a sound wave when it reaches your ear? First, the sound wave is collected by the outer ear. Next, the sound wave makes your eardrum vibrate. This causes three tiny bones in your inner ear to vibrate. These vibrations pass through the inner ear to nerves. The nerves send a message to your brain, and you hear a sound.

Protect Your Hearing

It is important to protect your ears. Never put a finger or pencil in your ear. You may hurt the parts inside. Loud sounds can damage your ear as well. Loud sounds have a lot of energy. They can damage the parts inside the ear.

This construction worker must protect his ears.

Quick Check

Predict What might happen to your hearing if you listen to loud music often?

Critical Thinking Which makes your eardrum vibrate faster, a high sound or low sound?

Lesson Review

Visual Summary

Sound is produced when an object vibrates. Sound can travel through solids, liquids, and gases.

Sounds can be compared by using volume and pitch.

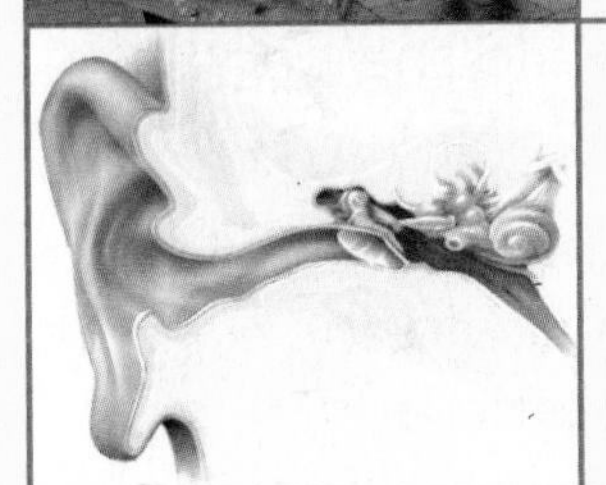

You hear sounds when vibrations travel through your ear.

Make a FOLDABLES™ Study Guide

Make a Trifold Book. Use it to summarize what you learned about sound.

Think, Talk, and Write

1. **Main Idea** What do you need to do to make a sound?

2. **Vocabulary** What is the difference between pitch and volume?

3. **Predict** How would cymbals sound if you tapped them together lightly? How would they sound if you crashed them together?

What I Predict	What Happens

4. **Critical Thinking** List five different sounds you hear. How are these sounds the same? How are these sounds different?

5. **Test Prep** **Objects that vibrate quickly make sounds with**
   A high volume.
   B low volume.
   C high pitch.
   D low pitch.

Writing Link

Persuasive Writing
It is important to protect yourself from loud sounds. Loud sounds can harm your hearing. Find out how you can protect your hearing. Then write a paragraph telling others what you learned.

Music Link

Make an Instrument
Put on goggles. Stretch rubber bands of different thicknesses around a shoe box. Then use the rubber bands to make sounds. How can you change the pitch? How can you change the volume?

LOG ON e-Review Summaries and quizzes online at www.macmillanmh.com

Be a Scientist

Materials

3 plastic bags

tuning fork

water

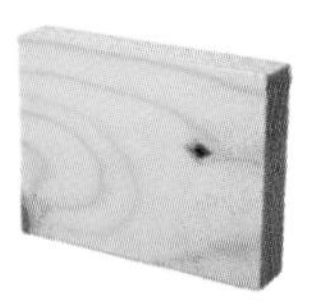

wooden block

Structured Inquiry

How does sound move through different types of matter?

Form a Hypothesis

You just learned that sound travels through solids, liquids, and gases. How does the state of matter affect how sound travels? Write a hypothesis.

Test Your Hypothesis

1. Fill a plastic bag with air and seal it. Hold the bag against your ear.
2. **Experiment** Tap the tines of the tuning fork against the bottom of your shoe. Then hold the base of the tuning fork against the plastic bag. Listen to the sound it makes.
3. Fill a plastic bag with water. Seal it and hold it against your ear.
4. **Experiment** Tap the tuning fork and hold it against the bag. Record any differences you hear.
5. Place a wooden block in a plastic bag. Squeeze out as much air as you can and seal the bag. Hold the bag against your ear.
6. **Experiment** Tap the tuning fork and hold it against the bag. How is the sound different now? Record your observations.

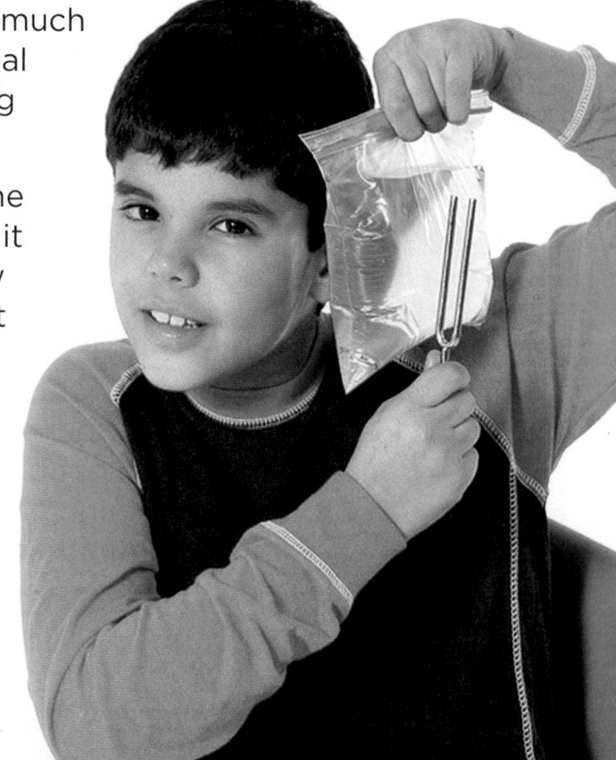

Step 4

Draw Conclusions

7. How did the tuning fork sound different through the different materials?
8. **Interpret Data** Through which material was the sound loudest?
9. **Infer** Does sound travel best through a solid, a liquid, or a gas?

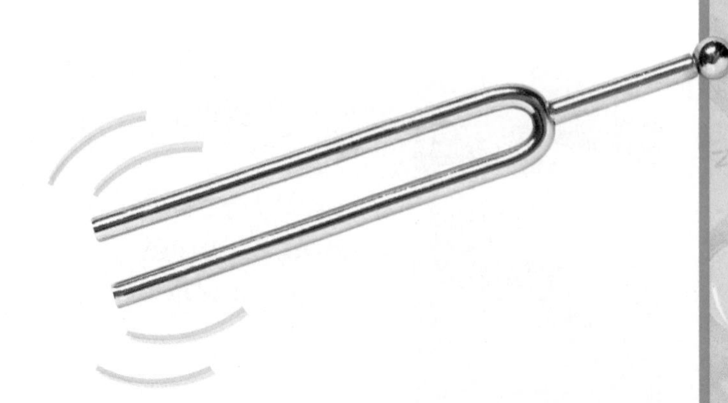

Guided Inquiry

How does sound move through different solids?

Form a Hypothesis

Sound can be stopped, slowed down, or absorbed by different solids. How does sound travel through different solids?

Test Your Hypothesis

Design an experiment to investigate how sound travels through different solids. Decide on the materials you will need. You may want to try plastic, wooden, and metal objects. Write out the steps you will follow. Record your results and observations.

Draw Conclusions

Did your results support your hypothesis? Why or why not?

Open Inquiry

What other questions do you have about sound? For example, what objects block sound the best? Design an experiment to find out.

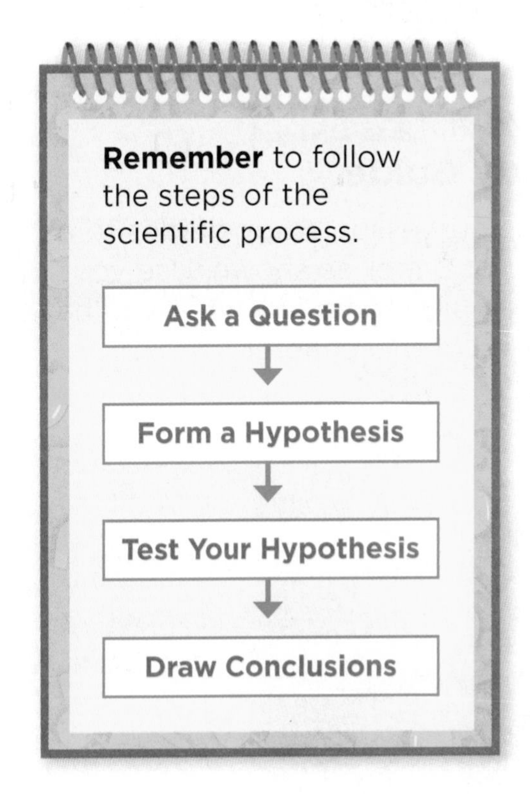

3-I.5. Use tools safely, accurately, and appropriately when gathering data.

CHAPTER 7 Review

Visual Summary

Lesson 1 An object is in motion when its position changes.

Lesson 2 Forces change an object's motion.

Lesson 3 Sounds are made when objects vibrate. Pitch and volume can be used to compare sounds.

Make a FOLDABLES™ Study Guide

Glue your lesson study guides to a piece of paper as shown. Use your study guide to review what you have learned in this chapter.

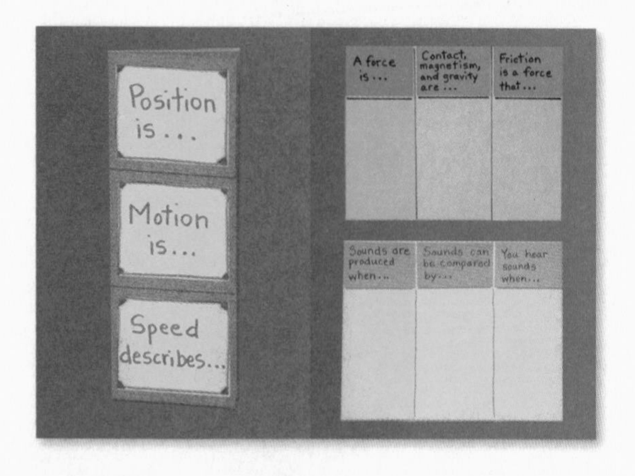

Vocabulary

Fill each blank with the best term from the list.

distance, p. 337	**pitch**, p. 359
force, p. 346	**sound**, p. 356
friction, p. 350	**speed**, p. 340
magnet, p. 348	**vibrates**, p. 356
motion, p. 338	**volume**, p. 358

1. An object in ______ is changing its position.
3-5.1
2. When an object moves back and forth very quickly, it ______.
3-5.5
3. How quickly an object moves is described as its ______.
3-5.2
4. When a guitar string vibrates, a ______ is made.
3-5.5
5. You can use a ______ to attract things made of iron.
6. The amount of space between two objects is described as their ______ from each other.
7. A push or pull is called a ______.
8. The highness or lowness of a sound is its ______.
3-5.8
9. You squeeze the hand brakes on a bike. The force that slows down the bike is ______.
3-5.3
10. The loudness of a sound is its ______.
3-5.7

LOG ON e-Review Summaries and quizzes online at www.macmillanmh.com

Skills and Concepts

Answer each of the following in complete sentences.

11. **Problem and Solution** A car has just traveled 100 kilometers. What else do you need to know to figure out its average speed?
3-5.2

12. **Persuasive Writing** What is your favorite kind of music? Write a paragraph explaining why you enjoy it. Include *volume* and *pitch* in your paragraph.
3-5.6

13. **Infer** Would you move faster down a water slide or a regular slide? Explain your answer.
3-5.4

14. **Critical Thinking** How do you know that something has moved?
3-5.1

15. What causes these guitar strings to make a sound?
3-5.5

16. What makes something move?
3-5

Performance Assessment

Mapping Your Motion

- Make a map of your classroom. Mark where the main objects are placed. For example, show the location of doors, windows, boards, and desks.
- For 5 minutes, slowly follow a path around the room. Stop once every minute. Mark an *X* on the map showing your location at the time that you stop.
- Who is moving faster: a student whose marks are far apart or one whose marks are close together? Compare maps with another student. Try to find out who moved faster. Explain how you know who moved at a greater speed.

South Carolina Activity

Every day we hear many different sounds. Carolina wrens sing, milk cows moo, and car horns honk. Look through newspapers or magazines to find pictures of objects that make the sounds of daily life in South Carolina. Cut out the pictures, and make a poster. On your poster explain what makes these sounds.

South Carolina Standards Practice

1 A student wants to find out the speed of a toy car. She uses a stopwatch to time the car's motion. What other tool does she need?

A a meterstick

B a graduated cylinder

C forceps

D a beaker

3-1.5

2 A rubber mallet is used to strike two different tuning forks.

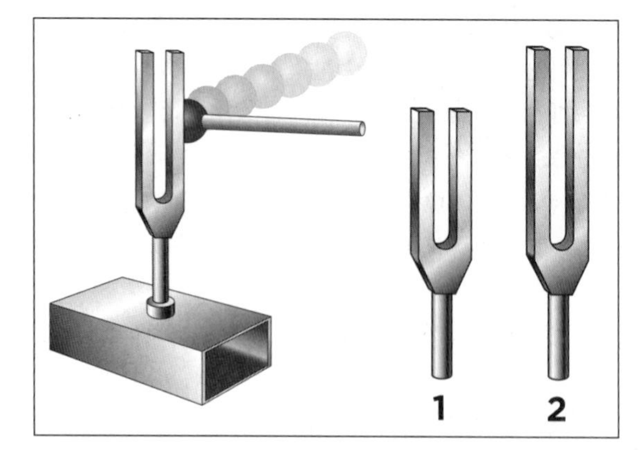

Which of these **best** explains the sounds they produce?

F Tuning fork 1 has a higher pitch because it is longer.

G Tuning fork 1 has a higher pitch because it is shorter.

H Tuning fork 2 has a higher pitch because it is longer.

I Tuning fork 2 has a higher pitch because it is shorter.

3-1.6

3 If you lifted each of the following objects the same distance, which object would need the **most** force?

A a pencil

B a feather

C a magazine

D a bowling ball

3-5.3

4 Which force pulls objects toward Earth?

F magnetism

G friction

H contact

I gravity

3-5.4

5 All sounds begin when something

A vibrates.

B spins.

C bends.

D shifts.

3-5.5

6 A scientist investigates whether loud sounds affect the growth of plants. What is the **most** important safety practice the scientist should follow?

F wearing goggles

G protecting the ears

H working with a partner

I handling plants with forceps

3-I.8

7 Examine the table below.

How Sounds Can Be Different	Cause of Difference	Description of Difference
volume	energy of waves	soft or loud
pitch		low or high

Which choice **best** completes the table?

A time of waves

B distance of waves

C speed of waves

D position of waves

3-I.6

8 The following are all metric measurements of distance **except**

F centimeters.

G liters.

H kilometers.

I meters.

3-5.1

9 An example of a contact force is a force that

A keeps the Moon orbiting Earth.

B keeps Earth orbiting the Sun.

C causes some metals to attract other metals.

D causes a bowling ball to knock down pins.

3-5.3

10 The **best** way for a drummer to increase the volume of his or her drumming would be to

F hit a smaller drum.

G hit a larger drum.

H hit the drum with smaller drumsticks.

I hit the drum with larger drumsticks.

3-5.7

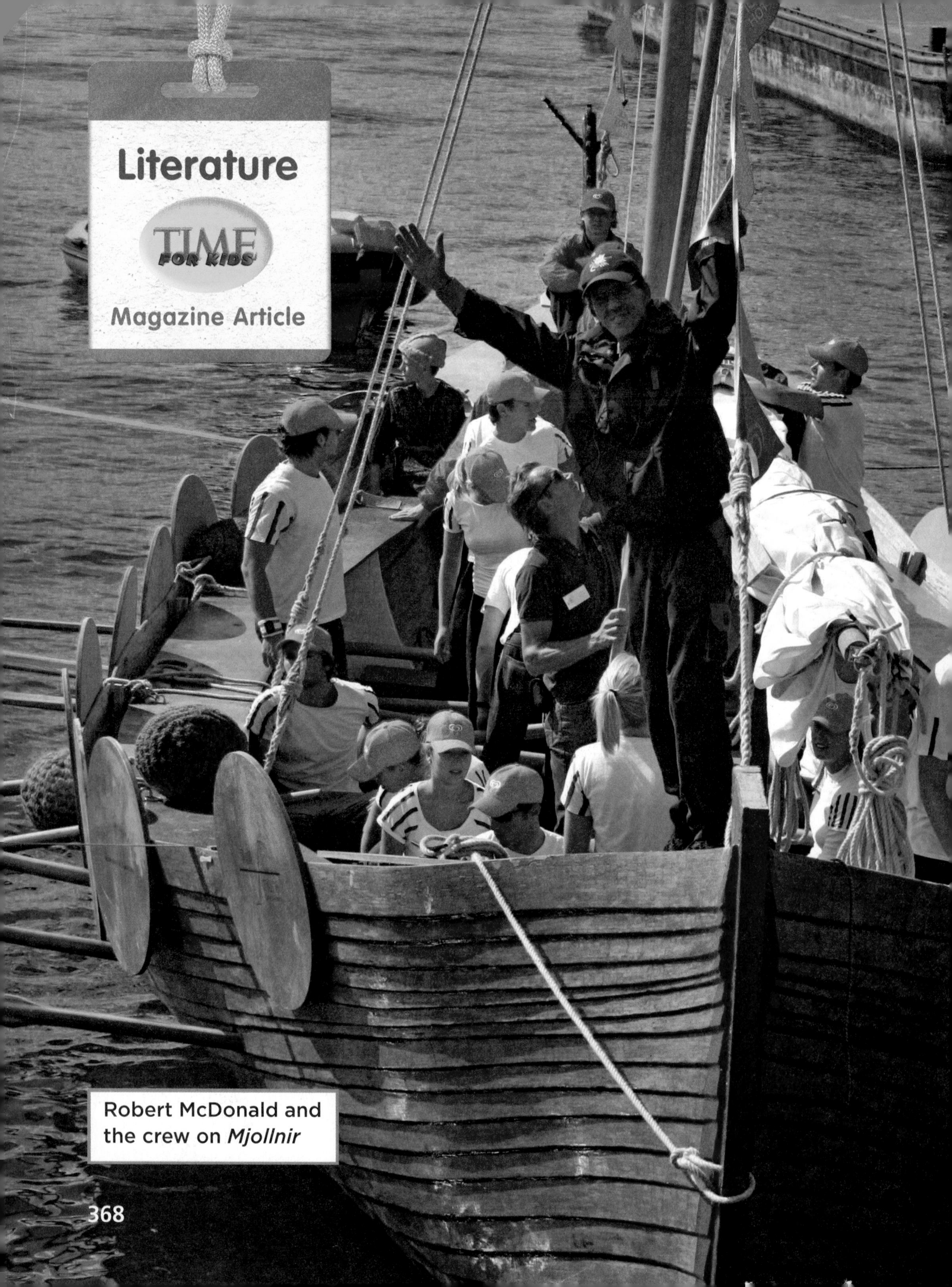

Robert McDonald and the crew on *Mjollnir*

from *Time for Kids*

The Good Ship Popsicle Stick

September 2, 2005

On August 16, former Hollywood stuntman Robert McDonald performed a record-breaking stunt. He floated a ship made of wooden ice cream sticks on a river that flows through the city of Amsterdam, in the Netherlands. And the boat didn't sink!

McDonald built the 50-foot-long replica of a Viking ship with 15 million ice cream sticks and more than two tons of glue. The 13-ton cruiser is named *Mjollnir* (MIL•ner), after the hammer of Thor, the Viking god of thunder.

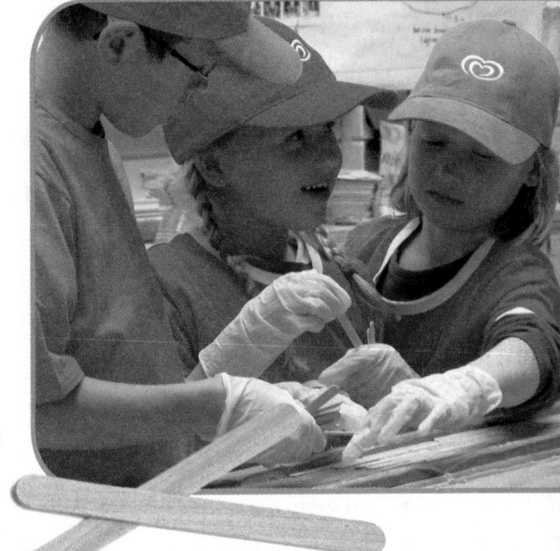

Captain Rob is the president of the Sea Heart Ship Foundation. The group's goal is to spread fun to kids in hospitals around the world. "I have a dream to show children they can do anything," he says. "If they can dream it, they can do it."

Write About It

Response to Literature This article is about a ship made from ice cream sticks. What words are used to describe the ship? Choose an object around you. Then use words to tell about it.

e-Journal Write about it online at www.macmillanmh.com

Environmental Chemist

Do you like helping keep plants and animals healthy? Are you concerned with keeping the environment clean? If so, then you might like to be an environmental chemist.

An environmental chemist is a kind of scientist. These scientists help keep the water, land, and air free of pollution. Pollution can hurt plants, animals, and people. Environmental chemists protect living things by helping clean up pollution. Environmental chemists also show people how to reduce pollution.

To become an environmental chemist, you should begin learning about the environment where you live. Start a recycling program in your home or at school to reduce waste. You could also join a group that helps protect the environment.

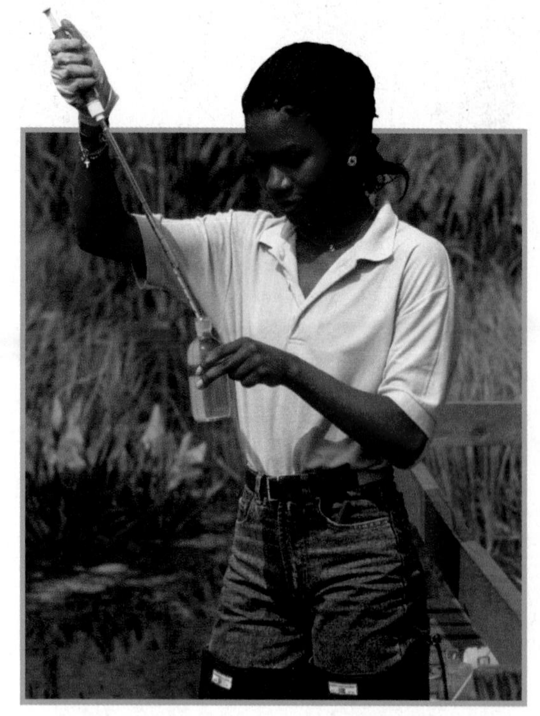

▲ This scientist is collecting data on water pollution.

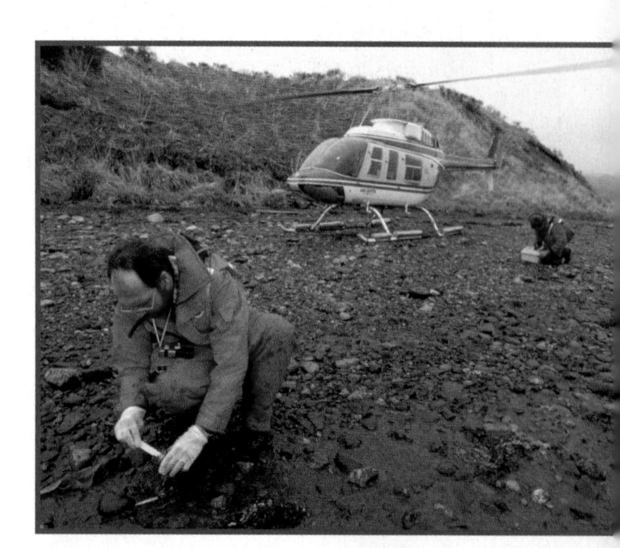

▲ This chemist is testing to see how much oil is left on a beach after a spill.

Here are some other Physical Science careers:

- carpenter
- lab technician
- chemical engineer
- pharmacist

LOG ON e-Careers at www.macmillanmh.com

Reference

Measurements

Units of Measurement

Temperature

▶ The temperature on this thermometer reads 86 degrees Fahrenheit. That is the same as 30 degrees Celsius.

Length and Area

▶ This student is 3 feet plus 9 inches tall. That is the same as 1 meter plus 14 centimeters.

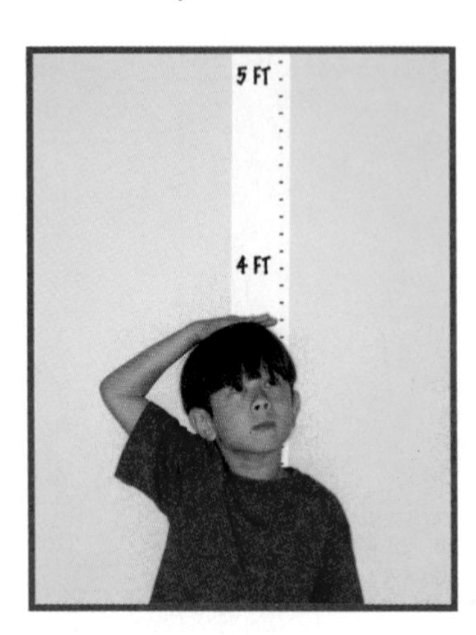

Mass

▶ You can measure the mass of these rocks in grams.

Volume of Fluids

▶ This bottle of water has a volume of 2 liters. That is a little more than 2 quarts.

Weight/Force

▶ This pumpkin weighs about 7 pounds. That means the force of gravity is 31.5 newtons.

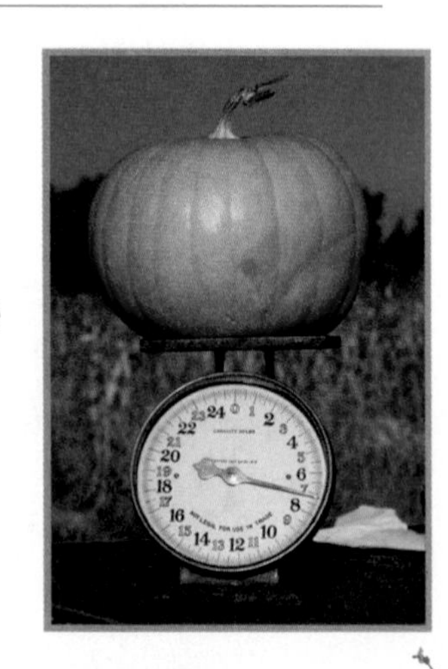

Speed

▶ This student can ride her bike 100 meters in 50 seconds. That means her speed is 2 meters per second.

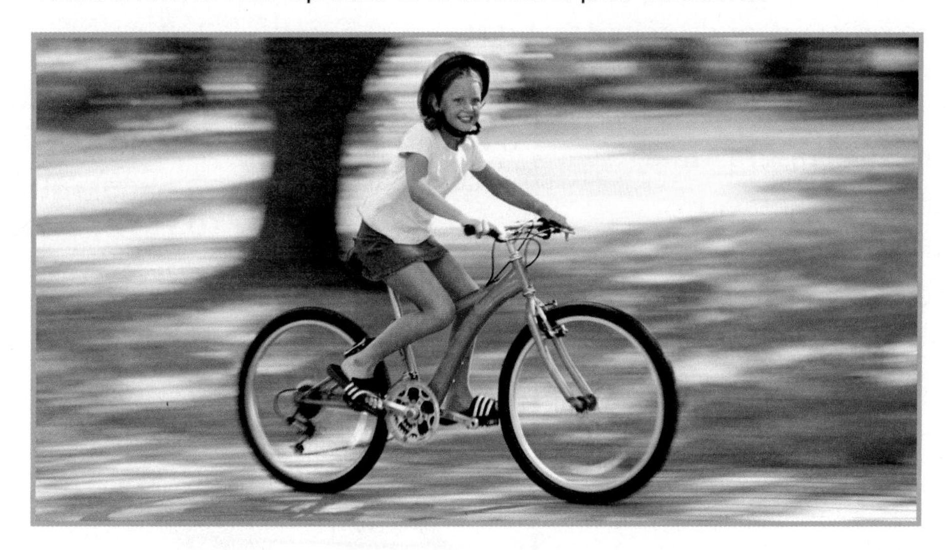

Table of Measures	
SI International Units/Metric Units	**Customary Units**
Temperature Water freezes at 0 degrees Celsius (°C) and boils at 100°C.	**Temperature** Water freezes at 32 degrees Fahrenheit (°F) and boils at 212°F.
Length and Distance 10 millimeters (mm) = 1 centimeter (cm) 100 centimeters = 1 meter (m) 1,000 meters = 1 kilometer (km)	**Length and Distance** 12 inches (in.) = 1 foot (ft) 3 feet = 1 yard (yd) 5,280 feet = 1 mile (mi)
Volume 1 cubic centimeter (cm^3) = 1 milliliter (mL) 1,000 milliliters = 1 liter (L)	**Volume of Fluids** 8 fluid ounces (fl oz) = 1 cup (c) 2 cups = 1 pint (pt) 2 pints = 1 quart (qt) 4 quarts = 1 gallon (gal)
Mass 1,000 milligrams (mg) = 1 gram (g) 1,000 grams = 1 kilogram (kg)	**Area** 1 square foot (ft^2) = 1 ft x 1 ft 43,560 square feet (ft^2) = 1 acre
Area 1 square meter (m^2) = 1 m x 1 m 10,000 square meters (m^2) = 1 hectare	**Speed** miles per hour (mph)
Speed meters per second (m/s) kilometers per hour (km/h)	**Weight/Force** 16 ounces (oz) = 1 pound (lb) 2,000 pounds = 1 ton (T)
Weight/Force 1 newton (N) = 1 kg x $1 m/s^2$	

Measurements

Measure Time

You measure time to find out how long something takes to happen. Stopwatches and clocks are tools you can use to measure time. Seconds, minutes, hours, days, and years are some units of time.

Try it Use a Stopwatch to Measure Time

1. Get a cup of water and an antacid tablet from your teacher.
2. Tell your partner to place the tablet in the cup of water. Start the stopwatch when the tablet touches the water.
3. Stop the stopwatch when the tablet completely dissolves. Record the time shown on the stopwatch.

0 minutes

25 seconds

75 hundredths (0.75) of a second

▲ Push the button on the top right of the stopwatch to start timing. Push the button again to stop timing.

Measure Length

You measure length to find out how long or how far away something is. Rulers, tape measures, and metersticks are some tools you can use to measure length. You can measure length using units called meters. Smaller units are made from parts of meters. Larger units are made of many meters.

Look at the ruler below. Each number represents 1 centimeter (cm). There are 100 centimeters in 1 meter. In between each number are 10 lines. Each line is equal to 1 millimeter (mm). There are 10 millimeters in 1 centimeter.

Try it Find Length with a Ruler

Place a ruler on your desk. Line up a pencil with the "0" mark on the ruler. Record the length of the pencil in centimeters.

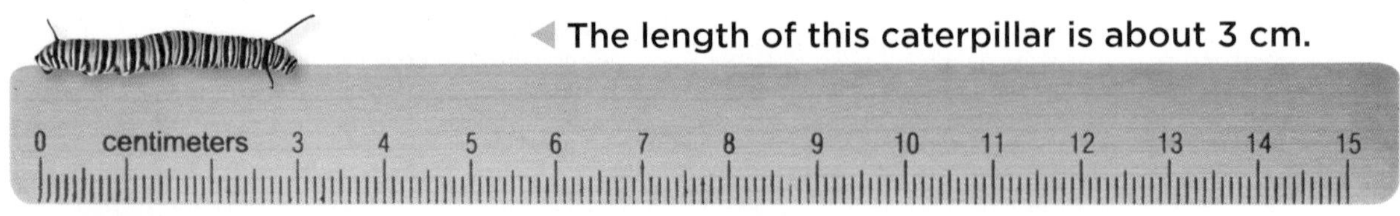

◀ The length of this caterpillar is about 3 cm.

Measure Liquid Volume

Volume is the amount of space something takes up. Beakers, measuring cups, and graduated cylinders are tools you can use to measure liquid volume. These containers are marked in units called milliliters (mL).

Try it Measure Liquid Volume

1. Gather a few empty plastic containers of different shapes and sizes.
2. Use a graduated cylinder to find the volume of water each container can hold. To start, fill the graduated cylinder with water, then pour the water into the container. Continue pouring this until the container is full. Keep track of the number of milliliters you add.

10 mL

▲ This graduated cylinder can measure volumes up to 100 mL. Each number on the cylinder represents 10 mL.

Measure Mass

Mass is the amount of matter an object has. You use a balance to measure mass. To find the mass of an object, you compare it with objects whose masses you know. Grams are units people use to measure mass.

Try it Measure the Mass of a Box of Crayons

1. Place a box of crayons on one side of a pan balance.
2. Add gram masses to the other side until the two sides of the balance are level.
3. Add together the numbers on the gram masses. This total equals the mass of the box of crayons.

Measure Force/Weight

You measure force to find the strength of a push or pull. Force can be measured in units called newtons (N). A spring scale is a tool used to measure force.

Weight is a measure of the force of gravity pulling down on an object. A spring scale measures the pull of gravity. One pound is equal to about 4.5 newtons.

Try it Measure the Weight of an Object

1. Hold a spring scale by the top loop. Put a small object on the bottom hook.
2. Slowly, let go of the object. Wait for the spring to stop moving.
3. Read the number of newtons next to the tab. This is the object's weight.

Measure Temperature

Temperature (TEM•puhr•uh•chuhr) is how hot or cold something is. You use a tool called a thermometer (thuhr•MOM•i•tuhr) to measure temperature. In the United States, temperature is often measured in degrees Fahrenheit (°F). However, you can also measure temperature in degrees Celsius (°C).

Try it Read a Thermometer

1. Fill a beaker with ice water. Then put a thermometer in the water.
2. Wait several minutes. Read the number next to the top of the red liquid inside the thermometer. This is the temperature.
3. Repeat with warm water.

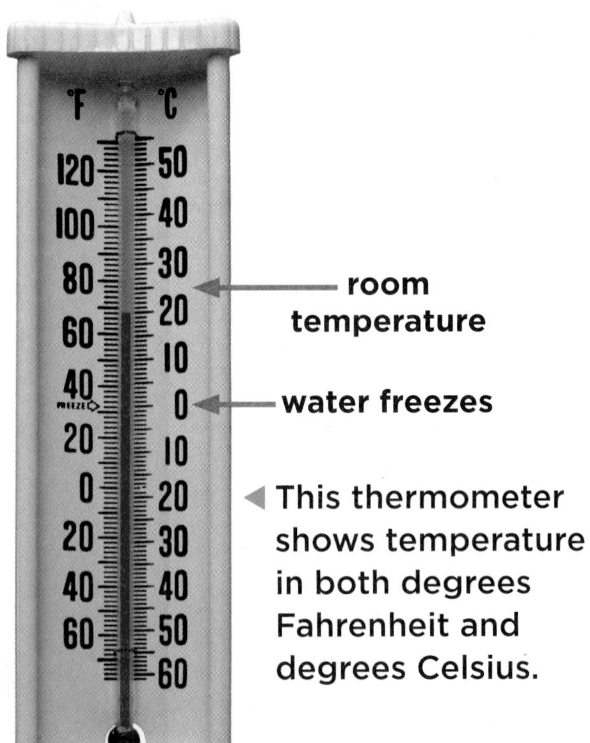

◀ This thermometer shows temperature in both degrees Fahrenheit and degrees Celsius.

Tools of Science

Use a Microscope

A microscope (MYE•kruh•skohp) is a tool that magnifies objects, or makes them look larger. A microscope can make an object look hundreds or thousands of times larger. Look at the photo to learn the different parts of a microscope.

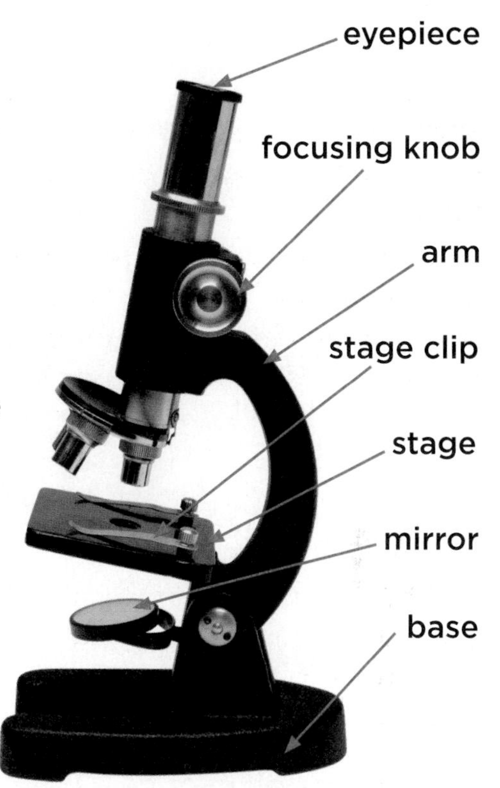

Try it Examine Salt Grains

1. Move the mirror so that it reflects light up toward the stage. ⚠ **Be Careful**. Never point the mirror at bright lights or the Sun. This can cause permanent eye damage.
2. Place a few grains of salt on a slide. Put the slide under the stage clips on the stage. Be sure that the salt grains are over the hole in the stage.
3. Look through the eyepiece. Turn the focusing knob slowly until the salt grains come into focus. Draw a picture of what you see.

Use a Hand Lens

A hand lens is another tool that magnifies objects. It is not as powerful as a microscope. However, a hand lens still allows you to see details of an object that you cannot see with your eyes alone. As you move a hand lens away from an object, you can see more details. If you move a hand lens too far away, the object will look blurry.

Try it Magnify a Rock

1. Look at a rock carefully. Draw a picture of it.
2. Hold a hand lens above the rock so that you can see the rock clearly.
3. Fill in any details on your original drawing that you did not see before.

Tools of Science

Use a Calculator

Sometimes during an experiment, you have to add, subtract, multiply, or divide numbers. A calculator can help you carry out these operations.

Try it Convert from °F to °C

Water boils at 212°F. Use a calculator to convert 212°F into degrees Celsius.

1. Press the [ON] key. Then, enter the number 212 by pressing [2][1][2].
2. Subtract 32 by pressing [-][3][2].
3. Multiply by 5 by pressing [x][5].
4. Finally, divide by 9 by pressing [÷][9]. Press [=]. This is the temperature in degrees Celsius.

Now, convert 100°F into degrees Celsius.

Use a Camera

During an experiment or nature study, it helps to observe and record changes that happen over time. Sometimes it can be difficult to see these changes if they happen very quickly or very slowly. A camera can help you keep track of visible changes. Studying photos can help you understand what happened over the course of time.

Try it Gather Data From a Photo

The photos below show a panda eight days after birth and then several months later. What differences do you notice? How has the panda changed over those months? Now think of something else that changes over time. With the help of an adult, use a camera to take photos at different times. Compare your photos.

Computers

Use a Computer

A computer has many uses. You can use a computer to get information from compact discs (CDs) and digital videodiscs (DVDs). You can also use a computer to write reports and to show information.

The Internet connects your computer with computers around the world, so you can collect all kinds of information. When using the Internet, visit only Web sites that are safe and reliable. Your teacher can help you find safe and reliable sites to use. Whenever you are online, never give any information about yourself to others.

Try it Use a Computer for a Project

1. Choose an environment to research. Then use the Internet to find out about this environment. Where is the environment located in the world? What is the climate like in the environment? What kinds of plants and animals live there?
2. Use DVDs or other sources from the library to find out more about your chosen environment.
3. Use the computer to write a report about the information you gathered. Then share your report with others.

Organizing Data

Make Maps

Locate Places

A map is a drawing that shows an area from above. Many maps have numbers and letters along the top and side. The letters and numbers help you find locations. The Buffalo Zoological Garden, for example, is located at D4 below. To find it, place a finger on the letter D along the side of the map and another finger on the number 4 at the top. Then move your fingers straight across and down the map until they meet. Now find B1? What is there?

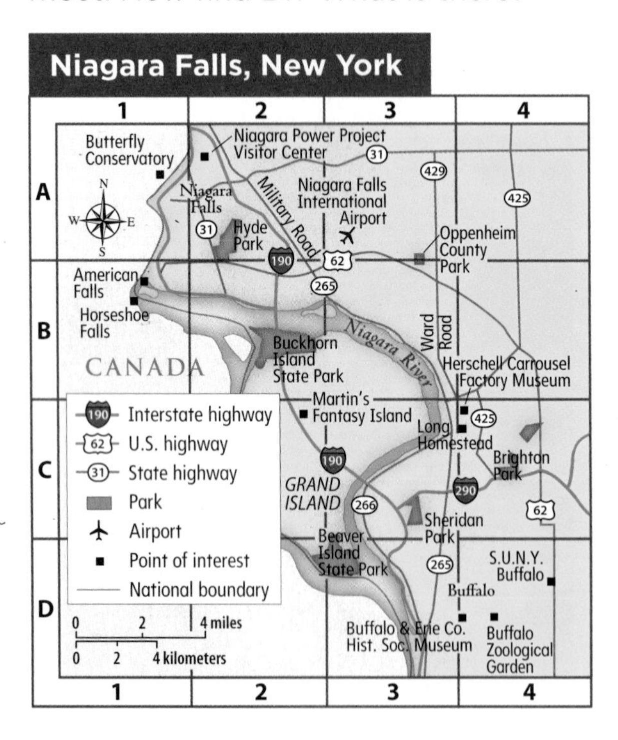

Try it **Make a Map**

Make a map of an area in your community. It might be a park or the area between your home and school. Include numbers and letters along the top and side. Use a compass to find north, and mark north on your map.

Idea Maps

The Niagara Falls map shows how places are connected to each other. Idea maps, on the other hand, show how ideas are connected to each other. Idea maps help you organize information about a topic.

Look at the idea map below. It connects ideas about water. This map shows that Earth's water can be fresh water or salt water. The map also shows three sources of fresh water. You can see that there is no connection between "rivers" and "salt water" on the map. This can remind you that salt water does not flow in rivers.

Try it **Make an Idea Map**

Make an idea map about a topic you are learning in science. Your map can include words, phrases, or even sentences. Arrange your map in a way that makes sense to you and helps you understand the connection between ideas.

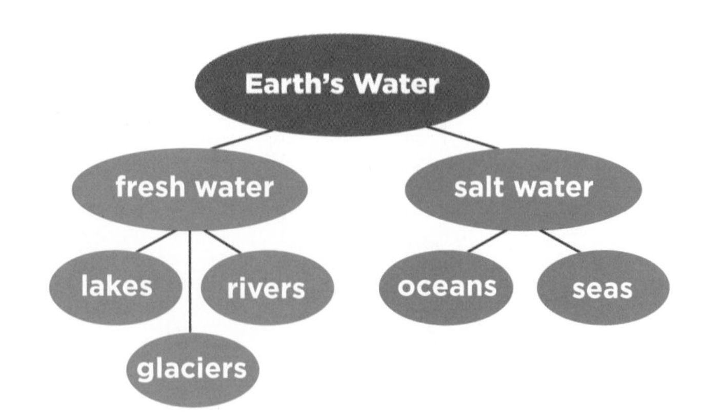

Make Charts

Living	Nonliving
tree	rock
chipmunk	puddle
bird	cloud

Charts are useful for recording information during an experiment and for communicating information. In a chart, only the column or the row has meaning but not both. In this chart, one column lists living things. A second column lists nonliving things.

Try it **Organize Data in a Chart**

Take a survey of your class. Find out each student's favorite kind of pet. Make a chart to show this information. Remember to show your information in columns or in rows.

Make Tables

Tables also help to organize data, or information. Tables have columns that run up and down and rows that run across. Column and row headings tell you what kind of data they hold.

The table below shows the properties of some minerals. Which mineral in the table has a white streak? Which mineral is yellow in color?

Try it **Organize Data in a Table**

Collect a few minerals from your teacher. Observe the properties of each. Make a table like the one shown. Use the same column headings. Record the properties of each mineral.

Mineral Identification Table

	Hardness	Luster	Streak	Color	Other
pyrite	6-6.5	metallic	greenish-black	brassy yellow	called "fool's gold"
quartz	7	nonmetallic	none	colorless, white, rose, smoky, purple, brown	
mica	2-2.5	nonmetallic	none	dark brown, black, or silver-white	flakes when peeled
feldspar	6	nonmetallic	none	colorless, beige, pink	
calcite	3	nonmetallic	white	colorless, white	bubbles when acid is placed on it

Organizing Data

Make Graphs

Graphs also help organize data. Graphs make it easy to notice trends and patterns. There are many kinds of graphs.

Bar Graphs

A bar graph uses bars to show data. What if you want to find the warmest and coldest months for your city? Every month you find the average temperature in the newspaper. You can organize the temperatures in a bar graph so you can easily compare them.

Month	Temperature (°C)
January	6
February	8
March	10
April	13
May	16
June	19
July	22
August	20
September	19
October	14
November	9
December	7

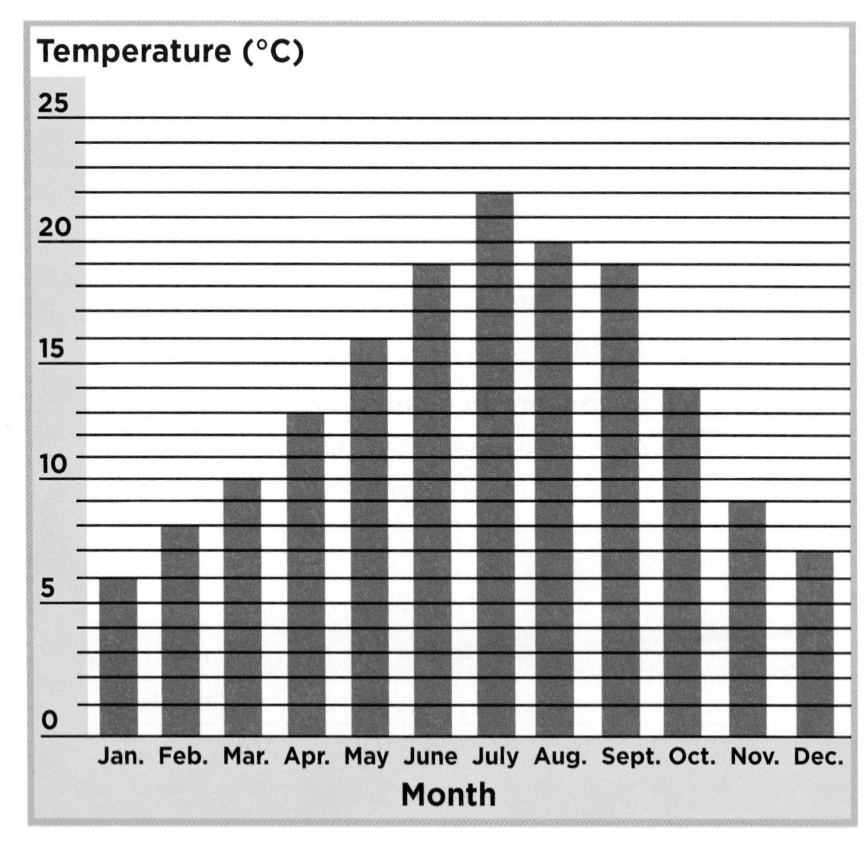

1. Look at the bar for the month of April. Put your finger at the top of the bar. Move your finger straight over to the left to find the average temperature for that month.
2. Find the highest bar on the bar graph. This bar represents the month with the highest average temperature. Which month is it? What is the average temperature for this month?
3. Look at the bars of the graph. What pattern do you notice in the temperatures from January to December?

Pictographs

A pictograph uses symbols, or pictures, to show information. What if you collect information about how much water your family uses each day?

Water Used Daily (liters)	
drinking	10
showering	100
bathing	120
brushing teeth	40
washing dishes	80
washing hands	30
washing clothes	160
flushing toilet	50

You can organize this information into a pictograph. In the pictograph below, each bucket means 20 liters of water. A half bucket means half of 20, or 10, liters of water.

1. Which activity uses the most water?
2. Which activity uses the least water?

Water Used Daily	
drinking	
showering	
bathing	
brushing teeth	
washing dishes	
washing hands	
washing clothes	
flushing toilet	

= 20 liters of water

Line Graphs

A line graph can show how information changes over time. What if you measure the temperature outdoors every hour starting at 6 A.M.?

Time	Temperature (°C)
6 A.M.	10
7 A.M.	12
8 A.M.	14
9 A.M.	16
10 A.M.	18
11 A.M.	20

Now organize your data by making a line graph. Follow these steps.

1. Make a scale along the bottom and side of the graph. Label the scales.
2. Draw a point on the graph for each temperature measured each hour.
3. Connect the points.
4. How do the temperatures and times relate to each other?

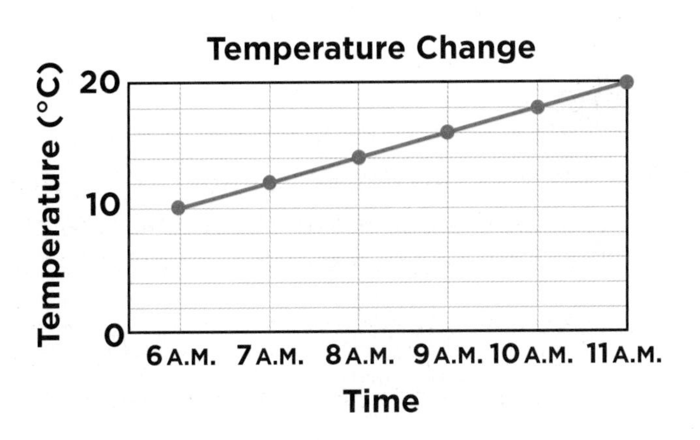

Human Body Systems

The Skeletal System

Feel your elbows, wrists, and fingers. What are those hard parts? Bones! Bones make up the skeletal system. The skeletal system is one of many body systems. A body system is a group of organs that work together to perform a specific job.

The skeletal system is made up of 206 bones. Each bone has a particular job. The long, strong leg bones support the body's weight. The skull protects the brain. The hip bones help you move. Together, bones do important jobs to keep the body active and healthy.

- ▶ Bones support the body and give the body its shape.
- ▶ Bones protect organs in the body.
- ▶ Bones work with muscles to move the body.
- ▶ Bones store minerals and produce blood for the body.

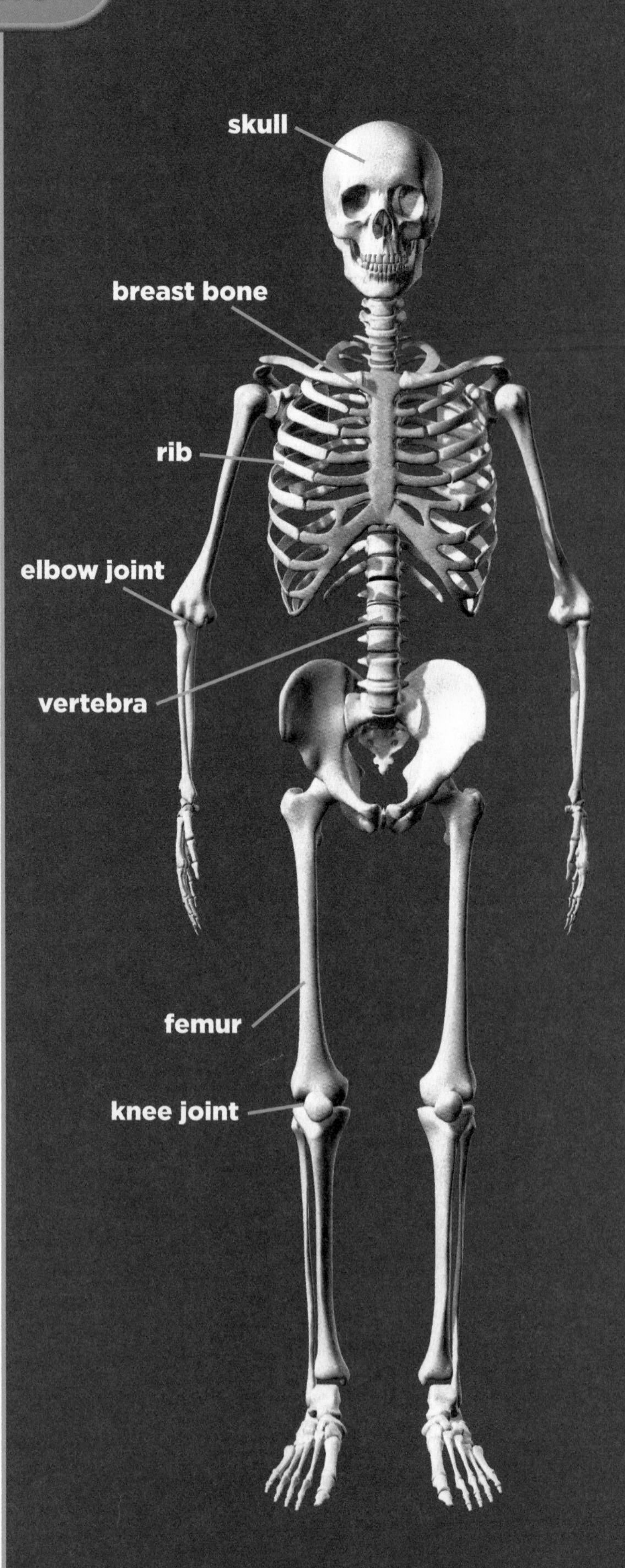

Joints

A joint is a place where two or more bones meet. There are three main types of joints.

Immovable joints form where bones fit together too tightly to move. The 29 bones of your skull meet at immovable joints. Partly movable joints are places where bones can move a little. Ribs are connected to the breastbone with these joints. Movable joints, like the knee, are places where bones can move easily. The knee lets the bones of your leg move.

The Muscular System

Together, all the muscles in the body form the muscular system. Muscles allow the body to move. Without muscles, you would not be able to run, smile, breathe, or even blink.

Most muscles are attached to bones and skin. These are called skeletal muscles. To move bones back and forth, skeletal muscles usually work in pairs. Each pulls on a bone in a different direction. When you want to move, your brain sends a message to a pair of skeletal muscles. One muscle contracts, or gets shorter. It pulls on the bone and skin. The other muscle relaxes to let the bone move.

▲ **There are 53 muscles in your face. You use 12 of them whenever you smile.**

◀ **To bend his arm, this boy's biceps contract while his triceps relax.**

Some muscles work without you even thinking about it. The heart is made of muscle. It pumps blood throughout the body even while you sleep. Smooth muscle in the lungs helps you breathe. Smooth muscle in the stomach helps you digest food.

Human Body Systems

The Circulatory System

The body's cells need a constant supply of oxygen and nutrients. The circulatory (SUR•kyuh•luh•tawr•ee) system is responsible for sending these things throughout the body. The circulatory system is made up of the heart, blood vessels, and blood.

Blood rich in oxygen travels from the lungs to the heart. The heart is an organ about the size of a fist. It beats about 70 to 90 times each minute, pumping blood through the blood vessels.

Blood vessels are tubes that carry blood. There are two main types of blood vessels. Arteries are blood vessels that carry blood away from the heart. Veins carry blood back to it.

Blood contains plasma, red blood cells, white blood cells, and platelets. Plasma is the liquid part of blood. It carries nutrients and other things the body needs. Red blood cells carry oxygen to all the cells of your body. Red blood cells and plasma also carry wastes, such as carbon dioxide, away from cells. White blood cells work to fight disease. Platelets keep you from bleeding too much when you get a cut.

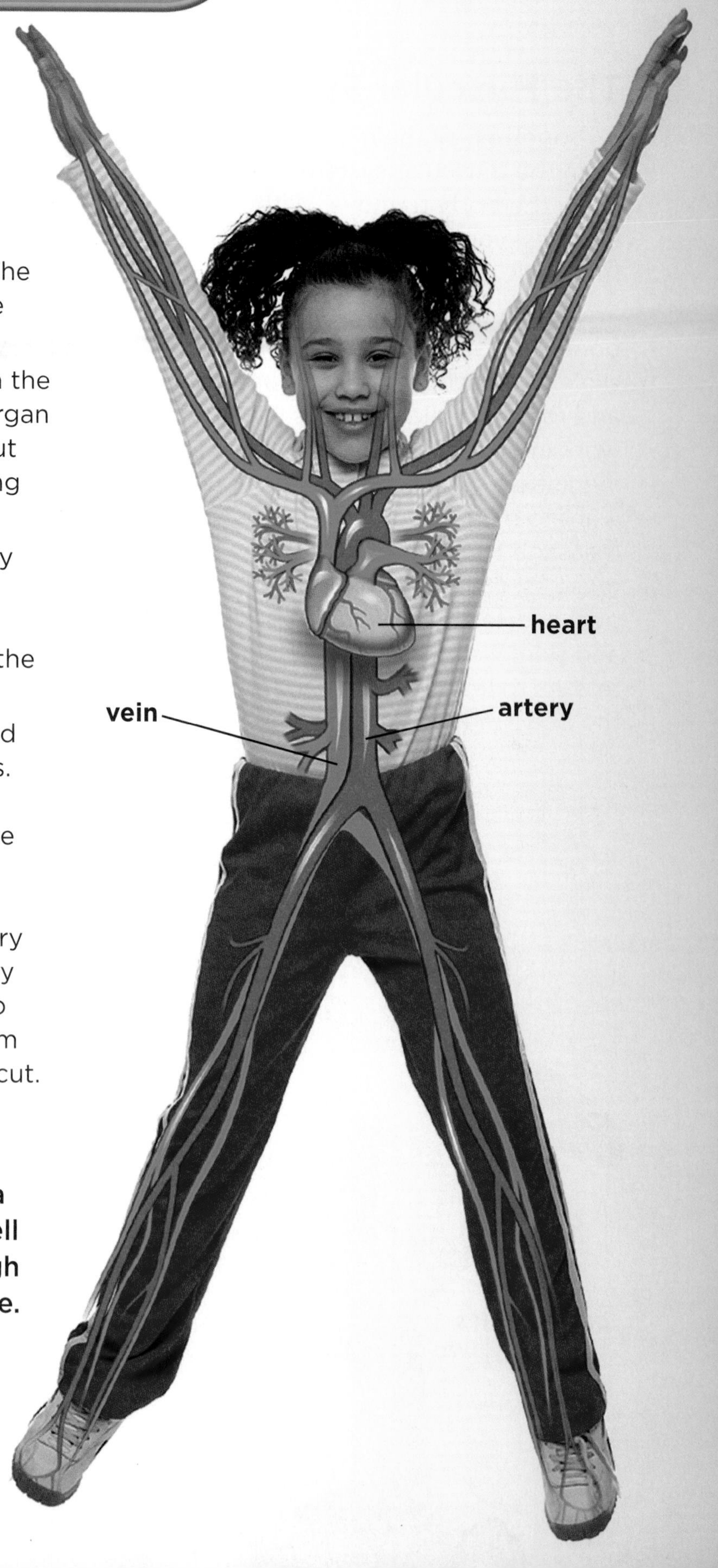

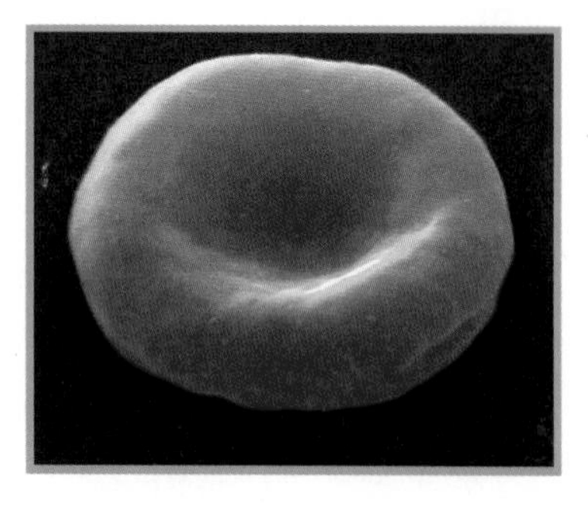

This is how a red blood cell looks through a microscope.

The Respiratory System

The respiratory (RES•puhr•uh•tawr•ee) system helps the body take in oxygen and give off carbon dioxide and other waste gases. All of the cells in your body require oxygen to work properly. You take in oxygen from the air when you breathe.

Every time you inhale, a muscle called the diaphragm (DYE•uh•fram) contracts. This makes room in your lungs for air. Air is taken in through the nose or mouth. This air travels down the throat into the trachea (TRAY•kee•uh).

In the chest, the trachea splits into two bronchial (BRONG•kee•uhl) tubes. Each tube leads to a lung. Inside each lung, the bronchial tube branches off into smaller tubes called bronchioles (BRONG•kee•ohlz). At the end of each bronchiole are millions of tiny air sacs. Here, red blood cells release carbon dioxide, a waste gas, and absorb oxygen. When you breathe out, the diaphragm relaxes. This causes the lungs to deflate and push carbon dioxide out of your body through the nose and mouth.

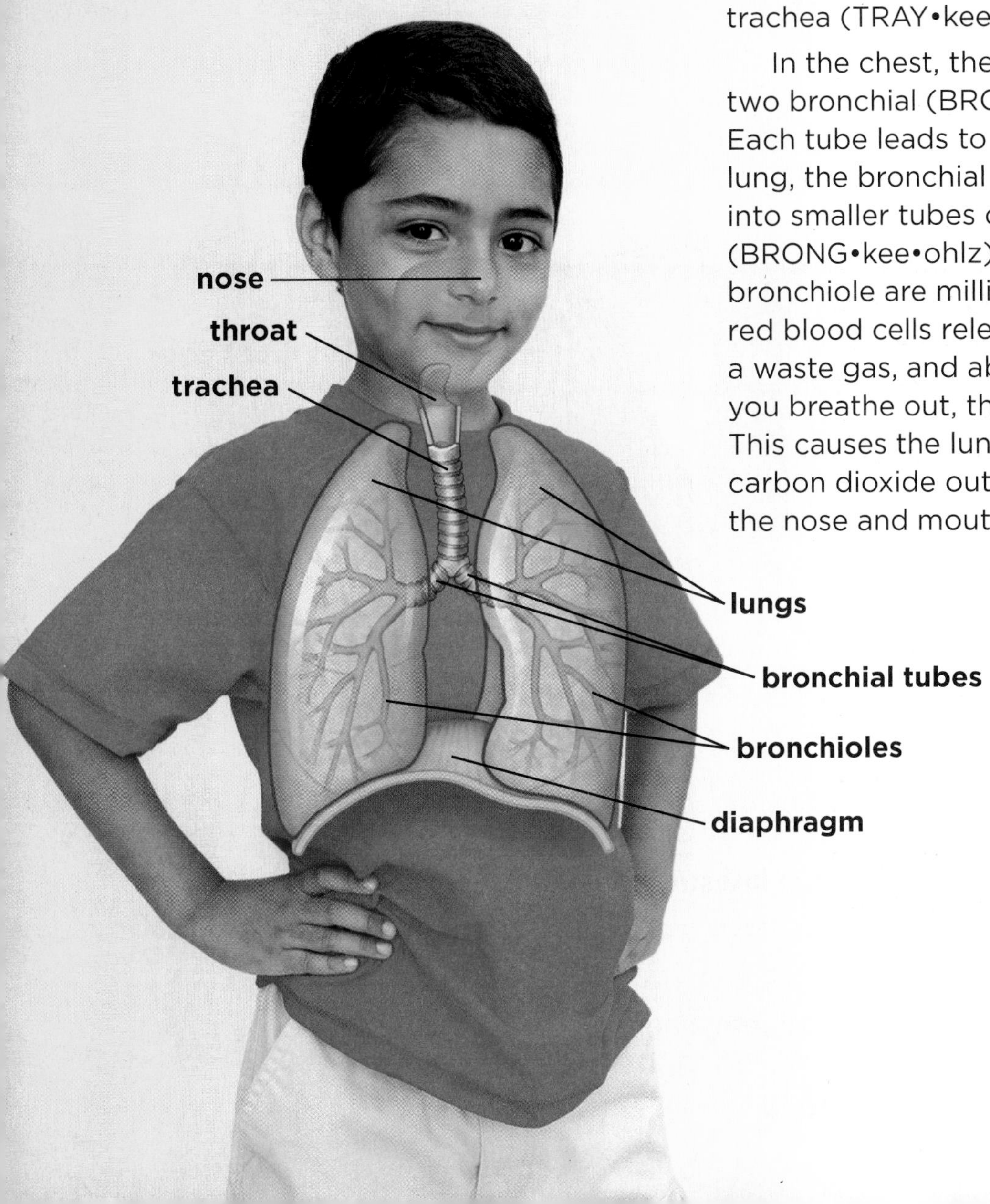

nose
throat
trachea
lungs
bronchial tubes
bronchioles
diaphragm

Human Body Systems

The Digestive System

The digestive (dye•JES•tiv) system is responsible for breaking down food into nutrients the body can use. Digestion begins when you chew food. Chewing breaks food into smaller pieces and moistens it with saliva. Saliva helps food travel smoothly when you swallow. The food travels down your esophagus (i•SOF•uh•guhs) and into your stomach.

Inside the stomach food is mixed with strong, acidic juices. This causes the food to break down further, making it easier for your body to absorb nutrients from the food.

After passing through the stomach, food moves into the small intestine (in•TES•tin). This is where most nutrients are absorbed. The small intestine is a narrow tube about 6 meters (20 feet) long. It is coiled tightly so it fits inside the body. As food passes through the small intestine, digested nutrients are absorbed into the blood. The blood then carries these nutrients to other parts of the body.

After food has passed through the small intestine, it enters the large intestine. The large intestine removes water from the unused food that is left. Then the unused food is removed from the body as waste.

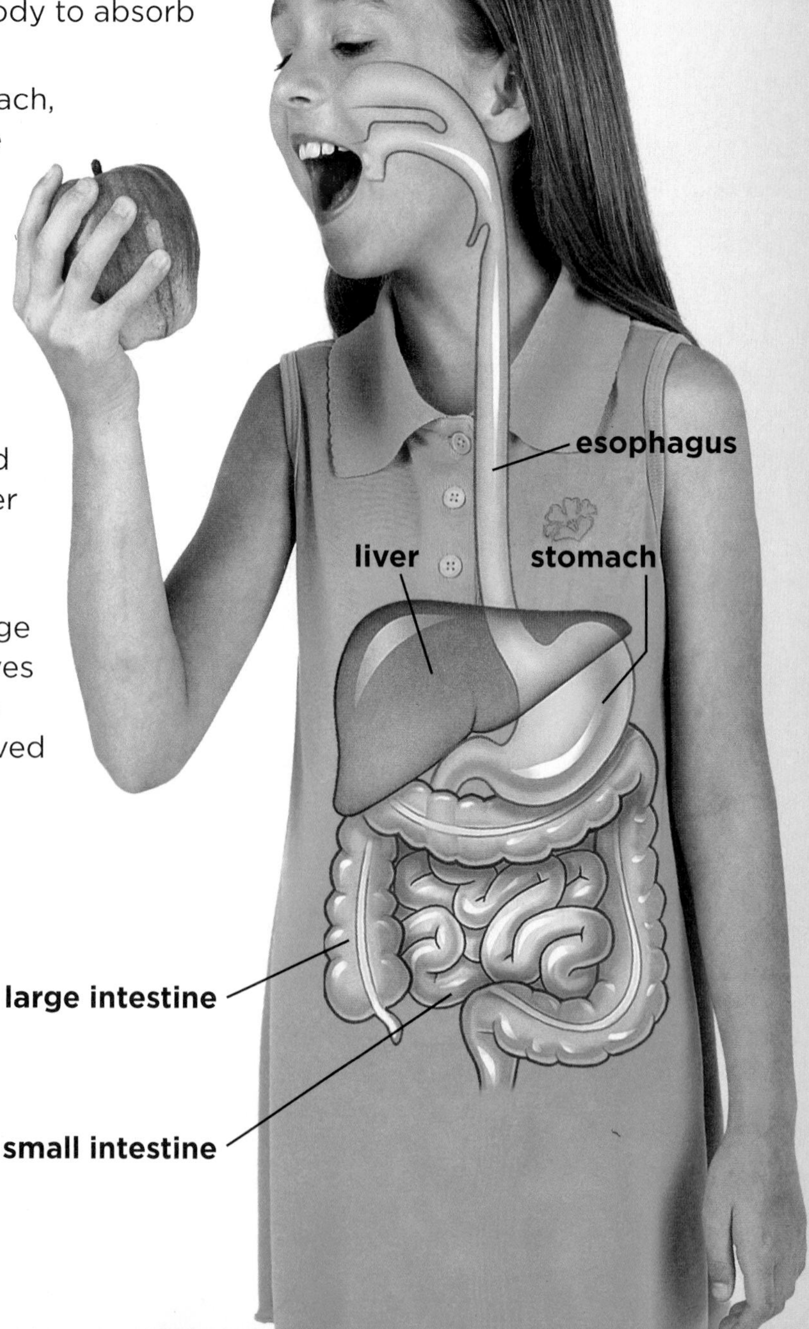

The Excretory System

The excretory (EK•skri•tawr•ee) system gets rid of waste products from your cells. Waste products are materials the body does not need, such as extra water and salts. The liver, kidneys, bladder, and skin are some organs of the excretory system.

Liver, Kidneys, and Bladder

The liver filters wastes from the blood. It changes wastes into a chemical call urea and sends the urea to the kidneys. Kidneys turn urea into urine. Urine flows from the kidney to the bladder. It is stored in the bladder until it is pushed out of the body through the urethra.

Skin

The skin takes part in excretion when a person sweats. Sweat glands in the inner layer of skin produce sweat. Sweat is made up of water and minerals that the body does not need. Sweat is excreted onto the outer layer of the skin. Sweating cools the body and helps it maintain an internal temperature of about 98°F (37°C).

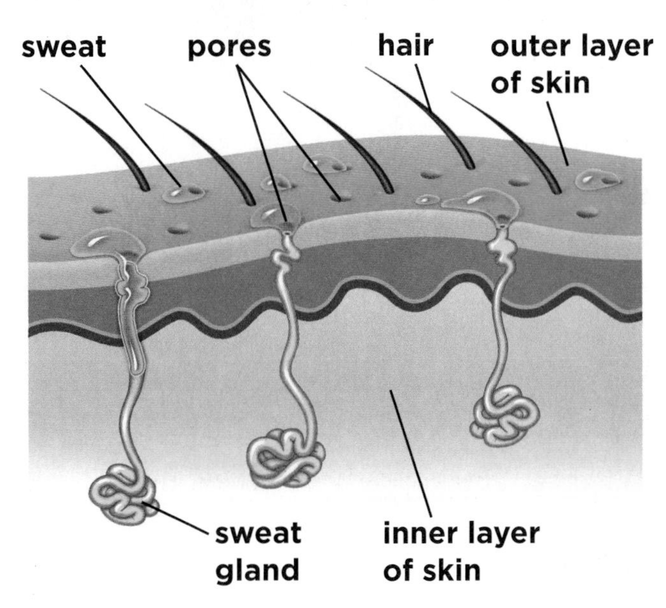

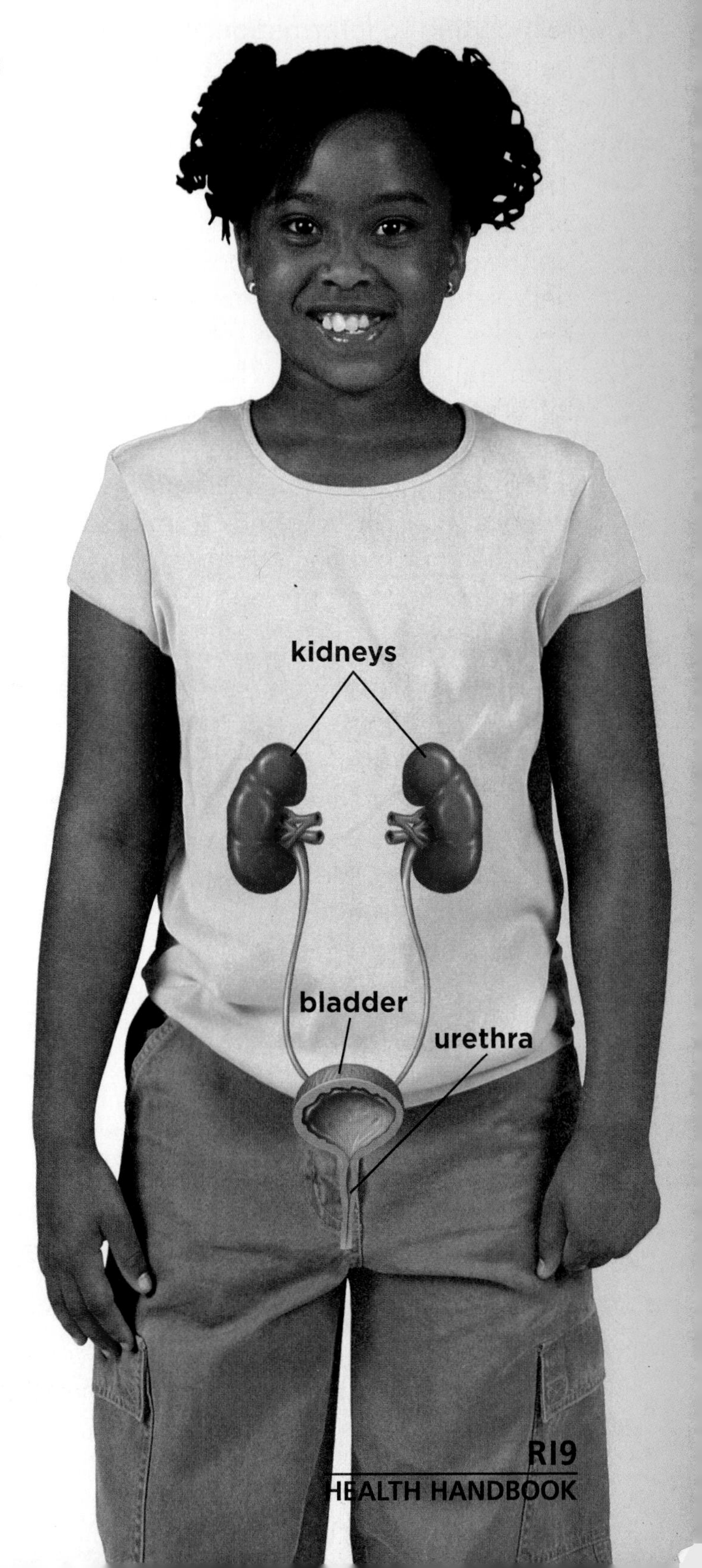

The Nervous System

The nervous system is responsible for taking in and responding to information. It controls muscles and helps the body balance. It allows a person to think, feel, and even dream.

The nervous system is made up of two main parts. The first part, the central nervous system, is made up of the brain and spinal cord. All other nerves make up the second part, the peripheral (puh•RIF•uhr•uhl) nervous system. Nerves from the peripheral nervous system receive sensory information from cells in the body. They pass this information on to the brain through the spinal cord. When the brain receives this information, it makes decisions about how the body should respond. Then it passes this new information back through the spinal cord to the nerves, and the body responds.

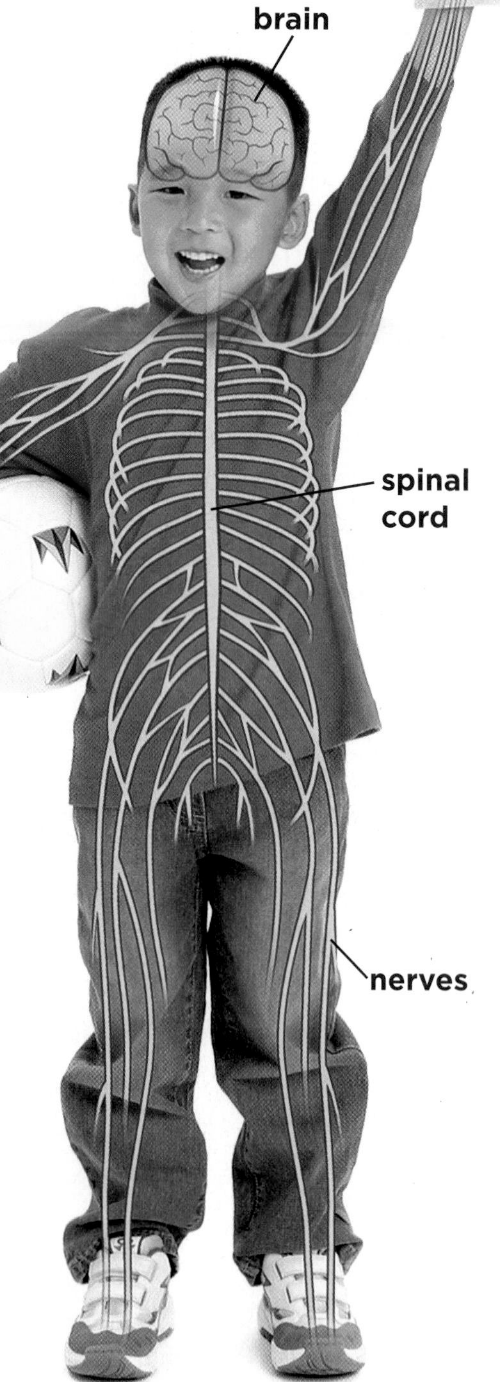

The Brain

The brain has three main parts, the cerebrum (suh•REE•bruhm), the cerebellum (ser•uh•BEL•uhm), and the brain stem. The cerebrum is the largest part of the brain. It stores memories and helps control information received by the senses. The cerebellum helps the body keep its balance and directs the skeletal muscles. The brain stem connects to the spinal cord. It controls heartbeat, breathing, and blood pressure.

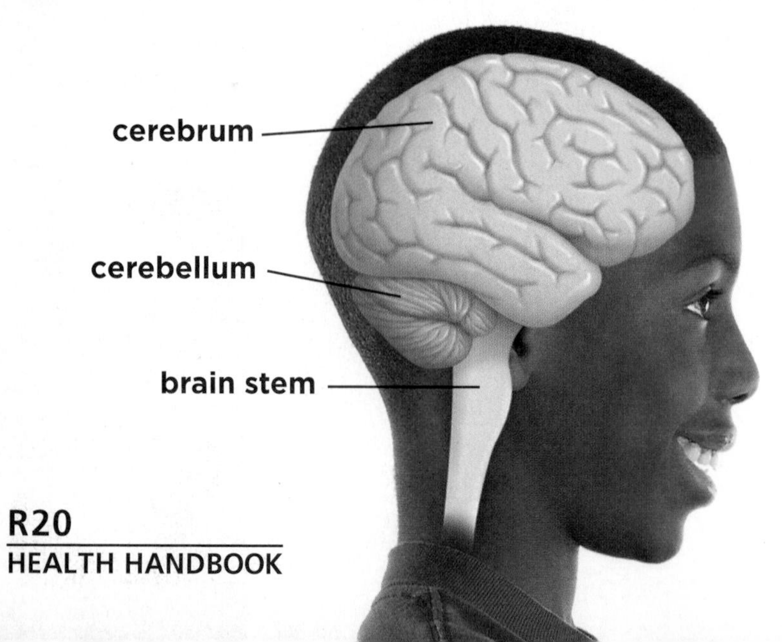

The Senses

Different nerves in the body take in information from the environment. These nerves are responsible for the body's sense of sight, hearing, smell, taste, and touch.

Sight

Light reflects off an object, such as a leaf, and into the eye. The reflected light passes through the pupil in the iris. Cells in the eye change light into electrical signals. The signals travel through the optic nerve to the brain.

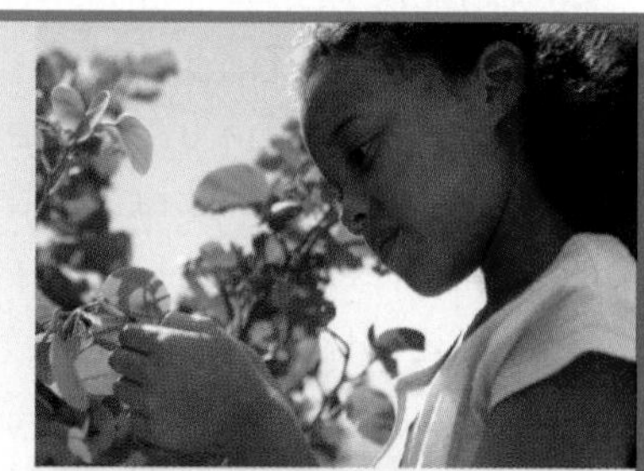

Hearing

Sound waves enter the outer ear. They reach the eardrum and cause it to vibrate. Cells in the ear change the sound waves into electrical signals. The signals travel along the auditory nerve to the brain.

Smell

As a person breathes, chemicals in the air mix with mucus in the upper part of the nose. When they reach certain cells in the nose, those cells send information along the olfactory nerve to the brain.

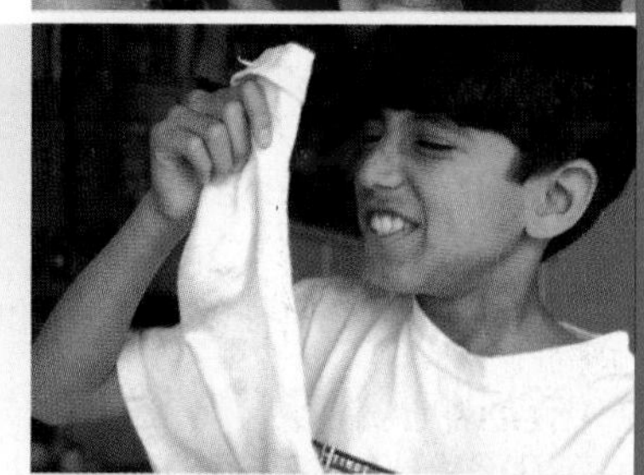

Taste

On the tongue are more than 10,000 tiny bumps, called taste buds. Each taste bud can sense four main tastes—sweet, sour, salty, and bitter. The taste buds send information along a nerve to the brain.

Touch

Different nerve cells in the skin give the body its sense of touch. They help a person tell hot from cold, wet from dry, and hard from soft. Each cell sends information to the spinal cord. The spinal cord then sends the information to the brain.

Immune System

The immune system protects the body from germs. Germs cause disease and infection. Most of the time, the immune system is able to prevent germs from entering the body. Skin, tears, and saliva are parts of the immune system. They work to kill germs and keep them out of the body.

When germs do find a way into your body, white blood cells help find and kill them quickly before you become ill. White blood cells are part of the blood. They travel through blood vessels and lymph (LIMF) vessels. Lymph vessels are similar to blood vessels. However, instead of carrying blood, they carry a fluid called lymph. Many white blood cells are made and live in lymph nodes. Here, they filter out harmful materials from the body.

White blood cells are not always able to kill germs before the germs start to reproduce in your body. When germs reproduce, they cause illness. Even while you feel ill, the immune system works to kill and remove germs until you are well again.

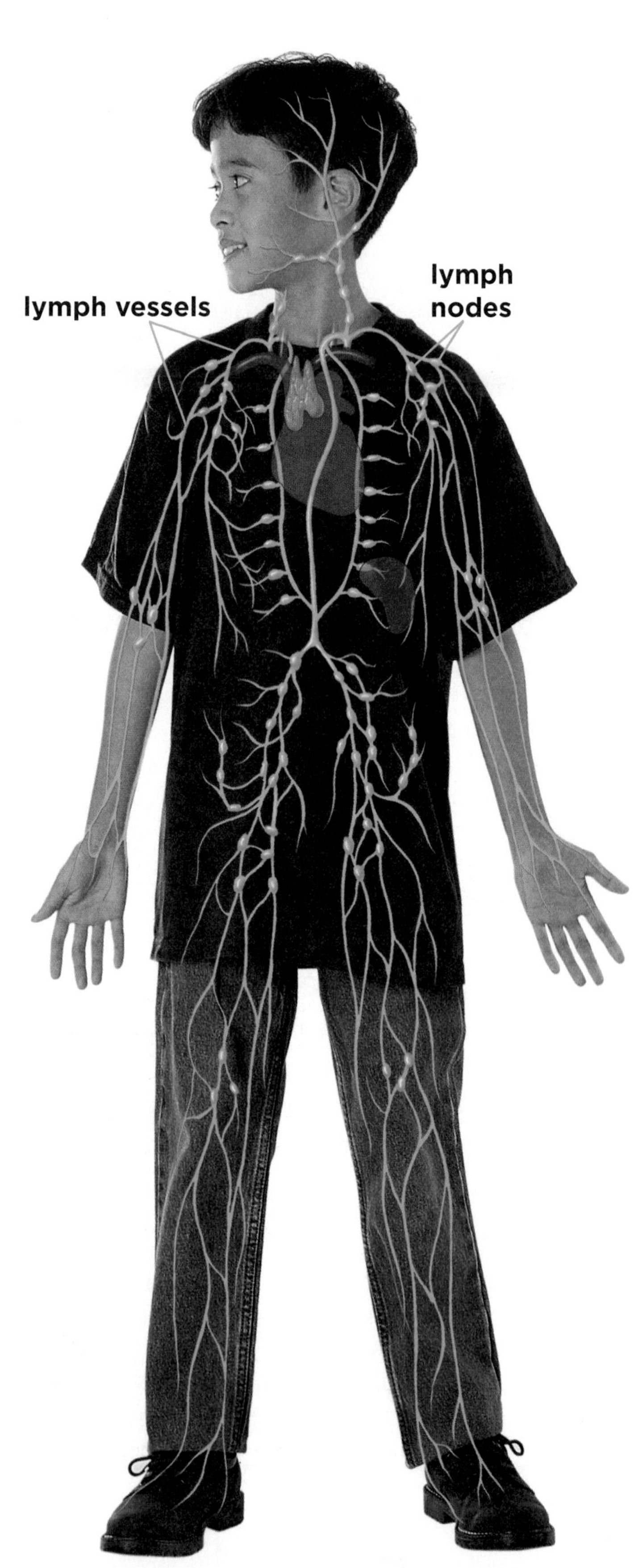

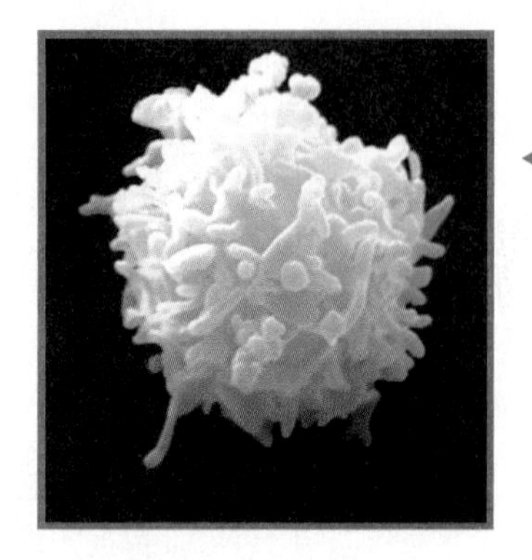

◀ **This is how a white blood cell looks through a microscope.**

Viruses and Bacteria

One of the main types of germs that makes the body ill are viruses. Illness from a virus like a cold or flu can be a big deal. Yet, viruses themselves are very small. In fact, you need a special microscope, an electron microscope, to look at a virus.

Viruses need to be inside living cells, called hosts, in order to reproduce. As they reproduce, viruses take nutrients and energy from the cell. They can even produce harmful materials that make the body itch or have dangerously high temperatures.

The other main type of germ that can make the body ill is bacteria. Bacteria are tiny, one-celled organisms. They can live on most surfaces and are able to reproduce outside of cells. Some bacteria can have a harmful effect on the body. Other bacteria, however, are good for the body. Some bacteria in your body, for example, help you digest food.

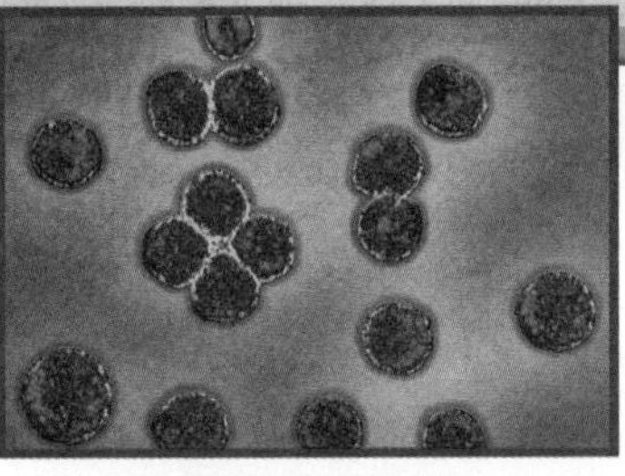

▲ A cold virus as seen through a microscope.

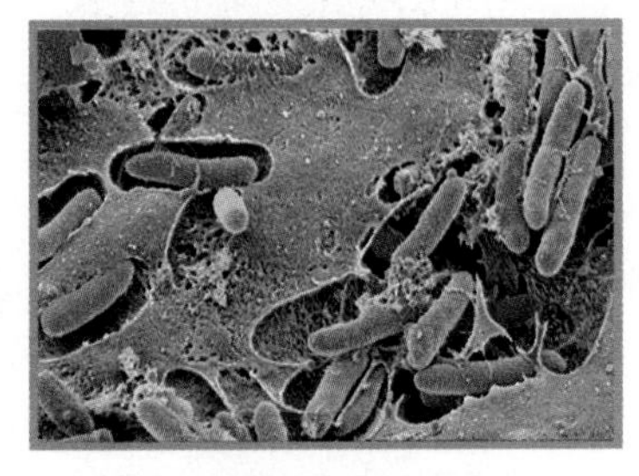

▲ *E. coli* bacteria as seen through a microscope.

You can help your body defend itself against germs. Here's what you can do.

▶ Eat healthful foods. This helps your body get all of the nutrients it needs to stay healthy. A healthy body is better able to fight germs.

▶ Be active. Being active makes your body fit. A fit body is better able to fight germs.

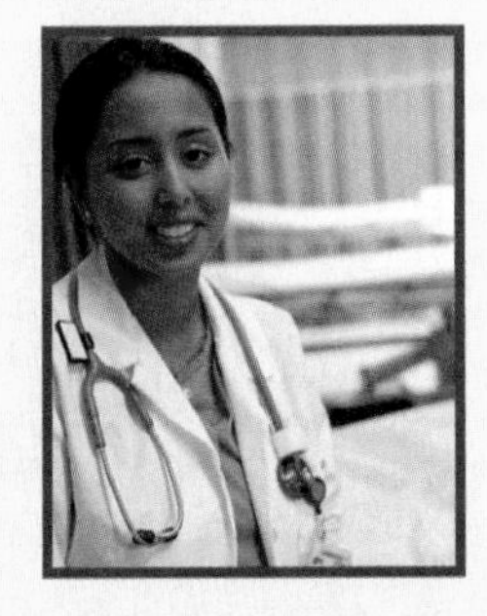

▶ Get a yearly check-up. Make sure you get all of your immunizations. Follow directions when taking medicines given to you by a doctor.

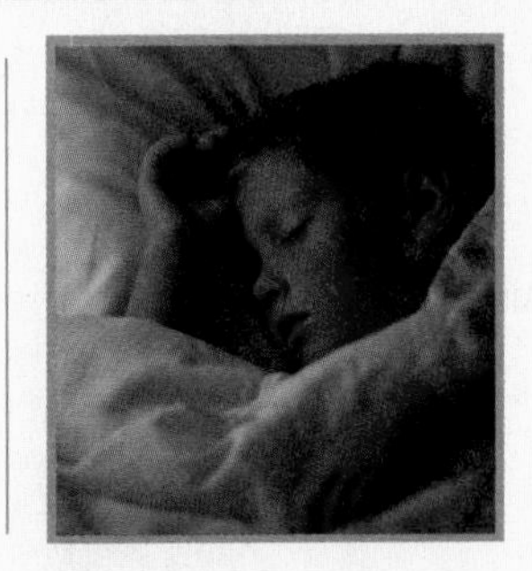

▶ Get plenty of rest. You need about 10 hours of sleep every night. Sleeping helps repair your body. Get extra rest when you are ill.

▶ Do not share cups or utensils with other people. Germs can be on objects you touch. Wash your hands, especially before eating and drinking. By washing your hands, you kill germs and make it harder for harmful things to get into your body.

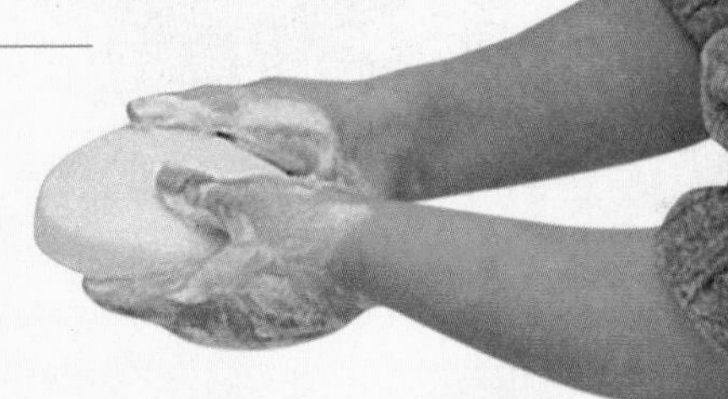

Healthy Living

Nutrients

Nutrients are materials in foods that help the body grow, get energy, and stay healthy. By eating a balance of healthful foods, your body gets the nutrients it needs to do all of these things.

There are six kinds of nutrients—carbohydrates, vitamins, minerals, proteins, water, and fats. Each nutrient helps the body in different ways.

carbohydrates

Carbohydrates

Carbohydrates are the main source of energy for the body. Starches and sugars are two types of carbohydrates. Starches come from foods like bread, pasta, and cereal. They provide long-lasting energy. Sugars come from fruits and can be used immediately by the body for energy.

Vitamins

Vitamins help keep the body healthy. They also help to build new cells in the body. The table below shows some vitamins and their sources.

Vitamin	Sources	Benefits
A	milk, fruit, carrots, green vegetables	keeps eyes, teeth, gums, skin, and hair healthy
C	citrus fruits, strawberries, tomatoes	helps heart, cells, and muscles function
D	milk, fish, eggs	helps keep teeth and bones strong

Minerals

Minerals help form new bone and blood cells. They also help your muscles and nervous system work properly. Here are some minerals and their sources.

Mineral	Sources	Benefits
calcium	yogurt, milk, cheese, and green vegetables	builds strong teeth and bones
iron	meat, beans, fish, whole grains	helps red blood cells function properly
zinc	meat, fish, eggs	helps your body grow and helps to heal wounds

Fats

Fats help the body use other nutrients and store vitamins. Fats also help the cells of the body to work properly. They even help keep the body warm. Fats can be found in foods such as meats, eggs, milk, butter, and nuts. Oils also contain fats. Though some fats help the body, some fats can cause health problems.

Water

Water is one of the most important nutrients. About $\frac{2}{3}$ of the body is made up of water! Water makes up most of the body's cells. It helps the body remove waste and protects joints. It also prevents the body from getting too hot.

Proteins

Proteins are a part of every living cell. Proteins help bones and muscles grow. They even help the immune system fight diseases. Foods high in protein are milk, eggs, meats, fish, nuts, and cheese.

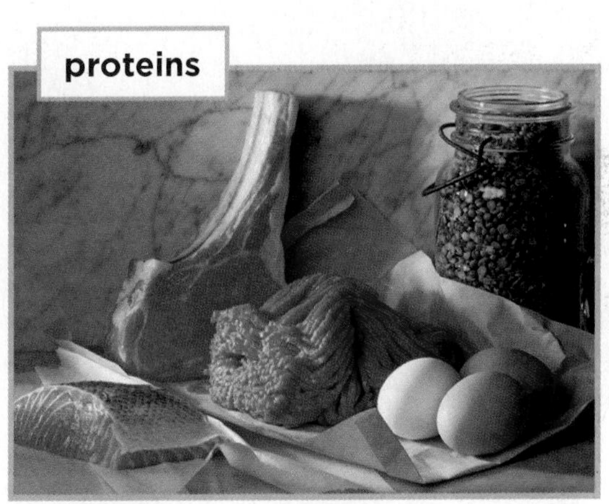

Healthy Living

Stay Fit

MyPyramid

You can use MyPyramid as a guide to healthful eating. The pyramid will show you the amounts of foods you should eat from each of the five food groups. A food group is foods with the same kinds of nutrients. To find the correct amounts of foods that are right for you, visit www.MyPyramid.gov

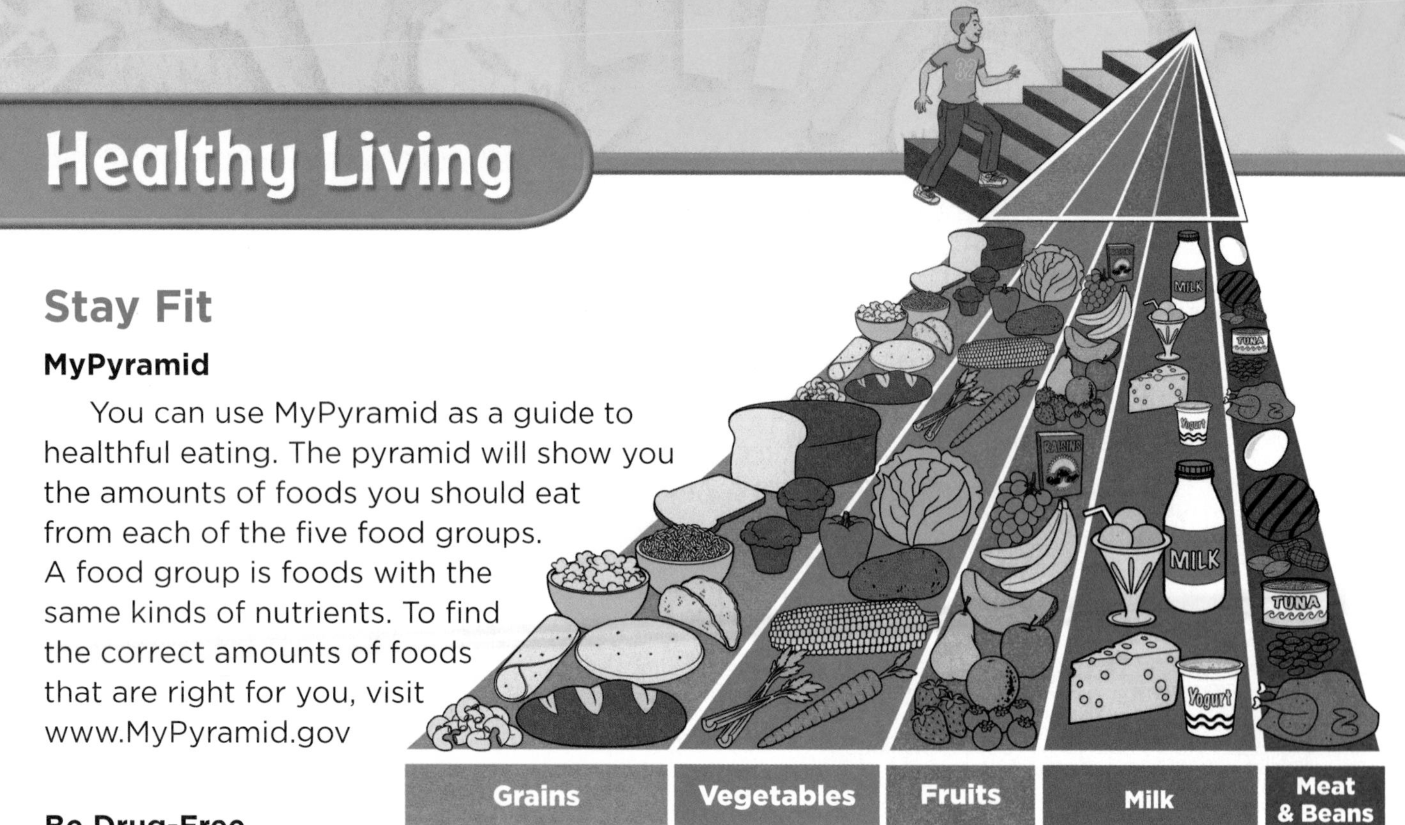

Be Drug-Free

Do not use cigarettes, illegal drugs, or alcohol. These things can harm your body. They can keep you from growing properly and becoming fit.

Be Physically Active

You need to be physically active for at least 60 minutes every day. When you are physically active, you become physically fit. When you are physically fit, your heart, lungs, bones, joints, and muscles stay strong. You keep a healthful weight and lower the risk of disease. You do not have to be on a sports team to be physically active. You just need to move your body. Running, biking, and swimming are just some ways to be physically active.

by Dinah Zike

Folding Instructions

The following pages offer step-by-step instructions about how to make Foldables study guides.

Half-Book

Fold a sheet of paper ($8\frac{1}{2}$" x 11") in half.

1. This book can be folded vertically like a hot dog or . . .

2. . . . it can be folded horizontally like a hamburger

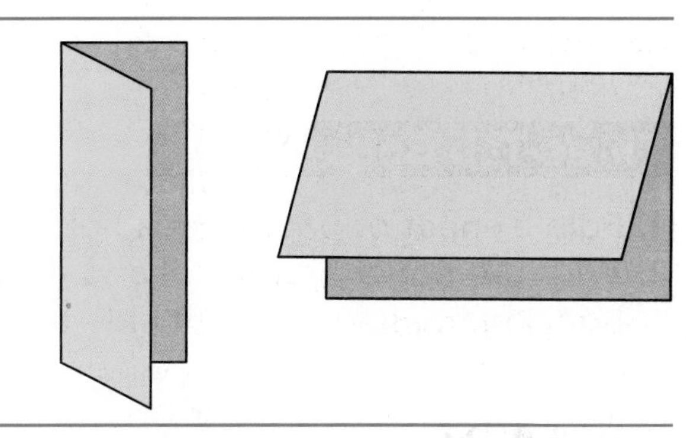

Folded Book

1. Make a Half-Book.

2. Fold in half again like a hamburger. This makes a ready-made cover and two small pages inside for recording information.

Pocket Book

1. Fold a sheet of paper ($8\frac{1}{2}$" x 11") in half like a hamburger.

2. Open the folded paper and fold one of the long sides up two inches to form a pocket. Refold along the hamburger fold so that the newly formed pockets are on the inside.

3. Glue the outer edges of the two-inch fold with a small amount of glue.

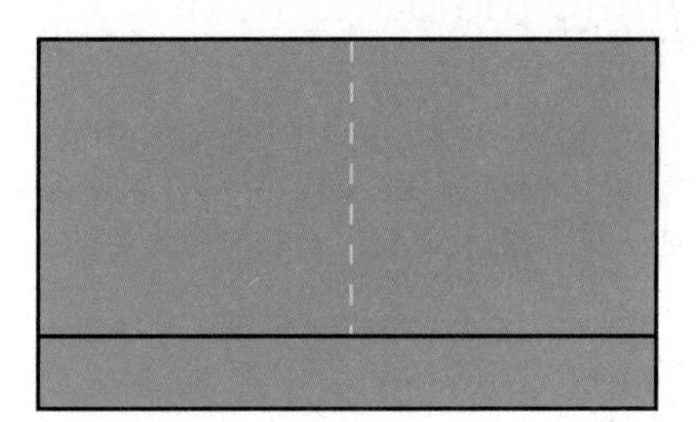

Shutter Fold

1. Begin as if you were going to make a hamburger, but instead of creasing the paper, pinch it to show the midpoint.

2. Fold the outer edges of the paper to meet at the pinch, or midpoint, forming a Shutter Fold.

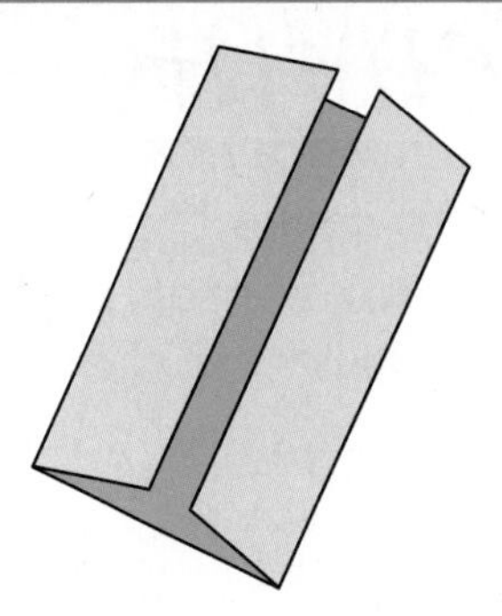

Trifold Book

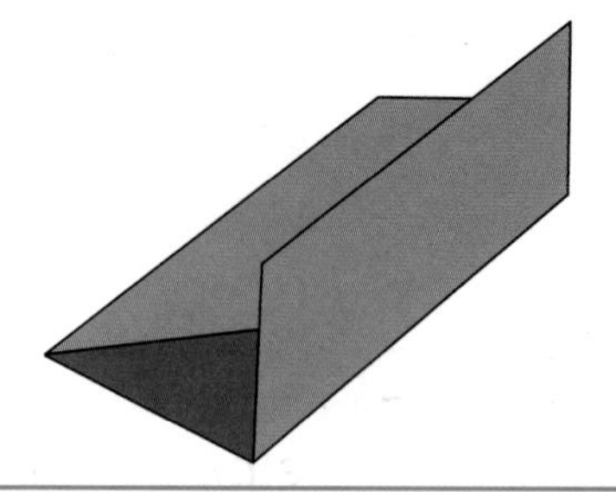

1. Fold a sheet of paper ($8\frac{1}{2}$" x 11") into thirds.
2. Use this book as is or cut into shapes.

Three-Tab Book

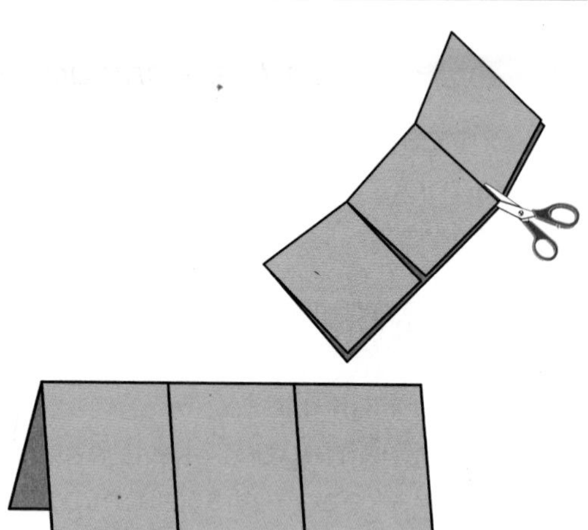

1. Fold a sheet of paper like a hot dog.
2. With the paper horizontal and the fold of the hot dog up, fold the right side toward the center, trying to cover one half of the paper.
3. Fold the left side over the right side to make a book with three folds.
4. Open the folded book. Place one hand between the two thicknesses of paper and cut up the two valleys on one side only. This will create three tabs.

Layered-Look Book

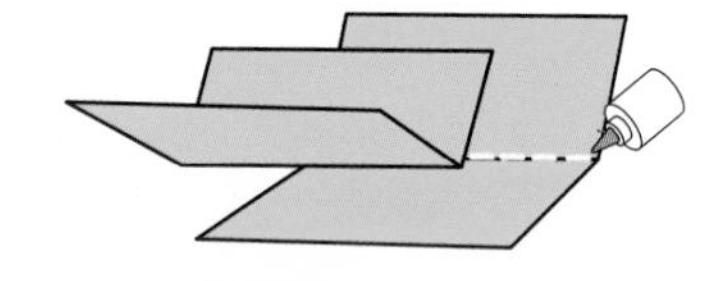

1. Stack two sheets of paper ($8\frac{1}{2}$" x 11") so that the back sheet is one inch higher than the front sheet.
2. Bring the bottoms of both sheets upward and align the edges so that all of the layers or tabs are the same distance apart.
3. When all the tabs are an equal distance apart, fold the papers and crease well.
4. Open the papers and glue them together along the valley, or inner center fold, or staple them along the mountain.

Folded Table or Chart

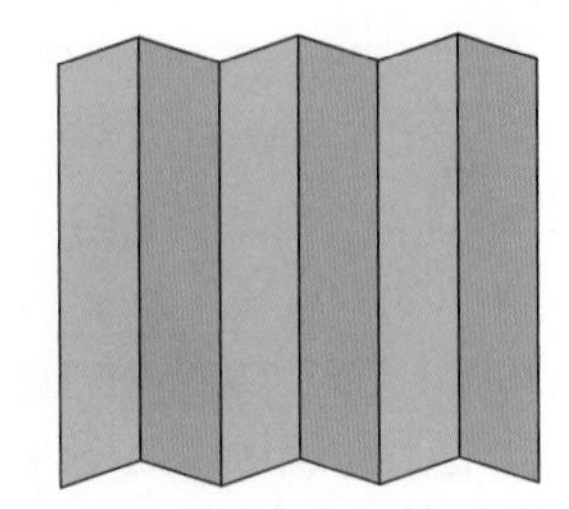

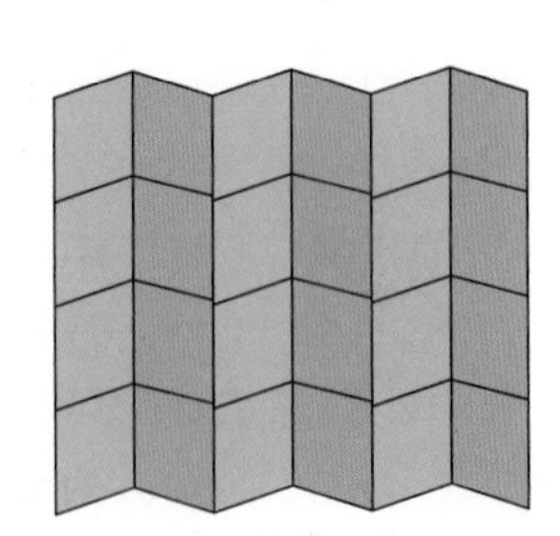

1. Fold the number of vertical columns needed to make the table or chart.
2. Fold the horizontal rows needed to make the table or chart.
3. Label the rows and columns.

Glossary

Use this glossary to learn how to pronounce and understand the meanings of Science Words used in this book. The page number at the end of each definition tells you where to find that word in the book.

adaptation (a′dəp·tā′shən) A feature or behavior that helps a living thing survive in its environment. (p. 62) *Sharp teeth are one adaptation that helps a bear survive.*

algae (al′jē) Tiny plantlike organisms that use water, air, and sunlight to make food. (p. 132)

arctic tundra (ärk′tik təndrə) A cold habitat above the arctic circle. (p. 118)

blubber (blə′bər) A thick layer of fat found in large mammals. (p. 122)

boil (boil) To change from a liquid to a gas. (p. 321) *Water will boil if you heat it on the stove.*

camouflage (kam′ə·fläzh′) An adaptation that allows an organism to blend into its surroundings. (p. 90)

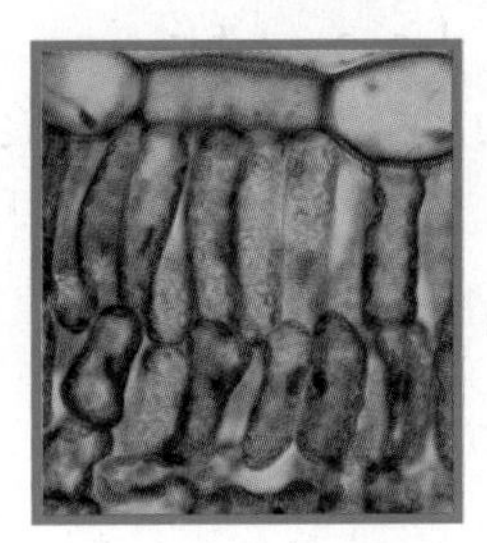

cell (sel) The basic building block that makes up all living things. (p. 28) *You can use a microscope to see that a leaf is made up of many tiny cells.*

climate (klī′mət) The pattern of weather at a certain place over a long time. (p. 56) *The Canadian tundra has a cold climate.*

community (kə mū′ni tē) All the living things in one place that interact. (p. 162) *All the organisms in this pond make up a community.*

competition (kom′pə·tish′ən) The struggle among organisms for water, food, or other needs. (p. 149) *There is competition for water between foxes.*

Pronunciation Key

The following symbols are used throughout the Macmillan/McGraw-Hill Science Glossaries.

a	**at**	e	**e**nd	o	h**o**t	u	**u**p	hw	**wh**ite	ə	**a**bout
ā	**a**pe	ē	m**e**	ō	**o**ld	ū	**u**se	ng	so**ng**		tak**e**n
ä	f**a**r	i	**i**t	ôr	**f**o**r**k	ü	r**u**le	th	**th**in		penc**i**l
âr	c**a**re	ī	**i**ce	oi	**oi**l	ů	p**u**ll	th	**th**is		lem**o**n
ô	l**a**w	îr	p**ier**ce	ou	**ou**t	ûr	t**ur**n	zh	mea**s**ure		circ**u**s

′ = primary accent; shows which syllable takes the main stress, such as **kil** in **kilogram** (kil′ e gram′).
′ = secondary accent; shows which syllables take lighter stresses, such as **gram** in **kilogram**.

LOG ON e-Glossary at www.macmillanmh.com

condense (kən·dens′) To change from a gas to a liquid. (p. 322) *When water vapor in the air cools and condenses, it can form dew.*

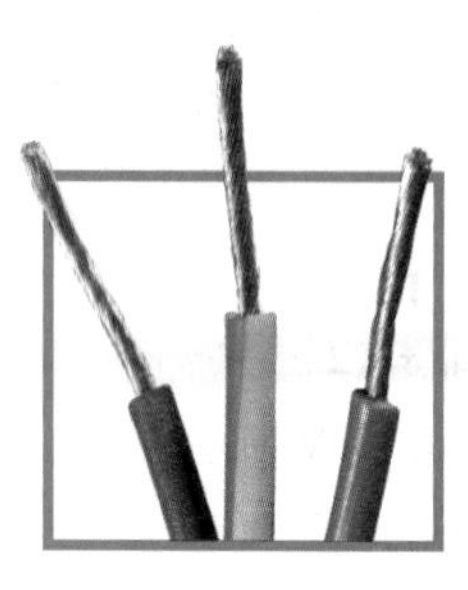

conductor (kən·duk′tər) A material which heat or electric current moves through easily. (p. 314) *Copper is a good conductor of heat and electric current.*

cone (cōn) A plant structure where seeds are made in some nonflowering plants. (p. 39)

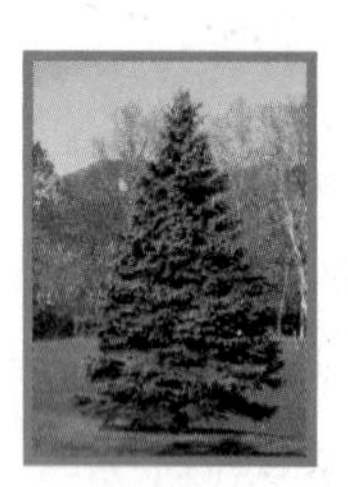

coniferous (kon·i′fər·əs) A kind of forest ecosystem that stays green all year long. (p. 109)

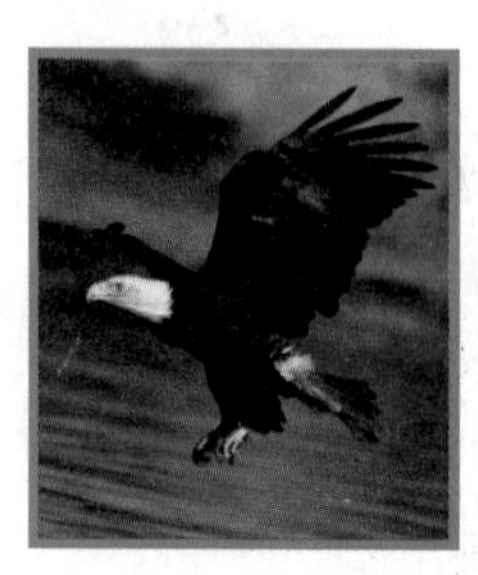

consumer (kon·sü′mər) An animal that eats plants or other animals. (p. 71) *Eagles eat fish, snakes, and other small organisms so they are consumers.*

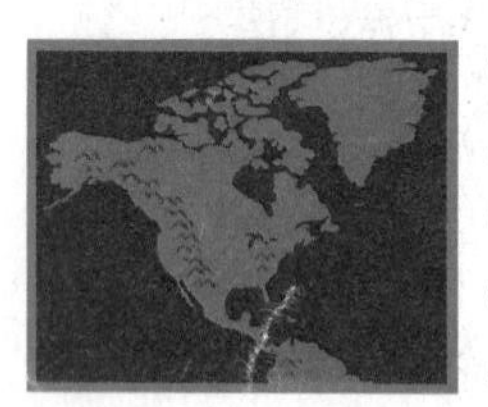

continent (kon′tə·nənt) A great area of land on Earth. (p. 235) *You live on the continent of North America.*

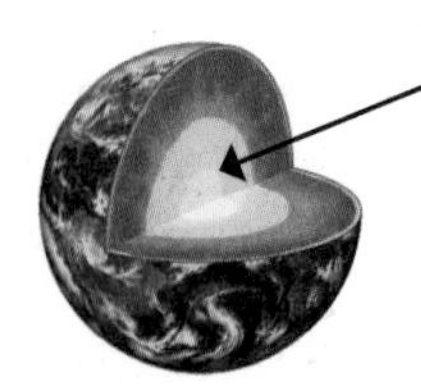

core (kôr) Earth's deepest and hottest layer. (p. 240)

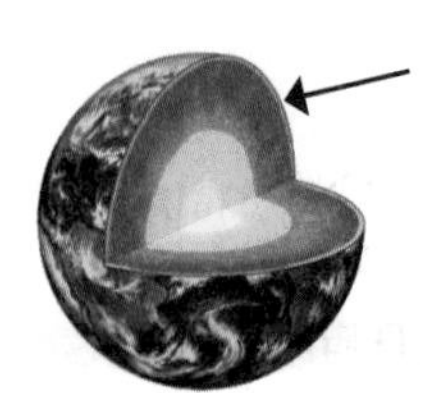

crust (krust) Earth's outermost layer. (p. 240)

D

deciduous (di·si′jə·wəs) A kind of forest ecosystem with many trees that lose their leaves in the winter. (p. 109)

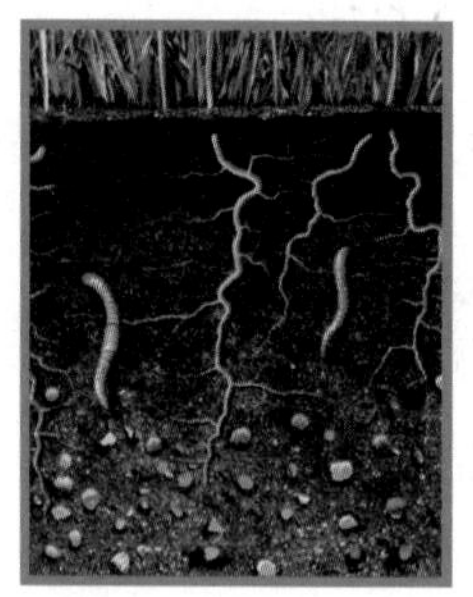

decomposer (dē′kəm·pō′zər) An organism that breaks down dead plant and animal material. (p. 71) *Worms are decomposers that eat dead leaves that fall to the ground.*

deposition (dep′ə·zi′shən) The dropping off of weathered rock. (p. 258)

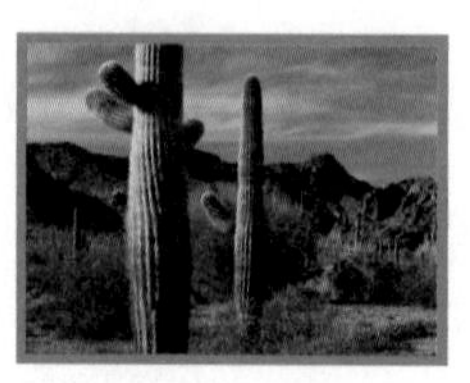

desert (dez′ərt) A habitat that has a dry climate. (p. 86)

LOG ON e-Glossary at www.macmillanmh.com

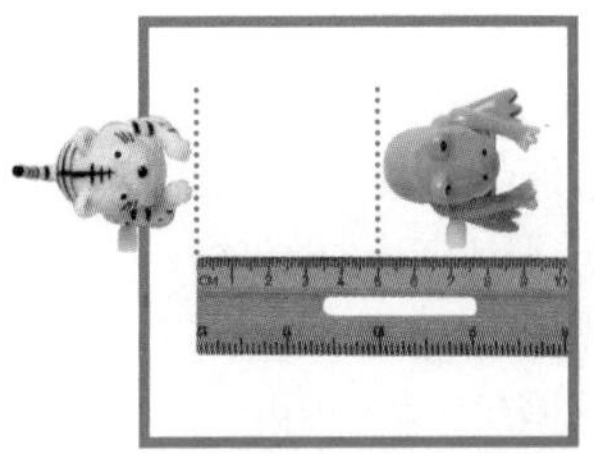

distance (dis′təns) The amount of space between two objects or places. (p. 337) *The distance between these two toys is five centimeters.*

drought (drout) When there is an unusual lack of rain in an area for a long period of time. (p. 158)

earthquake (ûrth′kwāk′) A sudden movement in Earth's crust. (p. 246) *An earthquake caused this road to crack.*

ecosystem (ē′kō·sis′təm) The living and nonliving things that share an environment and interact. (p. 68)

egg (eg) An animal structure that protects and feeds some very young animals such as birds. (p. 47)

element (el′ə·mənt) A building block of matter. (p. 284) *Gold is an element.*

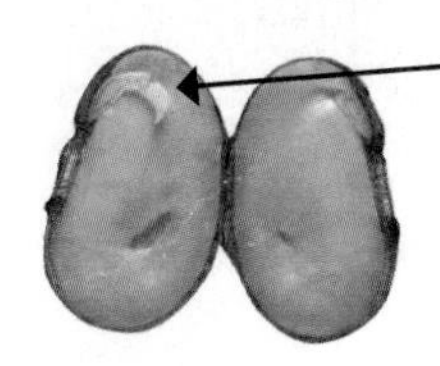

embryo (em′brē·ō) A young organism that is just beginning to grow. (p. 34)

endangered (en·dān′jərd) Having very few of a kind of organism left; close to becoming extinct. (p. 164) *Bengal tigers are endangered animals because there are very few of them left in the world.*

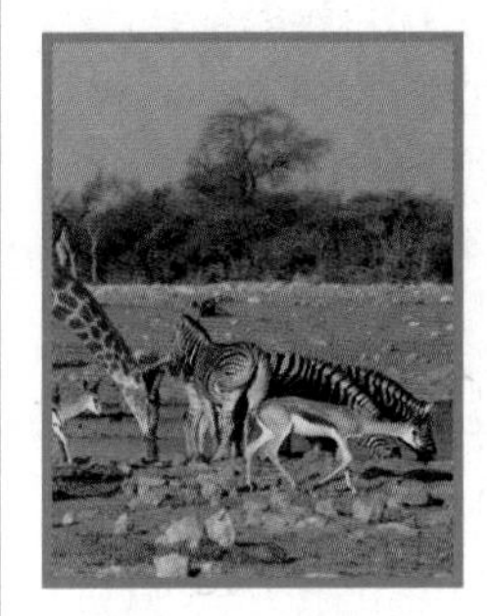

environment (en·vī′rən·mənt) All the living and nonliving things that surround an organism. (p. 26) *Water, soil, rocks, trees, and zebras are parts of the giraffes' environment.*

erosion (i·rō′zhən) The movement of weathered rock. (p. 258) *Erosion happens when water in this stream carries rocks away.*

evaporate (i·vap′ə·rāt′) To slowly change from a liquid to a gas. (p. 321) *These wet clothes will dry when the water in them evaporates.*

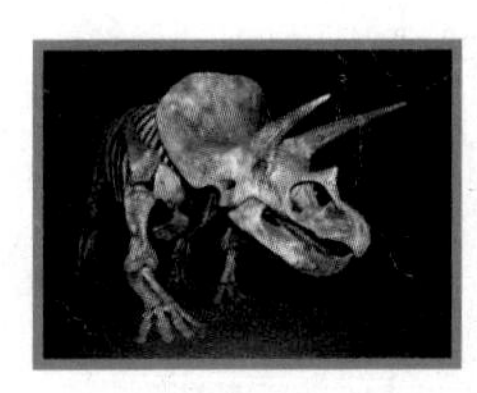

extinct (ek·stingkt′) Died out, leaving no more of that type of organism alive. (p. 170) *Many dinosaurs became extinct millions of years ago.*

flood (flud) Water flowing over land that is usually dry. (pp. 158, 250)

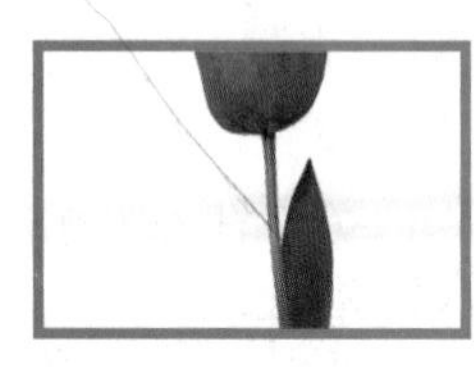

flower (flou′ər) A plant structure where seeds are made. (p. 36)

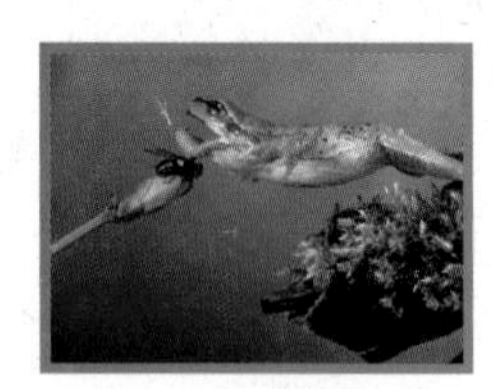

food chain (füd chān) A series of organisms that depend on one another for food. (p. 70)

food web (füd web) Several food chains that are connected. (p. 72)

force (fôrs) A push or a pull. (p. 346)

forest (fôr′ist) An ecosystem with many trees. (p. 106)

fossil (fos′əl) The trace or remains of something that lived long ago. (pp. 170, 218)

freeze (frēz) To change from a liquid to a solid. (p. 323) *You can freeze juice to make a juice pop.*

friction (frik′shən) A force that occurs when one object rubs against another. (p. 350) *Friction between a break pad and a rim stops a bike.*

fruit (früt) A plant structure that grows around seeds. (p. 37)

fuel (fū′əl) A material that is burned for energy. (p. 220) *Wood and gasoline are examples of fuels.*

gas (gas) Matter that has no definite shape or volume. (p. 303) *These balloons are filled with a gas called helium.*

gills (gilz) A structure some animals use to take in oxygen from water. (p. 134)

glacier (glā′shər) A large sheet of ice that moves slowly over land. (p. 258)

LOG ON e-Glossary at www.macmillanmh.com

grassland (gras′land) A habitat that is covered in grasses. (p. 96)

gravity (grav′i·tē) A pulling force between two objects, such as you and Earth. (p. 294) *Gravity pulls these skydivers toward Earth.*

H

habitat (hab′i·tat′) The home of a living thing. (p. 56) *A pond is a habitat for many fish.*

heat (hēt) A form of energy that moves from a hot object to a cold object. (p. 311) *The Sun is Earth's main source of heat.*

hibernate (hī′bər·nāt) To rest or sleep through the cold winter. (p. 112)

humus (hū′məs) Decayed plant and animal material in soil. (p. 208) *Humus makes soil look dark.*

I

igneous rock (ig′nē·es rok) A rock that forms when melted rock cools and hardens. (p. 199)

insulator (in′sə·lā′tər) A material that heat or electric current does not move through easily. (p. 314) *Plastic is a good insulator of electric current.*

L

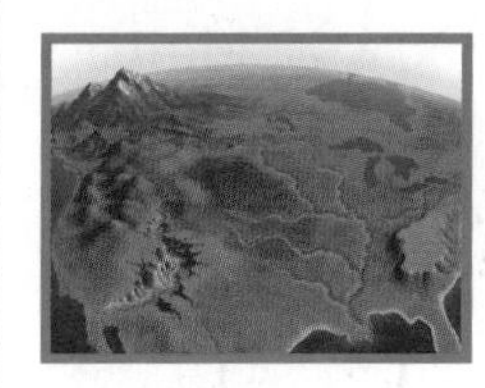

landform (land′fôrm′) A feature of land on Earth's surface. (p. 236)

landslide (land′slīd′) The rapid movement of rocks and soil down a hill. (p. 250)

larva (lär′və) The stage in some insects' life cycles which comes after hatching. (p. 47)

lava (lä′və) Melted rock that flows onto land. (p. 248)

life cycle (līf sī′kēl) All the stages in an organism's life. (p. 38)

liquid (lik′wid) Matter that has a definite volume but no definite shape. (p. 302)

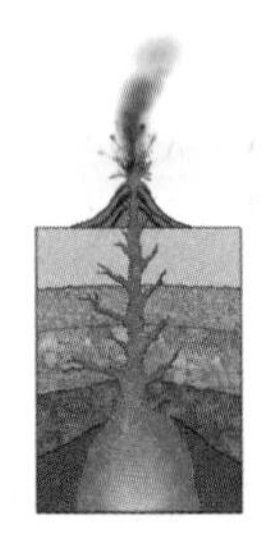

magma (mag′mə) Melted rock that is below Earth's surface. (p. 248)

magnet (mag′nit) An object with a magnetic force; magnets can attract or repel certain metals. (p. 348)

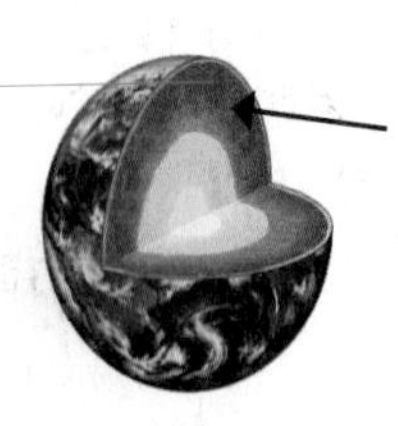

mantle (man′təl) The layer of Earth below the crust. (p. 240)

mass (mas) A measure of the amount of matter in an object. (p. 281)

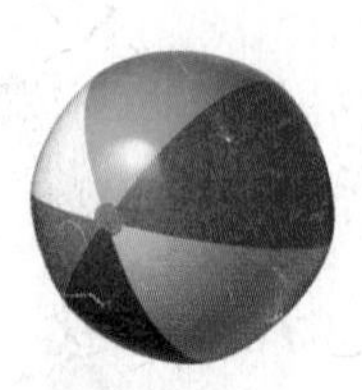

matter (mat′ər) Anything that has volume and mass. (p. 280)

melt (melt) To change from a solid to a liquid. (p. 320) *This snowman will melt on a warm day.*

metamorphic rock (met′ə·môr′fik rok) A kind of rock that has been changed by heating and squeezing. (p. 201)

metamorphosis (met′ə·môr′fə·sis) A series of changes in which an organism's body changes form. (p. 47) *A tadpole becomes a frog through metamorphosis.*

metric system (met′rik sis′təm) A system of measurement. (p. 290) *A centimeter is a unit in the metric system.*

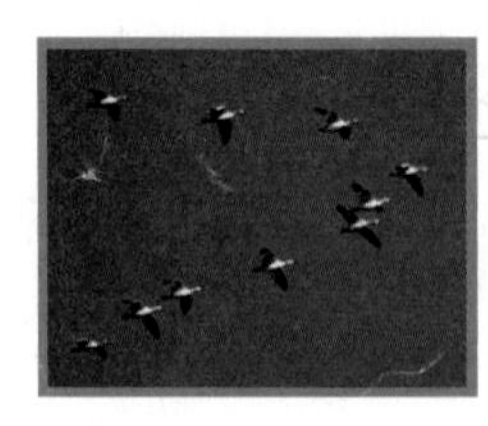

migrate (mī′grāt) To move to another place. (p. 124) *These geese migrate south when the weather gets cold.*

mimicry (mim′i·krē) An adaptation in which one kind of organism imitates another in color or shape. (p. 110)

mineral (min′ə rəl) A solid, nonliving substance found in nature. (p. 194)

e-Glossary at www.macmillanmh.com

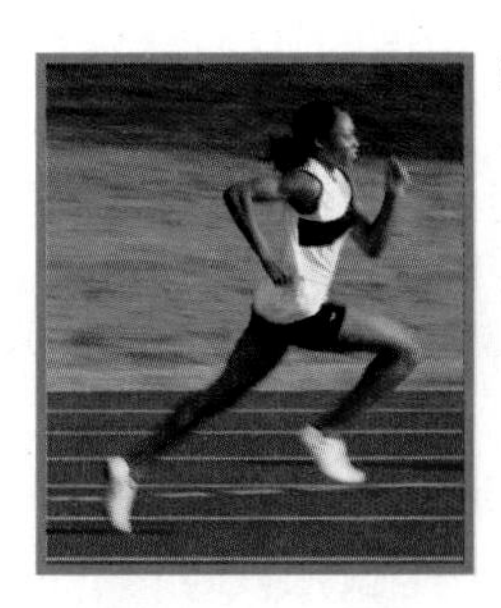

motion (mō′shən) A change in the position of an object. (p. 338)

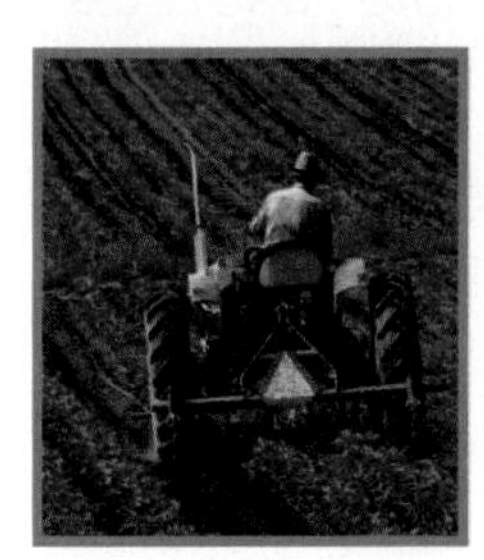

natural resource (nach′ər əl rē′sôrs′) A material on Earth that is necessary or useful to people. (p. 212) *Plants and soil are natural resources.*

nocturnal (nok·tûr′nəl) An adaptation in which an animal is active during the night and asleep during the day. (p. 90)

nonrenewable resource (non′ri·nü′ə·bəl rē′sôrs′) A resource that cannot be replaced or reused easily. (p. 221) *Oil is a nonrenewable resource. Once it is used up, it is gone forever.*

ocean (ō′shən) A large body of salt water. (pp. 131, 234)

organism (ōr′gə·niz·əm) A living thing. (p. 24) *Koala bears and eucalyptus trees are organisms.*

pan balance (pan bal′əns) A tool used to measure mass. (p. 292)

permafrost (pər′mə·frost) A layer of soil that is always frozen. (p. 119)

pitch (pitch) How high or low a sound is. (p. 358) *A whistle has a high pitch.*

pollination (pol′ə·nā′shən) When pollen moves from the male part of a plant to an egg, after which a seed can form. (p. 37)

pollution (pə·lü′shən) What happens when harmful materials get into water, air, or land. (p. 150)

population (pop′yə·lā′shən) All the members of a single type of organism in an ecosystem. (p. 162)

position (pə·zish′ən) The location of an object. (p. 336)

producer (prə·dü′sər) An organism, such as a plant, that makes its own food. (p. 70)

property (prop′ər·tē) Any characteristic of matter that you can observe. (p. 281) *A sweet taste is a property of this pineapple.*

pupa (pū′pə) The stage of some insects' life cycles before becoming an adult. (p. 47)

recycle (rē·sī′kəl) To turn old things into new things. (p. 152) *Plastic can be recycled to make new bottles and other products.*

reduce (ri·düs′) To use less of something. (p. 152) *When you fix a leaky faucet, you reduce your use of water.*

renewable resource (ri·nü′ə·bəl rē′sôrs′) A resource that can be replaced or used again and again. (p. 221) *Wind is a renewable resource.*

reproduce (rē′prə·düs′) To make more of one's own kind. (p. 25)

resource (rē′sôrs) Substances in the environment that help an organism survive. (p. 148) *Flowers are a resource for butterflies.*

respond (ri·spond′) To react to something. (p. 24) *When the weather gets cool in the fall, this tree responds by losing its leaves.*

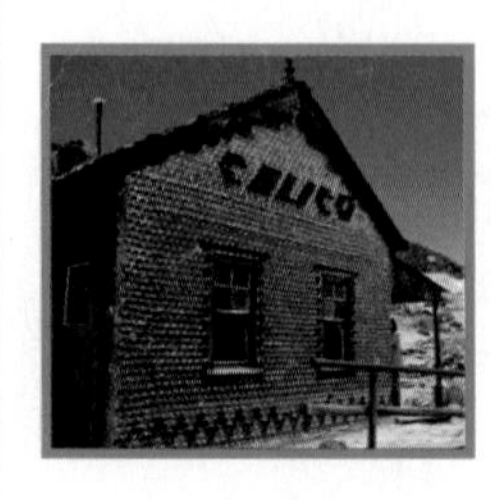

reuse (rē·ūz′) To use something again. (p. 152) *Old bottles were reused to make this building.*

LOG ON e-Glossary at www.macmillanmh.com

rock (rok) A nonliving material made of one or more minerals. (p. 198)

sediment (sed′əmənt) Tiny bits of weathered rock or once-living animals and plants. (p. 200)

sedimentary rock (sed′ə·mən′tə·rē rok) A kind of rock that forms from layers of sediment. (p. 200)

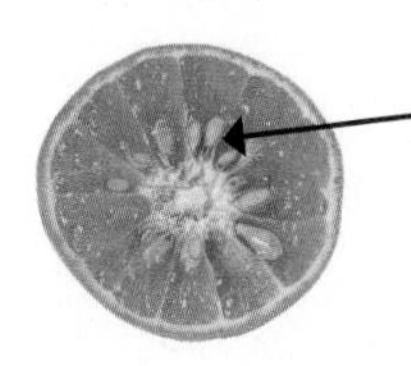

seed (sēd) A structure that can grow into a new plant. (p. 34)

shelter (shel′tər) A place in which an animal can stay safe. (p. 60) *A nest is a shelter for young birds.*

soil (soil) A mixture of minerals, weathered rocks, and decayed plant and animal matter. (pp. 56, 208)

solar energy (sol′ər en′ûr·jē) Energy from the Sun. (p. 222)

solid (sol′id) Matter that has a definite shape and volume. (p. 300)

sound (saund) A form of energy that you hear when an object vibrates. (p. 356)

speed (spēd) How fast an object moves over a certain distance. (p. 340)

state of matter (stāt uv mat′ər) A form of matter, such as solid, liquid, and gas. (p. 300)

structure (struk′chər) A part of an organism; a thing that help living things get or make what they need. (p. 59)

temperate (tem′pər·ət) An environment that has a mild climate and four seasons. (p. 97) *The prairies of Northern America are temperate grasslands.*

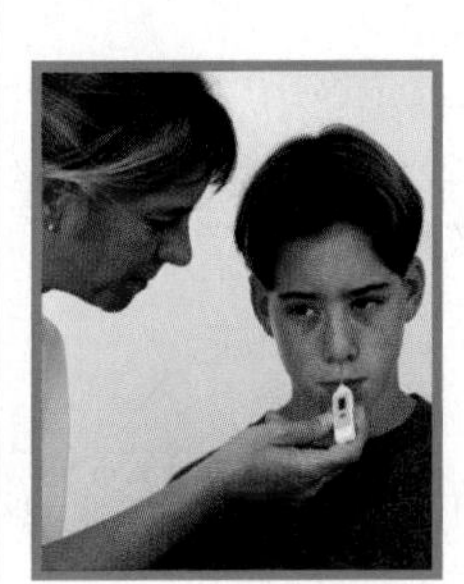

temperature (tem′pər·ə·chər) A measure of how hot or cold something is. (p. 310) *When you visit the doctor, she measures your body's temperature.*

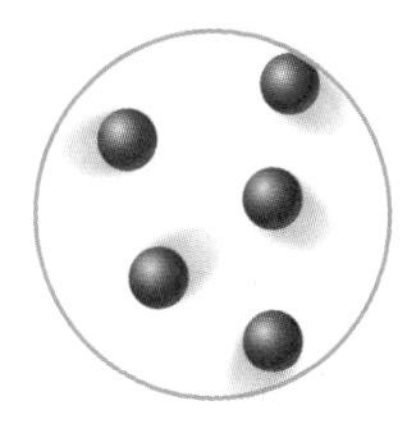

thermal energy (thûr′məl en′ər·jē) The energy of moving particles of matter. (p. 310)

thermometer (thûr′mom′i·tər) A tool that is used to measure temperature. (p. 312)

tropical (trä′pi·kəl) Coming from a region near the equator with warm temperatures all year round. (p. 97)

V

vibrate (vī′brāt) To move back and forth quickly. (p. 356) *A guitar string vibrates after you pluck it.*

volcano (vol′kā·nō) A mountain that builds up around an opening in Earth's crust. (p. 248)

volume (vol′ūm)
1. A measure of how much space an object takes up. (p. 281)

2. How loud or soft a sound is. (p. 358) *A whisper has a low volume.*

W

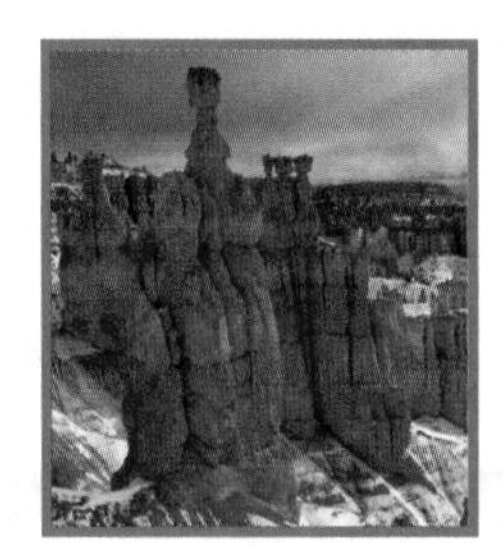

weathering (weth′ər·ing) The breaking down of rocks into smaller pieces. (p. 256) *Weathering caused these interesting rock shapes to form.*

weight (wāt) A measure of the pull of gravity on an object. (p. 294)

LOG ON e-Glossary at www.macmillanmh.com

Index

Note: Pages followed by an asterisk indicate activities.

G

H

I

N

O

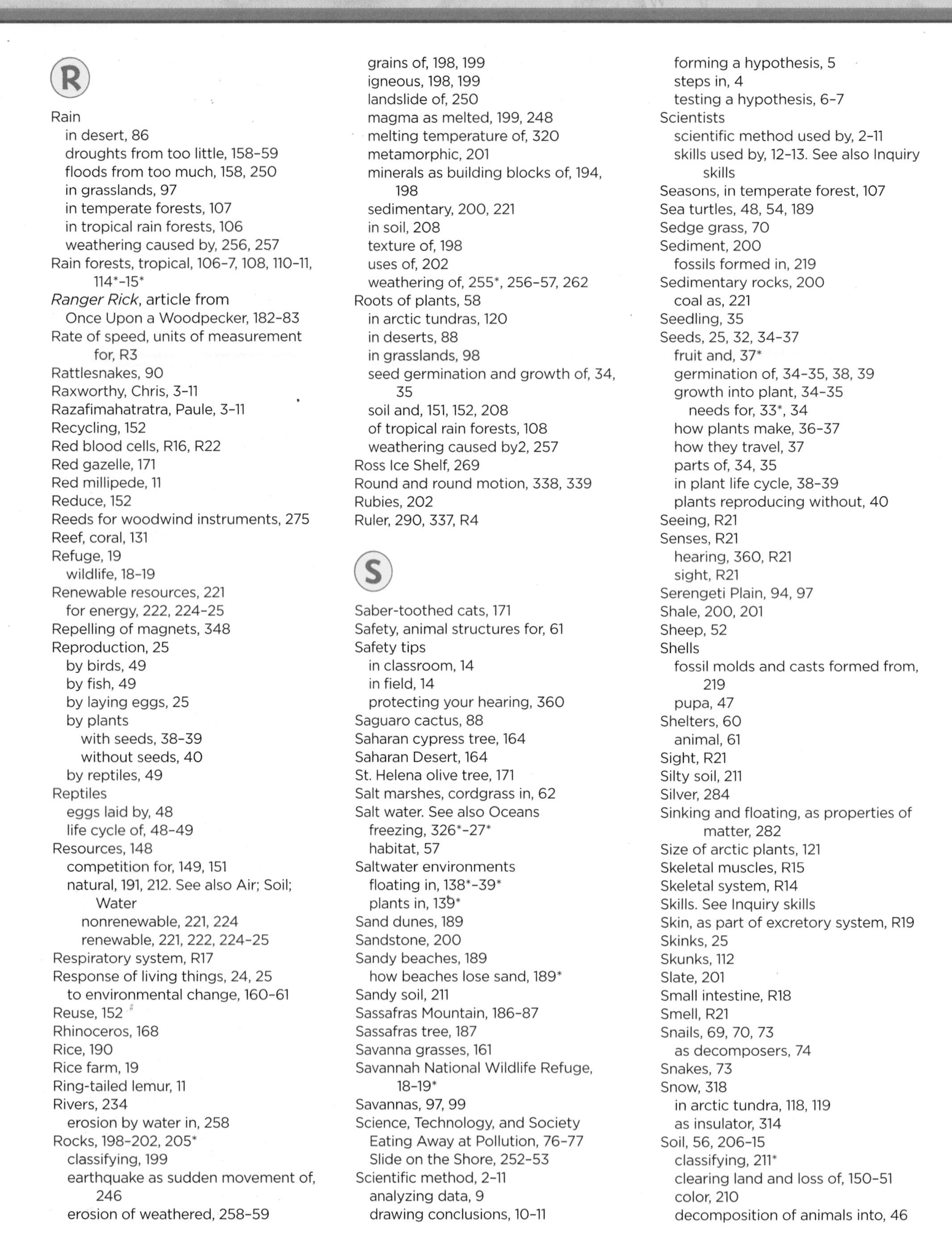

R

S

T

Science Content Standards

Scientific Inquiry

3-1 The student will demonstrate an understanding of scientific inquiry, including the processes, skills, and mathematical thinking necessary to conduct a simple scientific investigation.

- **3-1.1** Classify objects by two of their properties (attributes).
- **3-1.2** Classify objects or events in sequential order.
- **3-1.3** Generate questions such as "what if?" or "how?" about objects, organisms, and events in the environment and use those questions to conduct a simple scientific investigation.
- **3-1.4** Predict the outcome of a simple investigation and compare the result with the prediction.
- **3-1.5** Use tools (including beakers, meter tapes and sticks, forceps/tweezers, tuning forks, graduated cylinders, and graduated syringes) safely, accurately, and appropriately when gathering specific data.
- **3-1.6** Infer meaning from data communicated in graphs, tables, and diagrams.
- **3-1.7** Explain why similar investigations might produce different results.
- **3-1.8** Use appropriate safety procedures when conducting investigations.

Habitats and Adaptations

3-2 The student will demonstrate an understanding of the structures, characteristics, and adaptations of organisms that allow them to function and survive within their habitats. (Life Science)

- **3-2.1** Illustrate the life cycles of seed plants and various animals and summarize how they grow and are adapted to conditions within their habitats.
- **3-2.2** Explain how physical and behavioral adaptations allow organisms to survive (including hibernation, defense, locomotion, movement, food obtainment, and camouflage for animals and seed dispersal, color, and response to light for plants).
- **3-2.3** Recall the characteristics of an organism's habitat that allow the organism to survive there.
- **3-2.4** Explain how changes in the habitats of plants and animals affect their survival.
- **3-2.5** Summarize the organization of simple food chains (including the roles of producers, consumers, and decomposers).

Earth's Materials and Changes

3-3 The student will demonstrate an understanding of Earth's composition and the changes that occur to the features of Earth's surface. (Earth Science)

- **3-3.1** Classify rocks (including sedimentary, igneous, and metamorphic) and soils (including humus, clay, sand, and silt) on the basis of their properties.
- **3-3.2** Identify common minerals on the basis of their properties by using a minerals identification key.
- **3-3.3** Recognize types of fossils (including molds, casts, and preserved parts of plants and animals).
- **3-3.4** Infer ideas about Earth's early environments from fossils of plants and animals that lived long ago.
- **3-3.5** Illustrate Earth's saltwater and freshwater features (including oceans, seas, rivers, lakes, ponds, streams, and glaciers).
- **3-3.6** Illustrate Earth's land features (including volcanoes, mountains, valleys, canyons, caverns, and islands) by using models, pictures, diagrams, and maps.
- **3-3.7** Exemplify Earth materials that are used as fuel, as a resource for building materials, and as a medium for growing plants.
- **3-3.8** Illustrate changes in Earth's surface that are due to slow processes (including weathering, erosion, and deposition) and changes that are due to rapid processes (including landslides, volcanic eruptions, floods, and earthquakes).

Heat and Changes in Matter

3-4 The student will demonstrate an understanding of the changes in matter that are caused by heat.

- **3-4.1** Classify different forms of matter (including solids, liquids, and gases) according to their observable and measurable properties.
- **3-4.2** Explain how water and other substances change from one state to another (including melting, freezing, condensing, boiling, and evaporating).
- **3-4.3** Explain how heat moves easily from one object to another through direct contact in some materials (called conductors) and not so easily through other materials (called insulators).
- **3-4.4** Identify sources of heat and exemplify ways that heat can be produced (including rubbing, burning, and using electricity).

Motion and Sound

3-5 The student will demonstrate an understanding of how motion and sound are affected by a push or pull on an object and the vibration of an object. (Physical Science)

- **3-5.1** Identify the position of an object relative to a reference point by using position terms such as "above," "below," "inside of," "underneath," or "on top of" and a distance scale or measurement.
- **3-5.2** Compare the motion of common objects in terms of speed and direction.
- **3-5.3** Explain how the motion of an object is affected by the strength of a push or pull and the mass of the object.
- **3-5.4** Explain the relationship between the motion of an object and the pull of gravity.
- **3-5.5** Recall that vibrating objects produce sound and that vibrations can be transferred from one material to another.
- **3-5.6** Compare the pitch and volume of different sounds.
- **3-5.7** Recognize ways to change the volume of sounds.
- **3-5.8** Explain how the vibration of an object affects pitch.

Credits

Cover Photography Credits: (bkgd) Natural Selection Stock Photography; (inset) Pete Oxford/Steve Bloom Images/Alamy.

Illustration Credits: All illustrations are by Macmillan/McGraw-Hill except as noted: ix: John Kaufmann. 6: Joe LeMonnier. 8: Joe LeMonnier; Marta Pernas. 17: Karen Minot. 19: Karen Minot. 21: Wendy Smith. 38: Fiammetta Dogi. 39: Fiammetta Dogi. 40: Fiammetta Dogi. 41: Fiammetta Dogi. 68–69: Fiammetta Dogi. 72–73: Fiammetta Dogi. 75: Fiammetta Dogi. 87: Mike DiGiorgio. 97: Mike DiGiorgio. 98: Sandra Williams. 101: Sam Tomaselo. 107: Mike DiGiorgio. 108: Sandra Williams. 119: Mike DiGiorgio. 148–149: Fiammetta Dogi. 162: Fiammetta Dogi. 163: Fiammetta Dogi. 187: Karen Minot. 189: Karen Minot. 209: John Kaufmann. 220–221: John Kaufmann. 227: John Kaufmann. 231: John Kaufmann. 234–235: John Kaufmann. 236–237: John Kaufmann. 238–239: John Kaufmann. 240: John Kaufmann. 241: John Kaufmann. 247: John Kaufmann. 248: Steve Weston. 273: Karen Minot. 275: Karen Minot. 293: Peter Gunther. 301: Peter Gunther. 302: Peter Gunther. 303: Peter Gunther. 309: Stephen Durke. 313: Peter Gunther. 321: Stephen Durke. 324: Peter Gunther. R25: Kate Sween. R26: Barb Cousins. R27: Barb Cousins. R28: Barb Cousins. R29: Steve Oh. R30: Barb Cousins; Tom Leonard. R39: John Kaufman; Karen Minot. R40: Stephen Durke; Fiammetta Dogi. R41: John Edwards, Inc.; John Kaufmann. R42: Fiammetta Dogi; Stephen Durke. R43: John Kaufmann; Fiammetta Dogia R44: John Kaufmann. John Kaufmann; Denise Ortakales; Fiammetta Dogi; Steve Weston. R47: John KaufmannR48: Karen Minot; Wendy Smith. R50: Karen Minot. R51: John Kaufmann; Karen Minot. R53: Peter Gunther; John Kaufmann.

Photography Credits: All ph otographs are by Macmillan/McGraw-Hill or are by Michael Scott for Macmillan/McGraw-Hill except as noted below: vi: Mimotito/Digital Vision/Getty Images; (t) Annie Griffiths Belt/National Geographic/ Getty Images. vii: Michael P. Gadomski/SuperStock. viii: Owaki-Kulla/CORBIS; (b) B. Runk/S. Schoenberger/Grant Heilman Photography. ix: (r) Mark A. Schneider/ Photo Researchers; (c) Roger Weller, Cochise College; (l) B. Runk & S. Shoenberger/ Grant Heilman Photography. x: Masterfile Royalty Free; MMH. xi: Photodisc/Getty Images; (b) Tim McGuire/CORBIS. xii: (tc) Royalty-Free/CORBIS; (tr) age fotostock/ SuperStock; (br) Geostock/Getty Images; (bl) Roger Phillips/DK Images. xiii: (tr) Mark A. Schneider/Photo Researchers; (br) Bran X Pictures/PunchStock. xiv: (cl) Image Source/SuperStock; (br) Jayme Thornton/The Image Bank/Getty Images. 1: Frans Lanting/Minden Pictures. 2: (tr) The Macmillan McGraw Hill Companies Inc./Ken Cavanagh Photographer; (tl) The Macmillan McGraw Hill Companies Inc./ Jacques Cornell Photographer; (bl) Stockbyte. 2–3: Michael Melford/NGS Images. 3: (l) Courtesy American Museum of Natural History; (r) Courtesy American Museum of Natural History. 4–5: Mike Powles/Jupiter Images. 6: Courtesy American Museum of Natural History. 7: Courtesy American Museum of Natural History. 8–9: Burke/ Triolo Productions/Brand X Pictures/Getty Images; Fabrice Bettex/Alamy. 9: (tr) Nick Garbutt/Taxi/Getty Images; (r) The McGraw-Hill Companies Inc./Ken Cavanagh Photographer; (r) Burke Triolo Productions/Brand X Pictures/Getty Images. 10: (tr) Mitsuhiko Imamori/Minden Pictures; (l) Piotr Naskrecki/Minden Pictures; (b) Chris Hellier/CORBIS. 11: (br) Pete Oxford/Minden Pictures; (bl) Wolfgang Kaehler/CORBIS; (t) Piotr Naskrecki/Minden Pictures. 12: (tc) Stockbyte/PunchStock; (cl) Stockdisc/ PunchStock; (c) Stockdisc/PunchStock; (cr) Royalty-Free/CORBIS. 13: (tr) Siede Preis/ Getty Images; (tl) Photodisc/Getty Images; (br) Comstock/PunchStock; (cl) Simon Murrell/Alamy; (tc) Stockdisc/PunchStock. 16: Myron Brenton/Omni-Photo Communications; (inset) Tony Arruza/CORBIS. 17: Matthew Ward/DK Images. 18: Raymond Gehman/CORBIS; (inset) Altrendo Nature/Getty Images. 19: Mimotito/ Digital Vision/Getty Images. 20–21: Zigmun Leszczysnki/Animals Animals/Earth Scenes; (t to b) Kike Calvo/Visual&Written SL/Alamy; Joseph Van Os/Getty Images; Lester V. Bergman/CORBIS; Zigmun Leszczysnki/Animals Animals/Earth Scenes; Craig K. Lorenz/Photo Researchers; Amos Nachoum/CORBIS. 22–23: Joseph Van Os/ Getty Images. 23: Royalty-Free/CORBIS. 24: Arco Images/Alamy. 25: (t) Zigmund Leszczynski/Animals Animals/Earth Scenes; (b) Gary Vestal/Photographer's Choice/ Getty Images. 26: (b) David Cavagnaro/Visuals Unlimited; (t) Bob Jensen/Bruce Coleman Inc. 27: (t) Kike Calvo/Visual&Written SL/Alamy; (b) Blickwinkel/Alamy. 28: (t) Image100 Ltd.; (br) Lester V. Bergman/CORBIS; (bl) Burke/Triolo Productions/ Getty Images. 29: (t to b) Zigmund Leszczynski/Animals Animals/Earth Scenes; (2) David Cavagnaro/Visuals Unlimited; (3) Lester V. Bergman/CORBIS. 32–33: Keith Neale/Masterfile. 34: (c) J. Brown/OSF/Animals Animals/Earth Scenes; (r) J. Brown/ OSF/Animals Animals/Earth Scenes; (l) Roger Phillips/DK Images. 35: (l) J. Brown/ OSF/Animals Animals/Earth Scenes; (c) J. Brown/OSF/Animals Animals/Earth Scenes; (r) Roger Standen/Science Photo Library/Photo Researchers; (t) Nigel Cattlin/Holt Studios International Ltd./Alamy. 36: (t) Michael P. Gadomski/SuperStock; (b) Hans Pfletschinger/Peter Arnold Inc. 37: (t to b) Stockdisc/PunchStock; Digital Vision/ Getty Images; Stockdisc/PunchStock; Blinkwinkel/Alamy. 38: AGE Fotostock/SuperStock. 39: Susan Cruz. 40: (t) Nigel Cattlin/Alamy. 40–41: (b) DK Images. 41: (t) J. Brown/OSF/ Animals Animals/Earth Scenes. 42: Roger Phillips/DK Images. 44–45: Frans Lanting/ Minden Pictures. 46: (cw from top) Philippe Clement/Nature Picture Library; Stephen Dalton/Photo Researchers; George Bernard/NHPA; Stephen Dalton/Minden Pictures. 47: (cw from top) Perennou Nuridsany/Photo Researchers; Troy Bartlett/Alamy; Bill Beatty/Visuals Unlimited; Ted Kinsman/Photo Researchers. 48: (cw from top) Gerard Lacz/Animals Animals/Earth Scenes; Kevin Schafer/CORBIS; James Watt/Animals Animals/Earth Scenes; D. Fleetham/OSF/Animals Animals/Earth Scenes. 49: (t to b) Photodisc/Getty Images; Siede Preis/Getty Images; Photodisc/Getty Images; Jane Burton/ Nature Picture Library; LUTRA/NHPA; Norbert Wu/Minden Pictures. 50: (cw from top) Juniors Bildarchiv/Alamy; Mitsuaki Iwago/Minden Pictures; Anup Shah/ImageState/ Alamy. 51: (t to b) Stephen Dalton/Photo Researchers; (2) James Watt/Animals Animals/ Earth Scenes; (3) Juniors Bildarchiv/Alamy. 52: Rene Morris/Taxi/Getty Images. 53: Lee Karney/US Fish & Wildlife Service. 54–55: Georgette Douwma/Photographer's Choice/Getty Images. 55: Michael Scott. 56: Jim Brandenburg/Minden Pictures. 57: (t) Annie Griffiths Belt/National Geographic/Getty Images; (b) Andre Seale/Alamy. 58–59: (bkgd) Dorling Kindersley. 60: (t) John Cancalosi/naturepl.com; (b) Richard Du Toit/ naturepl.com. 61: Frank and Joyce Burek/PhotoDisc/Getty Images. 62: QT Luong/terragalleria.com. 63: (t) Annie Griffiths Belt/National Geographic/Getty Images; (tc) Dorling Kindersley; (bc) QT Luong/terragalleria.com. 64: Photodisc/Getty Images. 65: (tl) Creatas/PunchStock; (tc) Creatas/PunchStock; (tr) Creatas/ PunchStock; (tcl) Photodisc Collection/Getty Images; (tc) Digital Vision/ PunchStock; (tcr) Creatas/PunchStock; (bcl) Creatas/PunchStock; (bc) Alan & Sandy Carey/Getty Images; (bcr) IT Stock/PunchStock; (bl) Digital Vision/PunchStock; (bc) Alan & Sandy Carey/Getty Images; (br) Royalty-Free/CORBIS. 66: Yva Momatiuk/John Eastcott/Minden Pictures. 70: (cl) Royalty-Free/CORBIS; (bl) C. Milkens/OSF/ Animals Animals/Earth Scenes; (br) Stephen Dalton/Minden Pictures; (tl) Jim Allan/ Alamy; (tr) James Carmichael Jr./ NHPA. 71: (bl) Animals Animals/Earth Scenes; (br) Steve Maslowski/Photo Researchers; (tl) Michael Gadomski/Animals Animals/Earth Scenes; (tr) Alan & Sandy Carey/Getty Images. 74: Gary Braasch/CORBIS; (inset) Eye of Science/Photo Researchers. 75: Stephen Dalton/Minden Pictures; Gary Braasch/ CORBIS. 76–77: (bl) Brian Sytnyk/Masterfile. 77: (r) Dr. Dennis Kunkel/Visuals Unlimited; (l) Ken Graham/Accent Alaska. 82–83: Ian West/Oxford Scientific/ PictureQuest. 84–85: (bkgd) Roy Ooms/Masterfile. 86–87: David L. Brown/PictureQuest. 89: (b) D. C. Lowe/Superstock; (tl) Jay Syverson/CORBIS. 90: (t) Daniel Heuclin/NHPA; (c) John Cancalosi/naturepl.com; (b) Ralph A. Clevenger/CORBIS. 91: (t) David L. Brown/PictureQuest; (c) Daniel Heuclin/NHPA. 94–95: (bkgd) Manoj Shah/Stone/ Getty Images. 96: (t) Annie Griffiths Belt/CORBIS; (b) Darlyne A. Murawski/ National Geographic/Getty Images. 97: Friedrich von Hörsten/Alamy. 98: Richard Hamilton Smith/CORBIS. 99: Danita Delimont/Alamy. 100: (br) James Warwick/The Image Bank/Getty Images; (bl) Paul Souders/The Image Bank/Getty Images; (t) PhotoLink/Getty Images. 101: (b) PhotoLink/Getty Images; (t) Friedrich von Hörsten/ Alamy. 102: (inset) Courtesy of Ana Luz Porzecanski; (tl) Franz Lanting/Minden Pictures. 102–103: Gabriel Rojo/Nature Picture Library. 103: (r) Franz Lanting/Minden Pictures. 104–105: (bkgd) Mike Dobel/Alamy; (bkgd) age fotostock/Superstock; (b) Stuart Westmorland/Stone/Getty Images. 107: Daniel Templeton/Alamy. 109: (b) Andrew Butler/The National Trust Photolibrary/Alamy; (t) Siede Preis/Getty Images. 110: (br) Michael and Patricia Fogden/Minden Pictures; (t) Breck P. Kent/Animals Animals -

Earth Scenes; (bl) Brian P. Kenney/Animals Animals. 111: PhotoLink/Getty Images. 112: (c) age fotostock/Superstock; (b) Digital Zoo/Digital Vision/Getty Images; (t) Paul Sterry/Worldwide Picture Library/Alamy. 113: (c) age fotostock/Superstock; (t) Daniel Templeton/Alamy; (b) Paul Sterry/Worldwide Picture Library/Alamy. 116–117: (bkgd) Steven Kazlowski/Peter Arnold, Inc. 118: B & C Alexander/NHPA. 120: (b) Simon Murray; Papilio/CORBIS; (t) B & C Alexander/NHPA. 121: (inset) Kevin Schafer/NHPA; (r) Paal Hermansen/NHPA. 122: (l) Fritz Polking/Peter Arnold, Inc.; (r) Stephen J. Krasemann/DRK PHOTO.COM. 122–123: (t) D. Robert & Lorri Franz/CORBIS. 123: (b) Graham Hatherley/naturepl.com; (t) B & C Alexander/NHPA. 124: (c) Doug Allan/naturepl.com; (b) Rich Kirchner/NHPA; (t) Lynn M. Stone/naturepl.com. 125: (tc) Kevin Schafer/NHPA; (bc) Fritz Polking/Peter Arnold, Inc. 126: Ariel Skelley/Corbis. 127: C Squared Studios/Getty Images. 128: (t) Keith Neale/Masterfile; (c) Frans Lanting/Minden Pictures; (b) David Stoecklein/CORBIS. 128–129: (bkgd) Kevin Schafer/Alamy. 129: (bl) J. Brown/OSF/Animals Animals/Earth Scenes; (tc) Frans Lemmins/Zefa/CORBIS; (tr) Lee Karney/US Fish & Wildlife Service. 130–131: (bkgd) Christ Newbert/Minden Pictures. 131: (b) Siede Preis/Getty Images. 132: (t) Ralph A. Clevenger/CORBIS; (l) Flip Nicklin/Minden Pictures. 132–133: (b) Marty Snyderman/Stephen Frink Collection/Alamy. 134: (t) Jack Jackson/Robert Harding Picture Library Ltd./Alamy; (b) Mark Harmel/Alamy. 135: (b) Andre Seale/Alamy. 136: (c) Norbert Wu/Minden Pictures; (b) Jeffrey L. Rotman/CORBIS; (t) Rudie Kuiter/oceanwideimages.com. 137: (t) Chris Newbert/Minden Pictures; (c) Ralph A. Clevenger/CORBIS; (b) Mark Harmel/Alamy. 141: (tl) age fotostock/Superstock; (tr) Breck P. Kent/Animals Animal-Earth Scenes; (bcr) Stephen J. Krasemann/DRKPhoto.com; (bl) Darlyne A. Murawski/National Geographic/Getty Images. 144–145: Jim Brandenburg/Minden Pictures. 145: (t to b) Nigel J. Dennis/Photo Researchers; David Cavagnaro/Visuals Unlimited; T. O'Keefe/PhotoLink/Getty Images; Arco Images/Alamy; Annie Griffiths Belt/CORBIS; Wardene Weisser/Bruce Coleman, Inc. 146–147: Claude Ponthieux/Alt-6/Alamy. 150: (t) T. O'Keefe/PhotoLink/Getty Images; (b) Chip Porter/Stone/Getty Images. 151: Robert W. Ginn/PhotoEdit. 152: (t) Stephen Saks/Lonely Planet Images; (b) Photodisc/Getty Images; (inset) Scott Mitchell/Stone/Getty Images. 153: T. O'Keefe/PhotoLink/Getty Images; Photodisc/Getty Images. 155: Kari Marttila/Alamy. 156–157: Curt Maas/AGStockUSA. 158: Nguyen/ Dong/UNEP/Peter Arnold Inc. 159: (t) Bureau of Land Management; (cr) Hal Beral/CORBIS; (br) Mark Turner/PictureQuest. 160: (t) Nigel J. Dennis/Photo Researchers. 160–161: (b) Steve Bloom Images/Alamy. 161: (inset) Rod Patterson/ABPL/Animals Animals. 164: (b) Arco Images/Alamy; (t) FAN Travelstock/Alamy. 165: (t to b) Nguyen/Dong/UNEP/Peter Arnold Inc.; Rod Patterson/ABPL/Animals Animals. 166: John Cancalosi/Peter Arnold, Inc. 167: Lynn M. Stone/Bruce Coleman Inc. 168–169: Annie Griffiths Belt/CORBIS. 170: Russ Merne/Alamy. 171: (t) Topham/The Image Works; (b) Dr. Rebecca Cairns-Wicks/ARKive. 172: (bl) Chris Howes/Wild Places Photography/ Alamy; (cr) Albert Copley/Visuals Unlimited; (tr) The Natural History Museum, London. 173: The Natural History Museum, London. 174: (b) Wardene Weisser/Bruce Coleman, Inc.; (t) Windland Rice/Bruce Coleman Inc. 175: (t) Russ Merne/Alamy; (c) The Natural History Museum, London; (b) Wardene Weisser/Bruce Coleman, Inc. 176: (inset) (c) The Natural History Museum, London; (inset) Image Farm; (c) Bettmann/CORBIS. 176–177: (c) John Sibbick/Natural History Museum Picture Library. 177: (t) Stan Honda/AFP/Getty Images. 178: (t to b) Claude Ponthieux/Alt-6/Alamy; Curt Maas/ AGStockUSA; Annie Griffiths Belt/CORBIS. 179: (t) Photodisc/Getty Images; (b) Chris Howes/Wild Places Photography/Alamy. 182–183: Arco Images/Alamy. 183: Joe McDonald/Visuals Unlimited. 184: (br) Jack Dykinga/Getty Images; (t) Penny Tweedie/ CORBIS; (b) Paul Nicklen/NGS Images. 186: John C. Stevenson/Animals Animals/Earth Scenes; (inset) Brian Sytnyk/Masterfile. 187: Hal Horowitz/CORBIS. 188: SBR/ Popperfoto/Robertstock/IPNstock; (inset) J. Savage Gibson/Alamy. 189: Dave King/ Dorling Kindersley/Getty Images. 190–191: Don Smith/Alamy. 192–193: GC Minerals/ Alamy. 194: (r) Mark A. Schneider/Photo Researchers; (c) Roger Weller, Cochise College; (l) B. Runk & S. Shoenberger/Grant Heilman Photography. 195: (t) Roger Weller, Cochise College; (b) ER Degginger/Photo Researchers. 196: (1) Ben Johnson/Photo Researchers; (6) Lawrence Lawry/Photo Researchers; (2) Andy Crawford/DK Images; (3) Randy Allbritton/Getty Images; (4) Wally Eberhart/Visuals Unlimited; (5) Image Farm Inc./Alamy. 199: Joyce Photographics/Photo Researchers. 200: (t) Wally Eberhart/Visuals Unlimited; (c) Jonathan Blair/CORBIS. 200–201: William Manning/CORBIS. 201: (t) Jerome Wyckoff/Animals Animals/Earth Scenes; (c) Dr. Parvinder Sethi; (b) Roger Weller, Cochise College. 202: (t) Roger Weller, Cochise College; (b) Profimedia.CZ s.r.o./Alamy; (c) Richard Cummins/SuperStock. 203: (t to b) Roger Weller, Cochise College; (2) William Manning/CORBIS; (3) Richard Cummins/SuperStock. 204: (c) Lester Lefkowitz/The Image Bank/Getty Images; (r) Richard Nowitz/National Geographic Image Collection. 206–207: Joseph Van Os/Getty Images. 208: Jacana/Photo Researchers; (inset) B. Runk/S. Schoenberger/Grant Heilman Photography. 210: (l) Franck Jeannin/Alamy; (r) Ian Francis/Alamy. 211: (bl) The McGraw-Hill Companies, Inc./Jacques Cornell photographer; (bc) The McGraw-Hill Companies, Inc./Jacques Cornell photographer; (br) The McGraw-Hill Companies, Inc./Jacques Cornell photographer. 212: (t) Richard Hamilton Smith/CORBIS; (b) David Frazier/The Image Works. 213: (t to b) Jacana/Photo Researchers; (2) Ian Francis/Alamy; (3) David Frazier/The Image Works. 214–215: Lee White/CORBIS. 215: Bran X Pictures/PunchStock. 216–217: B. Runk/S. Schoenberger/Grant Heilman Photography. 218: (b) B. Runk/S. Schoenberger/Grant Heilman Photography; (t) Tom Bean/CORBIS. 219: B. Runk/S. Schoenberger/Grant Heilman Photography. 220: (br) Andrew J. Martinez/Photo Researchers. 220–221: Owaki-Kulla/CORBIS. 221: (bl) Photodisc/Getty Images. 222: (c) Kimimasa Mayama/Reuters/CORBIS; (b) Jeremy Woodhouse/Masterfile; (t) Toshiyuki Aizawa/Reuters/CORBIS. 223: (t to b) Tom Bean/CORBIS; Owaki-Kulla/CORBIS; Jeremy Woodhouse/Masterfile. 224: (l) Wisconsin Historical Society; (r) Klaus Guldbrandsen/Photo Researchers. 224–225: (bkgd) Cristina Pedrazzini/Photo Researchers, Inc. 225: (l) Tommaso Guicciardini/Photo Researchers; (r) Warren Gretz/NREL/US Department of Energy/Science Photo Library/Photo Researchers. 226: (t to b) GC Minerals/Alamy; Joseph Van Os/Getty Images; B. Runk/S. Schoenberger/Grant Heilman Photography; Toyohiro Yamada/Getty Images. 227: (t) Owaki-Kulla/CORBIS; (b) Roger Weller, Cochise College. 230–231: Brand X Pictures/PictureQuest. 231: (t to b) Chad Ehlers/Minden Pictures; Lloyd Cluff/CORBIS; Greg Vaughn/Alamy; Yva Momatiuk/John Eastcott/Minden Pictures; Tom & Pat Leeson/Photo Researchers. 232–233: Chad Ehlers/Minden Pictures. 235: Brand X Pictures/PunchStock. 242: Fred Hirschmann/Science Faction/Getty Images. 244–245: Lloyd Cluff/CORBIS. 246: Daniel Sambraus/Photo Researchers. 249: Greg Vaughn/Alamy. 250: (t) Reuters/CORBIS; (b) Josh Ritchie/Getty Images. 251: (t to b) Daniel Sambraus/Photo Researchers; Greg Vaughn/Alamy; Reuters/CORBIS. 252: (t) Craig Lovell/CORBIS; (b) Mark Edwards/Peter Arnold, Inc. 252–253: Vince Streano/CORBIS. 254–255: Tom Bean/CORBIS. 256: Scott Darsney/Lonely Planet Images. 257: (t) Yva Momatiuk/John Eastcott/Minden Pictures; (b) Louis Psihoyos/IPN Stock. 258: (t) Tom & Pat Leeson/Photo Researchers; (b) WildCountry/CORBIS. 259: Bernhard Edmaier/Photo Researchers. 260: (l) CORBIS; (r) Danny Lehman/CORBIS. 261: (t to b) Scott Darsney/Lonely Planet Images; Bernhard Edmaier/Photo Researchers; CORBIS. 262: Altrendo Travel/Getty Images. 263: Danita Delimont/Alamy. 264: (t to b) Chad Ehlers/Minden Pictures; Lloyd Cluff/CORBIS; Tom Bean/CORBIS. 265: Tom & Pat Leeson/Photo Researchers. 268: (inset) yourexpedition.com. 268–269: (bkgd) Higdon Photographic Art Studio/SuperStock. 269: (inset) yourexpedition.com. 270: (t) Tony West/CORBIS; (b) David Hiller/Photodisc/Getty Images. 272: Rob Harling/Alamy. 274: South Carolina Philharmonic Orchestra. Photo by Brad Allen/High Contrast Studios. 274: (inset) Johner Images/Getty Images. 275: C Squared Studios/Getty Images; Photodisc/Getty Images. 276–277: Studio City/eStock Photo/Alamy. 278–279: Royalty-Free/CORBIS. 280: Paul Barton/CORBIS. 281: (c) Stockdisc Classic/Alamy; (t) Brand X Pictures/PunchStock; (b) Stockdisc/PunchStock. 282: (t) Matthias Stolt/FAN travelstock/Alamy; (b) Burnett-Palmer/Visual & Written/Bruce Coleman Inc. 284: (tl) C Squared Studios/Getty Images; (tr) V&A Images/Alamy; (cr) Stockbyte Silver/Alamy; (br) Royalty-Free/CORBIS. 285: (t to b) Paul Barton/CORBIS; Burnett-Palmer/Visual & Written/Bruce Coleman Inc.; Royalty-Free/CORBIS; Lawrence Lawry/Photo Researchers. 286: (inset) Photo by Denis Finnin. Copyright American Museum of Natural History. 286–287: NOAO/AURA/NSF/Photo Researchers. 288–289: Alexis Rosenfeld/Photo Researchers. 290: (c) Burke/Triolo/Brand X Pictures/Jupiter Images; (r) Frank Gaglione/Photodisc/Getty Images. 292: Ablestock/Hemera Technologies/Alamy. 294: NASA. 295: NASA. 298–299: David Wall Photography/Danita Delimont. 300: Ariel Skelley/CORBIS. 301: (cr) Gary S. Chapman/The Image Bank/Getty Images; (cl) Duomo/CORBIS; (tr) Comstock Images/Alamy.

302: Mauritius/age fotostock. 304: (c) David Young-Wolff/PhotoEdit; (t) Richard Hutchings/PhotoEdit; (b) Tom Stewart/CORBIS. 305: Comstock Images/Alamy. 306: (l) SW Productions/Photodisc/Getty Images; (r) C Squared Studios/Getty Images. 308–309: Schlegelmilch/CORBIS; Peter Gridley/Stock Connection Distribution/Alamy. 309: (t to b) Blickwinkel/Alamy; Peter Gridley/Stock Connection Distribution/Alamy; David Young-Wolff/Alamy; Yoav Levy/Phototake; Chad Ehlers/Stock Connection Distribution/Alamy. 310–311: Heather Perry/National Geographic/Getty Images. 312: (b) Blickwinkel/Alamy; (t) Royalty-Free/CORBIS; (cr) John A. Rizzo/Getty Images. 313: John A. Rizzon/Getty Images. 314: (b) JTB Photo/Alamy; (t) Lisa Romerein/The Image Bank/Getty Images. 315: (t to b) Heather Perry/National Geographic/Getty Images; Royalty-Free/CORBIS; Lisa Romerein/The Image Bank/Getty Images; CAB. 316: BananaStock/PunchStock. 317: (bl) C Squared Studios/Getty Images; (tr) Stockbyte Silver/PunchStock. 318–319: Ei Katsumata/Alamy. 320: Masterfile Royalty Free. 321: (tr) Ablestock/Hemera Technologies/Alamy; (tl) Ablestock/Hemera Technologies/Alamy. 322: (b) Steve Bloom Images/Alamy; (t) Viesti Associates. 323: Michael Newman/PhotoEdit. 324: Royalty-Free/CORBIS. 325: (t to b) Masterfile Royalty Free; Michael Newman/PhotoEdit; Royalty-Free/CORBIS. 326: Michael DeYoung/CORBIS. 328: (t to b) Royalty-Free/CORBIS; Alexis Rosenfeld/Photo Researchers; David Wall Photography/Danita Delimont. 329: (c) Stockbyte Silver/Alamy; (r) Jack Hollingsworth/redchopsticks/Getty Images. 332–333: Schlegelmilch/CORBIS. 333: (t to b) Kwame Zikomo/SuperStock; Franco & Bonnard/Sygma/CORBIS; Michael Newman/PhotoEdit; Jeff Greenberg/Peter Arnold, Inc./Alamy; Alan Schein Photography/CORBIS; Steve Cole/Photodisc Red/Getty Images. 334–335: blickwinkel/Alamy. 336: Kwame Zikomo/SuperStock; Purestock/PunchStock. 338: (l) Franco & Bonnard/Sygma/CORBIS; (c) Franco & Bonnard/Sygma/CORBIS; (r) Franco & Bonnard/Sygma/CORBIS; (t) Michael Prince/CORBIS. 339: (tl) Reuters/CORBIS; (tr) Duomo/CORBIS; (bl) Mark Junak/Stone/Getty Images; (br) Jason Molyneaux/Masterfile. 340: (b) Zoomstock/Masterfile; (c) Geostock/Getty Images. 341: (t to b) Kwame Zikomo/SuperStock; Mark Junak/Stone/Getty Images; Geostock/Getty Images; Zoomstock/Masterfile. 342: (l) NRM/SSPL/The Image Works; (r) NRM/SSPL/The Image Works. 343: (t) Underwood & Underwood/CORBIS; (b) Robert Mullan/Alamy. 344–345: Tsuneo Nakamura/Volvox Inc./Alamy. 346: Michael Newman/ PhotoEdit. 347: (c) Jim Cummins/CORBIS; (b) Tim McGuire/CORBIS; (t) Tim Pannell/CORBIS. 348: (t) Jose Luis Pelaez, Inc./Blend Images/Alamy; (bl) Richard T. Nowitz/CORBIS. 349: Andi Duff/Alamy. 350: (b) Niehoff/imagebroker/Alamy; (t) Reuters/CORBIS. 351: (t to b) Michael Newman/PhotoEdit; Andi Duff/Alamy; Niehoff/imagebroker/Alamy. 354–355: David Young-Wolff/Alamy. 356: David Gregs/Alamy; (inset) Yoav Levy/Phototake. 357: (t) Brandon Cole Marine Photography/Alamy; (c) Image Source/PunchStock; (b) Jayme Thornton/The Image Bank/Getty Images. 358: (t) Joe Raedle/Getty Images; (b) Alan Williams/Alamy. 359: (b) P. Narayan/AGE Fotostock. 360: Michael Newman/Photoedit. 361: (t to b) Brandon Cole Marine Photography/Alamy; P. Narayan/AGE Fotostock; CAB. 364: (t to b) blickwinkel/Alamy; Tsuneo Nakamura/ Volvox Inc./Alamy; Marc Steinmetz/VISUM/The Image Works; Jim Corwin/Index Stock. 365: (bl) Tony Freeman/PhotoEdit; (bc) Steve Harper/Grant Heilman Photography; (br) C Squared Studios/Getty Images; (tc) Gary Kreyer/Grant Heilman Photography; (tr) Royalty-Free/CORBIS; (tl) Niehoff/imagebroker/Alamy. 368–369: Peter Dejong/ AP/Wide World Photos. 370: (t) Colin Cuthbert/Newcastle University/Photo Researchers; (b) Natalie Fobes/CORBIS. R11: (tr) Leonard Lessin/Photo Researchers; (bl) Jonathan Nourak/PhotoEdit. R12: (tl) David Young-Wolff/PhotoEdit; (bl) Randy Faris/CORBIS; (tr) The McGraw-Hill Companies, Inc./Ken Cavanagh Photographer; (cr) Ingram Publishing; (br) PhotoLink/Getty Images. R13: BananaStock/PunchStock. R14: Amos Morgan/Getty Images. R16: (t) Frans Lanting/Minden Pictures; (b) Burke/Triolo/Brand X Pictures/Jupiter Images; (t) Getty Images. R18: (t) Myrleen Ferguson Cate/PhotoEdit; (bl) Gerry Ellis/ Globio/Minden Pictures; (br) Katherine Feng/Globio/Minden Pictures. R19: BananaStock/ PunchStock. R24: Roger Harris/Photo Researchers. R25: MIchael Newman/PhotoEdit. R26: Eye of Science/Photo Researchers. R27: Dan Bigelow/Getty Images. R28: Ingram Publishing/Alamy. R29: Amos Morgan/Getty Images. R30: Scholastic Studio 10/Index Stock. R31: (t to b) Royalty-Free/CORBIS; Hoby Finn/Getty Images; Cindy Charles/PhotoEdit; IT Stock Free/PunchStock; ImageState/PunchStock. R32: (bl) Eye of Science/Photo Researchers. R33: (cw from top) Dr. Gopal Murti/Visuals Unlimited; Dr. Gary D. Gaulger/PhotoTake; Brand X Pictures/PunchStock; Ryan McVay/Getty Images; Steven Mark Needham/FoodPix/Jupiter Images. R34: (cw from top) PhotoTake, Inc./Alamy; C Squared Studios/Getty Images; Burke Triolo Productions/Getty Images; Stockdisc/PunchStock; C Squared Studios/Getty Images; Stockdisc/PunchStock; Burke Triolo Productions/Getty Images; PhotoAlto/PunchStock. R35: (br) Steven Mark Needham/FoodPix/Jupiter Images; (cr) Pornchai Mittongtare/FoodPix/Jupiter Images; (tl) Burke Triolo Productions/Getty Images; (cl) Jonell Weaver/Getty Images. R36: (b) Ariel Skelley/CORBIS. R39: (cw from top) First Light/Getty Images; Lee Karney/US Fish & Wildlife Service; Image100/Alamy; Tim Flach/Stone/Getty Images; Darrell Gulin/Getty Images. R39: David Fischer/Photodisc Red/Getty Images. R40: (cw from top) Digital Vision/PunchStock; Royalty-Free/CORBIS; C Squared Studios/Getty Images; Michael Newman/PhotoEdit; James Sparshatt/CORBIS; Lester V. Bergman/CORBIS; Gregory G. Dimijian/Photo Researchers. R41: (cw from top) Viesti Associates; Royalty-Free/CORBIS; WildCountry/CORBIS; Alan & Sandy Carey/Getty Images; John A. Rizzo/Getty Images; Siede Preis/Getty Images; David Hebden/Alamy. R42: (cw from top) David L. Brown/PictureQuest; Stockbyte Silver/Alamy; Nigel Cattlin/Holt Studios International Ltd./Alamy; Alan & Sandy Carey/Getty Images; Siede Preis/Getty Images; Lloyd Cluff/CORBIS; Nguyen/Dong/UNEP/Peter Arnold Inc. R43: (cw from top) Alan Thornton/Stone/Getty Images; Russ Merne/Alamy; Creatas/PunchStock; Josh Ritchie/Getty Images; Susan Cruz; Fritz Rauschenbach/Zefa/CORBIS; Michael Newman/PhotoEdit; G.K. & Vikki Hart/Getty Images; Ablestock/Hemera Technologies/Alamy; Tom & Pat Leeson/Photo Researchers; Joseph Van Os/Getty Images. R44: (cw from top) Russell Illig/Getty Images; Jonathan Blair/CORBIS; Michael Newman/PhotoEdit; Jack Jackson/Robert Harding Picture Library Ltd./Alamy; Bernhard Edmaier/Photo Researchers; Andi Duff/Alamy; Image100/PunchStock; Design Pics/age fotostock; Digital Vision/Getty Images; Niehoff/imagebroker/ Alamy; (cl) ImageState/Punchstock. R45: (cw from top) Heather Perry/National Geographic/Getty Images; Steve Cole/Photodisc Red/Getty Images; Bonnie Sue Rauch/ Photo Researchers; David Hebden/Alamy; Comstock Images/PictureQuest; Royalty-Free/CORBIS; NewStock/Alamy; Daniel Aguilar/Reuters/CORBIS; Bran X Pictures/PunchStock; Paul Sterry/Worldwide Picture Library/Alamy. R46: (cw from top) Reuters/ CORBIS; Chad Ehlers/Stock Connection Distribution/Alamy; Troy Bartlett/Alamy; Dan Bigelow/Getty Images; Creatas/PunchStock; BananaStock/PunchStock; Siede Preis/Getty Images; Masterfile Royalty Free. R47: (cw from top) Ablestock/Hemera Technologies/Alamy; Royalty-Free/CORBIS; Bill Beatty/Visuals Unlimited; Siede Preis/Getty Images; C Squared Studios/Getty Images; Reuters/CORBIS; Royalty-Free/CORBIS; Brand X Pictures/PunchStock; Ei Katsumata/Alamy; Stephen Dalton/Photo Researchers; Dr. Parvinder Sethi. R48: (cw from top) Dr. Merlin D. Tuttle/Photo Researchers; Purestock/PunchStock; Owaki-Kulla/CORBIS; Eckhard Slawik/Photo Researchers; Ulana Switucha/Alamy; Siede Preis/Getty Images; StockTrek/Getty Images; Photodisc/PunchStock; Royalty-Free/CORBIS; Burke/Triolo Productions/Getty Images. R49: (cw from top) Hans Pfletschinger/Peter Arnold Inc.; Royalty-Free/CORBIS; Stockdisc/PunchStock; Sebastien Baussai/Alamy; Creatas/PunchStock; Photodisc/Getty Images; C Squared Studios/Getty Images; Royalty-Free/CORBIS; Royalty-Free/CORBIS; Kwame Zikomo/SuperStock; Brian Sytnyk/Masterfile; Annie Griffiths Belt/National Geographic/Getty Images. R50: (cw from top) Richard Megna/Fundamental Photographs; Gary Vestal/Photographer's Choice/Getty Images; Stephen Saks/Lonely Planet Images; Jerome Wyckoff/Animals Animals/Earth Scenes; Creatas/PunchStock; IT Stock/PunchStock; Zigmund Leszczynski/Animals Animals/Earth Scenes; Glen Allison/Getty Images; Richard Megna/Fundamental Photographs. R51: (cw from top) Tony Freeman/PhotoEdit; Digital Vision/PunchStock; Brand X Pictures/PunchStock; The McGraw-Hill Companies, Inc./Jacques Cornell photographer; Royalty-Free/CORBIS; Comstock Images/Alamy; John A. Rizzo/Getty Images; Liane Cary/AGE fotostock. R52: (cw from top) David Gregs/Alamy; Susan Cruz; Alan & Sandy Carey/Getty Images; TRBfoto/Getty Images; Russell Illig/Getty Images; NASA/JPL/Cornell University; Royalty-Free/CORBIS; Paul Barton/CORBIS; Brand X Pictures/PunchStock; Jacques Cornell. R53: (cw from top) Burke/Triolo/Brand X Pictures/Jupiter Images; Craig K. Lorenz/Photo Researchers; Yoav Levy/Phototake; Royalty-Free/CORBIS; Brand X Pictures/PunchStock; Philippa Lewis/Edifice/CORBIS; Photodisc Collection/Getty Images; Royalty-Free/CORBIS.